The up 'Granite City' express leaving Aberdeen for Glasgow, hauled by 'BR5' 4-6-0, No 73005 (British Railways).

The Class '6' 'Pacific', No 72009, Clan Stewart, *of which only 10 were built* (British Railways).

BRITISH LOCOMOTIVES OF THE 20th CENTURY

O.S.Nock

Volume 2 1930~1960

Guild Publishing London

This edition published 1984 by Book Club Associates
by arrangement with Patrick Stephens Limited.
Reprinted March 1985

Photoset in 10 on 10 pt Baskerville by Manuset Limited,
Baldock, Herts. Printed in Great Britain on 115 gsm
Fineblade coated cartridge, and bound, by Anchor
Brendon Limited, Tiptree, Colchester, Essex.

Contents

Preface

When the British railways were approaching the 1930s the nation itself was in sombre mood. The catastrophic Wall Street crash had been one of the more spectacular symptoms of rapidly deepening world recession which, on the railways of Great Britain, manifested itself in rapidly dwindling volumes of what had been staple traffics. Nevertheless a brave attempt was made to sustain, and even to improve, the standards of passenger travel and, faced by the urgent need to obtain more economical locomotive operation, some interesting technical developments were in hand. In a chronology of this kind it is not easy to draw a strict date-line of demarcation between one volume and the next and, if one mentions 1930, the first new chapter—dealing with the second phase of Gresley's work as Chief Mechanical Engineer of the LNER—does open with references to locomotives introduced a little previous to that year, but the work of which belongs almost entirely to the 1930s and after.

To locomotive enthusiasts, if not to railway shareholders, the 1930s were halcyon years, and the first few chapters of this second volume recall with relish the exciting advances in train speed and the monumental record of July 1938 when the Gresley streamlined 'Pacific' Mallard set up the world-record, for all time, with steam traction, of 126 mph. But while the enterprise of the British railways in passenger scheduling seemed to be having no bounds, particularly on the two great lines running north from London, the later years of that decade were clouded by the increasingly serious prospect of another major war. While the railway managements, and especially the civil engineering and signalling departments, became concerned with questions of air raid precautions, locomotive progress and the prospects of still more interesting developments continued unabated. But when war did come, in September 1939, all was very suddenly changed.

While it was not to be expected that the six years of the Second World War would have anything but a stultifying effect on the development of British locomotive design in its more advanced respects, the lean years proved to be not without interest. The postulation of features of design practice dictated by the conditions of mounting austerity, in which the railways of Britain were operated, became a constant challenge. Indeed, in meeting the circumstances of the hour, much ingenuity was shown in both design and works procedure that was to prove of lasting benefit in later years. This was reflected in 1975,

when the time came to celebrate the 150th anniversary of the inauguration of the British main line railway network. My great friend, the late Roland C. Bond, and I were invited to collaborate in presenting the Clayton Memorial Lecture of that year to the Institution of Mechanical Engineers and, after much consideration, we felt justified in titling the lecture '150 years of *uninterrupted* progress in Railway Engineering'.

After the war came nationalisation of the railways and, with the recurrent cold douches of uncertainty and successive reorganisations, the railways of Britain became the catspaw of party politics. The profession of locomotive engineering, tempered in the fire of two World Wars, and suffering the constraints inevitable in years of depression, has nevertheless a noble record of achievement to its credit, not least in the way dedicated railwaymen carried on from hand to mouth when the 'scrap steam' factions, in the Railways Board, in the press, and elsewhere, were simple and misguided enough to believe that the elimination of steam traction would see the end of all ills, financial and otherwise.

This volume traces the history of the British locomotive through the last years of steam when, by ingenious and enthusiastic development, the performance of some of the most famous classes was notably enhanced and indicated quite clearly that the steam locomotive had by no means reached its zenith of achievement. Again, as with Volume 1 of this work, I must express my deep appreciation, to the management and engineers of the nationalised British Railways, for the privilege of seeing so much of this work at first hand: in main works, in the two stationary testing plants, and in accompanying so many full dress road trials in the dynamometer cars. Supplementing these semi-official occasions there have been the innumerable times when I have been privileged to ride on the footplate of locomotives in ordinary service. There is, indeed, hardly a single modern type of express passenger, or mixed traffic locomotive that I have not ridden at sometime. To those who have granted me these privileges, and to the drivers and firemen, and the running inspectors, who made me so welcome on their engines, my deepest gratitude is due.

O.S. Nock
Bath, July 1983

LMS: the first Stanier 'Pacific', No 6200, The Princess Royal. *This photograph has been autographed by M. Stanier* (British Railways).

Nº 4830

1. The Gresley 3-cylinder designs

When consideration came to be given to the eventual replacement of the famous 'Atlantic' designs that had been such a tower of strength on the three constituents of the East Coast main line, and also on the Great Central, the economy in steam consumption, realised by the use of long travel valves, led to the production of a powerful 3-cylinder 4-4-0 modern design. The 'D49' Class of which the detail design and construction was done at Darlington, was in every way a main line job, with a 21¼ ton maximum axle load, and a tractive effort of 21,556 lb. This latter made the new engines equal or better than any of the Atlantics of the constituent companies of the LNER though the boiler was considerably smaller. It was, in fact, standard with that of the general purpose 0-6-0s, also designed at Darlington, of the 'J38' and 'J39' Classes. These latter were in some ways a follow-up to the very successful Worsdell 'P2' and 'P3' Classes of the North Eastern Railway.

In view of its use alongside the North Eastern and North British 'Atlantics', the boiler proportions of the 'D49' are interesting, as indicating the extent to which 'full regulator-short cut-off' working was expected to require less steam from the boiler than older traditional methods. In actual working the 'D49', good though it was, never came to supplant the 'Atlantics', either on the North Eastern or the North British section, as the foremost second-line power behind the 'Pacifics'. When first introduced in Scotland, I believe the load limits on the East Coast main line north of Edinburgh were the same as those for the 'Atlantics'; but in actual practice they came to be regarded as 'one coach less'. When I was travelling a lot, and footplating north of Edinburgh the running people put a 'D49' on to a top link job only when an 'Atlantic' was not available. In the North Eastern Area, at the same time, the 'D49s' were used to great advantage on the express services originating from Leeds, Hull, and cross-country-wise from Newcastle. The relative boiler proportions are shown in the subjoined table.

LNER boiler proportions

Class	**D49**	**NE 'Z'**	**NB '868'**
Type	4-4-0	4-4-2	4-4-2
Heating surfaces (square feet)			
Tubes	1,226.28	1,672.5	1,619.0
Firebox	171.50	185.0	184.8
Superheater	246.1	437.0	385.0
Grate area (square feet)	26	26.63	28.5
Boiler pressure (lb per square inch)	180	175	180
Tractive effort (lb)	21,556	19,300	23,400

Left *LNER: one of the highly successful 'V2' 2-6-2 express mixed traffic locomotives in passenger service on the Great Central line was engine No 4830 working the 6.20 pm Marylebone to Bradford express on the GW & GC joint line near Saunderton* (H.K. Harman).

Below *LNER: the 3-cylinder 4-4-0, No 2753,* Cheshire*; one of the later Walschaerts gear 'D49' Class, built at Darlington in 1929* (British Railways).

LNER: one of the final batch of the 3-cylinder 4-4-0 'Hunt' series with larger steam and exhaust valves, Class 'D49/4', No 365, The Morpeth, *built at Darlington in December 1934* (British Railways).

The 'engine' of the 'D49' was a beautifully designed piece of machinery. The first order was for 28, and most of them had Walschaerts gear with the Gresley derived motion for the valves of the inside cylinder. But the layout differed from that of the 'Pacifics' and the 'K3' Moguls in that the rocking shafts for actuating the 2:1 gear were behind the cylinders instead of in front, thereby avoiding the factor of expansion in the valve spindles that had to be taken into account on the larger engines. Another feature that made the original batch of 'D49s' very speedy engines was that the standard type of piston valve was used, of 8 inch diameter, which was very large in relation to the cylinder diameter of 17 inches.

In contrast to the massively impressive connecting and coupling rods of the 'Atlantics', particularly those of the North British and of the North Eastern 'V' Class, the motion work of the 'D49s' looked light almost to the point of flimsiness; but the use of high-tensile alloy steel made this lightness possible. The first batch of these engines, with piston valves, were mostly based in Scotland and were named after 'shires'; but there could be no appropriate territorial allocation, because quite half the names were of English counties. Some duplicated names currently borne by 'Experiment' Class 4-6-0s of the former LNWR, then in LMS ownership.

It was a time when Gresley was interested to find out if the use of poppet valves, rather than piston valves would improve the overall efficiency of his engines; and six of the first batch of 'Shires', turned out in 1928 were fitted with Lentz oscillating-cam poppet valves actuated by the ordinary Walschaerts motion. A further two had rotary cam poppet valves driven by a longitudinal shaft, actuated by a bevel gear off the driving axle. This was an extremely simple mechanism, and a further 40 engines with this gear were built in 1932-5. There were 20 engines with piston valves; of the six with OC poppet valve gear all but one were named after English shires, No 318, *Cambridgeshire*; 320, *Warwickshire*; 322, *Huntingdonshire*; 327, *Nottinghamshire* and 335, *Bedfordshire*. However, to my knowledge, none

Class	**D49/1**	**D49/3**	**D49/2**	**D49/4**
Name series	'Shires'	'Shires'	'Hunts'	'Hunts'
Valve gear	Walschaerts (Piston)	Walschaerts OC Lentz	RC Poppet	RC Poppet larger valves
Total in class	20	6	17*	25

* Includes the two experimental RC engines of 1929, which were renamed after 'Hunts' in 1932.

LNER: the first 'D17' Class 3-cylinder 4-6-0, No 2800, Sandringham, *with a small GER type tender and Westinghouse brake, which was built in 1928* (British Railways).

of them penetrated anywhere near those counties. At the opposite extreme was the sixth—329, *Inverness-shire*, equally remote, so far as 'D49' workings were concerned. The two original RC poppet valve gear engines were 336, *Buckinghamshire*, and 352, *Leicestershire*. Their heavy maximum axle-loading of 21¼ tons precluded their use on any part of the old Great Eastern system, and the only trial of one of them on the Great Northern line was not a success.

Experience with Nos 336 and 352, put into traffic in 1929 was such that the further batches, with RC poppet valve gear, were built in 1932-3, and 1934-5, the last named with larger steam and exhaust valves. The complete stud of 'D49' Class engines, by February 1935 consisted of four varieties (see table opposite). One would imagine that in these days the naming of a class of locomotives after famous 'Hunts', with the figure of a fleeing fox incorporated in the nameplate, would not be universally popular, when there is in certain quarters so much opposition to blood sports; but the 'Hunts' survived, and did much excellent work. The first of the 1932 series, No 201, *The Bramham Moor*, was the prototype of a fine '0' gauge model in the Hornby series, one of which ran on my own model railway for many years.

The 'Hunts' worked mostly in the North Eastern Area. At Neville Hill shed (Leeds) they had a prestige job with the morning Leeds-Glasgow express which they worked as far as Newcastle. It was one of the few East Coast trains that passed Darlington without stopping. The schedule, in the 1930s, was 87 minutes for the 80.1 miles from York to Newcastle, but I have timed it in 82½ minutes, with a 285-ton load and engine No 370, *The Rufford*. I had many runs with 'D49' Class engines both piston and poppet valves, both on and off the footplate, and invariably found them very lively and free running engines. In certain quarters they were reputed to be rough riding, but I never experienced this, and the 'Hunts' in particular were extremely smooth and quiet in their going. I cannot, however, say that they were very *comfortable* engines to ride. In the North Eastern tradition they had wide 'tool boxes' on either side of the cab, and I usually found myself sprawling over the one on the right-hand side with my legs dangling in the direct line of the fire! Most of my runs were made with fairly light trains, on which they worked very easily, and with good economy; but by far the best run was quite unpremeditated.

In 1936 I was travelling from Kings Cross to Edinburgh on the Thursday before Easter, and the 1.20 pm express was divided. I do not know how the relief portion, leaving at 1.5 pm, was loaded, but on the main part we had 16 on, six of which were due to be detached at Newcastle. North of that point the relief portion was evidently expected to be the heavier of the two trains, and the regular engine, a 'Pacific' and its crew, was allocated to it, and had left some little time before the main train arrived in Newcastle. A spare engine, the 'D49' 4-4-0 No 249, *Aberdeenshire*, was waiting for the 10-coach second portion. But when we arrived, so great was the crowd of passengers waiting, that on the spur of the moment the station supervisor decided to send three of the coaches, which should have been detached, forward to Edinburgh, with the result that the little 'D49' had to take 13, 412 tons tare, and 435 tons loaded. Furthermore, the two conditional stops included in the schedule, at Dunbar and Drem, were both to be called at. It was inevitable that time would be lost, but in the circumstances it was remarkably little, seeing that the schedule was planned for 'Pacific' haulage and a normal load of about 350 tons. The finest intermediate run was from Alnmouth to Berwick, with a steeply adverse start, 32.1 miles in 36¼ minutes, start to stop, with a maximum speed of 77 mph near Beal.

Provision of greater power for the Great Eastern lines also became a major consideration in the later 1920s. The Great Eastern Railway had always cherished its proud traditions of first-class enginemanship, highlighted in the nightly run of the Hook Continental boat express from Liverpool Street to Parkeston Quay, 68.7 miles in 82 minutes. At first sight this might not seem a very exacting schedule; but with a 64-ton 4-6-0 locomotive with no more than 44 tons adhesion, and a regular load of 420 to 450 tons, it was one of the toughest assignments anywhere in the country—albeit not one of very long duration. The élite quartet of top-link enginemen at Parkeston Quay, who had the exclusive handling of the job, treated it with the devotion and expertise bestowed upon the working of a Royal Train. That the engines had to be thrashed, good and hard, went without saying, and coal consumption was astronomical; but until the sittings of the Bridge Stress Committee, the obstacle in the way of larger locomotives was the limitation upon axle loading compelled by the nature of Great Eastern permanent way, and its underline bridge structures. The 'Claud Hamilton' Class of 4-4-0s in their non-superheated days had a maximum axle-load of 16½ tons, and the 4-6-0s had 16, 14, and 14 tons respectively on their leading, second and third coupled axle.

The work of the Bridge Stress Committee made it clear that in a carefully balanced 3-cylinder 4-6-0 an axle load of up to 18½ tons could be accepted on the Great Eastern main lines. Both the detail design, and construction of the first batch of the new engines was entrusted to the North British Locomotive Company and, as was to be expected, they made an excellent job of it. Named after stately homes in East Anglia, and known as the 'Sandringham' Class, the new engines provided the only instance of a divided drive among the Gresley 3-cylinder locomotives. The inside cylinder drove the leading pair of coupled wheels and, as in the 4-4-0 'Shires', the 2:1 link mechanism providing the derived motion for the inside cylinder piston valve was behind, instead of in front of that cylinder. With an excellent boiler and firebox, a pressure of 200 lb per square inch and long-lap, long-travel valves, the 'Sandringhams' proved as efficient in working as they were handsome to look upon.

LNER: one of the football club series of 'B17' 4-6-0s with standard tender, No 2862, Manchester United, *was the first of a series built by Robert Stephenson & Company in 1937* (British Railways).

LNER: the standard 'A3' 'Pacific', No 2599, Book Law, *in Newcastle Central station* (the late W.B. Greenfield).

Connoisseurs of locomotive running, however, were not for long to see how they would have coped with maximum loading on that exacting schedule of the outward bound 'Hook Continental'; because, in deference to *force majeure*, an additional 5 minutes was inserted into the schedule.

The first batch, consisting of 10 engines, was the only one built by the North British Locomotive Company. Subsequent batches, taking the running numbers up from 2810 to 2861 were built at Darlington, with no modifications from the original, except the brake equipment. The first 15, including all the NBL batch and the first five from Darlington, were dual fitted; then came 27 with steam brake on the engine and vacuum for the train, while from No 2843 onwards the brake was vacuum for both. Down to engine No 2847 they were fitted with short Great Eastern pattern tenders. A number of these later engines were stationed at Gorton, and began taking a share in the double-home working between Manchester and Marylebone, as well as working to Parkeston Quay with the North Country Continental train. By the time the running numbers had reached 2847 it would seem that the stock of 'stately homes' was exhausted, and for the next batch someone with a flair for popular publicity hit upon the idea of naming them after Association football clubs, and incorporating the club colours and a football in the nameplate.

It was then that the 'Sandringhams' really began to 'hit the headlines' in the realm of locomotive performance; for the first batch of 'football clubs' went to Leicester, and the incomparable top-link there, who for many years had done magnificent work with the Great Central 'Atlantics', took to the new engines immediately and were soon toppling their own notable records daily. This new batch, beginning with No 2848, *Arsenal*, was the first of the class to have the standard LNER 4200-gallon tenders, instead of the small GER type demanded by the size of some of the turntables in East Anglia. My great runs on the former GCR line were not confined to those with the Leicester men because, very early one summer morning in 1936, I went down from Marylebone on the 2.32 am Newspaper express, on the footplate of No 2841, *Gayton Hall*, and clocked some very exciting running, with a maximum speed of 90 mph in the descent of Whetstone bank towards Leicester. The 'Sandringhams', like the 'D49' 4-4-0s were certainly not the least of Gresley's very successful 3-cylinder designs.

Of course the 'neon-lights' display of Gresley locomotive prowess continued to be the East Coast main line and, following the dynamometer car trials of 1928 between the standard 180 lb engine No 4473 and the modified 220 lb engine No 2544, *Lemberg*, the new standard 220 lb variety, Class 'A3' was evolved. The new engines, of which No 2743, *Felstead*, was the first (built Doncaster, August 1928), had 19 inch diameter cylinders, but was otherwise unchanged from those that had been rebuilt from Class 'A1' with 20 inch diameter cylinders. The standard engines of Class 'A3' had a higher tractive

FLYING SCOTSMAN
L N E R
2795

L N E R
465

COCK O THE NORTH
2001
L N E R

effort than that of the original Class 'A1' engines, but in Gresley's own time no further rebuilding of the former with 220 lb boilers took place and, until the general introduction of the streamlined 'A4' Class from 1937 onwards, the 'A1' and 'A3' engines were used indiscriminately on the heaviest and fastest East Coast express. In 1935 one of the London based 'A3' engines, No 2750, *Papyrus*, was used for the high speed dynamometer car test runs between London and Newcastle prior to the building of the 'Silver Jubilee' streamlined train. On the return trip a maximum speed of 108 mph was attained, the British record at that time.

The 'A3s' like the 'D49' 4-4-0s and the 'Sandringhams' had left-hand drive. It was no small step to take on the LNER, because on all its English constituents right-hand drive had been traditional for very many decades, and it was the kind of change that could be very upsetting to footplatemen. But with the coming of colourlight signalling it was a very necessary change, albeit one to be introduced gradually. It was a long time before the great majority of main line engines on the LNER in England were left-hand drive. It was indeed a right-hand drive 'A1' Pacific that was indirectly the cause of a hair-raising 'near miss' from disaster at Northallerton, in 1935. The North British had always been a left-hand drive railway.

The next new 3-cylinder locomotive in the standard range designed under the direction of Mr Gresley, was the powerful 'V1' 2-6-2 tank, for fast outer suburban, and longer distance local services in Scotland and in the North Eastern area. Though incorporating the principles of design, now well established on the LNER, the new engines incorporated for the first time the use of a single 'monobloc' steel casting to include all three cylinders, the valve chests, steam and exhaust passages, and the smokebox saddle. In this way all pipe joints external to the smokebox were avoided. All three steam chests were in line with their centres at an inclination of 1 in 30, while the inside cylinder was inclined at 1 in 8 to enable the inside crosshead and connecting rod to work above the leading coupled axle. The valve gear was Walschaerts, with the 2:1 lever mechanism of the derived gear for actuating the valves of the inside cylinder operated from forward extensions of the outside valve spindles, as on the 'Pacifics'. The 'V1's were powerful engines for the duties involved with a tractive effort of 22,404 lb. The 78 engines of this class were all built at Doncaster, between 1930 and 1939.

On the East Coast main line north of Edinburgh, although the introduction of 'Pacifics' on certain turns had enabled the maximum unpiloted loads to be increased to 480 tons northbound and 420 tons southbound, not many of the big engines could be spared from Haymarket shed, especially in the summer, when they were most needed, and when even these increased maxima were frequently exceeded. Double-heading with the 'Pacifics', although resorted to in cases of exceptional loading south of Edinburgh, was not permitted on the line north to Aberdeen, and reliance continued to be placed on those great stalwarts, the North British 'Atlantics', assisted when necessary by 'Scott' Class 4-4-0s. It was to meet the most extreme cases of loading that the giant 'P2' Class 2-8-2s were introduced in 1934, with a tractive effort of 43,462 lb and an adhesion weight of no less than 80½ tons. The use of three cylinders and skilful balancing of the reciprocating parts made a maximum axle load of 20.5 tons acceptable, over a route that included the Forth and Tay Bridges, as well as numerous smaller structures. North of Kinnaber Junction the East Coast trains used the former Caledonian line, so that the weight diagram combined with the dynamic augment had also to satisfy the civil engineer of the LMS.

The first two 'P2' engines differed from each other in respect of the valve gear, No 2001, *Cock o' the North*, having RC poppet valves, and No 2002, *Earl Marischal*, the standard arrangement of Walschaerts gear, with the conjugated gear for the piston valves of the inside cylinder. Originally the valve gear fitted to No 2001 was capable of giving fine adjustments of the cut-off, and on dynamometer car test runs made between Kings Cross and Grantham, soon after the engine was built, the cut-offs reported were 10, 12, 15, 20, 22, 25, and 30 per cent. But when the engine went into regular service in Scotland in 1935, making two return trips from Edinburgh to Dundee and back daily, the cam arrangement of the valve gear had been changed, and only three steps were available, namely 18, 25 and 35 per cent. These naturally did not give sufficiently fine adjustments to provide for the greatly varying demands for steam over this route of constantly fluctuating gradients, and

Opposite page, top to bottom

LNER: a standard 'A3', No 2795, Call Boy, *working the up Flying Scotsman—non-stop from Edinburgh to Kings Cross—near Barkston* (M.W. Earley).

LNER: 3-cylinder 2-6-2 suburban tank engine Class 'V1', introduced in 1930. The 82 engines of this class were built at Doncaster (British Railways).

LNER: the pioneer 2-8-2 express engine of 1934, No 2001, Cock o' the North, *as originally built with RC poppet valve gear and tested at Vitry, France* (British Railways).

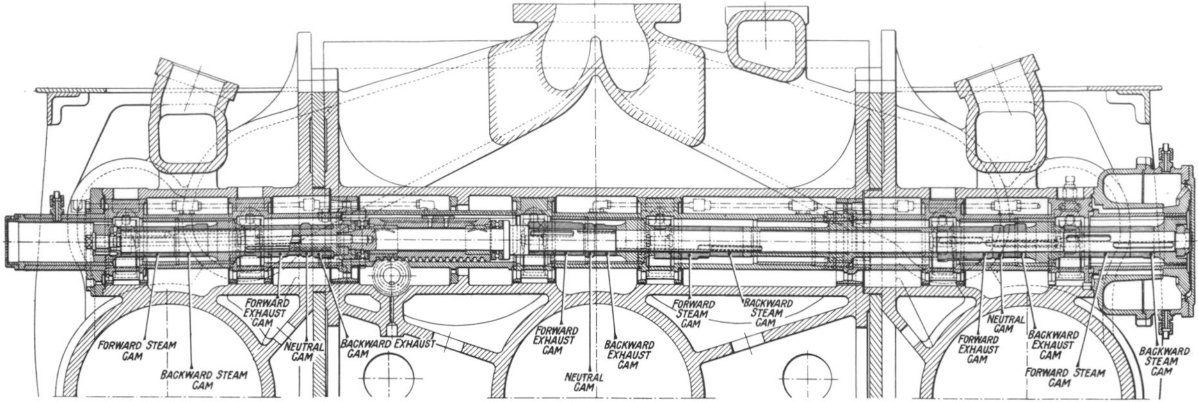

LNER: the 'D49' Class 4-4-0s with poppet valves—cross-section through cylinders and camshaft.

drivers had to make adjustments of power output by varying the regulator opening. On her initial trials No 2001 astonished the testing staff by running easily up to 85 mph though nothing approaching such speeds were required on the Edinburgh-Aberdeen route.

In the earliest tests an output of 2,000 drawbar horsepower was registered in the dynamometer car but, at the end of 1934, Gresley arranged for the engine to be shipped over to France for 'full-dress' trials on the Vitry stationary plant. This, one feels, was as much a remonstrance on his part (against the lack of any similar plant in Great Britain) as a desire, or need for more precise performance data. While in France the engine was put through some constant speed trials on the Paris-Orleans main line and, on one run at a speed of 68 mph, an output of 1,910 drawbar horsepower was sustained for 35 minutes. The French engineers considered that the sharp blast, leading to a certain amount of fire throwing, was responsible for a basic coal consumption of 3.25 lb per drawbar horsepower hour, which they thought was rather high. When I rode on the engine between Dundee and Edinburgh in August 1935 I noticed, late at night, a good deal of fire throwing when steaming hard. Even with a gross load of 530 tons the maximum demands were not more than intermittent; but when working in 25, and still more so in 35 per cent cut-off, there was a continuous rain of red hot particles from the chimney. The engine steamed freely, and for the hardest work the regulator did not appear to be more than three-quarters open; the steam chest pressure was never more than 5 lb per square inch below the boiler pressure.

Constructionally the two engines 2001 and 2002

LNER: one of the final batch of non-streamlined 'Pacifics', No 2500, Windsor Lad, *built at Doncaster, 1934, and having a perforated pipe steam collector instead of conventional dome* (British Railways).

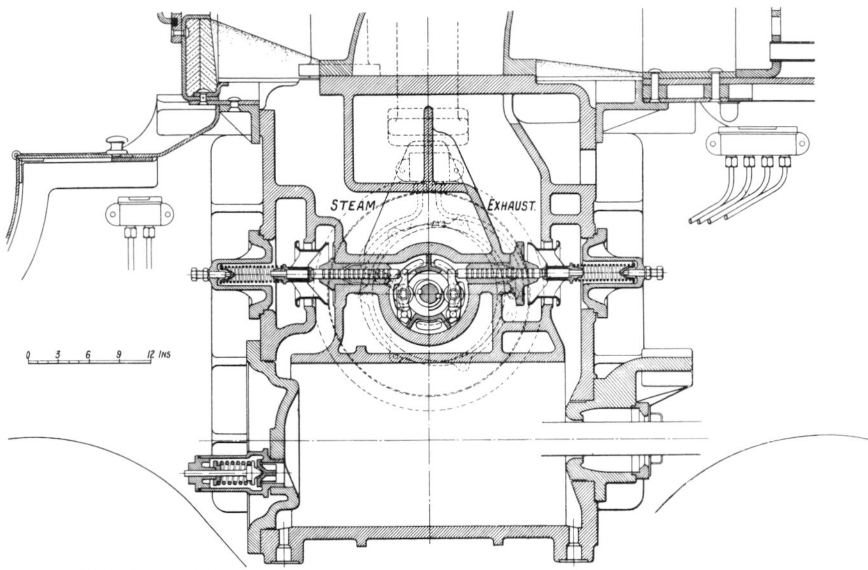

Above *LNER: the 'D49' Class 4-4-0s with poppet valves—longitudinal section through cylinders and valves.*

Below *LNER: the Sandringham Class 3-cylinder 4-6-0 for East Anglia.*

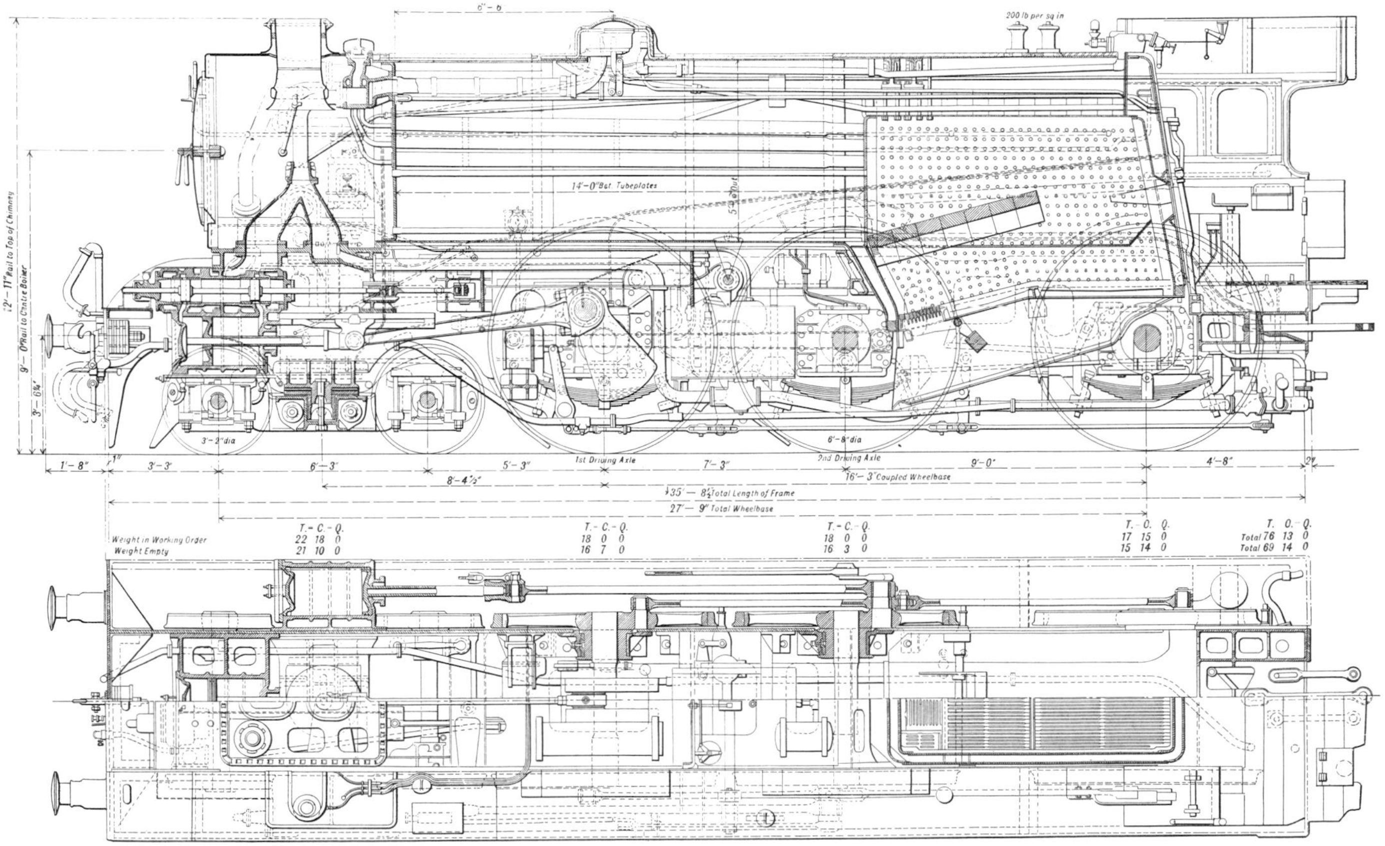

had some interesting features. They had the monobloc casting design, as first used on the 'V1' 2-6-2 tank engines, but in a much larger form, with 21 inch by 26 inch cylinders. That for the *Cock o' the North* can be studied from the accompanying drawing (below). The twin orifice blastpipe and double chimney arrangement, also illustrated, had incorporated with it a series of petticoats. Although not intended for continuous high speed running, the top of the boiler was arranged with a smoothed exterior and, with the chimneys not projecting above its top line, careful experiments were made with models in the wind tunnel of the aeronautical department of the City and Guilds (Engineering) College, South Kensington, to determine the ideal shape of the deflector screens at the front.

These experiments proved very effective with the sharp blast on *Cock o' the North* but, on the comparative engine with ordinary piston valves and the relatively soft blast when working at short cut-offs, the single screen on either side of the smokebox was not enough. Exhaust steam beating down obscured the driver's look-out and additional screens had to be fitted, outboard from the original ones. These, although somewhat unsightly, were entirely successful. Admittedly my own impressions were formed after no more than a few footplate journeys, but I though that No 2002, *Earl Marischal*, was the better of two magnificent locomotives. The way this latter engine, with loads of more than 500 tons, got away with its trains, and climbed the heavy gradients southbound between Aberdeen and Dundee was deeply impressive.

On No 2002, when the regulator was fully opened there was no drop in steam pressure between that in the boiler and the steam chests, giving evidence to the excellent design of all stages in the steam circuit. It began with the entry to the regulator. Although it was not apparent externally, because of the 'air-smoothing' on the top of the outer casing of the boiler, these engines were the first on the LNER to have the so-called 'banjo dome'. This is shown in the accompanying drawing (below) and consisted of a series of slots through which steam entered the passage leading to the regulator. This itself had exceptionally large openings to steam, but the collector had a total area of slots equal to twice the area of the regulator valve when the latter was fully open, thus obviating, very successfully any 'wire drawing' in the steam flow. Again, so far as the front-end was concerned, while the drawing below

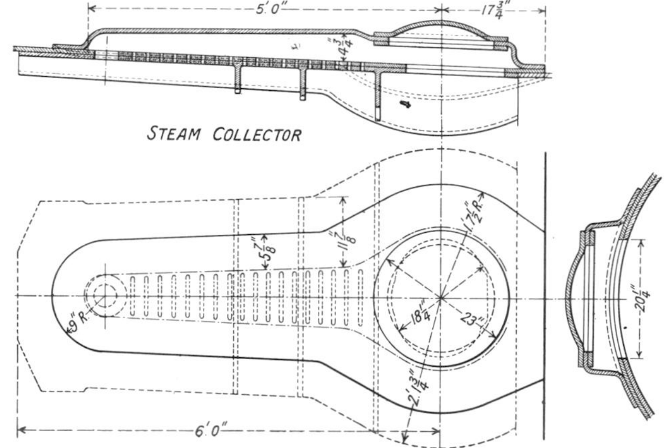

Right *LNER: the steam collector (sometimes called the Banjo Dome) on the 'P2' and the final batch of 'A3' engines.*

Below *The* Cock o' the North: *the smokebox, showing the Kylchap exhaust arrangement.*

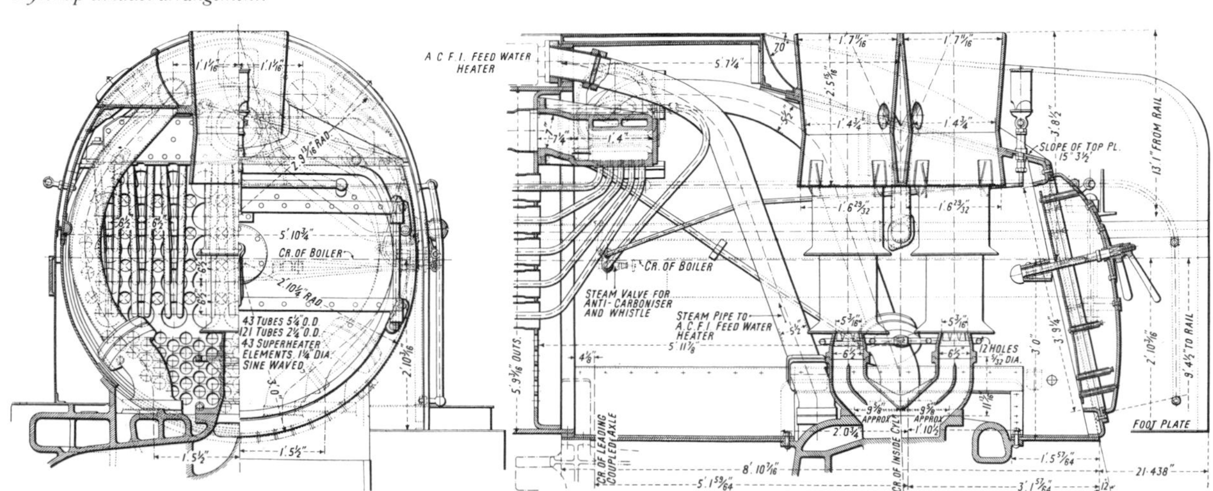

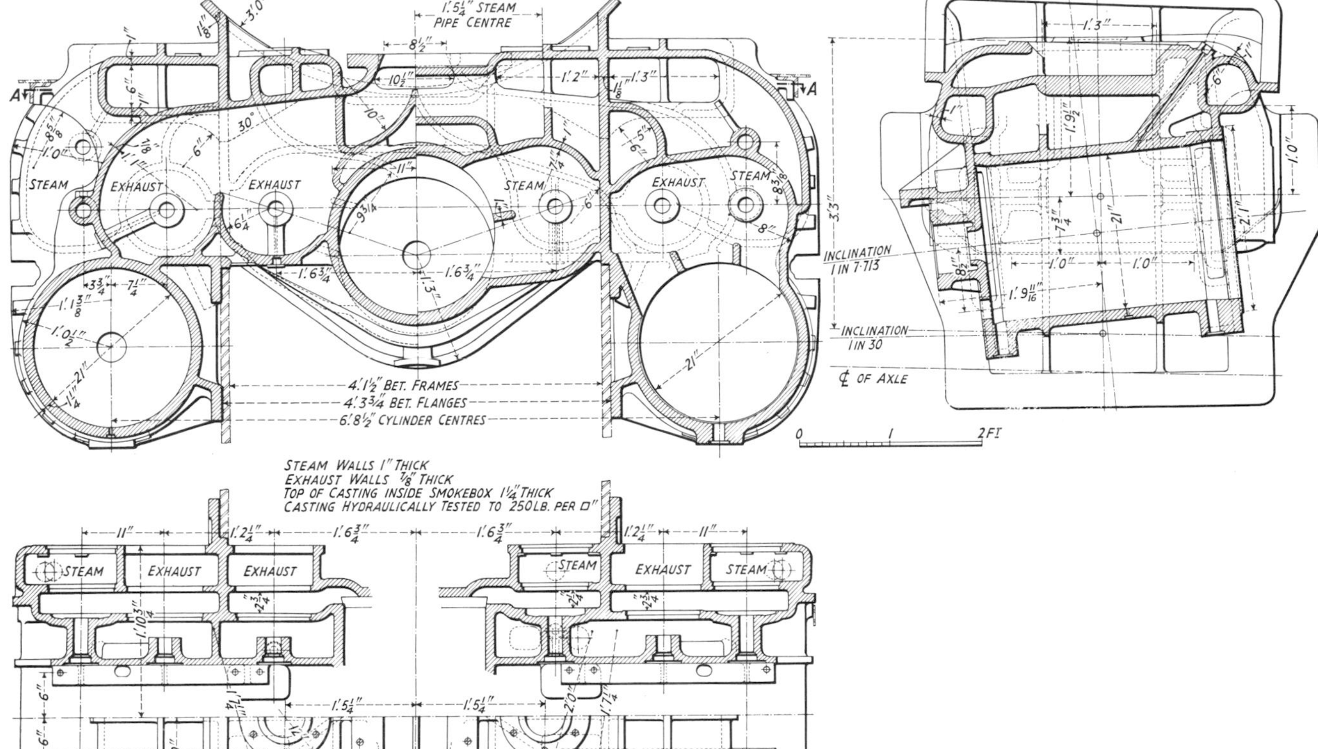

LNER: Cock o' the North—*sectional drawings showing design and construction of 'monobloc' castings.*

shows the cross-section of the cylinder casting for the *Cock o' the North*, with separate steam and exhaust valves in the RC valve arrangement, the second engine, the *Earl Marischal* also had a single 'monobloc' casting embracing the entire front-end, even including the outside steam pipes leading to the steam chests of the outside cylinders.

The 'banjo dome', if one may continue to call it so, made its first 'public' appearance on a new batch of 'A3' Pacifics, in which the first three, No 2500-2, were completed at Doncaster in July 1934, actually before the second 2-8-2. There were nine of these engines and, so far as I can recall, none were at first stationed in London, though those based at Gateshead became frequent visitors, and one or two of those at Haymarket came to Kings Cross in the summer with the non-stop 'Flying Scotsman'. The new 'Pacifics' had the standard 'A3' front-end, not including the monobloc casting design of the 'P2' Class 2-8-2s. The 'banjo dome' rather spoiled the traditional appearance of the Gresley 'Pacifics', though, of course, it became a familiar enough fitting in later years. It next appeared in June 1936, on the first of the 'V2' 2-6-2s, 'Green Arrow' Class.

I am passing over for the moment the memorable introduction of the 'A4' streamlined 'Pacifics' in 1935, because the general subject of locomotive streamlining is discussed in a chapter of its own. It is now the 'V2s' which need special attention. In the 'P2s' Gresley had introduced a new wheel diameter in his standard range of locomotives, 6 feet 2 inches, and this had permitted speeds up to 85 mph to be readily attained; and so, in what was officially designated a 'mixed-traffic' engine, the same wheel diameter was combined with a shortened version of the standard 'A3' boiler, and the 'monobloc' casting front-end. The cylinders were slightly reduced from those of the 'Pacifics', 18½ inches in diameter, instead of 19 inches, but the piston valve diameter was increased to 9½ inches. The result

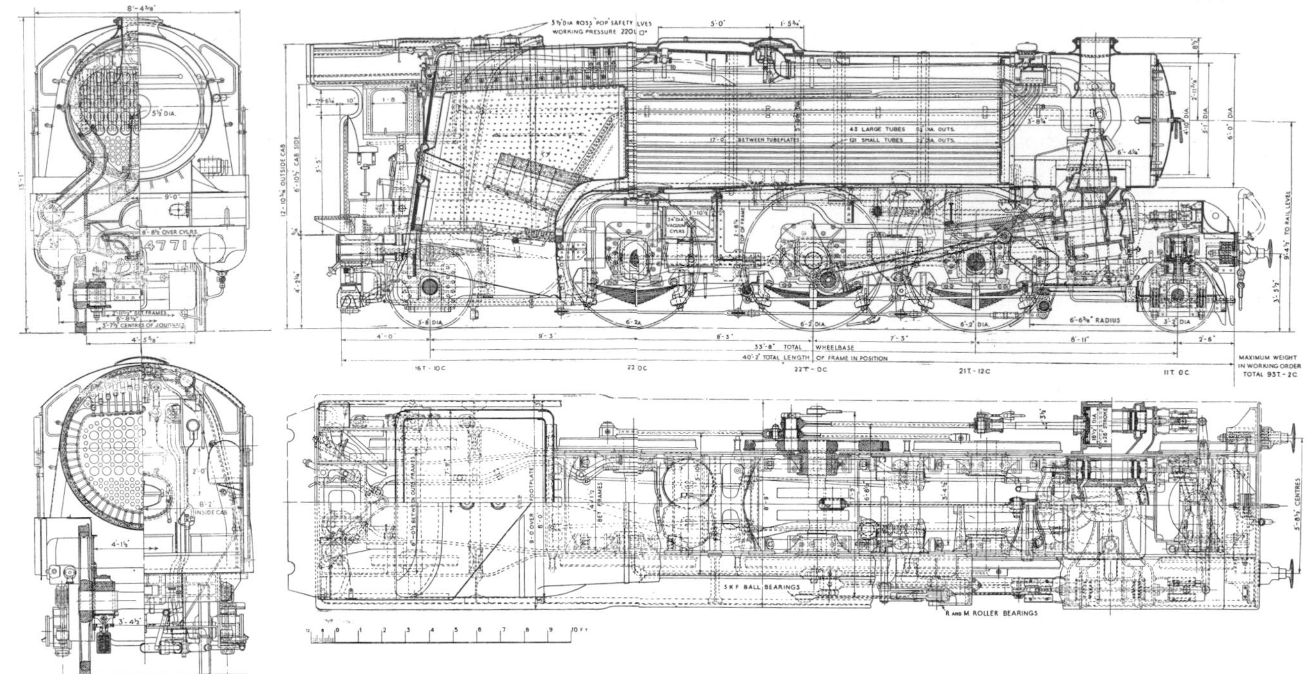

Above *LNER: the 3-cylinder 2-6-2 mixed traffic 'V2' engine, the 'Green Arrows'.*

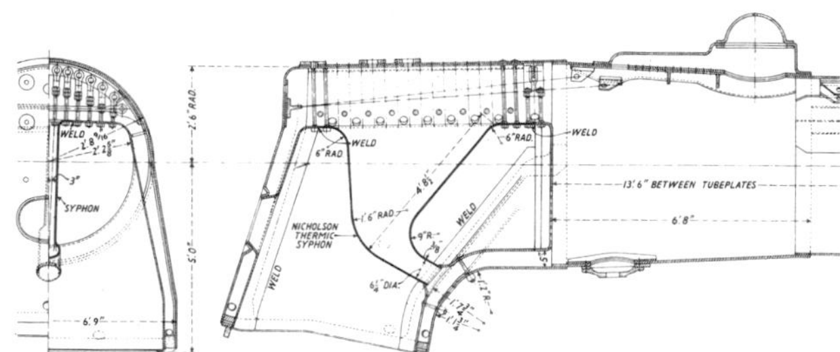

Left *LNER: the 'V4' 2-6-2—detail of the wide type steel firebox, with a single Nicholson thermic siphon.*

Below *LNER: one of the later 2-8-2 express engines, having Walschaerts valve gear and the standard Gresley conjugated motion, No 2003,* Lord President. *The front end streamlining followed that of the 'A4' 'Pacific' engines* (British Railways).

LNER: one of the later 2-8-2s (Class 'P2') No 2006, Wolf of Badenoch, *climbing the bank out of Aberdeen with an express for Edinburgh* (M.W. Earley).

was an outstandingly successful design, capable of top class express passenger service, even in the Southern Area, south of Doncaster, where by the year 1934 the schedules were becoming very fast. In some quarters the desirability of using engines with a leading pony truck on such duties was questioned; but the 'V2' engines proved very smooth and steady riders at speeds up to 90 mph. Only five of these engines were built in 1936, until the design had been fully tried out; and then a further 20 were added in 1937, to be followed by very many more in later years.

LNER: the first of the very powerful Class 'K4' 3-cylinder 'Moguls' for the West Highland Line was No 3441, Loch Long. *The other five engines of the class were named after Highland chieftains* (British Railways).

Gresley, like all Great Northern locomotive men, abhorred double-heading and, having successfully solved the problem of the East Coast main line north of Edinburgh with the 'P2' Class of 2-8-2, of which four more examples were built in 1936, he turned his attention to the difficult problem of the West Highland (where until 1937, no larger engines than the ex-Great Northern 2-6-0s of the 'K2' Class had been permitted to run). The limitations there in the conveyance of heavy summer loads were not only the exceptionally severe gradients, with long sections inclined at 1 in 60, but the continuously curving alignment of much of the route. With 2-cylinder locomotives balanced in the conventional way, axle-loading was limited to 18 tons, and in such conditions the maximum tonnage that could be taken single-headed was 220 tons. Gresley would have liked to build a 'Mogul' with the 'K3' type 6 foot diameter boiler; but, even with the reduced hammer blow from 3-cylinder propulsion, a maximum axle-load of less than 20 tons could not be

achieved, and so the new engines had a slightly longer version of that fitted to the 'D49' 4-4-0 and the 'J38' and 'J39' 0-6-0 goods engines.

The 'K4', of which the detailed designing and construction was done at Darlington Works, was an extremely interesting and successful locomotive. The three cylinders, 18½ inches diameter by 26 inches stroke, and their, associated 8 inch diameter piston valves, were incorporated in a single 'monobloc' casting, which also formed the smoke-box saddle, and with coupled wheels of 5 foot 2 inch diameter and a boiler pressure of 200 lb per square inch, the tractive effort was no less than 36,598 lb. As originally turned out in January 1937 the boiler pressure was limited to 180 lb per square inch; but the boiler was designed for 200 lb, and this latter was being worked to by the late summer of 1937, when I had the privilege of riding on the first engine of the class, No 3441, *Loch Long*. The load limit for this class was fixed at 300 tons and, except for certain trains in the height of the summer tourist season, the six engines of this class practically eliminated double-heading on the West Highland line. They steamed well and, with the efficient front end, used little more coal in working 300-ton trains than the 'K2' Class used with their maximum loads of 220 tons, although the total weight of the engine was only some 5 tons heavier, 68.4 against 63.7 tons in working order.

The last Gresley 3-cylinder design, the first two examples of which were completed only a few months before his regretted death, at the early age of 64 in 1941, was the 'V4' mixed traffic 2-6-2. This was intended to be a general service replacement for the many ageing 4-4-2 and 4-6-0 passenger engines of the pre-grouping companies, but to have a much higher route availability. The maximum static load on any axle was no more than 17 tons and, by the use of high tensile steels and modern constructional practices, the overall weight of the engine in working order was no more than 70.4 tons, a remarkable figure for a unit having a tractive effort of 27,420 lb—far greater than the various classes it was planned to replace. In the event, however, only two of them were built. I rode the first of them, No 3401, *Bantam Cock*, on the West Highland line in 1946, and noted how easily and comfortably she traversed the sharply curving stretches of line; but, with a tractive effort of 27,420 lb, she could not handle such heavy trains as the 'K4s', with their tractive effort of 36,598 lb. Although a beautiful piece of locomotive engineering, the 'V4' was never developed to its full maturity.

Gresley 3-cylinder designs: Phase two

Class	**D49**	**A3**	**B17**	**V1**	**P2**	**V2**	**K4**	**V3**	**V4**
Date	**1927**	**1927**	**1928**	**1930**	**1934**	**1936**	**1937**	**1939**	**1941**
Type	4-4-0	4-6-2	4-6-0	2-6-2T	2-8-2	2-6-2	2-6-0	2-6-2T	2-6-2
Cylinders (3)									
Diameter (inches)	17	19	17½	16	21	18½	18½	16	15
Stroke (inches)	26	26	26	26	26	26	26	26	26
Coupled wheel diameter (feet/inches)	6 8	6 8	6 8	5 8	6 2	6 2	5 2	5 8	5 8
Heating surfaces (square feet)									
Tubes	1,226.28	2,477	1,508	1,198	2,477	2,216	1,253.6	1,198	1,292.5
Firebox	171.5	215	168	127	237	215	168	127	151.6
Superheater	271.8	703	344	284	636	679.7	310	284	355.8
Grate area (square feet)	26.0	41.25	27.5	22.08	50	41.25	27.5	22.08	28.8
Maximum axle load (tons)	21.25	22.05	18.35	19.25	20.5	22.0	19.85	20	17
Total engine weight (tons)	66.0	96.25	77.25	84.0	110.25	93.1	68.4	86.8	70.4
Boiler pressure (lb per square inch)	180	220	200	180	220	220	200	200	250
Tractive effort (lb)	21,556	32,909	25,380	22,404	43,462	33,730	36,598	24,960	27,420
Number in class	76	32*	73	82	6†	184	6	10	2

* Total in 1937 includes five rebuilt from Class 'A1'.
† Includes four built with streamlined front end in 1936.

Right *Problems with smoke deflection: an experimental smokebox on 'A3' 'Pacific', No 2751,* Humorist *(British Railways).*

Below Humorist *was the first non-streamlined 'Pacific' to be fitted with the Kylchap exhaust arrangement of twin-orifice blastpipe and double chimney, in 1939* (British Railways).

Bottom *LNER: the last Gresley steam locomotive design, the second of the only two examples of Class 'V4', 3-cylinder mixed traffic 2-6-2s introduced in 1941. This engine has the wartime black-out screens* (British Railways).

2. Standardisation on the LMS

In 1931, sponsored by the LMS, there was published a finely illustrated 51-page paperback under the title *Locomotives of the LMS, Past and Present*, and among the 80 locomotives illustrated, eight in full colour, 10 were designated as standard designs. Four of these were so directly derived as to be very nearly pure Midland: the 3-cylinder compound 4-4-0; the 6 foot 9 inch version of the '2P' 4-4-0; the '4F' 0-6-0, and the '3F' 0-6-0 tank engine (Jinty). Four others may have been regarded as standard by the Derby hierarchy of the late 1920s, though they did not remain so for long. These were the parallel boilered tank engines of the 2-6-4 and 2-6-2 types; the LMS version of the ex-LNW 0-8-0 mineral engines, and the Horwich-designed 2-6-0. The ninth class, still strangely enough designated as a 'standard' as late as 1947, was the little short-wheel-base 'dock' 0-6-0 tank, of 1928, of which no more than 10 were ever built, and classed '2F'. The tenth of the standard classes of 1930-1 was the 'Royal Scot' 4-6-0 which, with the detail modifications made to it in Stanier's time, became one of the most outstanding passenger locomotive classes in Great Britain in the 1930s.

The four designs of 1926-30, although not eventually forming part of the major standardisation programme, under Stanier, are important in themselves, and equally in the large number of each that were built. The mixed traffic 2-6-0, which was designed at Horwich during the time when Hughes was still Chief Mechanical Engineer, was not built until after his retirement, though it was essentially a Lancashire and Yorkshire job. Apart from its basic dimensions, which are tabulated, interesting features were the unusually large diameter piston valves—11 inches—and the use of long-lap, long-travel valves. This was the result of experience with the ex-LYR 4-cylinder 4-6-0 passenger locomotives. The 2-6-0s, nicknamed the 'Crabs', from the look of their steeply inclined outside cylinders, and outside valve gear, were not exactly the most handsome of engines; but, despite coupled wheels no larger than 5 feet 6 inches, they were very free-running, and I noted one of them to run the 17.5 miles from Watford Junction to Euston in 19 minutes 6 seconds start to stop, with a gross trailing load of 285 tons. The 9 miles from Harrow to South Hampstead were covered in 7 minutes 27 seconds, an average speed of 72½ mph, with a maximum of 76½ mph.

The 2-6-4 tanks of the '2300' Class were to have been a typical Derby design; but, almost at the last minute, the valve gear was changed to have long-lap, and long-travel, with highly beneficial effects. On the outer residential trains from Euston these engines were regularly run with the gear linked up inside 10 per cent cut-off, and on the up journey from Watford Junction I have several instances of maximum speeds well over 80 mph. The smaller 2-6-2 tanks, with 5 foot 3 inch coupled wheels, were also very lively performers. On the other hand, the Derby-designed development of the ex-LNWR 'G2' freight 0-8-0 does not seem to have found such favour, although having a slightly higher tractive effort. The new standard LMS 0-8-0s, though generally similar so far as the boiler was concerned, had inside Walschaerts instead of Joy valve gear and this did seem to give the same 'punch' in getting away with a heavy load. In the event, the ex-LNW engines outlasted their LMS counterparts.

Turning now to the 'Royal Scots', the immediate aftermath of the trial running of the Great Western

LMS: the Midland Compound in its standardised form, with left-hand drive—a Derby-built example No 1102, of 1925 (British Railways).

LMS: new designs 1926-1930

Class	5F	4P	3P	7F
Type	2-6-0	2-6-4T	2-6-2T	0-8-0
Cylinders				
Diameter (inches)	21	19	17½	19½
Stroke (inches)	26	26	26	26
Coupled wheel diameter (feet/inches)	5 6	5 9	5 3	4 8½
Heating surfaces (square feet)				
Tubes	1,345	1,082	691	1,402
Firebox	160	138	104	150
Superheater	307	246	186	342
Grate area (square feet)	27.5	25.0	17.5	23.6
Boiler pressure (lb per square inch)	180	200	200	200
Tractive effort (lb)	26,580	23,125	21,486	29,747

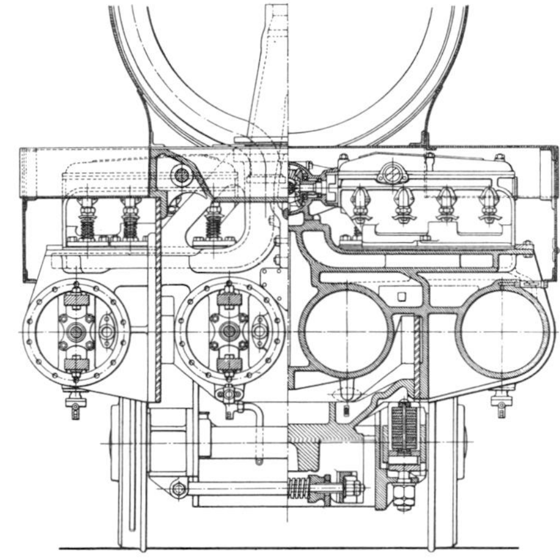

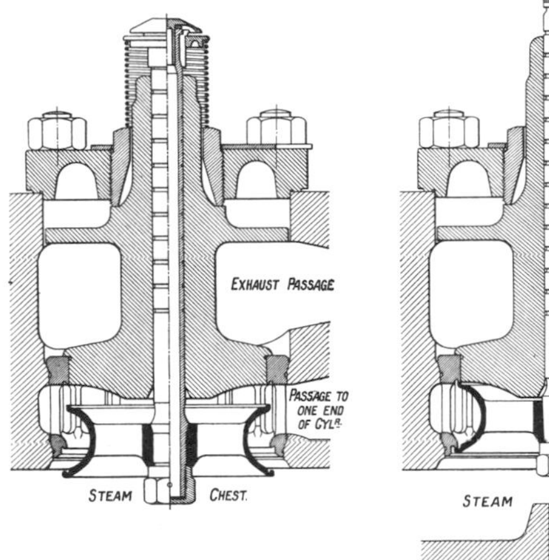

Above *LMS: cross-section of the cylinders of 'Claughton' 4-6-0, No 5908—the original boiler, fitted with Caprotti valve gear.*

Above right *LMS: cross sections through Caprotti valves.*

Below *LMS: the standard '2P' 4-4-0, based on the Fowler 7 foot rebuild, with 6 foot 9 inch coupled wheels* (British Railways).

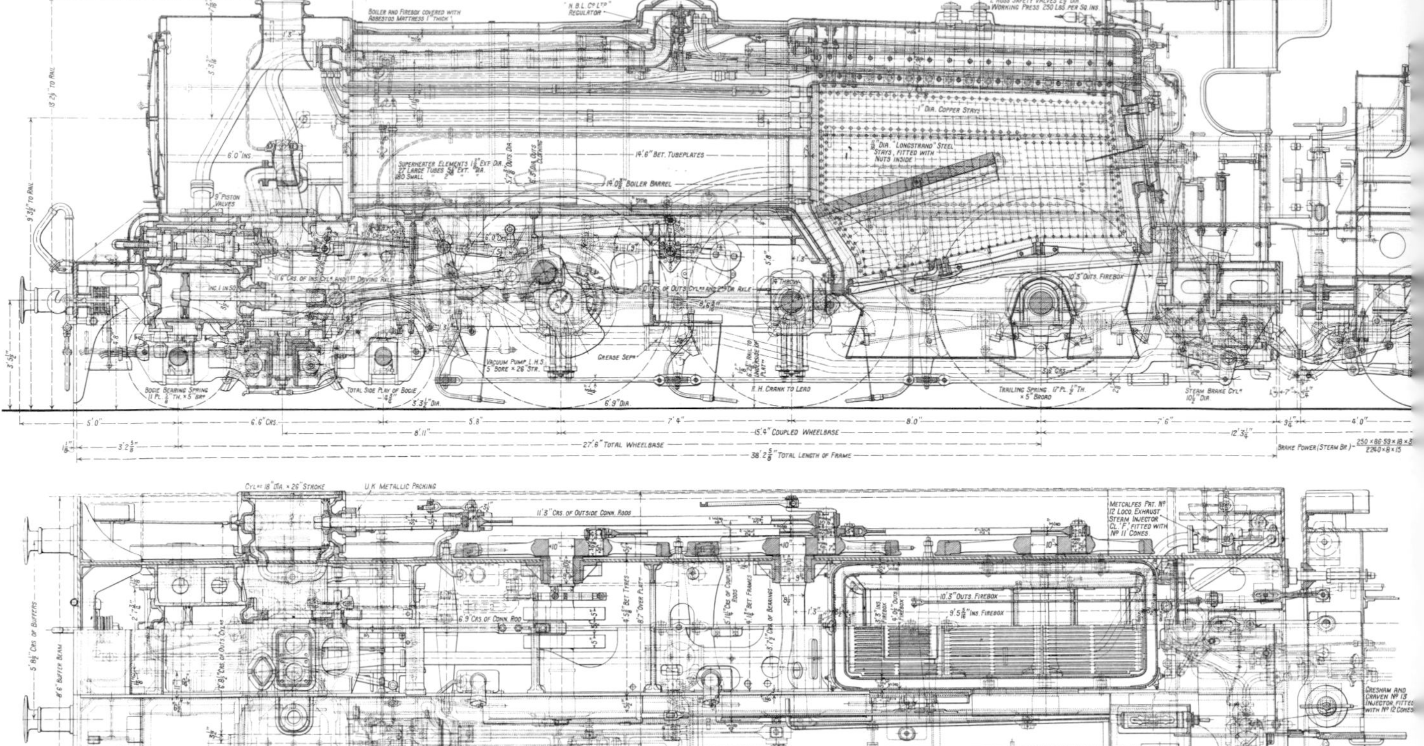

'Castle', in the late autumn of 1926, was rather pathetic. The operating department told the high management that a 4-6-0 of 'Castle' capacity would meet their needs and Fowler was instructed to get 50 built ready for the summer traffic of 1927. It was an unhappy and humiliating time for the CME's department of the LMS. There was not a hope of getting an entirely new express locomotive designed, let alone built in such quantities as the management had stipulated, in time for the summer traffic, and an appeal was made to the Great Western to build 50 'Castles'. This, of course, Swindon could not legally do, but Collett went further, and refused to supply a set of drawings. Thus rebuffed, Fowler next approached R.E.L. Maunsell, who proved more co-operative; in fact Clayton and Holcroft were delighted that so large a company as the LMS, in its extremity, should have sought the assistance of the Southern. The *Lord Nelson*, then brand new, was of the tractive capacity required, and a set of drawings was rushed up to Glasgow, to enable the North British Locomotive Company to tender for the 50 engines the LMS required. It was evident that the principal burden of getting a new design prepared had been passed to Herbert Chambers, Chief Locomotive Draughtsman at Derby; for it was he who went to Waterloo, and he who briefed the NB Loco Co, as to what was required.

For a locomotive class conceived in such traumatic circumstances, the 'Royal Scots' were an outstanding success; and for this the credit rests mainly upon the North British Locomotive Company. The men of the LMS can have contributed little. The operating department, not the CME, specified three cylinders; Chambers no doubt saw to it that the valve gear provided long laps, and long travel, and there were Midland features of detail design, such as bogie wheel brakes, solid manganese bronze coupled wheel axle-boxes, and the Schmidt type of piston rings. The boiler and firebox looked something like that of the *Lord Nelson*, but without the refinements of shaping that Clayton had carefully copied from Swindon practice; but in service, the NBL design on the 'Royal Scot' proved a more reliable steamer than that of the 'Nelson'.

However, it was, above all, the way the 'Scots' were plunged into the tremendous winter task of running the 15-coach 'Royal Scot' train non-stop over the 299.2 miles between Euston and Carlisle, in each direction, through the 1927-8 winter, with such regularity and excellent time-

Left *LMS: The 'Royal Scot' Class 4-6-0.*

Right *Somerset & Dorset Joint Railway: in 1925 an enlarged design of 2-8-0 was prepared at Derby. The machinery was the same as that of the earlier class of 1914, but the boiler was larger. Five engines, Nos 86-90, were built by Robert Stephenson & Co* (British Railways).

Below *LMS: the 'Royal Scot' Class 4-6-0 as originally built, before naming. Note also brakes on the bogie wheels, subsequently removed* (North British Locomotive Company).

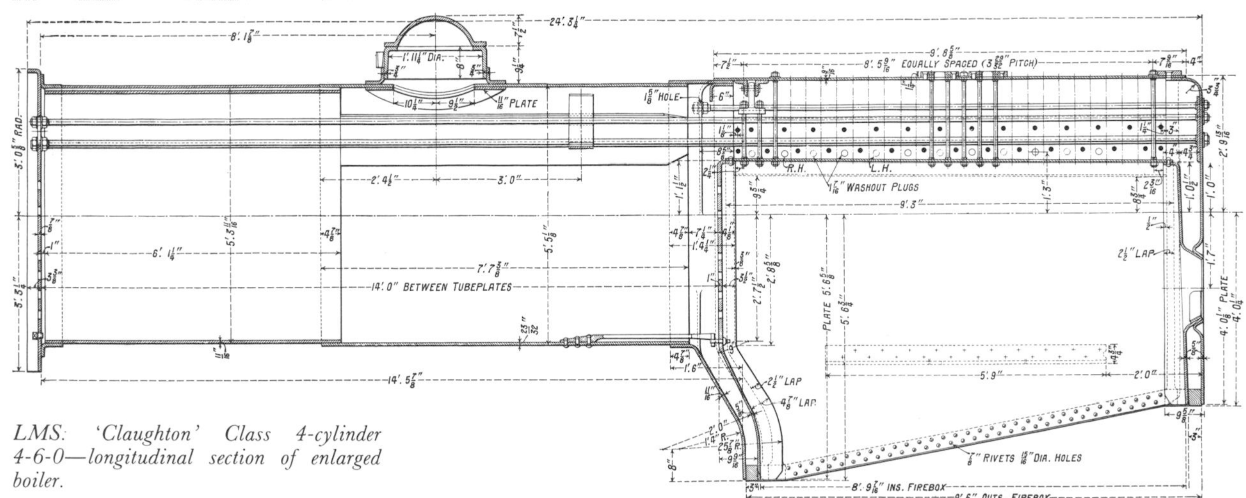

LMS: 'Claughton' Class 4-cylinder 4-6-0—longitudinal section of enlarged boiler.

keeping, that marked the design as a whole as a brilliant success. It is true that, before so very long, a number of details had to be altered in the light of continuing experience; but the introduction of the engines, and the non-stop running of the train itself, gave a tremendous and much needed boost to LMS morale as a whole.

When Fowler's compound 'Pacific' project was scotched in the summer of 1926 it became known that a larger boiler for the 'Claughtons' was being designed at Crewe, and that this might be the basis for the new first-line express passenger engine for the LMS. By that time the findings of the Bridge Stress Committee, though not yet published, were becoming known in locomotive engineering circles, and it would have been surprising if some of those at Crewe, with long memories, had not looked back to the original 'Claughton' boiler design of 1911, which was vetoed on account of weight by the civil engineer.

LMS: '6P' and '5XP' 4-6-0s

Class	'Royal Scot'	Rebuilt 'Claughton'	'Baby Scot'
Cylinders (number of)	3	4	3
Diameter (inches)	18	15 ¾	18
Stroke (inches)	26	26	26
Coupled wheel diameter (feet/inches)	6 9	6 9	6 9
Heating surfaces (square feet)			
Tubes	1,892	1,550	1,550
Firebox	189	183	183
Superheater	416	365	365
Grate area (square feet)	31.2	30	30.5
Boiler pressure (lb per square inch)	250	200	200
Tractive effort (lb)	33,150	27,577	26,520

Whatever may have been the background to it, rebuilding of some of the 'Claughtons' with larger boilers began early in 1928. The new boilers, carrying a pressure of 200 lb per square inch instead of 175, increased the weight of the engines by no more than 1¼ tons, and the tube heating surface was actually less, through the use of a slightly shorter barrel and 140 small tubes of $2\frac{1}{8}$ inches outside diameter, instead of 149 of $1\frac{7}{8}$ inches outside diameter, rather more closely spaced. The rebuilt engines, of which there were 20 in all, were very successful. Ten were fitted with Caprotti valve gear but, on dynamometer car tests between Manchester and Euston, the engines retaining their original valve gear proved more economical. Details

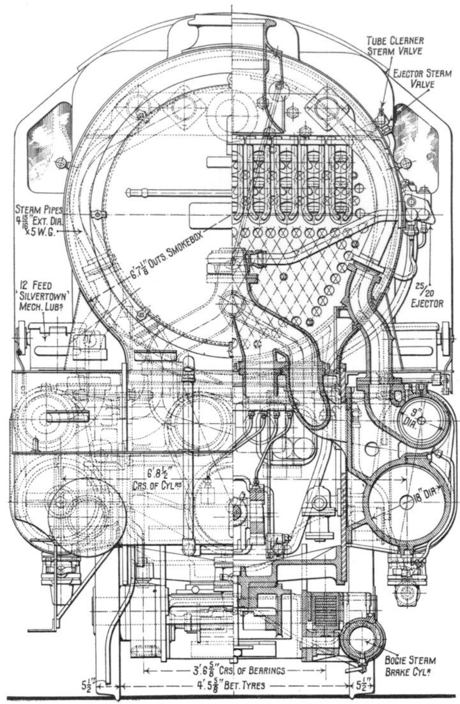

LMS: cross-sectional drawings of the 'Royal Scot'.

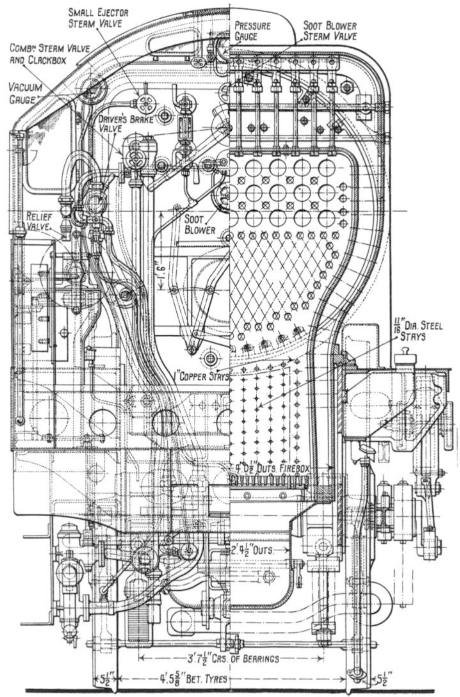

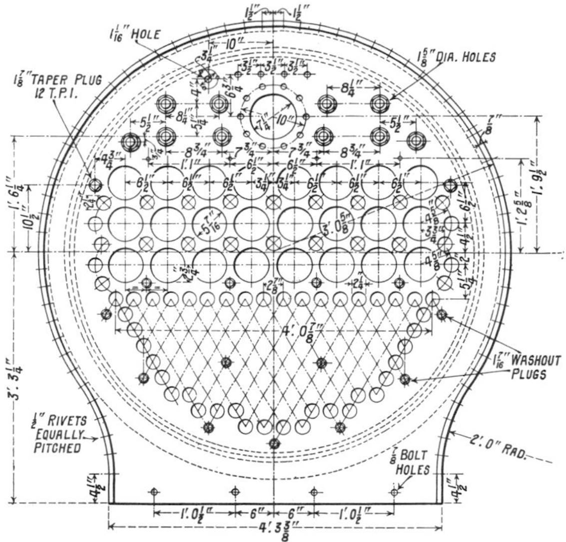

Above *LMS: rebuilt 'Claughton' engine—details of tube plate.*

Below *LMS: rebuilt 'Claughton'—cross-section through the firebox.*

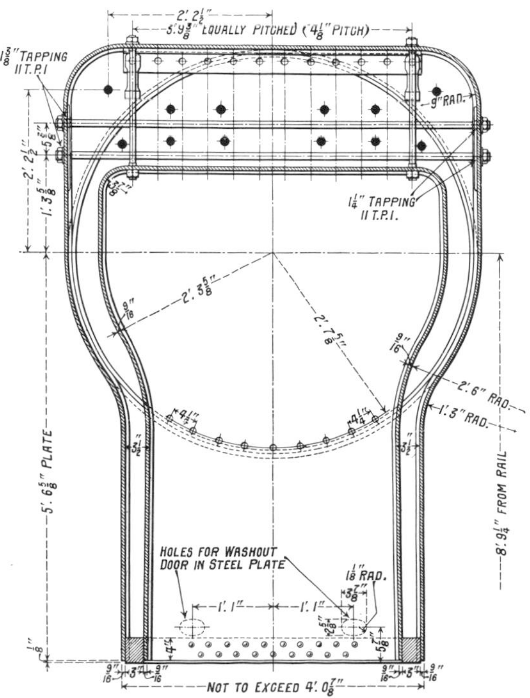

of these test runs were given later, in connection with reference to the alterations to the piston valves made on the 'Royal Scots'.

While Crewe had made a successful job of modernising the 'Claughton' engine, as it stood (retaining the completely balanced 4-cylinder engine layout) a design for a more complete renewal of engines of this class was prepared at Derby. This was a complete crossbreed, using the chassis and machinery of the 'Royal Scot', and the enlarged 'Claughton' boiler. Two prototypes, using some parts from the original engines, were built at Derby in 1930, and they had the rather clumsy official title, originally, of 'Three-cylinder Converted Claughton'. They had particularly the object of enhancing locomotive power on the Midland line, and more conversions, or more correctly replacements were authorised in 1932. It was then that the enginemen found a more homely, and really more appropriate name for them in the 'Baby Scots'. These handsome medium-powered engines came to have a curious history. It began in a positive blaze of glory, because in a series of dynamometer car test runs on Manchester to Euston expresses, via Stoke-on-Trent, running in competition with the two varieties of large-boilered 'Claughtons', they not only returned a lower basic coal consumption, but the class as a whole was showing a quite spectacularly low repair cost index. This yardstick of maintenance costs was based on the repair costs for the entire class in pence per mile, and was related only to the mileage covered in traffic, and not to the work done.

The 'Baby Scots' came to be spread over the whole LMS system, south of Glasgow, and a high proportion of their duties, particularly on the Midland Division, were on fairly light trains. In contrast, the rebuilt 'Claughtons' were all on the Western Division, on heavy trains like the Irish Mails, and the Liverpool and Manchester Scottish expresses between Preston and Carlisle. This could well account for some of the differences between their repair costs and those of the 'Baby Scots'—equally between those of the latter and the 'Royal Scots', on which the machinery was identical. In the following comparison the basis, with the index number 100, was the cheapest relatively modern LMS engine to repair, the 6 foot 9 inch '2P' 4-4-0.

Repair cost indices

Engine class	Index
'Royal Scot'	177
'Baby Scot'	118
Rebuilt 'Claughton'	175
Original 'Claughton'	200

This page, top to bottom

LMS: one of the 'Royal Scots' as received at Crewe, and photographed on the Old Chester main line, with a background of the gardens of the senior officers of the works (British Railways).

LMS: the Class '3P' small passenger tank engine of 1930 (British Railways).

LMS: the celebrated 2-6-4 tank engine design of 1927, having long-lap, long travel valves. The earliest engines of this class were painted in Midland red (British Railways).

Opposite page, top to bottom

LMS: one of the large-boilered 'Claughtons' retaining Walschaerts valve gear: No 5986 stationed at Preston (Locomotive Publishing Company).

LMS: a large boilered 'Claughton' fitted with the Caprotti valve gear—No 5927, Sir Francis Dent (British Railways).

LMS: Beyer-Garratt articulated 2-6-0 + 0-6-2 heavy mineral engine, with self-trimming rotating coal bunker, used on the Toton-Brent coal trains. Thirty of this type were supplied by Beyer-Peacock & Co, following successful experiments with three trial units introduced in 1927 (British Railways).

5986
L M S

5927
L M S

7971
LMS
7971

The difference between the original and the rebuilt 'Claughton' presumably lay in the boiler, because the layout of the machinery was unchanged, while the difference between the Royal and the Baby Scots can almost certainly be attributed to the relative severity of the work they were called upon to do.

The dynamometer car test runs between Manchester and Euston gave the following results:

'5X' 4-6-0 Test runs

Engine class	'Claughton' (Caprotti)	'Claughton' (Walschaerts)	'Baby Scot'
Average load (tons) rate	418	417	409
Average speed (mph)	52.9	52.7	52.5
Coal per dhp hour (lb)	3.53	3.25	3.12

The astonishing change in basic coal consumption from those recorded in earlier LMS trials requires some explanation. After the 'Royal Scots' had been in heavy main line service for several months it was found that they began to show a marked increase in coal consumption, to such an extent as to limit power output on the lengthy double-home duties, such as Euston-Carlisle, Crewe-Glasgow, and Crewe-Perth. There was not enough coal on the tenders. On prolonged investigation it was found that the trouble lay in steam leakage past the wide rings of the Schmidt type of piston valves, which had been standard on both the Midland and the LNWR since the introduction of superheating. The answer was to replace the original complex valves with solid valve heads having six narrow rings. This change was made not only to the 'Royal Scots' and the '5X' Claughtons, but also to the original 'Claughtons', and it brought their coal consumption down to little more than 3.5 lb per dhp hour, instead of the previous figure of around 4½ lb.

Sir Josiah Stamp had not been many years in the saddle as President of the Executive before he became convinced that no real progress in the locomotive department would be made until the deep seated rivalry between the establishments of Crewe and Derby could be eliminated. It was evident even in 1930 in the Derby response to the Crewe rebuilding of the 'Claughton' Class 4-6-0, into Class '5X': Derby must also have its version of Class '5X'. In 1930 Stamp decided that the first step towards an entirely new set-up should be made at

LMS: the application of R. C. Poppet valve gear to 'Horwich' type 2-6-0 locomotive.

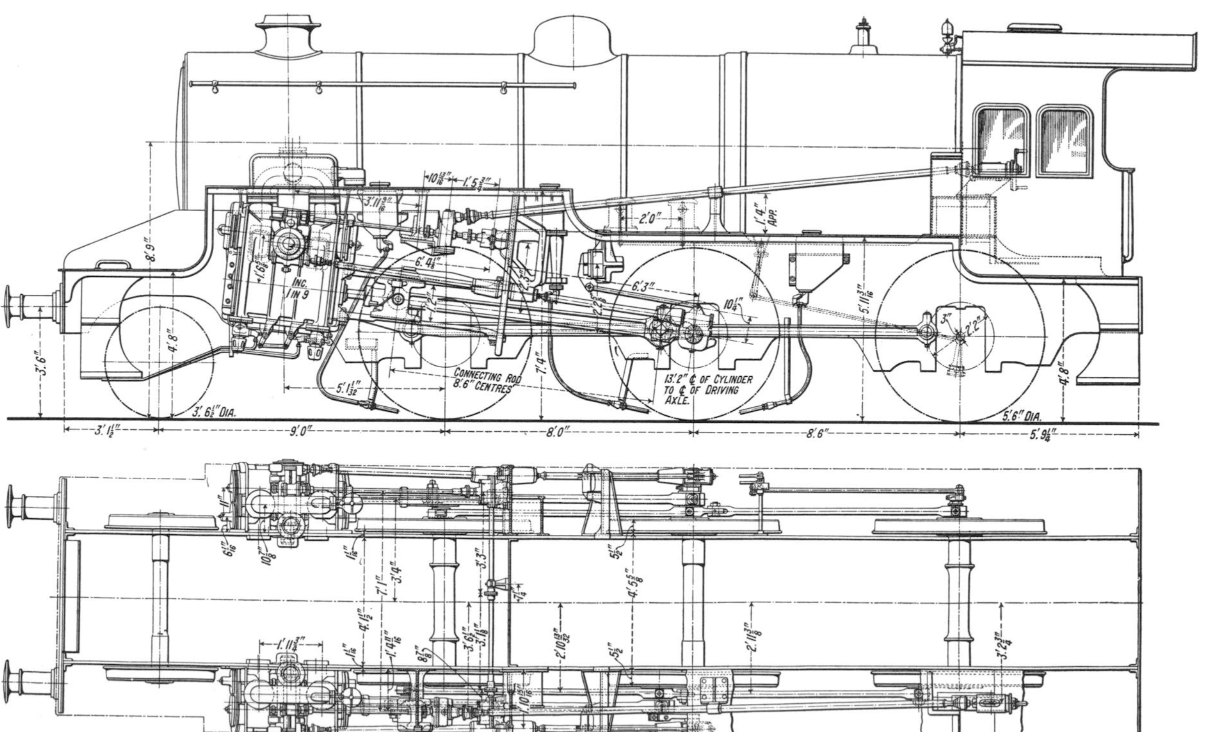

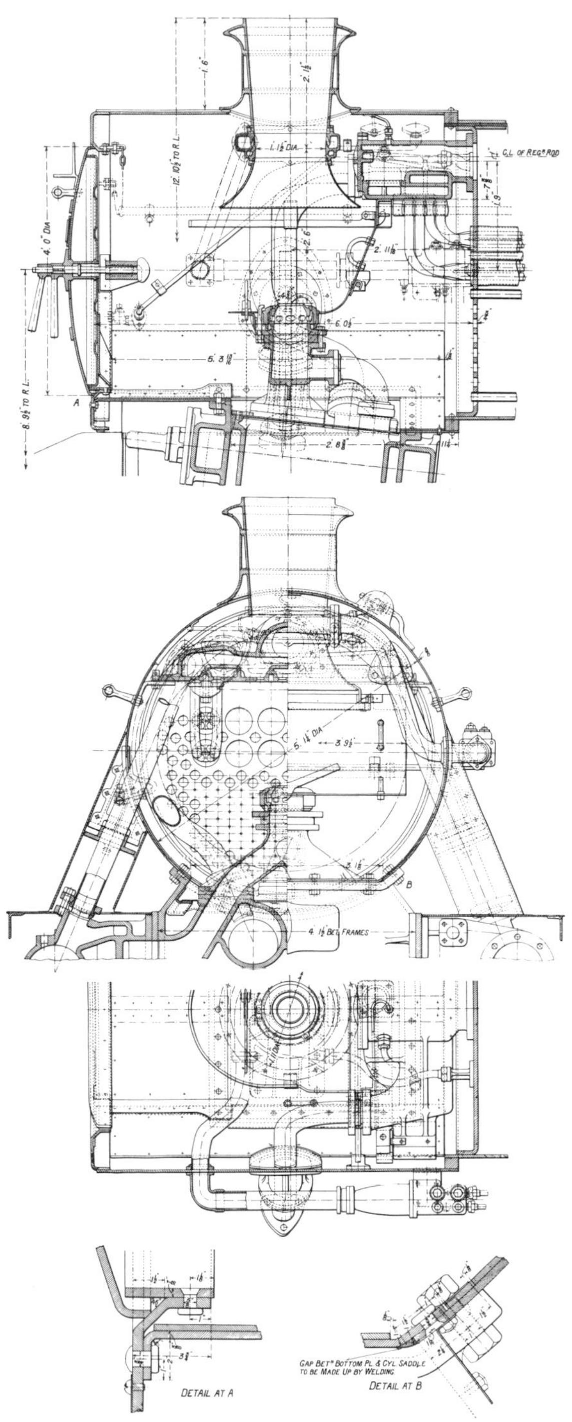

LMS: Stanier 3-cylinder 2-6-4 tank locomotive—details of front end.

the top. Earlier that year a very eminent scientist, Sir Harold Hartley, had joined the LMS as Vice President (Works and Ancilliary Undertakings) and Director of Scientific Research and, as from the beginning of 1931, Sir Henry Fowler was moved 'sideways', to become assistant to Sir Harold, with particular responsibilities for research. This, of course, was Fowler's particular *forte* and, no more than 60 years of age at the time, he might have looked forward to many fruitful years ahead. But benign old gentleman though he might have been, the sideways move in 1930 was not the first jolt that his professional status had received, and he retired after no more than two years' association with Sir Harold Hartley. In the meantime the locomotive department was having something of a shake-up further down the scale.

At that time two senior men might reasonably have had hopes of promotion. They were H.P.M. Beames, Mechanical Engineer, Crewe, who, prior to the merger with Lancashire and Yorkshire Railway in 1922, had been Chief Mechanical Engineer of the LNWR, and secondly, S.J. Symes, who had been personal assistant to Sir Henry Fowler at Derby, following a long and successful career in the locomotive department of the Midland Railway. In the event neither was chosen to succeed Fowler. Instead the opportunity was taken to combine the locomotive and the carriage and wagon branches of mechanical engineering under a single chief officer, as was the case on the other three 'grouped' railways in Great Britain, and E.J.H. Lemon, Carriage and Wagon Superintendent of the LMS since 1927, was appointed the new Chief Mechanical Engineer, with responsibility for locomotives in addition to its previous command.

The headquarters of the CME's department was moved to Euston and thence went S.J. Symes, in a continuance of his previous office as Personal Assistant. Beames was appointed Deputy Chief Mechanical Engineer, with headquarters henceforth at Derby. Lemon himself, however, had been earmarked for still higher things, and his tenure of office as Chief Mechanical Engineer was little more than one of caretaker. Stamp was convinced that the permanent incumbent must be a complete outsider, and much of the year 1931 was spent in finding the right man. How W.A. Stanier was chosen, and eventually persuaded to take the job, is a story I have told more than once*. We must now pass on to his notable work in the LMS.

From almost a lifetime's work on the Great Western, it is not surprising that he crossed to Euston with many strong views as to how locomotives should be designed and built; but the

* *William Stanier: An Engineering Biography.*

heart-warming theme pervading the whole of his distinguished career on the LMS was that he not only showed humanity as well as great skill in choosing his chief assistants, but turned their experience and advice to the lasting benefit of the railway as a whole. His mandate, to scrap and build new, was drastic, and in applying a little too literally the Great Western practices he knew so well the early results were no more than partially successful; but from the very outset he carried the staff with him and as difficulties arose they were surmounted by vigorous and enthusiastic team-work. It was the difference in basic organisation on the Great Western and the LMS that exacerbated some of the difficulties first experienced.

At Swindon the CME had total responsibility for locomotive running with a senior officer in charge, reporting direct to him. In Churchward's day the footplate inspectors were regarded as the 'eyes and ears' of the Drawing Office, and from end to end of the line the locomotives, large and small, were driven and fired as they were designed to be handled. Furthermore the inspectors themselves were nearly all promoted from the ranks of senior drivers, and were mostly held in high esteem by the engine crews. This ensured a two-way liaison. If any difficulties were experienced in working any class of engine the inspectors referred it back to headquarters, confident of a careful and sympathetic investigation into it. In many thousands of miles ridden on the footplates of Great Western locomotives I have seen the fruits of this long sustained tradition, in the most standardised, and assiduously practised methods of working. It is necessary to appreciate this tradition to understand how the design practice of Swindon survived in a difficult and changing environment.

Churchward's view that the boiler was at the heart of all problems connected with the steam locomotive has been quoted on countless occasions. To some it might seem like a glimpse of the obvious, seeing that if the boiler does not function properly the driving force of the locomotive is removed. But Churchward was of course looking to the finer points of boiler performance, not only in the economic production of steam, but in minimising maintenance costs. A major point in his development was to use just enough superheat to dry the steam admitted to the cylinders, but after it had done its work, to throw no heat away in the exhaust. The moderate degree of superheat attained in Great Western boilers was calculated just to do that; but—and it was an all important 'but'—if boiler pressure was not constantly and systematically maintained at, or very near to, the designed maximum, the steam after doing its work would be reduced to the point of condensation, and the designed efficiency of the engine very much impaired. The close and cordial relation between the Drawing Office and the footplate inspectors ensured that all firemen were brought up to understand the importance of maintaining steam pressure at or near the maximum value.

Things were different on the LMS. Not only was the authority for locomotive running vested in the operating, rather than the CME's department, but the majority of the superheater locomotives on the English constituents were equipped for a much higher degree of superheat and would not in consequence be subject to such a marked falling off in effectiveness by a drop in boiler pressure as were those of the Great Western. Even with a top link crew working maximum tonnage trains on 'Special Limit' timings I have personally seen boiler

Left *LMS: the 3-cylinder variant of the enlarged 'Claughton' 4-6-0, with the same machinery as the 'Royal Scots', and in consequence nicknamed 'Baby Scots'* (British Railways).

Right *LMS: a 'Royal Scot' visits Canada and the USA in 1933-4. Engine No 6152 was the one actually used, but it was renamed and numbered 6100,* Royal Scot, *and equipped with an electric headlight* (British Railways).

Below *LMS: the second of the Stanier 'Pacifics' of 1933, No 6201,* Princess Elizabeth, *at Euston after having worked the Royal Scot train throughout from Glasgow. Note the Caledonian type semaphore headcode.*

LMS: Stanier taper boilered version of the 2-6-0 already in wide use, built at Crewe 1933 (British Railways).

pressure allowed to drop 30 or 40 lb per square inch below maximum, and quickly raised again without any apparent loss in efficiency. Another point too: Great Western locomotives had the Ramsbottom type of safety valve, and with good firing this could be kept in a balanced position, with almost full pressure, 'sizzling', rather than fully blowing off, whereas with the 'pop' type of safety valve (favoured on all new LMS designs) there was no 'sizzling' position. If maximum pressure was reached, off they would go, with a 'bang' rather than a 'pop', and I have seen so much steam go to waste that the boiler pressure was lowered sometimes down by as much as 30 lb per square inch before the valves closed.

Stanier's mandate was to introduce as quickly as possible new designs that would eventually cover the entire working of the railway, and enable a large number of obsolescent designs to be scrapped; and, in less than two years, five new designs had been produced. These five, in ascending order of power, are shown in the table below.

Classes 1, 2 and 4 were equivalent in tractive power to the existing '2300' Class of 2-6-4 tank, to the Horwich 'crabs', and to the rebuilt 'Claughton' and 'Baby Scot' 4-6-0s. The 'Black Five' was something new on the LMS, though undoubtedly, inspired by the Great Western 'Hall' Class. Leaving the huge 'Pacifics' out of consideration for the moment, the first batch of 2-6-4 tanks, completed in 1934, had three cylinders. They were designed to provide a smooth starting torque and high acceleration with the heavy commuter trains of the London Tilbury and Southend line, and had heavier axle loading than the preceeding Fowler 2-6-4s, the weights on the coupled wheels being 18.25, 19.5 and 19.25 tons, against 17.0, 18.15, and 16.3 tons. This increase in weight led to a 'brush' with the Chief Civil Engineer, Alexander Newlands, he, who in his Highland days, had

Ref no	1	2	3	4	5
Class	**4P**	**5F**	**5P5F**	**5XP**	**7P**
Type	2-6-4T	2-6-0	4-6-0	4-6-0	4-6-2
Duty	3-cylinder passenger tank	2-cylinder mixed traffic	2-cylinder ('Black Five')	3-cylinder passenger (Jubilee)	4-cylinder heavy passenger (Princess Royal)

LMS: a boiler comparison

Class	**4P**	**4P**	**5F**	**5F**	**5XP***	**5XP**
Type	2-6-4T	2-6-4T	2-6-0	2-6-0	4-6-0	4-6-0
Engineer	Fowler	Stanier	Hughes	Stanier	Beames	Stanier
Heating surfaces (square feet)						
Tubes	1,082	1,011	1,345	1,479	1,552	1,462.5
Firebox	138	137	160	155	183	162.4
Superheater	246	160	307	232	365	277.5
Grate area (square feet)	25.0	25.0	27.5	27.8	30.5	29.5
Boiler pressure (lb per square inch)	200	200	180	225	200	225

* Rebuilt 'Claughton' and 'Baby Scot' Classes.

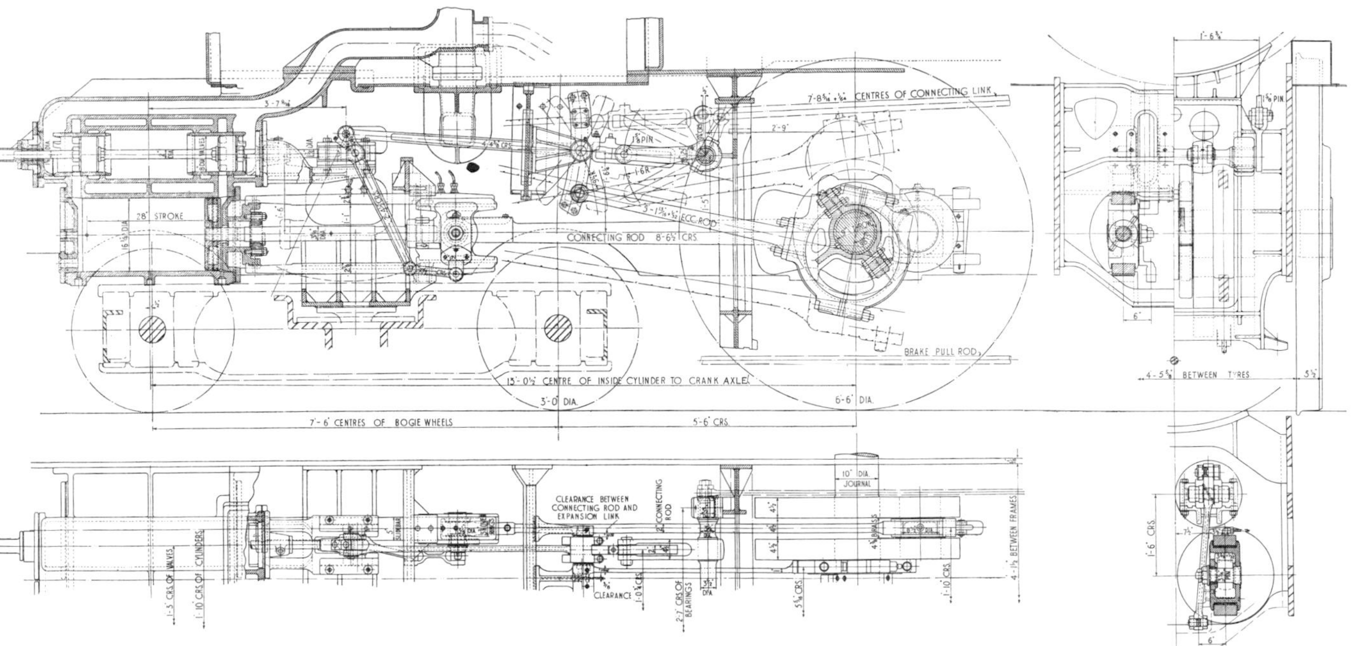

Above *LMS: 'Princess Royal' Class 4-6-2 engines—details of valve gear on inside cylinders.*

Below *LMS: 'Princess Royal' Class 4-6-2 engines—details of boiler with high degree superheat.*

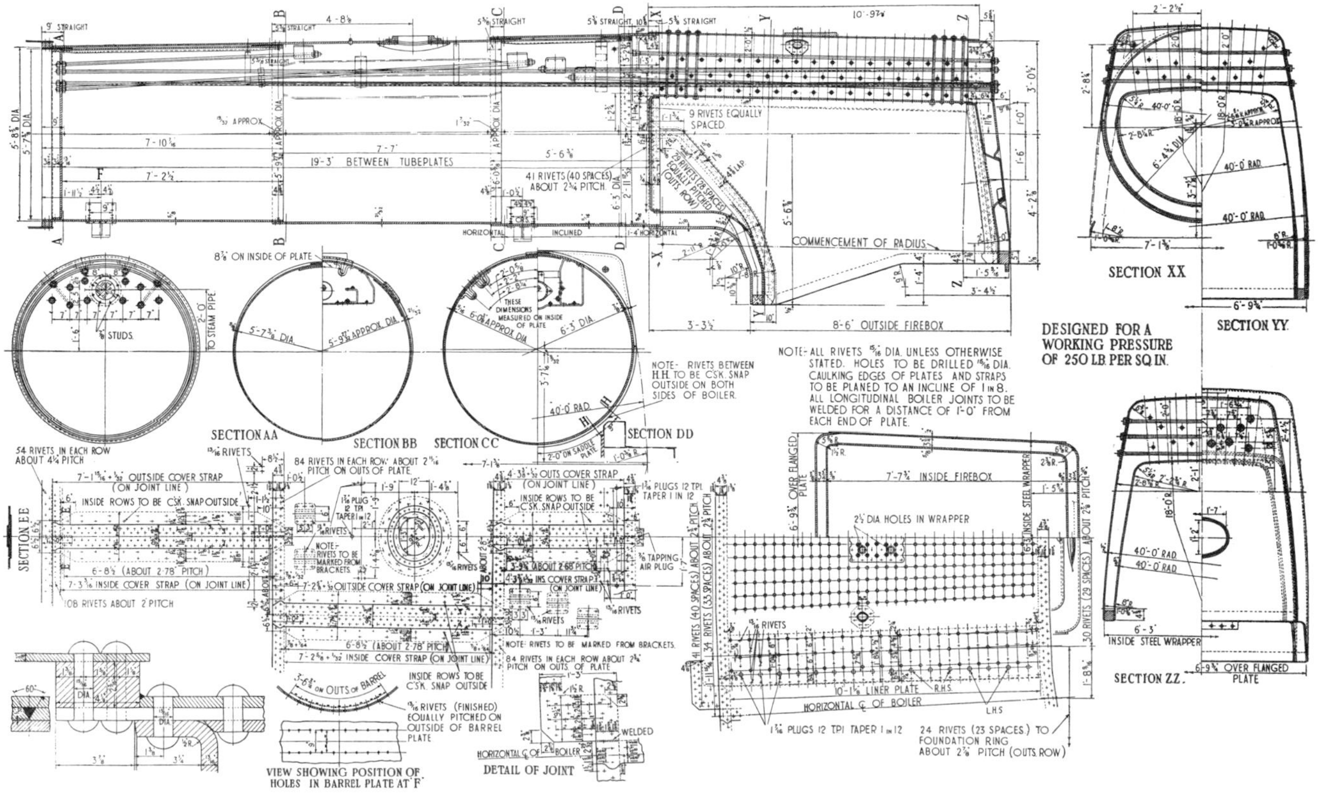

19'-3" BETWEEN TUBEPLATES

8'-6" OUTSIDE FIREBOX

COMMENCEMENT OF RADIUS

SECTION AA

SECTION BB

SECTION CC

SECTION DD

SECTION EE

SECTION XX

SECTION YY

SECTION ZZ.

DESIGNED FOR A WORKING PRESSURE OF 250 LB PER SQ IN.

NOTE- ALL RIVETS 15/16 DIA. UNLESS OTHERWISE STATED. HOLES TO BE DRILLED 15/16 DIA. CAULKING EDGES OF PLATES AND STRAPS TO BE PLANED TO AN INCLINE OF 1 IN 8. ALL LONGITUDINAL BOILER JOINTS TO BE WELDED FOR A DISTANCE OF 1'-0" FROM EACH END OF PLATE.

NOTE- RIVETS BETWEEN H.H. TO BE CSK. SNAP OUTSIDE ON BOTH SIDES OF BOILER.

7'-7¾" INSIDE FIREBOX

INSIDE STEEL WRAPPER

6'-9¾" OVER FLANGED PLATE

HORIZONTAL ℄ OF BOILER

24 RIVETS (23 SPACES) TO FOUNDATION RING ABOUT 2⅞" PITCH (OUTS ROW)

VIEW SHOWING POSITION OF HOLES IN BARREL PLATE AT 'F'

DETAIL OF JOINT

banned the use of the 'River' Class 4-6-0s in 1915. But when attention was politely drawn to the findings of the Bridge Stress Committee, and that the new engines had three, and not two, cylinders, objection was withdrawn, and the 37 engines of the class, 2500 and 2536, went into regular working on the Tilbury line. They were followed by a further series with two cylinders for general service on the LMS.

Excellent though the Tilbury 4-4-2 tanks were, and well liked by all who had to deal with them, the new 2-6-4s were so much more powerful, and so much master of their loads that they were appreciated from the start, no matter how different they were from the engines to which the men had been so long accustomed. But it was far otherwise with the new '5XP' 4-6-0s. The chassis and wheel spacing was the same as that of the 'Baby Scots', even to the retention of the 6 foot 3 inch spacing of the bogie wheels which the latter class had inherited from the 'Claughtons' they replaced, but the boiler, if one may call it so, was almost pure Great Western, except that for some reason it would not steam! Except that the barrel was one foot shorter, it was a slightly smaller version of the 'Castle', equally with a 14-element superheater, though the heating surfaces were less, consequent upon the shorter barrel: 1,462.5 square feet in the tubes, against 1,886, and 227.5 square feet in the superheater against 263 square feet. The shaping of the firebox was pure Swindon. Of course the LMS enginemen, both on the LNW and Midland sections, set out to drive and fire them in the same carefree style with which they had handled their own engines. Fluctuating boiler pressure did not help, but at first all was not well with the draughting on the '5XPs'. The 'Black Fives', which followed them into traffic later in 1934, though also suffering from too little superheat, seemed much more reliable at first.

Part of the trouble was that the management had been in such a hurry to get new engines that the 'Black Five' 2-cylinder mixed traffic 4-6-0s, and the '5XP' express passenger class were ordered in large quantities from the outset. There was no question of a few prototypes for trial. No fewer than 113 of the '5XP' Class were ordered straight off the drawing boards—53 from Crewe, 50 from the North British Locomotive Company, and 10 from Derby. The 'Black Fives' were launched with a first order for 50 tons from the Vulcan Foundry, in 1934. Following

LMS: The 'Black-5' mixed traffic 4-6-0, the later type with domed boiler and higher degree of superheat.

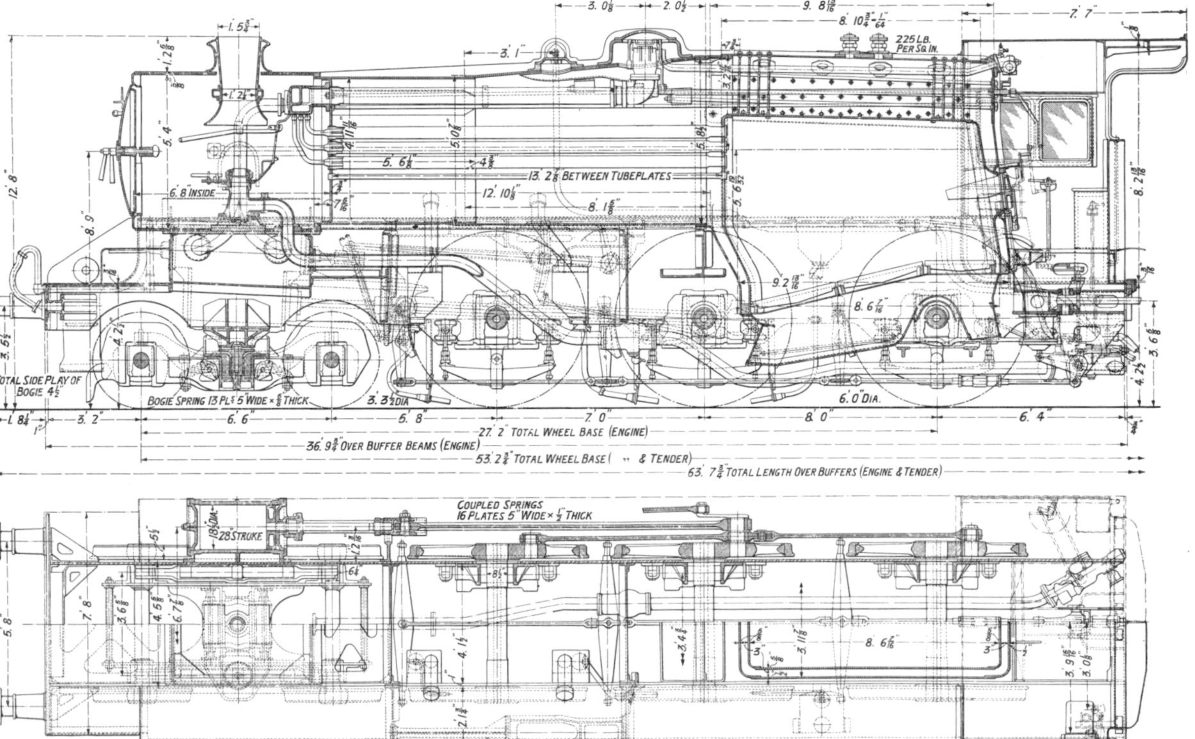

Right *LMS: one of the later engines of the Stanier 'Jubilee' Class 3-cylinder 4-6-0s, working on the Derby–Manchester line* (E.D. Bruton).

Below *LMS: the first of the Stanier '8F' 2-8-0s, as introduced in 1935 with domeless boiler. This design, as later developed, was adopted as a wartime standard for all the British railways* (British Railways).

Above *LMS: the famous Stanier 'Pacific' No 6201,* Princess Elizabeth, *with modified boiler and new type of tender. It was in this form that the engine made the London–Glasgow record non-stop runs in November 1936* (British Railways).

Right *LMS: the Stanier type of 2-6-4 tank engine with taper boiler and top feed* (British Railways).

LMS: the Stanier '3P' 2-6-2 tank engine in its later form, with larger domed boiler.

the completion of the order for '5XP' 4-6-0s at Crewe, the works there went on to build 20 'Black Five' 4-6-0s. These latter were numbered 5000 to 5019; the Vulcans which preceeded them were 5020 to 5069. Although the medium superheat '5XPs' did not get off to a very good start generally, some very fine work was done on some special dynamometer car test runs in 1934. For example, on the 4.35 pm Birmingham and Wolverhampton express from Euston, which then had two stops scheduled within the overall time of two hours, to Birmingham, one of the Crewe built '5XPs', No 5556, ran the 62.8 miles from Euston to Blisworth in 56 minutes 23 seconds start to stop with a load of 345 tons. The normal schedule is 63 minutes, but for test purposes this was cut to 59 minutes. It must be added, however, that the '5XP' engines rarely, if ever, rose to such heights of performance in ordinary service.

In the first phase of the Stanier transformation of the LMS motive power position it was, of course, the working of the two large 'Pacifics' engines, *The Princess Royal* and *Princess Elizabeth*, which tended to overshadow everything else. They were designed for through working over the 401 miles between Euston and Glasgow and, although when they were available they worked north one day and returned the next, it was hoped tht eventually the turn-round time at both Euston and Glasgow would be considerably less than the 16 hours when running the down and up 'Royal Scot' trains. There were four basic features of the design of these two engines that came to affect the daily performance.

In the details of the machinery that contributed to the value of nominal tractive effort these engines were identical to the 'Kings', though having four sets of valve gear. The valve events were the same. Secondly, there was the chassis, which was a beautiful piece of original design, and gave a superb ride. The original boiler which, like the smaller engines, had relatively low superheat, was not successful, and again suffered from ineffective draughting. In the last respect, the design of the 'King' was copied; when troubles occurred on the LMS, Stanier had the layout very carefully analysed and it was found that the gas-flow was markedly restricted at certain points. Finally, there was the design of the tender in which the coal did not readily trim forward, and which greatly increased the labour of firing on a long run.

While Stanier's own staff worked assiduously to diagnose and rectify these troubles it must be recorded that a small, though potentially dangerous, anti-Stanier faction developed in the Operating Department of the LMS. Maybe it was out of some jealousy, but also out of that isolationism which believed nothing good could come out of the Great Western, that fanned the flames. Prominent of this movement, if not actually the 'Leader of the Opposition', was D.C. Urie who, at the time of Stanier's appointment, was Divisional Mechanical Engineer (Glasgow). A son of R.W. Urie, the former CME of the London and South Western Railway, and Locomotive Superintendent of the Highland Railway after the retirement of C. Cumming, he had succeeded to the senior mechanical engineering post in Scotland after Pickersgill's retirement. In 1932, following Anderson's retirement, he was moved from the

LMS: the first taper-boiler 'Scot', No 6170, British Legion, *a replacement for the ill-fated super-pressure compound 4-6-0* Fury (British Railways).

CME's to the Operating Department as Superintendent of Motive Power. As such, of course, he had to use the Stanier locomotives, and it must be said that he was not very helpful when troubles arose. He referred to Stanier as 'that blue-pencil watchmaker'! Urie or not, the experience of 1934 sounded the death-knell of the brief LMS espousal of Great Western ideas about superheating, and the way in which the boilers of the Stanier standard engines were subsequently modified was an eye-opener.

The accompanying table shows the changes that were made to all the standard types, and they then became collectively the most reliable and free steaming engines that have ever run the rails in Great Britain. It was not only a matter of performance on the road. They were remarkably low in maintenance charges.

In this, of course, they were no different from their Great Western progenitors, but they were far less sensitive to varying footplate methods, and to variations in the fuel. The 'Black Fives', for example, were to be seen anywhere between Bristol

The Stanier standard locomotives

Class	**3P**		**4P**		**5P 5F**			**5XP**		**7P**		**8F**	
Type	2-6-2T		2-6-4T		4-6-0			4-6-0		4-6-2		2-8-0	
Boiler	1	2	1	2	1	2	3	1	2	1	2	1	2
Heating surfaces (square feet)													
Tubes	774.5	997	1,011	1,223	1,460	1,460	1,479	1,462.5	1,460	2,523	2,097	1,308	1,479
Firebox	103.9	111	137	143	156	171.3	171	162.4	181.1	190	217	155	171
Superheater	75.9	138	160	230	227.5	307	359	227.5	307	370	653	235	245
Grate area (square feet)	17.5	19.2	25.0	26.7	27.8	28.65	28.65	29.5	31	45	45	27.8	28.65
Boiler pressure (lb per square inch)	200		200		225			225		250		225	
Cylinders (number of)	2		2		2			3		4		2	
Diameter (inches)	17½		19 5/8		18½			17		16¼		18½	
Stroke (inches)	26		26		28			26		28		28	
Tractive effort (lb)	21.486		24,670		25.455			26,610		40,300		32,438	

and Wick while, when they had the modified boilers, the '5XP' 4-6-0s did equally good work anywhere on Western, Midland or Scottish Divisions. They came completely to eclipse (in popularity) the 'Baby Scots', except on the Euston-Wolverhampton trains. In 1935, engine No 5552, the first of the Stanier '5XPs', was given a special finish in black and stainless steel, and named *Silver Jubilee*, in honour of the great event of the year, the 25th anniversary of the reign of King George V. The engines themselves, named after the dominions, colonies and dependencies of the British Empire, became the 'Jubilee' Class.

It was not only the new engines which were greatly improved. Reference has already been made to the piston valves of the 'Royal Scots' and of the 'Claughton' Class engines. Stanier had not been on the LMS very long before he became shocked at the high incidence of hot axleboxes on the 'Royal Scots'—no less than 102 cases among the 70 engines of the class in the year 1932. These engines had manganese bronze boxes of the same design that had been standard on the larger Midland classes, and some detail features that could be regarded as 'fussy'. While the basic idea of using manganese bronze lay in its good conductivity it was not in itself a bearing material and was too soft to take a pressed-in brass. So separate bronze strips dovetailed into the parent metal had to be used to confine the white-metal bearing pads. It was a design that needed very careful fitting, and while it gave reasonably good service on the lightly-used Midland engines, its record, on heavily worked classes like the 'Royal Scots' was poor. The containing strips worked loose, and then the whole bearing disintegrated. At Crewe they had always used steel axle-boxes with pressed-in brasses; but in 1932 these were out of favour because of inadequate bearing surfaces. But an investigation into their bad record surprised Stanier all the more, because the Crewe design was the nearest LMS equivalent to the standard Great Western type, which was remarkably free from trouble, but even more so when he was assured by more than one ex-Crewe man that it had not been so in LNWR days.

One of these engineers, holding an eminent postion on an overseas railway, called on Stanier during his leave, and was shocked to hear of the crop of hot boxes, on ex-LNWR Classes—a situation quite unlike anything that prevailed in his own time at Crewe. At Stanier's invitation he paid a visit to Camden shed, and discovered to his astonishment that, on the Joy valve gear engines, the centre bearing on the driving axle had been removed, apparently on instructions from Derby. In consequence, when the engines were being worked hard, which they very often were, an inordinately heavy load was thrown upon the driving axle boxes

LMS: the 'Royal Scots' in their final and most brilliant form, with modified piston valves, new driving axle-boxes, and latest type of tender, No 6160, Queen Victoria's Rifleman (British Railways).

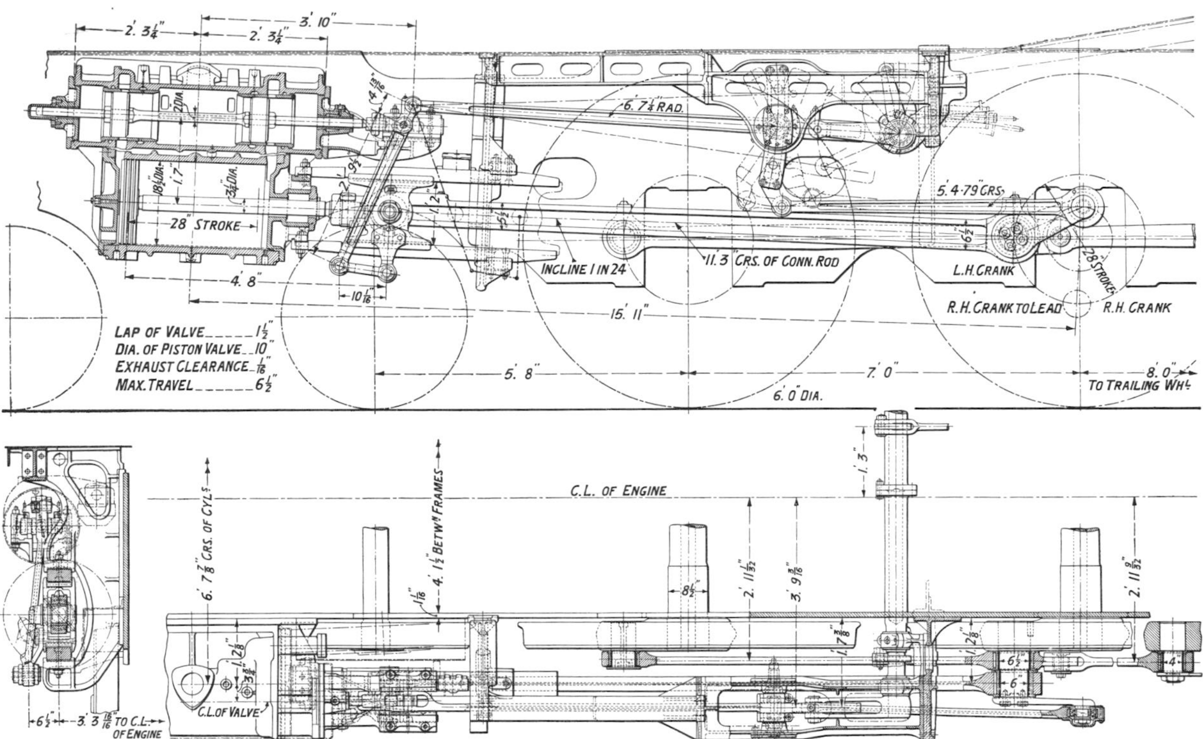

LMS: the 'Black-5'—general layout of valve motion.

in the main frames. Subjected thus to much more than their designed load it was not surprising that they ran hot and that frames cracked! But the Crewe axle box in its detail design was capable of much improvement, and on all Stanier's own engines on the LMS the Swindon type was used, with a steel box, with a thin whitemetal lining, not shrouded at the sides but only at the ends. It was also fitted to the 'Royal Scots', and it proved the finishing touch to a design of heavy express passenger locomotive, that gave outstandingly good service on the heaviest duties. The men found that they could thrash them with impunity. They would steam freely, on a coal consumption that was moderate in relation to the work done, and the monthly mileages they clocked up were prodigious.

It is always dangerous, and sometimes downright misleading, to make comparisons between the observed performance of locomotives in ordinary traffic; but I must add that up to the time of the Second World War certain of my own observations with engines of the 'Royal Scot' surpassed anything I had seen with locomotives of comparable tractive effort. Until the boilers of the 'Pacifics' had been modified, the 4-6-0s had frequently to deputise for the bigger engines, and they were not usually found wanting. Some individual performances may be set on record thus:

Royal Scot performance

Engine no	**6137**	**6142**	**6108**	**6108**	**6164**	**6137**	**6142**
Engine name	**Vesta**	**Lion**	**Seaforth Highlander**	**Seaforth Highlander**	**The Artists Rifleman**	**Vesta**	**Lion**
Location	Shap Incline	Standon Bridge	Castlemilk	Beattock	Grayrigg Bank	Berkhamsted	Hatch End
Speed (mph)	25	64	50	26	38	56	58½
Equivalent dhp	1,200	1,280	1,280	1,300	1,300	1,320	1,360

3. The veterans in excelsis

By the year 1932, when the nation itself was beginning its slow climb out of the great Depression, and renewed confidence in the future was shown by the notable accelerations of the Anglo-Scottish services on both the LMS and the LNER, the policies of standardisation and the building of new locomotives had not yet reached the stage when all the older types had been either demoted to secondary duties or withdrawn altogether. In consequence, some of the veterans which had been maintained in good condition were still regularly called upon for first class express duty, albeit of a nature somewhat below the severity of that demanded from the latest and largest engines. On the LNER, in particular, at the time of grouping, Gresley had been fortunate in inheriting from the constituents many locomotive classes capable of hard, reliable service on the road, if not necessarily measuring up to modern standards of thermal efficiency; and while the purse strings had perforce to be drawn tight where capital expenditure was concerned, they had to carry on, for some years at least. It so happened also that some of these ageing locomotives were called upon for harder work than at any time in their prime, to the approbation and delight of those who took detailed records of train running.

This was notably the case with the Robinson 'Atlantics' of the former Great Central Railway, which, in the haulage of the 6.20 pm London to Bradford express, as between Marylebone and Leicester had, every night in the year, a task of a severity unknown on the line in the most fiercely competitive pre-war years. Because of the heavy occupation of the Metropolitan Line at that hour with home going commuter traffic, the train took the longer route via High Wycombe, and was allowed 114 minutes non-stop for the 107.6 miles to Leicester, an average speed of 56.6 mph. Two slip coaches were carried, one detached at Finmere, and worked forward to give an excellent evening service to the succeeding stations of Brackley, Helmdon and Culworth, while the second was detached at Woodford, to serve the branch to Stratford-on-Avon. In consequence the train left Marylebone with a nightly load of 290 to 300 tons, whereas in pre-war days the loads of the principal expresses were rarely more than about 200 tons. While it could be argued that few of the Atlantics were then superheated a study of earlier work would suggest that this refinement in design did not make a great deal of difference to the performance, then at any rate.

When the modernisation of these engines, by the addition of superheaters, continued in the 1920s, their state, as modernised, was not uniform throughout the class in that some had 20 inch, and others 21 inch, diameter cylinders, while not all were fitted with piston valves instead of the original valves. But the work of the superheater 'Atlantics' on the 6.20 pm from Marylebone to Leicester was uniform enough in its consistent and thrilling excellence. I made a number of journeys on this train, and one could always tell by the sharpness of the exhaust beat that the engines were being worked very hard, especially in the early stages. The timetable allowed 45 minutes to cover the first 36 miles, to passing Princes Risborough. That may not seem very severe, but actually with speed restrictions over the junctions at Neasden and Northolt, and then

Left *Great Central Railway: flashback to early days on the London Extension, and two-tone carriage liveries—the 3.15 pm ex-Marylebone, non-stop to Sheffield, near Harrow, hauled by 'Atlantic' No 260* (R.J. Purves).

Right *Great Central Railway: another early shot of the 'Sheffield Special', with two-tone carriages, a light load, and engine No 261* (the late C. Laundy).

through High Wycombe station, with adverse gradients to follow each time, and no chance of developing any real express speed, it was very hard indeed. The schedule was planned for a load of about 180 tons, but several times I saw it kept with 300 tons.

By the time Princes Risborough was passed, however, the train was dashing down the northern slopes of the Chiltern Hills, on one occasion reaching 88 mph and then we would continue, without a moment's let-up, for the next hour. There were long uphill stretches inclined at 1 in 176, where the speed rarely fell below 55 mph; the slightest easing of the grade would see the speed go shooting up to well over 60, and when the train did get on to a really racing descent (like that from Catesby Tunnel down to Braunston) one could be sure of clocking another '80'. Just beyond Rugby the LMS main line was crossed on a long lattice girder viaduct and it often seemed as though the Great Central drivers were going particularly hard there, to show their rivals a thing or two! Then there was the final dash for Leicester. Often, in my experience, with time well in hand the drivers could at last steam their engines lightly there; but if they were a bit tight for time, having had, perhaps, a speed restriction for track repairs, on the way from London that descent could be taken like a thunderbolt with speeds between 87 and a full 90 mph. This may not sound anything very special in these days of HSTs doing 125 mph as a matter of routine; but in the 1930s, with engines built 30 years earlier, it was terrific.

And then, what of their 'Atlantics' counterparts on the Great Northern Line? Few among those who were fully conversant with locomotive operation in Great Britain at that time would, I should imagine, care to dispute an assertion that their working provided some of the major railway phenomena of the day. I am writing now of the years from 1932 onwards, when the oldest of them, the now-preserved 251, was just 30 years old. Their rise to fame was no more than gradual, quite unlike engines one could name which hit the headlines of the technical press no more than weeks after they were first steamed. There is no doubt indeed that many experienced observers of locomotive practice considered that H.A. Ivatt's '251', of 1902, was a somewhat ill-balanced design, in the relative proportions of cylinders and boiler. Certainly this engine, and the 81 of the class which followed it, came in for thinly-disguised, unfavourable comparison with the LNWR 'Precursor' Class 4-4-0s—much smaller engines, but which were doing some quite oustanding work at the time. Neither was Ivatt's first essay into superheating with them conspicuously successful; for in building the 1452-1461 series, in 1910, he reduced the boiler pressure from the original 175 to 150 lb per square inch, no doubt in the hope of reducing the boiler maintenance charges.

The tabulated details show the stages by which Gresley developed the 'Atlantics' from the first superheated version of 1910, in which Ivatt used the Schmidt type of superheater. In his own first development, using the Robinson superheater, the main feature was to keep the boiler pressure near to the original pressure of the non-superheater engines; but the major point in Gresley's development of this design (as discussed in detail later) was to go to a 32-element superheater of the Robinson type in 1919 on engine No 1403, providing no less than 570 square feet of superheater heating surface. I always have felt it was a great pity no 'full dress' trials of these engines took place, in which comprehensive details of the boiler performance and

LNER: very early 'grouping' days—the 4-cylinder 4-6-0, No 1167, then named Lloyd George, *waiting to back down into Kings Cross, while the down Harrogate Pullman is passing.*

indicated horse-power could be recorded for posterity; because the end products, in respect of load haulage at speed, were so remarkable. The boiler, as originally designed by Ivatt, was always very free steaming, but in their non-superheated form the locomotives did not seem able to make the best use of the steam that was so readily available; and performance on the road seemed to confirm the views of those who suggested that the cylinders were too small.

The reduction in boiler pressure on the first Ivatt superheater engines also lessened their effectiveness. When Gresley began fitting the existing Ivatt engines with superheaters, during the First World War, he used the Robinson type of superheater with 24-elements, instead of the Schmidt, and no more than a slightly reduced boiler pressure. With the exceptionally heavy loads of war time, these newly superheated engines did some very fine work; but even this came to be completely surpassed when the same engines were fitted with 32-element superheaters, from 1919 onwards.

Certain observers of long experience in recording locomotive running confessed themselves brought almost to the point of disbelief that engines of such moderate basic dimensions—those contributing to the value of nominal tractive effort—could ever do such work, even with the evidence of their own watches before them. It was sometimes claimed that only superlative skill in driving and firing could have produced such results. The explanation was nevertheless simple enough. The very high degree of superheat imparted a correspondingly high degree of fluidity to the steam, so that it passed with great freedom through the valves, both at inlet and exhaust from the cylinders, and enabled exceptionally large volumes to be passed through freely. It was a comparable case to that of the London and North Western superheater 4-4-0s of the 'George the Fifth' Class, in 1911-6. Above all, however, the Great Northern 'Atlantics' were supremely easy engines to drive and fire, and in consequence were extremely popular with their crews. They had a notched-lever reverser, and this could be set for a cut-off of anything between 35 and 50 per cent, and left there for the whole of the journey. Any variations of power required could be made by adjustments of the regulator opening. Added to this, the mechanical design of the locomotive made the firing easy.

The trailing wheel mountings were provided with lateral play, with the spring resting on a plate that

GNR large boilered 'Atlantics'

Stage	1	2	3	4	5	6
Superheater (type)	—	Schmidt	Robinson	Robinson	Robinson	Robinson
Superheater (no of elements)	—	18	24	24	32	32
Valves (type)	slide	piston	slide	piston	slide	piston
Cylinders						
Diameter (inches)	18¾	20	18¾	20	19	20
Stroke (inches)	24	24	24	24	24	24
Heating surfaces (square feet)						
Tubes	2,359	1,909½	1,882	1,882	1,884	1,884
Firebox	141	143½	138	138	143	143
Superheater	—	343	427	427	570	570
Total	2,500	2,396	2,447	2,447	2,597	2,597
Grate area (square feet)	31	31	31	31	31	31
Boiler pressure (lb per square inch)	175	150	170	170	170	170
Nominal tractive effort (lb)	15,700	15,300	15,200	17,340	15,650	17,340

Right *LNER/GCR: 4-cylinder 4-6-0, No 6167 (formerly named* Lloyd George*), as fitted with Caprotti valve gear* (Caprotti Valve Gears Ltd).

Below *LNER/GCR: the era of 'flower-pot' chimneys, but no loss of performance—engine No 5263, on the GW & GC joint line near Saunderton with the 12.15 pm ex-Marylebone* (M.W. Earley).

LNER: the pioneer Great Northern large-boilered 'Atlantic', No 3251, on a Leeds–Kings Cross express south of Grantham in 1932 (M.W. Earley).

LNER: the up West Riding Pullman leaving the tunnel at Stoke summit hauled by superheated 'Atlantic' No 3284 (M.W. Earley).

LNER: the same splendid 'Atlantic' engine on the up 'Queen of Scots' Pullman near Grantham. This engine made one of the fastest runs recorded on this service (M.W. Earley).

was free to slide over the top of the axle box. It was not a trailing 'truck', and had no side control by springs or other means to keep the wheels central when on a straight road. As vehicles the engines rode very well, but to anyone not accustomed to it, the side-by-side motion at the cab end could be very disconcerting. If one looked ahead through the cab glass, however, it could be seen that the front of the engine was riding quite steadily, even at the highest speeds. The lateral swaying at the cab end was a bonus for the fireman, once he had learned to keep his feet! The firebox was very short and very wide and, other things being equal, great care would have to be taken in keeping the back corners filled. On steady engines like the Gresley 'Pacifics' the firemen developed a knack of giving the shovel a twist as it passed through the firedoor so as to shoot coal into the back corners. No such technique was necessary on the 'Atlantics'; the lateral swaying of the engine did the job for them, spreading the coal evenly over the grate. Similarly, the 'tail-wag', transmitted to the tender, 'shimmied' the coal forward and brought it conveniently to the shovelling plate.

When I began my footplate work in the mid-1930s the 'Atlantics' were enjoying a kind of 'St Martin's Summer' on the East Coast main line. While the 'Pacifics' had taken over all the heavier trains, like 'The Flying Scotsman' and the various sleeping car trains to Scotland, there remained the Pullman Limited expresses, the 'Queen of Scots' and the 'West Riding Pullman', each normally limited to seven cars, and with a full complement of passengers, making a load of about 290 tons. They were sharply timed—193 minutes non-stop for the 185.8 miles between Kings Cross and Leeds, in the case of the 'Queen of Scots', although the 'West Riding' stopped additionally at Wakefield, to detach two cars for Bradford. When the Pullman trains were first put on in 1923, W.G.P. Maclure, formerly of the Great Central, was Locomotive Running Superintendant of the Southern Area of the LNER, and he allocated two of the Robinson 4-cylinder 4-6-0s of the 'Lord Faringdon' Class to Copley Hill shed, Leeds, to work on these trains turn and turn about with Great Northern 'Atlantics' from Kings Cross shed. But, although they were on the job for some time and did some very fast running at times, I never managed to get a trip behind one of them, nor with one of the 'Director' Class 4-4-0s that suceeded them. By the time the 1932 accelerations came, the veteran Great Northern 'Atlantics' had the job to themselves.

Six runs on the Leeds-Kings Cross non-stop runs give, in summarised form, the kind of running that one came to expect from these engines in 1932-9. Two runs that I made in that period are not included in this summary, both on the 'Harrogate Sunday Pullman', which was allowed an extra 10-minutes for the Leeds-Kings Cross non-stop run. On the first of the two runs, at midsummer, we had the unusual luxury, on a Sunday, of a completely clear road, and an average speed of no more than 56.8 mph between Doncaster and Kings Cross was needed for time-keeping. On the second, on a bad winter's evening, we had a continuous succession of temporary speed restrictions in the earlier part of the journey; but the last came in the approach to Grantham, and we made a splendid run from there to Kings Cross, regaining seven minutes on the Sunday schedule, with an 8-car train of 325 tons. This run was a particularly memorable one for me personally, because it was the only time I ever travelled behind the pioneer, and now preserved, engine No 251. In darkness and bad weather, the descent from Stoke Tunnel to Peterborough was not as fast as usual (with the speed not exceeding 82 mph) but from Peterborough we went magnificently, averaging 65 mph over 67 miles, and improving on the very sharp weekday schedule of the 'Queen of Scots', with one Pullman over the normal load for that train. Our total time for the 105.5 miles from Grantham to Kings Cross was 104¼ minutes.

Of the six runs tabulated, No 1 was a very hard effort with the Sunday train, when there were many temporary speed restrictions, while No 2 was a grand piece of running on the 'Queen of Scots' just after a bank holiday, when there was one extra car on the train. Nos 4 and 5 were both made when the schedule was 195 minutes, thus showing almost exact timekeeping, in the face of several delays en route, but it was No 6 which really hit the headlines, and on that occasion I was fortunate enough to be on the footplate. The principal cause of delay that made up the difference between the actual time of 189 minutes 35 seconds and the net time of 176 minutes was repair to the water troughs at Werrington Junction, 3¼ miles north of Peterborough. This involved slowing down over the actual site where we would normally have been running at nearly 80 mph but, far worse, we had to stop at Peterborough to take water. And so our driver was running much harder than usual to make sure of a punctual arrival in London. Actually we were 3½ minutes early after one of the most exciting runs I have ever had, anywhere in the world. It was a remarkable testimony to the quality of the permanent way on the famous racing stretch down from Stoke Tunnel that even a wild Great Northern 'Atlantic' was riding quite steadily at our tremendous maximum speed of 93 mph. Nothing

Leeds-Kings Cross: 185.8 miles, Pullman trains

Run number	**1**	**2**	**3**	**4**	**5**	**6**
Engine no	280	284	1436	1444	1444	1456
No of Pullmans	7	8	7	7	8	7
Gross trailing load (tons)	295	325	285	300	335	290
Overall time (minutes/seconds)	209 55	191 15	193 00	195 25	194 45	189 35
Net time (minutes)	186½	181¼	188	190	190	176
Net average speed, Doncaster to Kings Cross (mph)	63.7	64.8	62.7	61.4	61.6	66.9
Maximum speed (mph)	84	88	85	82	85½	93

remotely approaching such a performance as this would have been expected from these engines when they were new, which registered a net gain of *17 minutes*, on the sharp timing of 193 minutes from Leeds to Kings Cross. I should add that the weather was fine and calm—too fine and hot to be comfortable in that confined little cab, sitting almost on top of the fire!

The fame achieved by the Great Northern 'Atlantics' in the 1930s did not by any means rest upon their haulage of the moderately loaded Pullman trains. There are 'accidents', in the best regulated of families, and the Gresley 'Pacifics' were not immune from these at times. My friend of Imperial College days, A.F. Webber, was travelling north by the 1.20 pm Scotsman from Kings Cross one afternoon, when a defect developed on the booked engine that necessitated its removal from the train at Grantham, and substitution of the only express engine immediately available, the Great Northern 'Atlantic' No 4415. This was no 'Pullman' load, but no less than 16 East Coast Joint Stock coaches, a gross trailing load of 545 tons behind the tender, to be hauled over the ensuing 82.7 miles to York in 90 minutes.

The driver and fireman were top-link Kings Cross men, who would know all about 'Atlantics', and they set about the job with such vigour that they not only kept schedule time, but regained 3 minutes of the time that had been lost changing engines at Grantham. Although the line is level at first, it was a delicate task getting this huge load under way, with an engine having only 36 tons adhesion weight, against the 66 tons of an 'A3' Pacific, and it took 8 minutes to cover the first 4 miles. Then came the welcome descent to the Trent Valley, on which speed was worked up to 74 mph; but the really amazing part of the exploit began when they had got down to the flat, and from Newark the line is level in the aggregate for the remaining 68 miles to York. There were two marked 'humps', first where the line climbs from the Trent valley to Markham Moor and then descends to Retford and secondly, in the shorter climb past Bawtry to Pipers Wood; but these can be taken in the stride. The only serious hindrance is the severe permanent speed restriction at Selby, over the swing bridge and the sharp curve that follows.

From the initial impetus of 74 mph through Newark the Great Northern 'Atlantic' went on to cover the 52.9 miles to Brayton Junction, where the slowing down for Selby begins, in a few seconds

Left *North Eastern Railway: one of the very handsome 'R1' 4-4-0s, crossing the River Tyne, with the midday Newcastle–Liverpool express* (R.J. Purves).

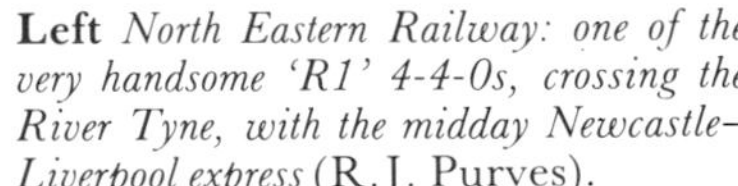

Right *LNER/NBR: the 'Atlantic' engine, No 9509,* Duke of Rothesay, *in 1935 stationed at Dundee, and maker of many fine runs.*

under 49 minutes—an extraordinary average for so grossly overloaded an engine of all but 65 mph. She took the Markham bank at a lowest speed of 53 mph and Pipers Wood at an extraordinary 67(!) and when slowing down to 24 mph for the cautious passage through Selby the 68.9 miles from Grantham start to that station had taken no more than 67½ minutes. With some slightly adverse gradients to follow it took some very hard work to get that enormous train going at express speed again, and they had not quite topped the '60' line when it was time to begin slowing down for York; but the journey from Grantham was completed in 4 seconds under 87 minutes, with a regaining of 3 minutes on schedule time. York had some help waiting for the hard pressed crew of the 'Atlantic' engine No 4415, because a 3-cylinder 4-4-0 of the 'Shire' Class was waiting to couple on ahead; and after that, with two engines, all was relatively easy.

Of course my friend lost no time in sending details of the Grantham-York epic to Cecil J. Allen, for his use in *The Railway Magazine.* At that time, in consideration of the large amount of correspondence received in connection with the 'British Locomotive Practice and Performance' feature, Allen made no more than formal acknowledgement, month by month, of the letters he had received, very rarely replying personally to any individual writer; so, despite the very exceptional nature of the data he had submitted, Webber was not altogether surprised to observe in the magazine no more than the usual formal notice of a letter having been received.

Two years elapsed, and then a similar experience came to Cecil J. Allen himself, on the same train, with the difference that the 'A3' Pacific that failed at Grantham was based at Gateshead, instead of Kings Cross, and that her crew, North Eastern men, had never been on a Great Northern 'Atlantic' before. Furthermore, the load was even heavier than previously, amounting to 17 coaches, totalling, with passengers and luggage, the somewhat staggering weight of 585 tons behind the total—just *double* the normal load of the 'Queen of Scots' Pullman. It did not take the Gateshead driver and fireman long to master the technique of handling one of these remarkable engines, No 4404 in this case, and on passing Newark they had practically tied with the time of the previous run, despite the heavier load. They fell behind to the tune of 2 minutes between Newark and Retford, with the minimum speed going up to Markham falling to 48 mph against 53; but from this point onwards they really began to pile it on, and, with a slightly faster passage through Selby and a more rapid recovery afterwards, they were actually ahead of No 4415 before the slowing down for York began. The exact times from Grantham on passing Chaloners Whin Junction, 80.7 miles, were 83 minutes 33 seconds, and 83 minutes 9 seconds.

As on the previous occasion York had a second engine, a North Eastern 'V' Class 'Atlantic', waiting to couple on ahead, and help on the rest of the run to Newcastle. Allen was bound for Tees-side and, by the strangest of coincidences, Webber, in the course of his professional work in the steel industry, was staying at the very same hotel where Allen was dining that evening. They had not previously met, but Webber, recognising him, introduced himself, and Allen, as might be imagined, was bursting with enthusiasm for the run he had just experienced; but when Webber tactfully reminded him of the similar run, details of which he had sent him two years earlier, Allen was slightly embarrassed, and confessed that he had been unable to believe that such a performance was possible. Despite Webber's high professional status it would seem that the lingerings of disbelief still persisted in Allen's mind for, shortly afterwards when he

GORDON CASTLE
H R

Above left *Highland Railway: a Peter Drummond 4-6-0, No 143,* Gordon Castle, *which was on first class main line work until the 1930s* (Locomotive Publishing Company).

Left *Southern Railway: a Drummond 'Paddleboat' 4-cylinder 4-6-0, as modernised by Maunsell, speeding through Byfleet on a Bournemouth express* (C.R.L. Coles).

Above *London & South Western Railway: a Dugald Drummond 'D15' class 4-4-0 (superheated) in its prime on a Waterloo–Bournemouth express* (Real Photographs).

'splashed' the story of his own run in *The Railway Magazine*, he *still* made no mention of the earlier and equally meritorious exploit. Technically, the outstanding feature of both runs was the exceptionally high drawbar pull constantly sustained in relation to the nominal tractive effort of the locomotives. Many years later, on one or other of the stationary testing plants, various modern locomotives were steamed up to the maximum capacity of their boilers, as will be described in detail later in this book; and it is when these 'all-out' efforts are compared with the emergency runs of the Great Northern 'Atlantics', 4415 and 4404, that the sense of disbelief can be understood, thus:

Ratio of drawbar pull to nominal tractive effort

Speed (mph)	LNER 'V2' 2-6-2	GWR 'King' 4-6-0	GNR Atlantic
55	29.7	27.8	38.0
60	26.7	24.3	34.0
65	23.8	21.2	31.0

So far as the 'Atlantics' were concerned these were no transitory 'flashes in the pan', but efforts sustained for well over an hour in each case, and they testify to the freedom with which large volumes of highly superheated steam could be passed through those relatively small cylinders, and to the freedom with which the boiler steamed, and to the relative ease with which the firebox could be kept replenished. The Great Northern 'Atlantics', when pushed to their limit, as these engines undoubtedly were, provide the nearest British counterpart (on a much lower scale of size and power to the traditional American methods of working), in which locomotives were driven for hours on end with the point of steam cut-off in the cylinders late in the piston stroke, fed from boilers, like those of the Great Northern 'Atlantics' that were large in relation to the cylinder volume.

One must not, however, bestow all the praise for these achievements on the component parts of the steam circuit, because the mechanical design of the Great Northern 'Atlantics' dates back to 1902 and must have been superb in its proportioning of the working parts, axle boxes, gudgeon pins, big-ends and such like, to transmit successfully the stresses induced by feats of haulage beyond the wildest dreams of those who made the original drawings! A final reflection upon these two runs, and of a *third* one, of which no more than summary details are available, is that it is a pity that no facilities then existed for making a full thermodynamic analysis of the performance of the 32-element superheater 'Atlantics' in maximum load conditions. There would surely have been much to be learned from such an analysis.

Space does not permit more detailed references to

other veteran locomotives which gave me glimpses of their past glories, in the 1930s; but it is hoped that a miscellany of pictures, and brief notes in the captions and thereafter, in no more than a single paragraph may help to convey something of the atmosphere the pictures recall. The 'R1' 4-4-0s of the North Eastern, not so grandly arrayed as of old, were working around Leeds when I was there on signalling business in the mid-1930s, while of North British 'Atlantics', and particularly of *Duke of Rothesay*, I have memories of some stirring footplate journeys. Still farther north, on the Highland line the Drummond 'Castles' were still in full blast, while in the south Dugald Drummond's beautiful 'D15' 4-4-0, displaced from the Bournemouth line was still acting as junior partners to the 'Schools' on the Portsmouth expresses prior to the electrification of that hilly route. On the old Brighton route to Portsmouth, the mid-Sussex line, the celebrated 'I3' superheated 4-4-2s were still on express passenger work, and these engines were yet again doing good work on the Oxted line to Tunbridge Wells, and to Lewes as late as 1947. One can never think of the Brighton line without the 'Gladstones', and my great friend, the late W.J. Reynolds, secured a memorable picture of a 'Gladstone', restored and alongside the Southern 'pride of the line', the *Lord Nelson*. Bill Soole's picture of Churchward's *Knight of the Bath*, on an up two-hour Bristol express recalls the 'wag', in Swindon Works who once referred to this engine as 'Friday Night', while the picture of the little 2-4-0 6 foot Jumbo of the LNWR then allocated to the 'Engineer Liverpool', but previously No 742 *Spitfire*, leads on to the next major subject; because lurking in the background can be seen one of the 'Claughton' Class 4-6-0s.

My reference earlier to the magnificent pre-war performances of the 'George the Fifth' Class 4-4-0s on the London and North Western Railway, aided by excellent cylinder and piston valve design and a high degree of superheat, prompts the question as to whether they had any opportunities for occasionally shining forth in their later years, despite being generally superseded by Midland compounds. Alas their chances of rising to any such occasion were sadly, and technically, inhibited by the action of their LMS owners in removing the centre bearing on the driving axle, thereby reducing the bearing area to about three quarters of its former value. Any attempt to coax pre-war standards of performance out of the engines, the 'Prince of Wales' Class 4-6-0s included, resulted in overheated bearings and cracked frames. Fortunately no such strictures applied to the 4-cylinder 'Claughton' Class 4-6-0s, and with them two stirring feats of performance came to my personal notice. It might be questioned as to whether these engines had quite such a claim to be termed veterans as the Great Northern 'Atlantics', seeing that they were introduced in 1913; but the improvements in design that made such outstanding engines of these latter dated, as previously mentioned, from 1919. It is true that the thermodynamic efficiency of the 'Claughtons' was much improved in the later 1920s by fitting the modified form of piston valves; but the boiler, cylinders, motion and high degree of superheat, dated from 1913.

The first run began quite ordinarily. I was travelling from London to Barrow-in-Furness just before the August Bank Holiday in 1929, and although the 5.20 pm express from Euston was running in two portions, the first was loaded practically up to the maximum then permitted to an unassisted 'Claughton' then 380 tons tare. This train scaled 370, but it was packed with passengers, and must have been at least 400 tons full. The engine was No 6021 carrying the name of the country residence of the great 19th century

Southern Railway: one of the Earle-Marsh superheated 'I3' Class express tank engines (P. Ransome Wallis).

Above *GWR: the Churchward 'Stars' still on first class duty—engine No 4015,* Knight of the Bath, *on the Bristol–Paddington two-hour non-stop express near Filton* (G.H. Soole).

Right *Stable-companion of* Gladstone *in the old Railway Museum at York, the 100 mph* City of Truro *of the GWR.*

Below *Southern Railway: a magnificent juxtaposition—*Gladstone, *restored to Stroudley's yellow livery, alongside* Lord Nelson (the late W.J. Reynolds).

LNWR: the 'Claughtons' as one likes to remember them, in the famous 'blackberry black'. Engine No 1191, Sir Frank Ree, *was only the third engine of this class of 130, being built at Crewe in 1913. It was the first engine to be completely rebuilt as a 'Baby Scot' in 1930* (British Railways).

Chairman of the LNWR Sir Richard Moon—*Bevere*. Engine and crew soon began to make light work of the job, and we were nearly 3 minutes early no farther out of London than Tring, 31.7 miles.

When we got to Rugby, crowds of additional passengers were waiting to board the train and, advised in advance that it was already packed, they had an extra coach waiting to be attached in rear. We now had 18 tons overload, by the rules of the day; but *Bevere* and her crew treated this with complete disdain and ran the next 51 miles to Stafford in exactly 52 minutes, start to stop, arriving there 4 minutes early. The situation at Rugby was then repeated; yet another coach was added, and we left with 426 tons tare, 46 tons overload and passengers standing in the corridors. I estimated that the gross load behind the tender was now 465 tons, and a maximum effort was now made up the rising gradients to Whitmore summit.

In Volume 1 I referred to the 'all-out' test runs carried out with one of the earliest 'Claughtons' in 1913. It is interesting to compare the performance of *Bevere* north of Stafford with what happened on that test run. In 1913, with the engine, *Ralph Brocklebank*, and a gross trailing load of 435 tons, they were passing Stafford at the prescribed reduced speed of 40 mph; *Bevere* was starting from rest, with a load of 465 tons. Comparative speeds over the next ten miles were thus:

The horsepower involved in this rapid up-grade acceleration was high, and with a fast concluding descent into Crewe, the arrival was nearly 2 minutes ahead of time despite this overload. There had been another remarkable 'Claughton' run in 1926 in the period of restricted train service following the General Strike of that year, when engine No 808 (LNW numbering) had to haul a very crowded 15-coach train from Stafford to Euston, weighing in all 505 tons behind the tender. The 86.9 miles to the stop at Bletchley were covered in 89½ minutes, and from the restart, Wembley, 38.6 miles, was passed in 40¾ minutes. A severe restriction for permanent way work delayed the final stages of the run, but the times on this journey were equivalent to a non-stop run of 137 minutes from Stafford to Euston, an average speed of 58.5 mph from start to stop. Both this run, and concluding stages of mine on the 5.20 pm down with *Bevere*, would have required firing skill of a very high order; because, although the firebox of these engines had a grate area almost the same as that of a Great Northern 'Atlantic', it was long and narrow, between the rearmost pair of coupled wheels, instead of short and wide, and the 'Claughtons' were very smooth riding engines, with no 'tailwag' to spread the coal about. Each shovelful stayed where the fireman put it.

The climax so far as 'Claughton' performance was concerned, and a climax as brilliant as anything

Distance (miles)	0.0	3.3	5.3	9.8
Location	Stafford	Great Bridgeford	Norton Bridge	Standon Bridge
Actual speed (mph)				
1913	40	59	61	66½
1929	0	50	53	58

London & North Western Railway: one of the 6 foot Jumbos 'Whitworth' Class, formerly No 742, Spitfire, *and built at Crewe in 1893 as* Engineer Liverpool.

achieved in the halcyon first years of the class in 1913-1916—if not actually more so!—came in 1933 in an emergency similar to those leading to such remarkable feats of the Great Northern 'Atlantics', Nos 4404 and 4415. In the previous summer the LMS had accelerated the evening express from Liverpool to Euston to run the 152.7 miles from Crewe to Willesden Junction non-stop in 142 minutes, a then-unprecedented average speed of 64.5 mph. No 'Pacifics' were then available, and a new range of engine loadings were established for this train, and the up 'Comet' that followed it, known as 'XL' Limits.

In this range the Class '6' engines (Royal Scots) were limited to a maximum load of 380 tons; Class '5X' (Baby Scots) to 340 tons, and because there were times foreseen when neither of these newer types might be available, particularly for the 'Comet', the Class '5' engines were also included in the 'XL' classification, with a maximum permitted load of 300 tons. Timekeeping being of prime importance, the slightest excess over these stipulated loads brought forth a pilot engine, and on Friday nights, even with 'Royal Scots' the train was regularly double-headed, usually with a Midland compound leading. I was living at Bushey at the time, and on fine summer evenings sometimes took a walk in the meadows beside the River Coln, north-eastwards from Watford, and would see the 'flyer' go streaking by; and on one such evening, June 23 1933, to be exact, I had a surprise.

I was too far from the line to be sure it *was* the Liverpool train, but it was going very fast and hauled by an unbuilt 'Claughton', which I could see was one of those carrying a name. I thought no more about it then; but many years later a friend who knew of my interest in LNWR locomotives sent me details of what had transpired on this very occasion. The load on that evening was 351 tons and, with no 'Royal Scot' or 'Baby Scot' available, Edge Hill shed had put on a 'Claughton', one of the three named after LNWR men who won the VC in the First World War, No 5967, *Lance Corporal J.A. Christie VC.* With 51 tons over the 'XL' Limit for Class '5' engines, a pilot was provided, one of the 6 foot 9 inch standard Class '2' 4-4-0s. The two engines together had not done particularly well between Crewe and Rugby and, with no greater hindrance than two slight checks, they had lost 50 seconds on schedule, on passing the latter station. Then, 2½ miles farther south, they stopped at Hillmorton signal box, to my friend's surprise, with all signals clear. It then transpired that something had gone wrong with the leading engine, and it was being coupled off, and run clear. With 51 tons overload the driver of the 'Claughton' would have been justified in asking for another pilot, being so near to Rugby, or otherwise lose time on the continuation of the journey to London. But he and his fireman must have been a couple of rare sportsmen, for they did neither and, going all-out for Willesden, made one of the truly classic runs of LMS steam history.

The uphill start from Hillmorton box to Kilsby Tunnel was tremendously vigorous, and they passed Welton, 5.1 miles, in no more than 7 minutes 35 seconds. Then they continued in a perfect riot of a speed run, covering the next 67.2 miles, on to Wembley, in a fraction under 55 minutes, an *average* speed of 73.5 mph. There was only one slight let-up in this tremendous effort. Approaching Castlethorpe troughs they were going

GWR: a picturesque rebuild of 1936, 'Duke' Class boilers fitted to 'Bulldog' Class double-frames. The earliest engines of this rejuvenated series were named after 'Earls', but the names were subsequently transferred to 'Castle' Class 4-6-0s, and the '3200' Class took up their nickname of the 'Duke-dogs'! (British Railways).

over 80 mph and, to lessen the chance of flinging water left and right when the scoop was lowered and not getting an advantageous fill-up, they checked the speed to about 60 mph; but afterwards, with plenty of water in the tender, they just threw in all they had, and averaged well over 1,000 horsepower at the drawbar while averaging just over 70 mph on the long rise from Wolverton to Tring.

Down the valley towards Watford the speed rose to, and was sustained at, 85 mph, and it can have been little less when I saw the train myself sweeping across the embankment between Watford Junction and Bushey. So they tore on, to cover the last 12.1 miles from Watford to the Willesden stop in no more than 10¾ minutes, clocking up another '80' near Wembley. In all, the 74.8 miles from Hillmorton to Willesden were covered in 65 minutes 48 seconds, start to stop, an average speed of 68.2 mph. So, despite the overload of 51 tons, which meant a gross load of 370 tons behind the tender, the two stout fellows on engine No 5967 not only kept the very fast sectional times of this prestige train, but actually regained more than 3 minutes.

The initial time to Welton, starting dead from Hillmorton, was almost exactly the same as that from passing Rugby at normal speed, and the splendid progress of the train thereafter can be appreciated from the following 'log' below.

The veterans were indeed 'in excelsis' on that June evening of 1933.

Location	Distance from Hillmorton (miles)	Schedule time from passing Rugby (minutes)	Actual time from Hillmorton (minutes/seconds)
Roade	20.3	21	20 10
Bletchley	33.5	32	31 11
Tring	48.5	46	44 00
Watford Junction	62.7	—	55 00
Willesden Junction	74.8	69	65 48

4. Notable unconventional designs

Once the basic steam locomotive (as exemplified admirably in the *Rocket*) had been developed to the stage of being a thoroughly reliable and very simple form of railway traction, at a time that could be vaguely indicated as around 1850, engineers began to consider means for improving its overall efficiency. At that time little more than 4 per cent of the heat energy contained in the fuel consumed was converted into useful work in hauling a train. Locomotive men looked enviously at stationary and marine steam plants in which condensers were used, and in which the overall efficiency could be as much as 15 per cent but, in the conventional steam locomotives, condensers could not be used, because the steam had to be exhausted to atmosphere, at a pressure something about 15 lb per square inch, and one lost the advantage of condensing it down to about 1 lb per square inch. Quite a lot of the latent energy in the steam was thrown away in the exhaust up the chimney; but that, in turn, was essential in a locomotive to provide draught on the fire.

There was, however, one feature of marine and stationary steam plant practice that could be applied to locomotives, and that was two-stage, or compound expansion of the steam; and in the latter part of the 19th century, compound locomotives of various kinds were built for trial on a number of the British railways. But, as was shown on the Great Western, however, a well-designed single expansion locomotive could show a thermal efficiency equal to that of the best compounds that had been produced at the turn of the century; and the introduction of superheating provided a notable increase in thermal efficiency. It was, however, the invention and rapid development of the steam turbine by Sir Charles Parsons which revolutionised the practice of motive power engineering, though not ultimately on railways. From his first experimental turbine of 1884, a tiny thing that developed no more than 10 horsepower, Parsons had progressed in 23 years to the mighty 74,000 horsepower turbines installed in the famous Cunard liners, *Mauretania* and *Lusitania*, which in 1907 captured the Blue Riband of the Atlantic crossing for Great Britain and held it for more than 20 years. Their steam consumption of about 14 lb per shaft horsepower hour was roughly half that of a good British steam locomotive of conventional design.

At a time when, even then, the price of coal was soaring, railway engineers began to think of turbine propulsion, and one of the earliest ventures came in 1910 from the North British Locomotive Company. This was an ingenious conception in which a condensing steam turbine was used to generate electricity, and supply power to traction motors. The boiler was of the locomotive type, superheated, supplying steam to the turbine which was coupled directly to a dc generator. The traction motors were built on to the four main driving axles of the locomotive. The exhaust steam from the turbine passed to a condenser and, together with the circulating condensing water, was delivered to a hot well from which it was pumped back to the boiler. There was no exhaust as such and the boiler was provided with forced draught from a small turbine-driven fan. The locomotive was mounted on two composite 8-wheeled bogies, each having a leading 4-wheeled bogie truck and four driving wheels. Beyond the fact that this novel locomotive ran some trials on the Caledonian and North British main lines from Glasgow, little was known of its progress. In a brochure issued by the manufacturers some years later it was explained that its development had been hindered by war conditions; but, since a full four years elapsed between its construction and the outbreak of war in August 1914, one may be fairly sure that little success had been attained with it.

The second attempt, also from the North British Locomotive Company, came in 1920—also turbo-electric, but this time using ac generators and traction motors. The condenser tubes were slowly rotated through cooling water. The locomotive developed about 1,000 horsepower at the rail, which was considered inadequate for contemporary main line work, and the project was criticised for its inordinately heavy weight of 155 tons. With the condenser and all its appurtenances, it was virtually carrying its own power station; but a poor steaming boiler, and serious water leakage led to its being scrapped after only four years.

The last attempt from the firm involved the rebuilding in 1924 of the 1910 locomotive, with two-stage expansion; the high pressure turbine drove on to the trailing bogie, and the low pressure on to the leading unit. In this project electrical drive was dispensed with, and the turbine drove through gearing on to the road axles. The condenser, which was placed at the leading end of the locomotive, was of the air cooled evaporative type with a turbine driven fan to boost the induced draught from the progress of the locomotive. Again, the overall weight of 135 tons was heavy in relation to the power output, not more than 1,000 horsepower. This locomotive also did no revenue earning service, but it was important in showing what might

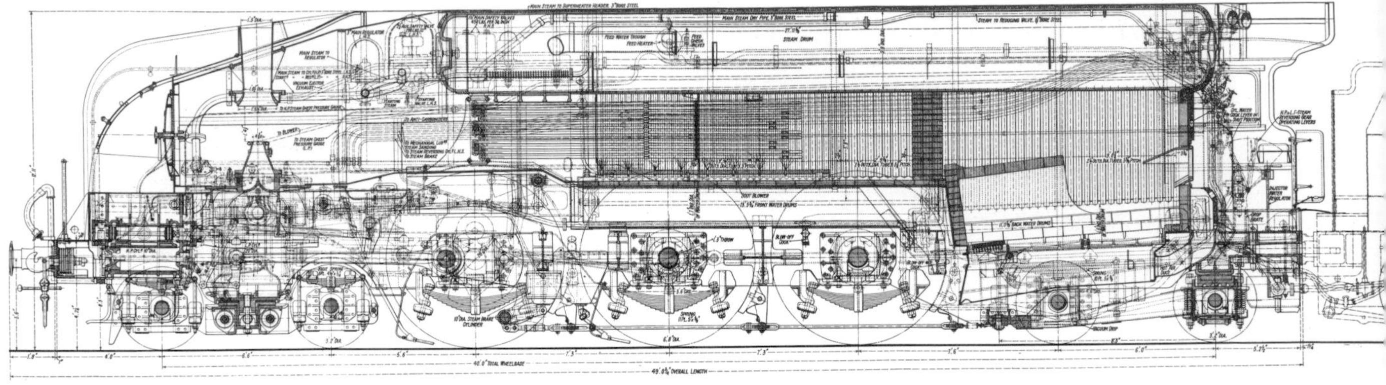

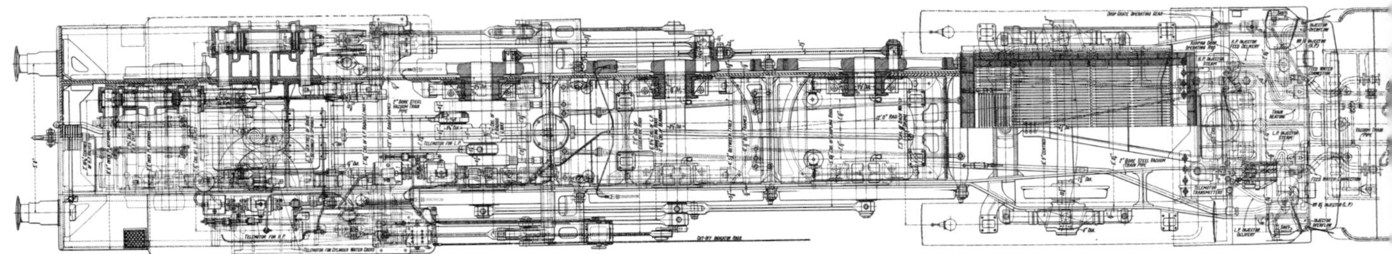

be done with a direct turbine drive, as distinct from electrical transmission.

The cause of turbine propulsion was then taken up by Beyer, Peacock & Co, who, in 1926, built a condensing turbine locomotive on the Swedish Ljungström principles; and this did a considerable amount of revenue-earning service on the Midland Division of the LMS between Manchester (Central) and St Pancras. It worked on duties normally undertaken by the 3-cylinder compounds 4-4-0s and, so far as ordinary timekeeping with the trains concerned, performed quite reliably. Seen from the chimney end it looked quite a 'proper' locomotive until one saw 6-coupled wheels underneath its very large tender. It was the size and weight of the condenser over again, because this engine doing the work of a 100-ton Midland compound weighed 143½ tons. It was never turned and looked odd in the extreme, with that immensely long tender, leading the way on one of the northbound Midland expresses from St Pancras to Manchester. For a time in 1927 it was running frequently on these trains; it was always an object of much curiosity at St Pancras. Sir Henry Fowler took much personal interest in it, though his own ideas towards the unorthodox were then running in different directions.

Theoretically the thermal efficiency of a locomotive, other things being equal, depends upon the pressure range, and in the conventional reciprocating type, needing a small amount of back pressure to induce the draught for combustion, the only way to increase the range would be to increase the initial pressure. In Great Britain in the early 1920s boiler pressures had not increased beyond the 225 lb per square inch standardised by Churchward some 20 years earlier for his largest engines on the Great Western but, other than that, most British locomotive engineers had endeavoured to keep boiler pressure down, being willing to sacrifice a little thermal efficiency in order to minimise maintenance charges on their boilers. On the London and North Eastern Railway, at the time of Grouping in 1923 and for a few years afterwards, H.N. Gresley was using a pressure of 180 lb per square inch, in his largest express passenger engines. But, in the knowledge that an increase to say 450 lb per square inch, in the direction to which certain American and Continental engineers were inclining, would give promise of an increase in thermal efficiency of at least 20 per cent, he began to give serious consideration to the construction of an experimental high pressure locomotive. In mind of contemporary success in marine practice he determined upon the use of the water-tube type of boiler, working at 450 lb per square inch.

As early as September 1924 he approached Mr Harold Yarrow, of Glasgow, whose firm were so well known as designers and builders of that type of boiler; but such were the differences between the

Left *LNER: the Gresley-Yarrow 4-cylinder compound 4-6-4 with Yarrow water tube boiler, No 10000.*

Above *LNER: the great experimental high pressure 4-cylinder compound 4-6-4 with Yarrow Water tube boiler, working at 450 lb per square inch* (British Railways).

Right *The Reid-MacLeod geared turbine condensing locomotive, built by the North British Locomotive Company, on test near Glasgow in 1927* (R. Haddon).

Right *The Beyer-Ljungstöm turbine locomotive tested on the LMS between Manchester and St Pancras* (British Railways).

Below *LNER: a broadside view of the Gresley-Yarrow experimental locomotive, which did a considerable amount of revenue-earning service on the East Coast main line* (British Railways).

working conditions in stationary and marine boilers, and those on locomotives, that no less than three years elapsed before a satisfactory design had been completed. Then, with authorisation secured for the construction of a large experimental locomotive, with a tractive capacity equal to the standard 'Pacifics', the order for the boiler was placed with Messrs Yarrow early in 1928, and for construction of the locomotive itself at Darlington Works, the latter in conditions of some secrecy.

The locomotive was built as a 4-cylinder compound and, having regard to the very high steam pressure, the high pressure cylinders were originally no more than 12 inches in diameter and the low pressure, 20 inches. The former were subsequently reduced to 10 inches to secure a more even distribution of the work between the high and low pressure cylinders. The wheel arrangement was conventional, except at the rear end, where there was a pair of carrying wheels with bearings in the main frames, as on the 'Pacifics', and in rear of this was a bissel truck, effectively making the wheel arrangement 4-6-4, or as some would have it 4-6-2 + 2. The general form of the boiler can be appreciated from the accompanying drawings. The locomotive was completed and ran its trial trip on December 12 1929. It was naturally the subject of intense interest and much curiosity at the time; but it was not until January 23 1931, when Gresley himself read a paper before the Institution of Mechanical Engineers, that any full authoritative information was released. The paper itself was a most absorbing document and covered no less than 106 pages in the proceedings of the Institution and the subsequent discussion was most interesting. At the time the locomotive had been in service for a year, and there was every promise of success.

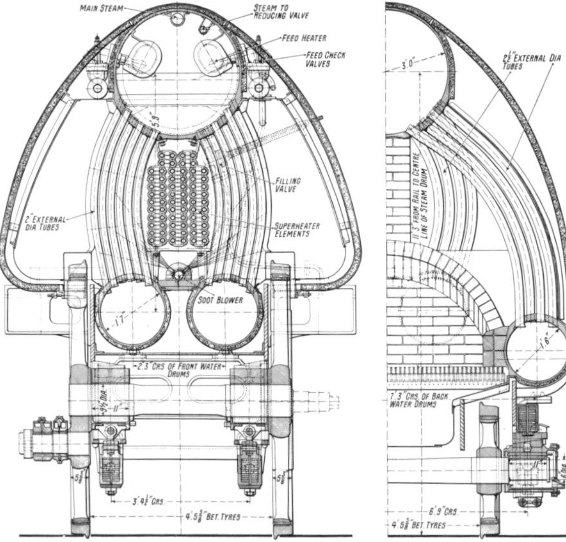

Engine No 10000, 'Old Hush-hush', as she had become known from the secrecy in which the earlier stages in her construction had been cloaked, was based at Gateshead shed, and during the summer of 1930 was working in the ordinary 'Pacific' link, including the long-mileage double-manned turn beginning with the 11.17 am non-stop Newcastle to Edinburgh, and back with the Glasgow-Leeds dining car train, through to York, on which the engine was remanned at Newcastle. On two successive days she worked on the summer non-stop 'Flying Scotsman'. The train then had the leisurely timing imposed when it was first put on, in 1928, namely 8¼ hours for the 392.7 miles, an average speed of no more than 46.3 mph. I was working near Kings Cross station at the time and, having received a 'tip off', I waited for some time after office hours to see her come in, which she did, dead on time at 6.15 pm. This was on July 31 1930, and she went back to Edinburgh non-stop on the following day. But the early promise of success was not fulfilled and No 10000 proved a troublesome and costly engine to maintain. As time went on she did less and less regular work and eventually was withdrawn—a great disappointment to her designer and to all who were associated with him in the project.

Sir Henry Fowler's experimental high pressure locomotive had an even shorter life, and did no revenue earning service at all. It was built by the North British Locomotive Company on a chassis almost identical to that of the 'Royal Scot' Class 4-6-0s, and the cylinder arrangement, as a 3-cylinder compound was designed to provide a nominal tractive effort of 33,200 lb, again equal to that of the 'Royal Scots'. The boiler, or boilers, were arranged on the Schmidt-Henschel principle, which had been applied to certain experimental locomotives in Germany. The composite boiler generated steam at three different pressures: at 1,400 lb per square inch, in a closed circuit water tube fire box; at 950 lb per square inch, for feeding to the inside high-pressure cylinder, and the exhaust from this mixed with steam generated at 250 lb per square inch, in the orthodox boiler barrel to the rear of the smokebox and then passed to the outside cylinders. What Sir Henry Fowler hoped to get from this complicated machine we are not to know because, during early trial running in Scotland, one of the high pressure water tubes burst, and caused a terrible blow-back

LNER: cross-sectional elevation through boiler and half-cross section through firebox of No 10000.

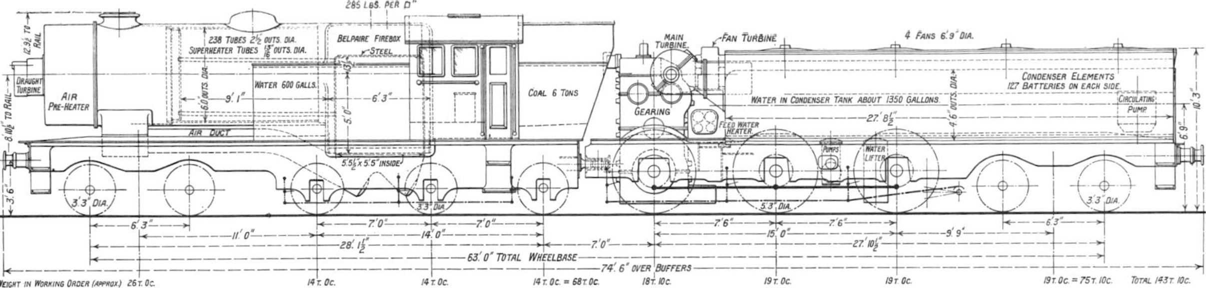

Above *Ljungström turbo-condensing locomotive, built by Beyer, Peacock & Co, and tested on the LMS.*

Right *The Reid-Ramsey turbo-electric locomotive of 1920* (North British Locomotive Company).

on to the footplate, killing one of the testing staff. No further running was attempted with the locomotive and yet another attempt at the unorthodox in design was ended.

The possibilities inherent in turbine drive for any form of motive power, so attractive in theory, had so far been clouded, where railway locomotives were concerned, by the complications introduced in providing for the condenser, and all its ancilliary equipment. But, at the end of the 1920s, a new aspect was introduced in turbine locomotive propulsion by the building, first in Germany and then in Sweden, of non-condensing turbine locomotives which, according to reports reaching this country, achieved a measure of success which was worth following up. It was the 2-8-0 freight engine designed by the Ljungström Company for the Grangesberg-Oxelösung Railway in Sweden which particularly attracted the attention of Sir William Stanier, after his appointment as Chief Mechanical Engineer of the LMS.

After preliminary discussions with Dr H.L. (later Sir Henry) Guy, Chief Engineer of the turbine division of Metropolitan Vickers Company, representatives of that firm and of the LMS visited Sweden to see the non-condensing turbine 2-8-0 in service; and, having been favourably impressed, Stanier asked Metropolitan Vickers, in association with Ljungström, to co-operate with the LMS in the design of a turbine driven 'Pacific' express passenger engine. Authorisation had already been given for the construction of three 'Pacific' engines, having a nominal tractive effort of 40,000 lb; but, in view of the favourable prospects with turbine drive, it was decided that one out of the three should be a turbine. The other two were the famous 6200 and 6201, *The Princess Royal* and *Princess Elizabeth*.

Although dispensing with a condenser meant that the pressure range (assuming the use of a boiler similar to those fitted to the ordinary 'Pacific' engines) would be no different, a very careful study of all the factors involved showed that turbine drive offered the possibility of improved performance under three broad headings:

1) Reduced coal and water consumption in relation to the work done at the drawbar.

2) A more powerful locomotive within the limits of weight imposed by the Civil Engineer.

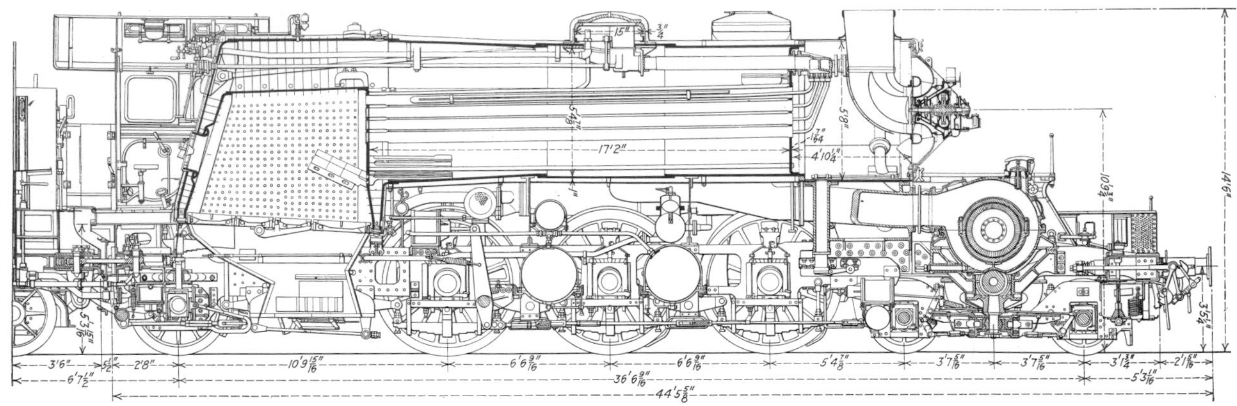

Above *German State Railways: non-condensing turbine locomotive.*

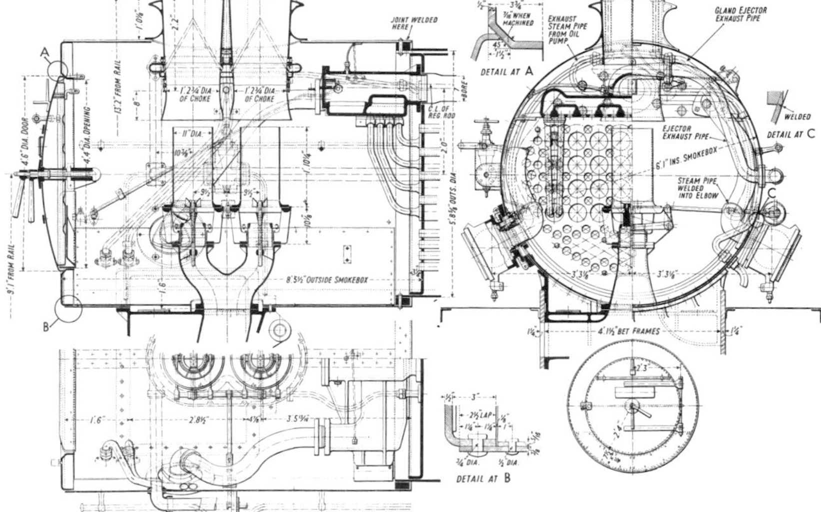

Left *LMS: the Stanier turbine locomotive, No 6202—details of the special smokebox arrangement.*

Below *LMS: No 6202—details of the boiler and firebox.*

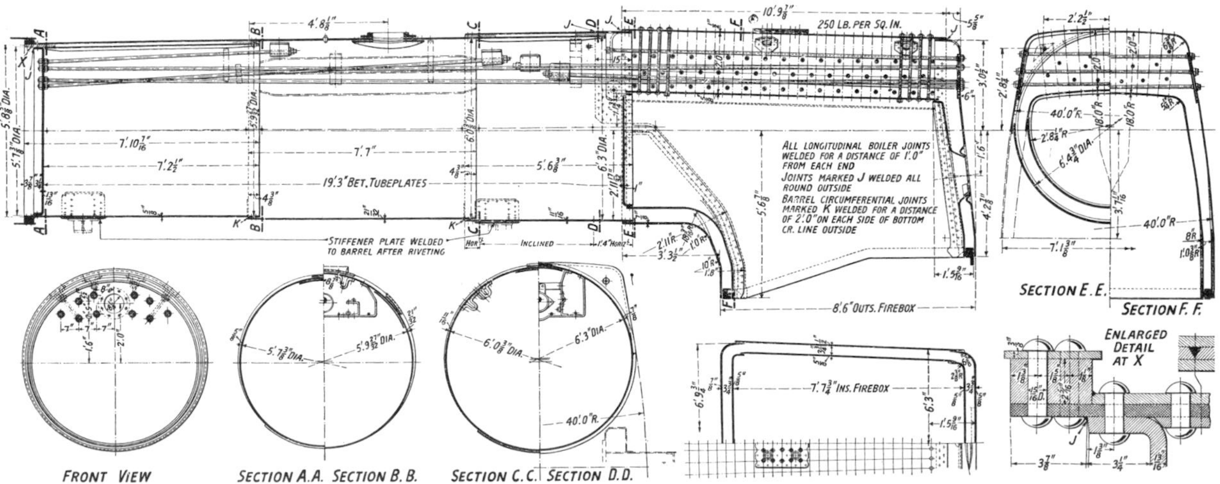

3) Greater availability.
Under the first heading, the hopes in this direction came from the possibility of improved thermal efficiency, from reduction of losses in the steam circuit, and the use of higher steam temperatures without the attendant troubles with lubrication.

The turbine-driven locomotive has a uniform torque, and a complete absence of 'hammer blow' arising from the movement of heavy reciprocating parts. In consequence of the latter, the Civil Engineer was prepared to allow a greater dead weight on the driving axles, and so to enable a higher starting tractive effort to be exerted. So far as the third consideration was concerned, the provision of a totally enclosed gear drive, with efficient lubrication was expected to reduce the frictional losses in the moving parts; to eliminate periodical examination needed on the pistons and valves of a reciprocating steam locomotive, and to give a higher thermal efficiency. By making possible higher mileages between shop repairs it was hoped to secure higher availability in traffic. As it was intended that the 'Pacific' engines, whether reciprocating or turbine, should work through between Euston and Glasgow, on duties requiring maximum power output at a wide range of speeds, the turbine was designed for maximum efficiency at a speed of 62 mph. With the same boiler and starting tractive effort of 40,000 lb it was expected that the turbine locomotive would have a tractive effort 30 per cent higher than the reciprocating 6200 and 6201 at all speeds above 35 mph.

Risking the charge of being wise after the event it does seem to have been rather venturesome to have embarked on this project with a huge locomotive of maximum power. It followed on the lines pursued by Gresley and Fowler in building their experimental locomotives to compete on level terms with the largest existing express passenger units, or so it was hoped. Certainly Stanier came nearest to success of the three, but it would seem in retrospect that the experience so dearly bought with the turbine driven 'Pacific' No 6202 could have been much more cheaply and conveniently obtained with a smaller locomotive. Nevertheless, the immense amount of care put into the design of all the various components resulted in a locomotive which was remarkably free from basic troubles. One of the most fundamental difficulties arose from an error of judgement in deciding the size of the reverse turbine. Separate turbines had to be provided for the forward and reverse direction of running and, in regard to the latter, it was evidently overlooked that at times it would be necessary to start and propel a heavy train from a terminal station. The reverse turbine was unfortunately inadequate for the job.

Although the first two Stanier 'Pacifics' on the LMS had the moderate degree of superheat customary on the Great Western Railway, it was realised at the outset that the attainment of

LMS: Sir Henry Fowler's experiment, with very high steam pressure at 900 lb per square inch, built by the North British Locomotive Company, and designed to do the same work as the 'Royal Scots' (North British Locomotive Company).

LMS: Sir William Stanier's non-condensing turbine locomotive, No 6202, which, but for the intermission of the Second World War, might have proved ultimately very successful (British Railways).

maximum economy from a non-condensing turbine locomotive demanded a high degree of superheat, and the LMS locomotive, No 6202, had from the outset a 32-element superheater, providing a free gas area through the flue tubes roughly double that of the original boilers fitted to the reciprocating 'Pacifics' Nos 6200-1, which was only 26 per cent of the total. The latter engines were subsequently fitted with 32-element superheaters identical to that first used on No 6202; though this latter was later equipped with a 40-element superheater having a superheater heating surface of no less than 832 square feet. All the time the locomotive was under very close observation while in ordinary revenue earning service and on dynamometer car trials conducted on service trains between Euston and Glasgow. It was put into ordinary traffic in June 1935, and at first worked principally between Euston and Liverpool, on rosters involving a daily mileage of 385.

Major interest, however, is shown for the series of dynamometer car test runs conducted on the 'Royal Scot' train, working daily over the 401 miles between Euston and Glasgow, in competition with later engines of the 'Princess Royal' Class, built at Crewe in 1935, and having boilers with 32-element superheaters. Trials with the turbine locomotive No 6202 were made with three variations of boiler. While the records of coal and water consumption in these trials (which extended over two years) did not reveal any very significant improvements in efficiency over the ordinary 'Pacific' engines, allowance must be made for the tests being made in ordinary service conditions and subject to the many factors of weather, traffic circumstances and such like that can have so pronounced an effect on test results, from day to day, on the same service trains with the same engines and crew. The summary results of the London-Glasgow trials, four return trips, in all cases except that with the turbine engine with her second boiler, were as follows:

Left *LMS: No 6202—arrangement of main turbine drive.*

Below *LMS: No 6202—plan view showing layout of main and reverse turbines.*

Right *LMS: No 6202—main and auxiliary framing.*

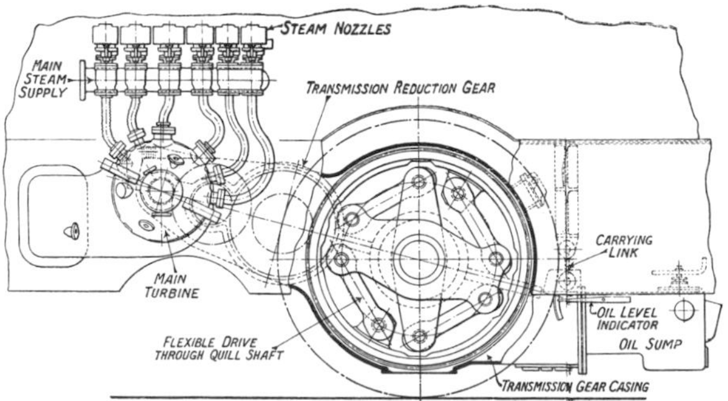

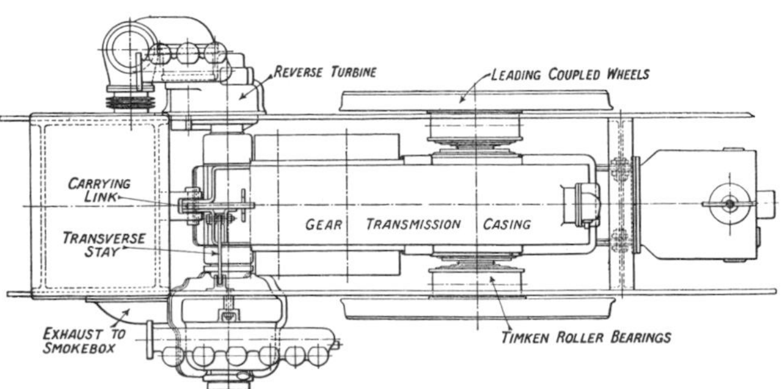

Engine No	**6212**	**6210**	**6202**	**6202**	**6202**
Boiler No	—	—	(1)	(2)	(3)
Total (miles)	1,608	1,608	1,608	1,207	1,608
Coal per dhp hour (lb)	3.22	2.98	2.97	2.86	2.78
Water per dhp hour (gallons)	26.9	24.7	24.0	22.1	24.8

Engines 6212 and 6210 were standard 'Pacifics' of the 'Princess Royal' Class with 32-element superheaters.

While the above summaries based generally on four return trips from Euston to Glasgow and back show a marginal superiority in favour of the turbine locomotive, both in coal and water consumption, the more significant details of performance are revealed when it comes to an examination of the best uphill running times; and these do go some way towards justifying the claim that the turbine locomotive would show a 30 per cent increase in tractive power over a reciprocating steam locomotive at speeds over 35 mph. The figures opposite relate to the 31.4 mile climb from Carnforth to Shap Summit, a vertical rise of 885 ft.

The times given in the table opposite are the fastest over each section recorded in the series of tests. While giving due regard to the maximum performance of the standard engine No 6210, which was exceptional for this class, the work of the turbine engine No 6202 was generally superior, particularly in respect of the severe final ascent from Tebay to Shap Summit. It therefore goes some way towards justifying the claim that the tractive

LMS comparative 'Pacific' tests: Carnforth-Shap Summit

Engine No			**6212**		**6210**		**6202(1)**		**6202(2)**		**6202(3)**	
Section	**Distance (miles)**	**Booked time (min)**	**Load (tons)**	**Time m s**	**Load (tons)**	**Time m s**	**Load (tons)**	**Time m s**	**Load (tons)**	**Time m s**	**Load (tons)**	**Time m s**
Carnforth-Oxenholme	12.7	14	477	13 35	512	15 30	474	12 55	475	14 05	489	12 10
Oxenholme-Tebay	13.0	16	507	17 20	482	14 10	470	16 20	486	14 55	484	16 00
Tebay-Shap Summit	5.7	10	507	9 30	512	8 40	470	8 50	486	7 10	484	7 35
Total	31.4	40	—	40 25	—	36 20	—	37 05	—	35 10	—	35 45

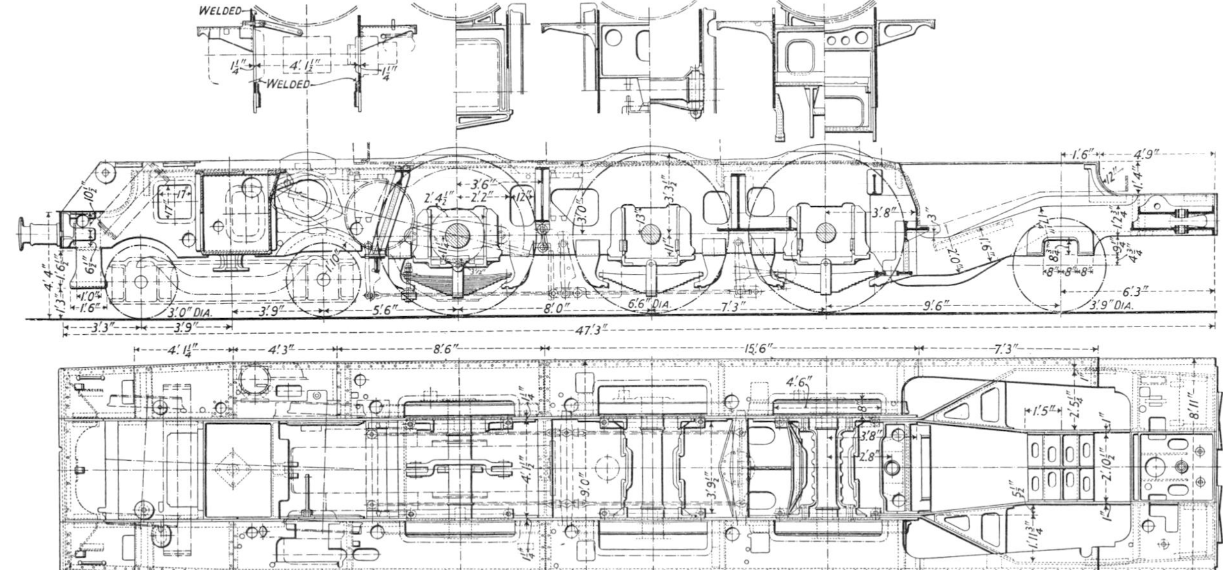

performance of the locomotive would be some 30 per cent superior to that of the comparable reciprocating locomotives.

In regular running on the Euston-Liverpool service the turbine engine worked with reliability and success. I travelled down one night on the 6.5 pm Merseyside Express, when the gross load behind the tender was 515 tons and, despite fog in places, there was some fast running, and Crewe, 158.1 miles, was passed on time in 164 minutes. The train was heavily delayed by fog afterwards but, allowing for delays, the net time to passing Crewe was 159 minutes. The engine also worked on the 5.25 pm up from Liverpool, which between Crewe and Willesden had the fastest start to stop run on the LMS, at an average speed of 64.5 mph. The maximum tare load specified for 'Pacifics' on this duty was 420 tons, but was often exceeded, and unlike the situation with the smaller engines (as mentioned in the preceeding chapter) loads in excess of this limit of as much as 60 tons were taken without loss of time. A very fast run stands to the credit of the turbine engine, when a load of 429 tons tare was conveyed, 455 tons gross. Because of checks farther north, the train was 5 minutes late in passing Weedon; but the ensuing 61.6 miles to Wembley were covered in 47½ minutes at an average speed of 77.8 mph and the train brought in to the stop at Willesden Junction on time.

Up to the outbreak of war in September 1939, the locomotive, although working in ordinary traffic, had been under close observation, and not entirely free from trouble. It had required a certain amount of specialised individual attention, and on this account it was considered wise to take the engine out of traffic. In any case, in the early stages of the war, the number of express passenger trains was greatly reduced, and those that remained were much decelerated. The locomotive was therefore stored in the Paint Shot at Crewe Works until July 1941, when the demand for maximum power locomotives had become urgent. Engine No 6202 was thereupon taken out of storage and returned to Edge Hill shed for working on the heaviest London-Liverpool trains. Its subsequent record of availability was not good. Little in the way of spare parts was carried in Crewe Works, and requirements had to be obtained from the turbine makers' works, at a time when the latter were intensely engaged on vital war-time production of their standard equipments. The LMS had to wait for the special parts for No 6202 to be fitted into an extremely busy schedule.

Then, in July 1943, there came a major failure of the final drive, and severe damage to the high speed pinion, and this put the locomotive out of service for a long time. While this could be regarded as part of the price one had to pay for experience in what was then still an unfamiliar field, it added to the poor record of availability in traffic that the locomotive was gradually gathering to itself. Since construction (and deducting the time that the locomotive was stored in the Paint Shop at Crewe) the average annual mileage was no more than 28,500, as compared to the war-time averages of 53,000 and 73,000 miles per annum for the 'Princess Royal' and 'Coronation' Classes of 'Pacific' engines. In peacetime conditions both these latter classes were averaging 80,000 miles per annum, whereas in the best year for the turbine, 1936, the total was 73,268 miles.

In January 1946 my great friend, the late R.C. Bond, who was then Deputy Chief Mechanical Engineer of the LMS, read a magnificently comprehensive paper before the Institution of Locomotive Engineers, covering in full and uncompromising detail the experience they had endured and enjoyed with No 6202, and concluding with what was hoped from it in the future. It was a remarkable document, enriched by the discussions that followed its presentation in London, Derby and Manchester. Bond concluded thus: 'On present indications, the next five years should show up the turbine locomotive in an increasingly favourable light. It has, in the author's opinion, already proved itself well worth persevering with, and it is not beyond the bound of possibility that a limited number of non-condensing turbine locomotives, in a more highly developed form based on the experience with No 6202, will be regularly employed on the heaviest and fastest express trains, with profit to their owners'.

This hopeful view of the future did not materialise but the text of Bond's paper, together with the many drawings included, provides a field of intensely interesting study for any who wish to delve deeper into the details of one of the nearest of near-misses in the history of the British locomotive.

5. The coming rivals of steam: electric—diesel

The later 1920s saw the last attempts on the British main line railways to restore the situation which had contributed so much to their prosperity in the years before the First World War. It was a losing battle. While long distance road haulage of heavy goods had not yet begun to make appreciable inroads upon what, for many of the old companies, had been a staple traffic, in rural areas, where small consignments were involved, road transport had already made a marked impact in its quickness and convenience. For the most opulent patrons the private motor car had begun to skim off some of the richest cream of long distance first class travel, while on the railways themselves increased running costs were leading to searching examinations towards means of economy. Outward signs like the decision of both the LMS and LNER to paint all locomotives black, save for a few selected express passenger classes, were no more than scratchings on the surface.

More serious, at the end of the decade, was the unmistakable evidence of deepening world-wide depression. While its effects were not so severe in Great Britain as in some other countries, particularly in the USA, they were bad enough. On the railways more economical ways of doing day to day jobs inevitably meant using fewer men; but, to relieve unemployment, the National Government, which had succeeded the minority Labour administration in the autumn of 1931, passed legislation enabling loans at advantageous interest rates to be made available to the railways to enable large works involving high capital expenditure to be undertaken. The Southern Railway took advantage of these facilities to embark upon the first-ever British scheme of main line electrification, between London and Brighton, with a short westward continuation along the south coast to Worthing. While it is interesting to recall that this great scheme was inaugurated and brought to fruition in the first stages of the national climb out of the great depression of the early 1930s, the technical aspect of the motive power involved are still more so, and are of course, the main considerations in this book.

One cannot set down in precise terms comparative figures for the overall efficiency of steam and electric locomotives, because the former constitute completely self contained power plants, including their own generating station, whereas the latter collect their form of power on the way, from conductor rails or an overhead power line. The overall efficiency in the latter case would have to include that of the remote central generating station, and of the transmission lines, before the current is actually collected on the locomotives. Despite varying conditions, however, it is generally considered that overall efficiency from the fuel used in the power station to horsepower at the rail in an electric locomotive is of the order of 20 per cent, against a very maximum in a first class steam locomotive of the late 1920s of about 8½ per cent,

London Brighton & South Coast Railway: one of the 'Elevated Electric' suburban trains entering Peckham Rye station (British Railways).

Great Western Railway: the first diesel-mechanical railcar, No 1, engined by the Associated Equipment Co, and introduced in 1934 (British Railways).

relating the heat in the coal to the work done in the cylinders. In addition to this there was the important advantage of electrification, as conceived on the Southern Railway, of one-man operation of the motive power.

Electric traction on railways south of the Thames had begun on the London Brighton and South Coast Railway in 1909, with the opening of the once-celebrated 'Elevated Electric' service on the South London line from Victoria through the southern suburbs via Peckham Rye, and round to London Bridge. Sir Philip Dawson was the consulting engineer and he designed and supervised the installation of the entire project. It involved no more than 9 miles of route, but its impact was sensational. On the electrified line, by far the greatest number of passengers were booked at Peckham Rye and, since the opening of the London County Council electric tramway system, bookings on the railway had slumped dramatically. The introduction of the 'Elevated Electric' brought an equally remarkable revival, thus:

Annual passenger bookings at Peckham Rye

1902: Before opening of LCC tram system	1,213,281
1909: Last year of steam trains	526,373
1910: First year of electric trains	1,051,263

Mr Philip Dawson, as he was then, came in for some severe criticism for advocating a system of electric traction radically different from what was then usual practice. On his recommendation the Brighton railway adopted 6,600 volts single-phase alternating current. One of the factors most seriously considered was the desirability of avoiding the use of conductor rails but, in adopting a line voltage *10 times* that used on the London Underground railways, Dawson and the Board of the LB & SCR were thinking in terms of a far wider application of electric traction than the 9 miles of the South London line, or indeed of the London suburban area at its fullest extent. It is, I think, fairly safe to say that had it not been for the First World War, the line to Brighton would have been electrified, according to the precepts of Sir Philip Dawson by about 1920! The General Manager, Sir William Forbes, like his celebrated uncle, James Staats Forbes of the London, Chatham and Dover, was a 'go-getter' of no mean order and, in the early 1900s he was in process of transforming the Brighton from one of the worst to one of the most go-ahead of all the British railways, and he had chosen a consultant after his own heart in Philip Dawson.

I have some vivid personal memories of him because, when I was taking a post-graduate course in railway engineering at the City and Guilds (Engineering) College, in 1924-5, he was one of the visiting specialist lecturers, and he lost no opportunities of extolling the system he had installed on the 'Bwighton', as he called it. (He could not pronounce his Rs.) Its merit for long distance electrification lay in reduced cost of the transmission system. At that time the LB & SCR was installing its third extension of the system, carrying the 6,600 volt single-phase network to Coulsdon, on the Brighton main line, and to Sutton; this work was completed in 1925. The rolling stock consisted of multiple unit trains. What Dawson had in mind for the contemplated extension to Brighton, we were not to know, because the grouping of the railways in 1923, and the amalgamation of the line with the London and South Western, put an entirely new complexion on the prospect of further development.

At the time of grouping, Sir William Forbes, having been in office since 1899, was much the senior of the three knighted General Managers of the constituents of the Southern Railway and, although he was then in his 67th year, there was no general understanding as to the time when senior executives were expected to retire. Indeed, the delay in appointing a General Manager of the Southern Railway until a full year after grouping, might well suggest that he had some hopes of getting the job. But Sir Herbert Walker, of the London and South Western, 12 years his junior, was preferred, and Forbes retired at the beginning of December 1923. The South Western had begun to electrify its suburban network on the 'third rail' system, at 650 volts, direct current, and Walker, an extremely strong personality, did not have much difficulty in persuading the Board of the Southern Railway to adopt the LSW, rather than the Brighton, system for the first electrification of the former South Eastern and Chatham lines. This was naturally a great disappointment to Brighton men, especially that it was on their line that the first extension of the then-standardised Southern system was applied to main line operation. Of course it could be argued that a line no more than 50 miles long was really no more than a glorified commuter run—which in fact it became; but for good or ill, the die was cast. The Southern Railway was irrevocably committed to low voltage direct current operation.

GWR: an interesting picture of a lightweight railcar, No 15, (note absence of conventional buffers) in a characteristic Brunel station with all-over roof at Thame, on the Princes Risborough to Oxford branch (M.W. Earley).

There was nevertheless a cloud on the horizon. In 1927 a Committee, under the chairmanship of Colonel Sir James Pringle, Chief Inspecting Officer of Railways at the Ministry of Transport, charged with making recommendation for a future British standard for main line electrification, came down strongly in favour of 1,500 volts, direct current, with overhead line collection, thereby ostracising both the Brighton and the South Western systems then extensively used in the southern suburbs of London. The recommendations of the Pringle committee were endorsed four years later by a committee under the chairmanship of Lord Weir, charged with the task of investigating the economic prospects of main line electrification in Great Britain. The report of the Weir committee was published in 1931, and received a somewhat lukewarm response from the technical press of the day. *The Railway Engineer*, for example, suggested that the economies forecast could be reached, or nearly reached, by improvements in steam locomotives at a vastly lesser capital cost. Nevertheless the recommendation of 1,500 volts dc for future electrification struck deep and was to be implemented in later projects; but not on the Southern!

When planning for the electrification to Brighton began in earnest the awkward fact that the line would still have to carry a mixed traffic had to be borne in mind. The original project included nothing east of the London-Brighton main line and, because multiple unit train sets were envisaged for all the new services, it meant that the Eastbourne, Hastings and Portsmouth trains, making a considerable portion of their mileage over the Brighton main line, would have to remain steam hauled. There could be no question of through portions for destinations on the Eastern and Western subsidiary lines being carried from London on the

Brighton trains and detached at Haywards Heath, or Three Bridges respectively. There were additionally the Continental Boat trains via Newhaven. In view of necessary retention of steam haulage out of both Victoria and London Bridge, it was at first thought that the 'Southern Belle' all-Pullman express would remain steam hauled. As the scheme developed, however, provision was made for the entire passenger service between London and Brighton, express and intermediate, to be worked by multiple unit electric trains.

Principal interest naturally centered around the new multiple unit express trains of which there were three varieties: 20 6-coach Pullman express units; three special 6-coach units for the 'City Limited' and three 5-coach all Pullman units for the 'Southern Belle'. The composition of these trains is shown in the table below.

These express set trains were designed so as to be coupled in multiple at times of heavy traffic and, of course, the special units for the 'City Limited' service at 8.45 am, from Brighton to London, and at 5 pm down in the evening, were exclusive to these trains and were regularly coupled in twin. The power equipment on each motor coach consisted of four 225 horsepower traction motors, in the case of the ordinary 6-car express units for a tare weight of 532 tons. With every seat taken this could involve a gross load of about 560 tons. The new trains for the 'Southern Belle' included the first motor Pullmans anywhere in the world, and these vehicles were also the heaviest passenger vehicles yet seen on the railways of Great Britain, having a tare weight of 62 tons. Prior to the introduction of the electric service (on New Year's Day 1933) the principal expresses to and from Victoria had been worked by the 'King Arthur' Class 4-6-0s, with the ex-LBSC 4-6-4 tank engines working the 'City Limited' to and from London Bridge. Although the power built into the new electric sets was considerably greater in relation to tare weight than that previously existing with steam traction, there was no appreciable acceleration of service at first, though it was evident that there was far more power in reserve.

The motorman's compartment in all the new trains was arranged for single-man operating and, although this might have seemed to presage a considerable reduction in footplate men at a time when unemployment was already severe, the new electric service, on a regular interval basis, was so lavish that there could have been very little reduction in the manpower required. Quite apart from the intermediate services there was a non-stop 60 minute express from Victoria to Brighton at every hour from 9 am till midnight, except at 5 pm Mondays to Fridays when the hourly timetable 'path' was taken from East Croydon southwards by the 'City Limited' from London Bridge. The Brighton 'opening' in 1933 was only the first phase in the Southern Railway electrification programme, which was continued in 1935, to Eastbourne and Hastings; to Portsmouth via Guildford, in 1937; and via the Mid-Sussex line, including the branches to Littlehampton and Bognor in 1938. With power taken from the grid of the Central Electricity Board, the voltage on the third rail was 750. In recording the rapid extension of the former London and South Western Railway's 'third rail' system of low voltage dc electrification, it is interesting to reflect upon how the course of British railway motive power engineering might have developed had the Brighton 'elevated electric' system prevailed from 1924 onwards, instead of the LSW 'third rail'. As it was, the last 'elevated' train ran on September 21 1929.

Parallel to the first introduction of a main line electric service in Great Britain, were the beginnings of diesel traction which, on the basis of thermal efficiency alone, gave promise of some welcome economies in railway operation. It was in 1930 that the diesel engine first began to receive seriously considered attention in the railway technical press. Attention was drawn to experimental locomotives operating on the continent of

Vehicle no	**6-coach express**	**6-coach City Limited**	**5-coach all Pullman**
1	Motor brake 3rd	Motor brake 3rd	Motor brake 3rd
2	Corridor 3rd	Corridor 1st	Pullman 3rd
3	Corridor Compo	Corridor 1st	Pullman 1st
4	Pullman Compo	Pullman Compo	Pullman 1st
5	Corridor Compo	Corridor 1st	Motor brake 3rd
6	Motor brake 3rd	Motor brake 3rd	—
Seats 1st	72	138	40
Seats 3rd	236	120	152
Tare weight (tons)	266	266	249
Total motor HP	1,800	1,800	1,800

GWR: the first diesel railcar to have standard railway buffers and drawgear, No 18, put into service in 1937, and here shown with a trailer (British Railways).

Europe with engines built by the Swiss firm of Sulzer Brothers Ltd. The Tyneside firm of Sir W.G. Armstrong Whitworth & Co Ltd built a remarkable diesel-electric train for the suburban service of the then-British owned Buenos Aires Great Southern Railway, consisting of a 5-car electric train which carried with it, permanently coupled, its own electric generating station in the form of a 1,200 hp diesel-electric power plant on a separate 12-wheeled carriage. Again, the two diesel generating sets, each of 600 hp, were built by Sulzer.

Manufacture of this design of diesel engine, under licence, was taken up by Armstrong Whitworth and, despite the prevailing depression, a considerable investment was made at their Newcastle works in providing extensive special plant for producing these engines cheaply and in quantities, and in a wide range of sizes. This enterprise, however, met with little response from the British main line railways. As a first venture, a 250 hp diesel-electric railcar was built and demonstrated to the LNER at Newcastle in November 1931; but Gresley was not impressed and it was not until some considerable time afterwards that the car was taken into the railway company's stock, together with the two similar ones built subsequently. They were the only diesel-electric railcars possessed by the LNER. The performance specification seemed attractive enough:

Weight in working order		42½ tons
Maximum speed		65 mph
Starting tractive effort		6,600 lb
Balancing speeds (fully loaded):		—
	Car only	When hauling 27 ton trailer
	mph	mph
On level track	56-60	50-55
On 1 in 200 gradient	48	41
On 1 in 100 gradient	48	30

The seating in the car itself was for 60 passengers, and another 90 could be accommodated in a trailer. From his subsequent attitude towards the German diesel-electric high speed 'Flying Hamburger' trains one could sense that Gresley had something of an aversion to diesels of any kind.

By contrast the Great Western entry into diesel traction was a complete success. The transmission throughout the fleet of railcars was, however, mechanical, with standard London bus engines manufactured by the Associated Equipment Company at their Southall Works beside the Great Western main line. To facilitate maintenance work a rail connection into the works was laid in from the adjoining Southall locomotive running shed. The first car, which was certainly experimental, was put into service in 1934. It had a single engine of 121 horsepower with a four-speed and reverse gearbox. Amusing stories are told of some of the drivers, and of the difficulties they found at first in changing gear. At that time, of course, few railwaymen below the upper echelons would have owned cars, and it was in any case many years before the days of pre-selector or automatic gear change. Car No 1, which had seating for 69 passengers, was an immediate success, and it led the way to more ambitious developments.

It was followed, in no more than five months, by the three 'express' railcars introduced on to the Birmingham-South Wales service. These had two 121 hp engines, while the passenger accommodation which was of a 'main-line', rather than of a local character, included a buffet compartment. They also proved very popular in providing a fast and quite luxurious service. The next 12, of which delivery began in July 1935, were larger, with a seating for 70 passengers, also having two of the standard AEC engines of 121 hp each. Car No 17, which was of the same overall size as the preceeding 12, was fitted for carrying parcels and had no passenger accommodation. Up to this time all the cars had been arranged for solo operation; but their popularity and the fluctuation in business from day to day made it desirable to have facilities for increasing the accommodation, and the 18th car, put into service in 1937, had standard railway type buffers and drawgear, and was designed to draw a tail load of up to 60 tons.

With the outbreak of war in 1939 all railcar services on the Great Western Railway were at first withdrawn. This, however, was not for long; indeed in 1940 not only had the cars been put back into service, not all of them on their former routes, but a further 20 of improved design were acquired. Of the new cars, four were arranged as twin-coupled units, with vestibule connections. One was designed to provide a second parcels-only car, and the remaining 15 were intended for local services. All had standard railway buffers and draw gear. The engines, as previously, were of AEC build, of the latest type, with a combined engine horsepower of 210, but things were made considerably easier for the drivers by use of a fluid flywheel, five speed, epicyclic gearbox with preselector control.

The four cars designed for twin operation were geared for a maximum speed of 70 mph, but I have personally timed one of them at 75 mph on the South Wales main line between Carmarthen and Haverfordwest. They gave every satisfaction, and it seemed that these diesel-mechanical cars would have been greatly multiplied for general use on branch lines, and on fast main line services of relatively light traffic. Only one man was required in the driver's cab, though at many sheds there were no separate railcar links, and drivers worked on rail cars and steam locomotives as required.

At the British Industries Fair in February 1932 the Hunslet Engine Company of Leeds exhibited the first main line diesel shunting locomotive to be seen in Great Britain. It had an engine developing 150 horsepower, purely mechanical transmission, and a pre-selector gear box. The final drive to the six wheels was by a jackshaft and outside coupling

GWR: one of the twin-coupled diesel railcar units, first introduced in 1940, here seen near Reading West station on a run to Newbury (M.W. Earley).

rods. Sir Harold Hartley, a Vice-President of the LMS, was keenly interested, because it gave promise of considerable economy on three separate counts: reduced fuel costs, increased availability (and therefore requiring fewer locomotives to do the same job) and single man operation. He authorised a sum of £30,000 for experimenting with diesel shunting locomotives to determine the most suitable type for standardisation. In the meantime two other firms, showing a preference for electric rather than mechanical transmission, entered the field; these were Sir W.G. Armstrong-Whitworth & Co, using the Sulzer type of diesel engine, and the English Electric Co, and examples of both designs were accepted for trial on the LMS, together with a few additional Hunslets.

Just at this time the distinguished Electrical Engineer of the LMS, Lieutenant Colonel F.A. Cortez-Leigh, was due to retire. As long ago as 1913 he had been appointed to the then-new office of Electrical Engineer to the London and North Western Railway, and he will always be remembered for the beautiful open-saloon type of multiple-unit trains on the services from Euston and Broad Street to Watford. Characteristic of the LNWR, they were unsurpassed for spacious comfort and immaculate riding. To succeed 'the Colonel' as he was usually known, Sir Harold Hartley brought in C.E. Fairburn, then Engineer and Manager of the Traction Department of English Electric. Prior to his appointment to this job, and following a brilliant career at Oxford, taking three 'firsts', he had been a pupil of Sir Henry Fowler on the Midland Railway, at Derby, and then gained valuable electrical installation experience on the Newport-Shildon freight line of the North Eastern Railway. With his subsequent industrial experience he was well suited to develop diesel traction on the LMS, though the mechanical part of the locomotives was Stanier's responsibility.

In 1936 delivery was taken of 20 new diesel-electric shunting locomotives of 350 horsepower, 10 each from Armstrong Whitworth, and English Electric. The differences between the mechanical parts of the transmission can be seen from the accompanying drawings, with the English Electric

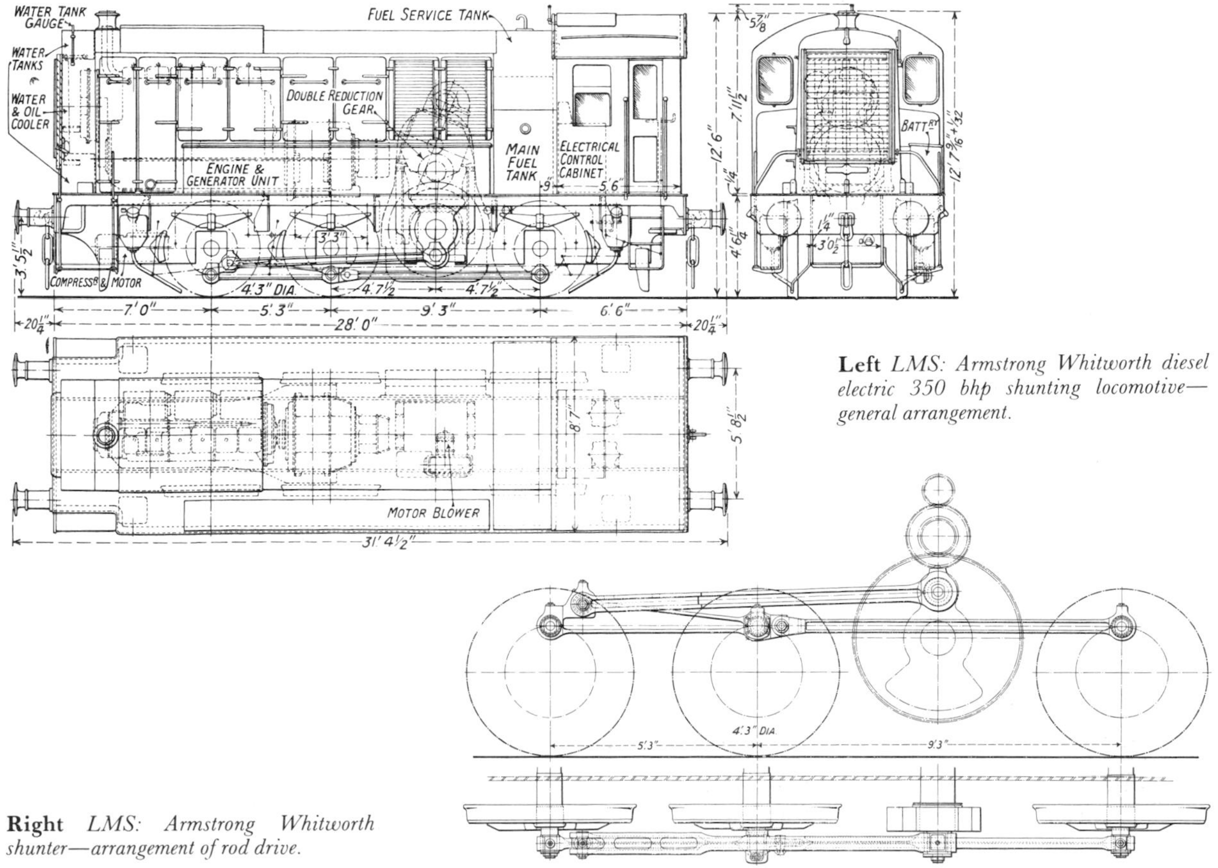

Left *LMS: Armstrong Whitworth diesel electric 350 bhp shunting locomotive—general arrangement.*

Right *LMS: Armstrong Whitworth shunter—arrangement of rod drive.*

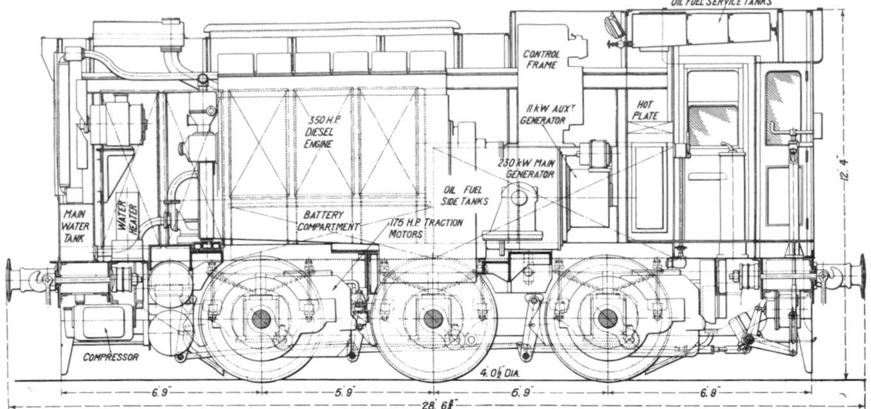

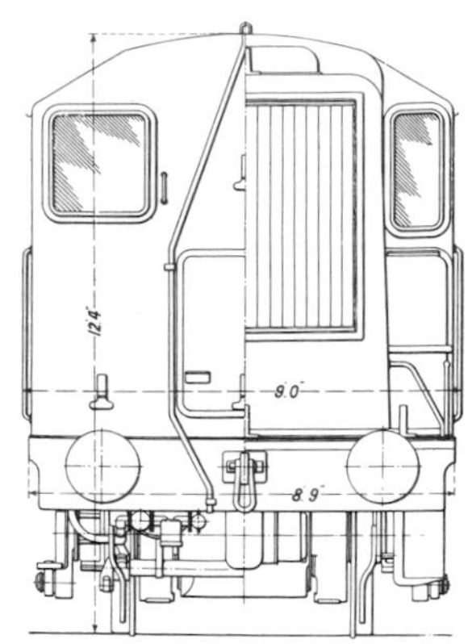

driving direct on to the middle pair of coupled wheels through a double reduction gear, and the Armstrong Whitworth driving on to a jackshaft, from which a connecting rod drove on to the coupling rod of the road wheels. In the former, both the diesel engine and the electrical equipment were of English Electric design and manufacture, while on the latter, the diesel engines were of the Armstrong-Sulzer type, and the electrical equipment was by Crompton Parkinson & Co. The 20 locomotives were soon launched into very severe railway service. Five locomotives of each design were assigned to Crewe south sorting sidings, while five of the English Electric units were stationed at Willesden. The remaining five Armstrong units were allocated to Carlisle. They were all subjected to the most intense utilisation, with each locomotive working 24 hours a day, for six days in the week.

That shunting can be the most demanding, and mechanically the most devastating of railway motive power service is generally acknowledged; but what was actually demanded from these 350 hp diesel shunters at Crewe and Willesden can be more truly appreciated from the results of some on-site observations made by a special correspondent of *The Railway Gazette*, and contained in an article contributed to that journal in 1937. This man spent some hours on the footplate of one of the Armstrong-Whitworth locomotives in the south sidings at Crewe, employed in splitting up loose-coupled arriving trains of from 50 to 70 wagons, and in making up similar trains for departure in adjacent marshalling sidings. A log of 20 minutes typical operation, showed something like 30 changes from forward to reverse direction of movement, with only two pauses of just over a minute's duration when the locomotive was not moving, and 50 individual pushes, or pulls. The

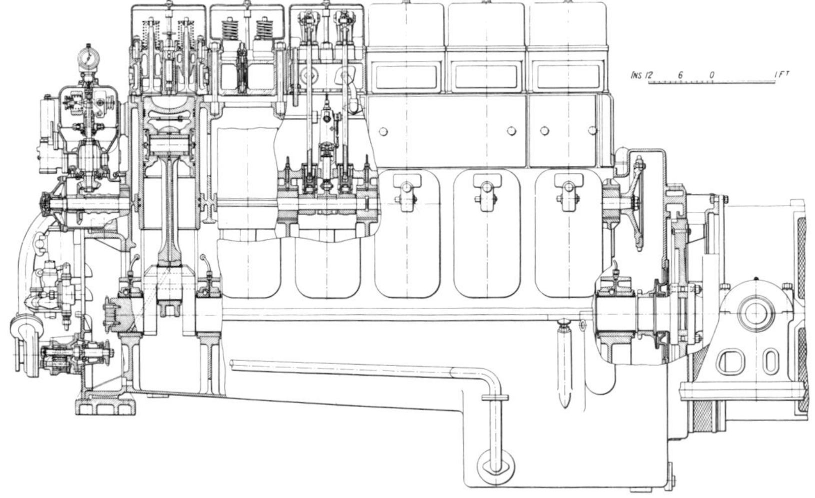

Above *LMS: English Electric-built 350 bhp diesel electric shunting locomotive.*

Right *Details of the 350 bhp Armstrong-Sulzer diesel engine.*

Left *LMS: English Electric diesel engine—longitudinal section and outside view.*

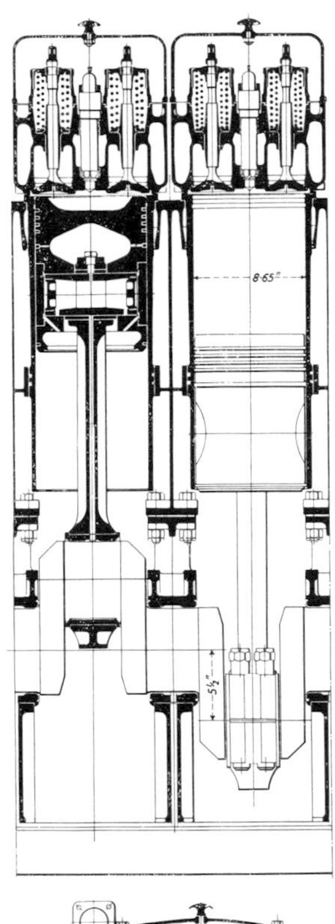

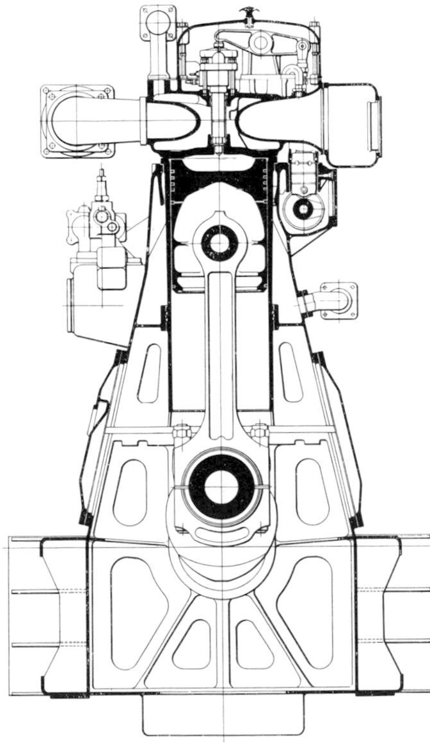

speed rarely exceeded 8 mph. It was noticeable that this demanding stop-start-stop kind of work did not result in any overheating of the engine. On one of the English Electric locomotives engaged in marshalling, as distinct from 'breaking up', service, the individual runs were of longer duration, and often at steady speeds of from 5 to 8 mph. At the same time, the moments when the locomotive was not in motion were equally brief. In one 20-minute spell of which a detailed log was kept, only one stop lasted longer than 20 seconds(!) and that was for 1 minute 15 seconds.

The overall performance of these two types of diesel-electric shunting locomotive was kept under close observation and, when the time came for additional units to be ordered, it was interesting to see that the design was a blend of the best features of the existing types. The mechanical portions followed those of the Armstrong Whitworth units, with geared jackshaft, and connecting rod drive. The frames and all these mechanical portions were made at Derby locomotive works. The diesel engine, and all the transmission equipment was of English Electric manufacture. The tractive effort was increased to 35,000 lb. I saw some of these new locomotives very efficiently at work just before the outbreak of war in 1939 in the newly-modernised hump marshalling yard at Toton, near Nottingham, which deals with the heavy coal traffic concentrated there for onward working southwards to the London area. A total of 20 of the new type was added in 1939.

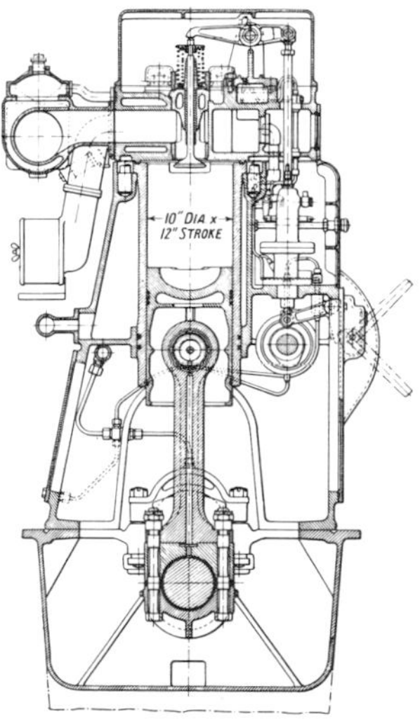

Above *LMS: cross-section of English Electric diesel engine.*

6. The streamline age

As the year 1935 approached, and with it the centenary of the Act of Incorporation of the Great Western Railway, there were many, quite apart from its most ardent supporters, who were wondering how this most important anniversary might be celebrated. Because of the grouping of the British railways in 1923, and the disappearance of all the other old companies, it was the only one likely to reach its century, unless the LMS, the LNER and the Southern lasted, as companies, until the year 2023. Supporters of the Great Western, rejoicing in the supremacy it seemed to hold in locomotive matters in the 1920s, were equally aware that in more recent years its thunder had to some extent been stolen by spectacular achievements on the LMS and LNER. There was speculation as to whether the great company would set up yet another milestone in 1935, comparable to the near-sensation created in 1927 with the production of the *King George V*. The feeling that something might, and ought to, be done was not confined to its many amateur supporters. It was also present in the Board Room.

It was a time when 'streamline' had become a catch word, to be applied, with singular promiscuity, to signal boxes, domestic kettles, toothbrushes—or, as Sir W.S. Gilbert might have put it, 'all goods from cough-mixtures to cables'! Certainly some members of the Locomotive Committee of the GWR Board had noted that certain new German and American trains were described as streamlined, and it was thought that the Great Western might show it was 'with it' by having some too. But C.B. Collett, their Chief Mechanical Engineer, just did not want to know. After Stanier's departure for the LMS he had become more insular than ever, and when he deigned to grant an interview to Charles S. Lake, the technical editor of *The Railway Gazette*, it was to upbraid him for devoting an altogether excessive amount of space 'to an engine *we* designed'—referring to the first Stanier 'Pacifics' on the LMS. When the chairman of the Locomotive Committee said he wanted some streamlined locomotives, Collett's reaction was churlish. He had a paperweight model of a 'King' on his desk. An office boy was sent out to buy some plasticine from a toy shop, and then Collett determined the form that the streamlining should take by smearing plasticine across the front and down the sides of the running plates, round the cylinders, and filling spaces behind the chimney and the safety valves, where eddies occur. A hemispherical blob on the front of the smokebox completed the job, and the paperweight thus decorated was sent into the drawing office for working drawings to be made.

The first, and only 'King' Class engine to be so treated was No 6014, *King Henry VII*, and when the official photograph was issued to the technical press early in 1935 it was accompanied by a note reading: 'The GWR is carrying out experiments in streamlining express locomotives with the object of reducing wind resistance and effecting economy in coal consumption. This will be followed by experiments of a similar type with engines of the "Castle" class'. I have never heard that any experiments were actually conducted, either with No 6014, or with the one 'Castle' so treated, No 5005, *Manorbier Castle.* I would imagine that the coverings had little more that a nuisance value in maintenance, especially the covering from the roof of the cab on to the tender. Stage by stage the shroudings were removed, until there was nothing left except the continuous splasher over the driving wheels and the prow-shaped front of the cab.

It was, of course, no more than a coincidence that the official photograph of the semi-streamlined *King Henry VII* was published in the same issue of *The Railway Magazine* that contained a very full account

of the record breaking performances of the LNER 'A3 pacific' engine No 2750, *Papyrus*, in working a high speed test train from Kings Cross to Newcastle and back (on March 5 1935) when, among other record making feats, a maximum speed of 108 mph was attained on the southbound journey. In 1936 Sir Nigel Gresley, as he had recently been honoured, was elected President of the Institution of Mechanical Engineers, and in his Presidential Address delivered in October of that year, he gave some interesting details as to how the first LNER streamlined train came to be constructed. He had become very interested in the running of various high-speed light-weight streamlined trains, in Germany, France and the USA, and I now quote, from his Presidential Address:

'I visited Germany in the latter part of 1934 and travelled on the *Flying Hamburger* from Berlin to Hamburg and back; I was so impressed with the smooth running of this train at a speed of 100 mph, which was maintained for long distances, that I thought it advisable to explore the possibilities of extra high-speed travel by having such a train for experimental purposes on the London and North Eastern Railway.

'I accordingly approached the makers of that train and furnished them with full particulars as to the gradients, curves and speed restrictions on the line between Kings Cross and Newcastle. With the thoroughness characteristic of the German engineers they made a very exhaustive investigation and prepared a complete schedule showing the shortest possible running times under favourable conditions and then added 10 per cent which they regarded as adequate to meet varying weather conditions and to have sufficient time in reserve to make up for such deceleration or delays as might normally be expected'.

The result of that 'exhaustive investigation' was disappointing. With a 3-coach articulated train, seating no more than 140 passengers, in accommodation much more cramped than that provided for *third* class passengers in Great Britain, the best that the German manufacturers could offer was a time of 4 hours 17 minutes in the up direction, and 4 hours 15½ minutes in the down. Sir Ralph Wedgwood, Chief General Manager of the LNER, on hearing of these proposals, suggested that better time could be made with one of the standard 'Pacific' engines with a train of ordinary coaches, providing more accommodation, in far greater comfort. This was convincingly shown by the great runs of March 5 1935. With a 6-coach train weighing 217 tons behind the tender, the northbound run of 268.3 miles was made in 237 minutes in spite of 7 minutes lost by checks, while the return took 231¾ minutes, including one speed restriction to 15 mph. The German proposals were thus put completely in the shade, by actual times of substantially less than four hours made by standard equipment.

Less than a month after these trial runs, the LNER announced that in October the new 'Silver Jubilee' high speed express would be introduced, running between Kings Cross and Newcastle in the level four hours, and that the train itself would be fully streamlined. Gresley's contracts with the leading French locomotive engineers of the day, and his experience with the 2-8-2 engines, *Cock o' the North* and *Earl Marischal*, had indicated that considerably greater economies and freedom in running were to be obtained from the *internal* streamlining of all stages in the steam circuit than from any fancy external shapes; and the new 'Pacific' engines authorised for the Silver Jubilee

Below Left *GWR: the partially streamlined 4-6-0, No 6014,* King Henry VII, *as thus modified in 1935* (British Railways).

Below *GWR: the partially streamlined 4-6-0, No 5005,* Manorbier Castle, *thus modified in 1935. In its original form this engine made the record Paddington–Swindon run of 77.4 miles in 60 minutes in May 1932* (British Railways).

This page, top to bottom

LNER: one of the first four Gresley 'A4' 'Pacifics' built specially for the Silver Jubilee train in 1935—No 2512, Silver Fox (British Railways).

LNER: one of the 'A4s' of 1937, No 4489, as originally painted in apple-green and named Woodcock. *This engine was one of the five set aside for working the 'Coronation' train, later painted in garter blue and named* Dominion of Canada (British Railways).

The hundredth LNER. 'Pacific', No 4498, named after the designer Sir Nigel Gresley (British Railways).

LNER: the northbound 'Coronation' at full speed, hauled by garter blue 'A4' No 4488, Union of South Africa (Real Photographs).

Horse power saved by streamlining

Speed (mph)		60	70	80	90
Horsepower required to overcome head-on air resistance	Standard 'A3' engine	97.21	154.26	230.51	328.49
	Proposed streamliner	56.39	89.41	133.61	190.40
Saving by streamlining		40.82	64.85	96.90	138.09

service differed from the standard 'A3' Class in having smaller cylinders, larger piston valves, a higher boiler pressure, and a slightly greater firebox heating surface. The boiler barrel was one foot shorter. These factors alone would make for a freer running engines but, with internal streamlining, the aggregate effect was profound. Gresley himself, however, was not at first convinced of the need for external streamlining; but some judicious prodding from Bulleid, who was then his chief assistant, led to some experiments being made in the wind tunnel at the National Physical Laboratory using scale models of a standard 'Pacific' engine, and of the proposed streamliner for the Silver Jubilee. The results obtained are shown above.

The wedge-shaped front, which was so effective in deflecting the exhaust steam clear of the cab look-out was derived from the Bugatti railcars running on the Paris-Deauville high speed service, on which Gresley and Bulleid together had some hair-raising rides; but Bulleid himself devised the aerofoil shape of the running plate and valences, after Gresley had suggested that the wedge-shaped front, à la Bugatti, did not look quite right on its own. Even with the wind tunnel test results before him, Gresley was still not convinced that the saving in horsepower was worth the extra cost of the fully streamlined casing; but again with a little encouragement from Bulleid, that it would be good for publicity, it carried the day. What would have been far more illuminating from a technical viewpoint would have been a scientifically conducted trial, on a stationary testing plant, to show the improvement resulting from the internal streamlining of the 'A4' Pacific, compared to that of the standard 'A3'. At that time, however, the only stationary testing plant in England was that of the Great Western, at Swindon; and even if it had then been of adequate capacity to absorb the maximum power of a Gresley 'Pacific' there would have been little likelihood of its being made available for testing an LNER locomotive.

When the first new streamlined 'Pacific' did emerge from Doncaster Plant in September 1935 it was to create an absolute sensation. The popular press loved it. The neophytes, whether they knew anything about locomotives or not, positively wallowed in a sea of panegyrics and, when on its demonstration run on September 27 1935, *Silver Link* attained a maximum speed of 112½ mph, the acclaim reached for the sky! It was the older ones among the ranks of the ever faithful railway enthusiasts who were inclined to shake their heads and ask, if in no more than whispers, what was the steam locomotive coming to. But equally as a commercial proposition and a piece of publicity the introduction of the Silver Jubilee train, and its four silver painted streamlined 'Pacifics' engines, was an outstanding success. Three out of the four engines, *Silver Link, Quicksilver* and *Silver Fox* were stationed at Kings Cross 'Top Shed', as it was known, while the fourth, *Silver King*, was at Gateshead. At first a specially selected link of four drivers at Kings Cross shed had the train to themselves, working between London and Newcastle on a 'double-home' basis; and the timekeeping was as immaculate as the mechanical reliability of the locomotives. There were, nevertheless, certain technical aspects of the LNER entry into the field of super-high speed running that gave considerable anxiety, and led to precautions in operating that could have been much of a hindrance on a main line with heavier traffic.

Not for the first time in British railway history the speed of locomotives had extended beyond the capacity to stop. At the time of grouping, although a majority of its constituents had hitherto used the air brake, the LNER decided to standardise on the vacuum and, in 1935, the traditional form of the brake was in use on the East Coast trains, in which all air for reducing the degree of vacuum in the brake cylinders throughout the train entered through the driver's brake valve. There was thus a sequential action in application of the brakes dependent upon the rate of propagation down the train pipe. Now while this might be thought advantageous on a short train like the 7-coach 'Silver Jubilee' it was not so for another reason. Although at one time it was customary to fit brakes to all the wheels of a locomotive, later practice, in the cause of simplification, was to omit brakes on the bogie wheels, and on the 'A4' streamlined 'Pacifics' a considerable proportion of the total weight of the engine was not braked. The disadvantage in the case of the 'Silver Jubilee' with its 103-ton engine, and a trailing load, including the tender with the train of 295 tons, will be appreciated in a comparison with the Flying Scotsman, on which the relevant figures, with an 'A3' engine were 96 tons against 560 tons of train. The 'Silver Jubilee', taking engine and train together had a higher proportion of unbraked weight; and because the power required for stopping is roughly proportioned to the *square* of the speed, the streamliner at its maximum service speed of 90 mph was obviously going to take more stopping, to use a colloquialism, than the 500-ton Flying Scotsman at 75 mph.

To provide the necessary safety margin, ruling out in ordinary service any bursts of speed up to 100 mph or more, the operating department arranged for the train to be 'double-blocked'—in other words, there had to be two block sections clear ahead of it, before 'line clear' was given, so as to give adequate braking distance from the highest speeds. Although this could be arranged in semaphore signalling territory, south of York and north of Darlington, by special instructions to the signalmen, the magnificently straight and almost dead level stretch between Northallerton, and the approaches to York had recently been equipped with colour light signalling, most of them working as automatics, and the distance between successive signals was too close to provide adequate braking distance for the 'Silver Jubilee' at 90 mph. The signals then were three-indication—green, yellow and red. So, on the finest stretch of the whole run, between London and Newcastle, the speed had to be limited to 70 mph to keep within the braking distance imposed by the colour light signalling. To ensure that there was no infringement of speed restrictions, the locomotives were fitted with an automatic speed recording instrument, and a graphic record taken of the speed throughout every trip. The charts from these instruments were removed from the locomotives immediately on arrival at Newcastle or Kings Cross, and sent for scrutiny to locomotive headquarters in London each day.

After the brilliant debut in 1935, the four silver 'A4s' settled down to hard reliable work. On Mondays to Fridays the duties on which they could be used, other than the 'Silver Jubilee' itself, were to some extent limited, because at both Newcastle and Kings Cross a second 'A4' was kept standing pilot until the streamliner was safely away. On Saturdays, however, the engine which had worked the down Jubilee on the Friday night returned to London on the up 'Flying Scotsman', and it was interesting to observe the performance of the 'A4s' with a typical East Coast load, usually about 520 tons behind the tender. Several times I personally recorded the attainment, on level track, of speeds of 75-76 mph with loads of more than 500 tons, and once of 79 mph. On the last mentioned occasion I was on the footplate and saw that the engine was working in 15 per cent cut off, with the regulator not quite full open.

In the late summer of 1936 it was announced that a second streamlined train would be introduced for Coronation Year, which would run the 392.7 miles between Kings Cross and Edinburgh in the level six hours. Until this time the LMS had stood aside from the super-high speed streamline business; but the prospect of an Anglo-Scottish streamliner was a challenge they could not ignore. By that time the initial troubles with the Stanier 'Pacifics' had been triumphantly overcome, and the 12 engines of the class were providing consistently splendid performance. With a view to rivalling the Coronation streamliner of the LNER, a special test run was organised in November 1936, non-stop from Euston to Glasgow, and a similar return trip on the following day, both ways scheduled in six hours. This was a similar test to that made on the LNER in 1935 with the 'A3' engine, *Papyrus*, except that the LMS 'Pacific' was to run the 401.5 miles from Euston to Glasgow, against the 268.3 miles to Newcastle. The LMS had no corridor tenders, and the question of manning on this special occasion was resolved by the carrying of two drivers and one fireman, the former having volunteered to take a share in the firing, as necessary. The engine chosen was No 6201, *Princess Elizabeth*.

Both runs were successfully made, northbound on November 16 in 5 hours 53½ minutes and returning next day in the still faster time of 5 hours 44¼ minutes despite an increase from seven to eight coaches in the load hauled. The latter represented an average speed of exactly 70 mph from start to stop, and it was remarkable that it was achieved with little in the way of exceptional high maximum speeds. At three points only between Crewe and Euston did the speed reach as much as 90-91 mph and the absolute maximum for the run, 95 mph, was attained on dead level track near Minshull Vernon, after having mounted the long gradual rise from Moore water troughs.

R.A. Riddles, then Principal Assistant to the Chief Mechanical Engineer, rode on the footplate on both of these record runs and, as in the case of the *Papyrus* runs on the LNER, the experience suggested that certain modifications in the design were desirable if a regular high speed service between London and Glasgow was to be introduced. It was then confidently expected that a 6-hour train would be introduced in the summer of 1937. Authority was given for the design and construction of five new high-speed 'Pacific' engines. It

so happened that Stanier himself was away for most of the time the new engines were being designed, as one of a two-man Committee of Enquiry into the working of the State Railways of India, and the design of the new 'Pacifics' was mainly in the hands of Riddles and the Chief Locomotive Draughtsman, T.F. Coleman. Between them they made a magnificent job of it.

Quite apart from the streamlining, which was distinctively different from that of the Gresley 'A4s', there were some important and significant changes in design from the 'Princess Royal' Class. Although retaining four cylinders, only two sets of valve gear were used, the valves of the inside cylinders being actuated through rocking shafts. The boiler had a considerably greater heating surface, and the superheater had 40 elements. The firebox was larger, but was notably easier to keep well furnished, while a great boon, from the fireman's point of view, was the provision of a steam operated coal pusher in the tender. This took much of the previous labour out of the firing on the long through runs between Euston and Glasgow. As on the Gresley 'A4s', the streamlining provided the show for the publicists, while the internal streamlining of all stages in the steam circuit was the real benefit in hauling a heavy train at high speed. The piston valves were no less than 9½ inches in diameter, for 16½ inch diameter cylinders, a notable increase over the 8 inch diameter valves of the 'Princess Royal' Class. They were very powerful and free-running engines.

With the completion of the first of them, No 6220, *Coronation*, in May 1937, the LMS entered into a speed competition with the LNER. The powers that were at Euston had evidently determined that the time had come for the maximum speed attainments of the Gresley 'A4' Pacifics to be seriously challenged, although the service timing for the 'Coronation Scot' train was disappointingly settled at 6½ and not the level six hours between London and Glasgow. But as to maximum speed, for naught except publicity, the efforts of June 1937 on both sides were somewhat

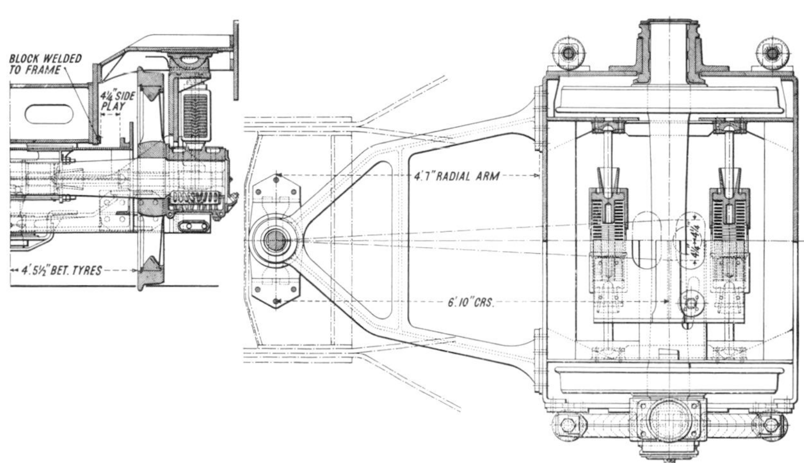

Above *LMS: one of the Stanier streamlined 'Pacifics' designed for the 'Coronation Scot' train in 1937—No 6222,* Queen Mary (British Railways).
Right *LMS: plan and part cross-sectional views of the trailing pony truck on Stanier 4-6-2s.*

mismanaged, as had also the LNER dynamometer car run with the southbound 'Silver Jubilee' on August 27 1936 with the engine *Silver Fox*.

In his book, *Last Giant of Steam*, Sean-Day-Lewis states that Bulleid was on the footplate on this last mentioned occasion. This was not so. The Chief Mechanical Engineer's representative in the dynamometer car on that test run was Edward Thompson, who succeeded to the post after Gresley's death in 1941. After Stoke summit had been passed he went through the corridor tender and somewhat belatedly told the driver to 'top a hundred'. The driver, who had begun a normal descent of the bank, with a probable maximum in the middle nineties, was taken completely by surprise, and to obey instructions had to start lengthening the cut-off when he was well down the bank. To get the record 113 mph the engine had to be 'thrashed' far beyond its normal limit, with the result that the big-end of the inside connecting rod overheated, and eventually the 'middle engine' almost completely disintegrated. They were very lucky to reach Kings Cross without having to stop.

The 'Invitation Run' of the 'Coronation Scot' on June 29 1937, with distinguished guests and a galaxy of the national press on board, included a misjudgment of another kind—an uncomfortably close call from outright disaster. On the down journey from Euston to Crewe, instructions had been given to limit the speed to a maximum of 90 mph except on the final descent from Whitmore to Crewe, where the line is splendidly straight, and those on the footplate were told to try for a maximum of 120 mph. But in mounting the very gradual rise from Stafford the engine was not unduly pressed, and the bank was topped at no more than 85 mph. Although acceleration thereafter was rapid it was too late and in trying to surpass the existing LNER record, the effort was prolonged until the train was perilously near to Crewe. It would not have been so bad if the special had not been routed into No 3 platform, involving the negotiation of three successive crossover roads! I was in the leading coach and it was not nice. The first crossover was struck at 57 mph and what might have happened had the engine overturned does not bear thinking about.

It was unfortunately to little avail. The stop watches of *four* independent recorders gave no higher maximum speed than 112½ mph; but in his post-luncheon speech at the Crewe Arms Hotel, E.J.H. Lemon, Vice-President of the LMS, said that the speed recorder on the locomotive had been very carefully examined and that the maximum had been 114 mph, and that the speed record held by the LNER had been broken. I am afraid there were

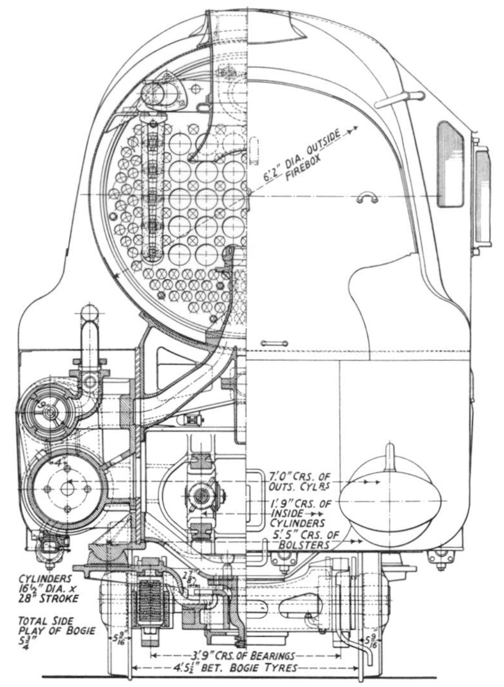

Above *LMS: part cross-section—part outside view of front end.*
Below *LMS: streamlined 4-6-2—part sections through firebox and smokebox.*

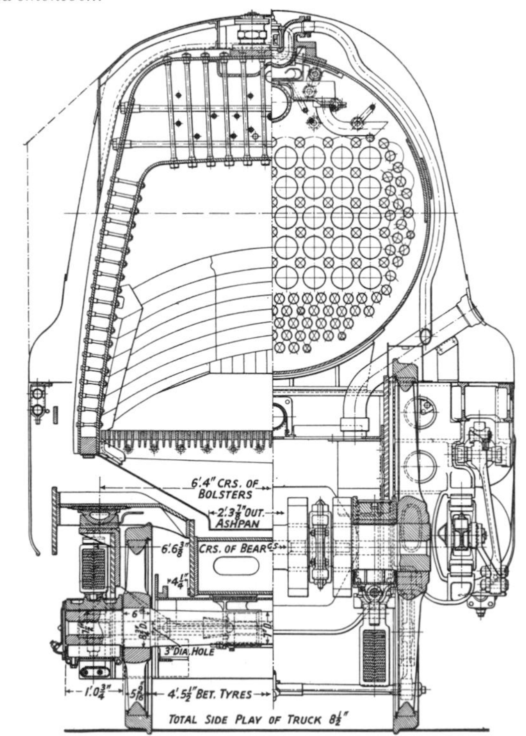

some among his hearers who just did not believe it!

The next day the rival 'Coronation' streamliner of the LNER was taken down to Grantham for a similar publicity outing, and the crew of the new 'A4' Pacific *Dominion of Canada*, resplendent in garter blue, were under definite instructions to beat the day-old LMS record. The new 'Coronation' train had a very attractive beaver-tail observation car at the rear end and, to avoid any remarshalling for the return journey, the whole train was taken four miles north of Grantham to be turned on the Barkston triangle. It was then held there until the return path was clear, and they were assured of a good clear road. That wait at Barkston was fatal to the chances of making a new record. It was a question of managing the fire during the waiting period. A locomotive inspector riding on the footplate overrode the better judgment of the driver and fireman, with unfortunate results in the firebox; and when they had topped the bank at Stoke Tunnel, and started on the racing descent to Peterborough, they began to run short of steam. To counteract this the driver lengthened the cut-off as much as he dared, but remembering what had happened to *Silver Fox* a year previously, enough was enough!

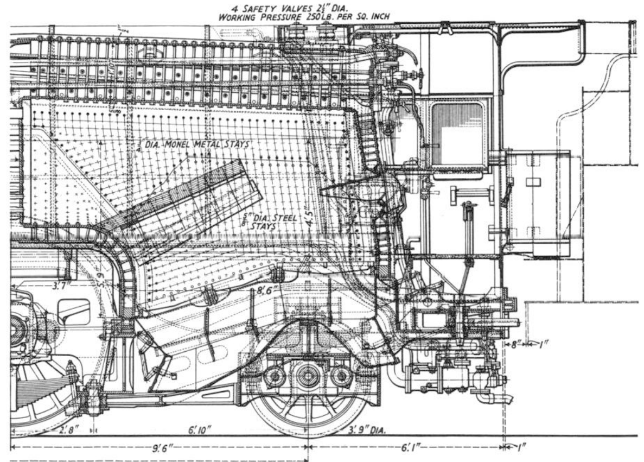

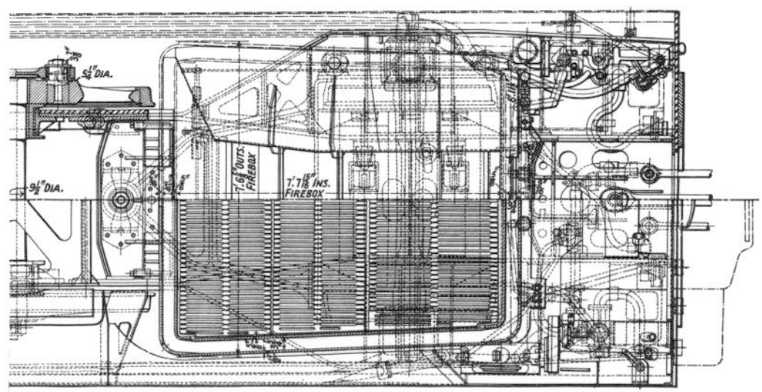

LMS: streamlined 4-6-2—firebox and cab end.

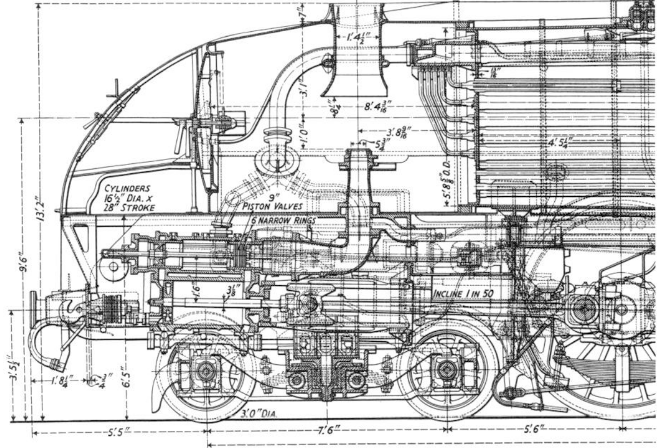

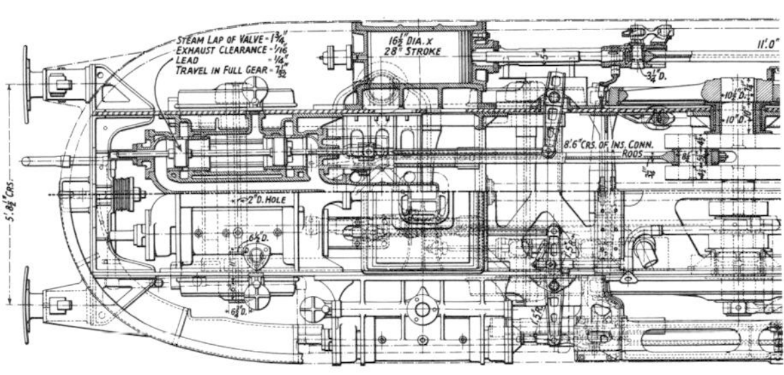

Above *LMS: the 'Princess-Coronation' Class 4-6-2—arrangement of the streamlined front-end.*

They did not exceed 109 mph much to Gresley's disappointment.

Speed stunts apart, the 6-hour 'Coronation' to Edinburgh was a much harder train to work than the 6½-hour 'Coronation Scot' to Glasgow. Although running to the same schedule as the 'Silver Jubilee' south of Newcastle, the 'Coronation' carried a 9-coach load totalling 325-tons behind the tender, against seven, for 235 tons. Moreover the one engine worked through over the 392.7 miles, with a change of crew intermediately. In contrast to the speed stunts it was very interesting to see how high a speed the 'A4' engines could attain, and sustain, in ordinary working conditions.

Not long after its first introduction, I was a passenger on the southbound 'Coronation', hauled by the *Commonwealth of Australia*. South of Newcastle the Gateshead based driver was making his first trip on the train and, by over-emphasising some of the permanent speed restrictions, he was a minute late on passing Grantham. The summit at Stoke Tunnel was topped at 64½ mph and then the engine was

allowed to run, with the reverser in 15 per cent, and the regulator practically full open. The speed rose to 106 mph, but what was more significant it was sustained at between 104 and 106 for nearly 10 miles, by which time the gradient had flattened out to little easier than dead level. Quite apart from the 'stunts' it was evident that the northern railways had got some magnificent locomotives in the Gresley 'A4s' and the Stanier 'Coronations'.

The winter of 1937-8 saw the first steps towards removal of the basic shortcomings of the fixed and moving equipment of the East Coast route. Plans were being made for adding a fourth-aspect to the signalling on the line between York and Northallerton, so as to permit 90 mph through the colour light area, while experiments began with an improved form of vacuum brake. The LMS was in process of adopting the Great Western 'direct admission' valve which, as its name implied, allowed air to enter the brake cylinders of each vehicle directly, instead of through the train pipe. But in the spirit of insularity which characterised much of the mutual relations between the one-time

Above *LNER: one of the 'A4' 'Pacifics' fitted with twin orifice, blastpipe and Kylchap double blastpipe—No 4903,* Peregrine, *on the up Yorkshire Pullman near Barkston* (M.W. Earley).

Below *LMS: non-streamlined 'Duchess' Class 4-6-2—cross-section at the front end.*

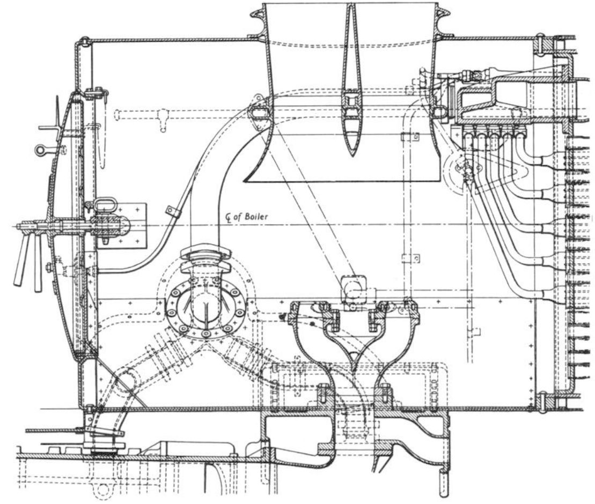

independent railway companies, Gresley would have nothing to do with the DA valve and instead favoured a product of my old firm, the Westinghouse Brake & Signal Company, who were then developing a 'quick-service application valve' QSA. On Sunday after Sunday in the late summer of 1938, tests were being made with the streamlined 'Coronation' train set that was in London at the week-end, and the results were encouraging. It was while those tests were in progress that Gresley showed his true attitude towards external streamlining.

My former chief, Captain B.H. Peter, then Managing Director of Westinghouse, was with Gresley one day when a clerk entered the room with a strip of paper. On the previous day when the southbound 'Coronation' train had arrived at Newcastle a defect on the engine was discovered that necessitated its removal from the train. An 'A3' Pacific, No 2595 *Trigo*, was commandeered at a moments notice, and the driver and fireman went to it in such style that although they had left Newcastle 8 minutes late they were on time by Retford, and practically kept the streamliners schedule onwards to Kings Cross in spite of 5 minutes lost through temporary speed restrictions for permanent way work. Gresley read the slip of paper giving details of what had happened on the previous day—a broad smile spreading over his face as he read it. Then he passed the paper over to his visitor, saying: 'There you are Peter; any of my bloody engines can do the job, whether they have a tin case on them or not!'

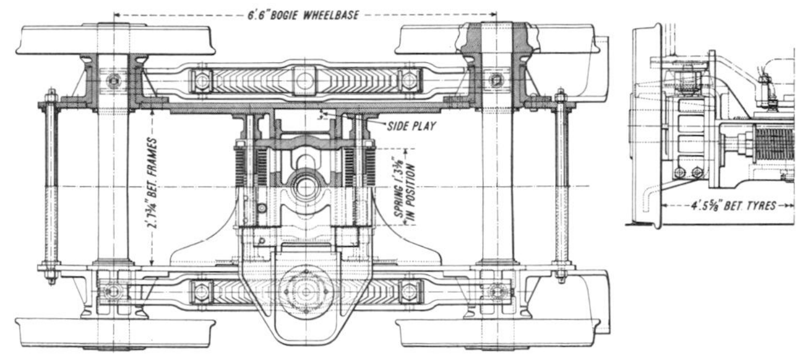

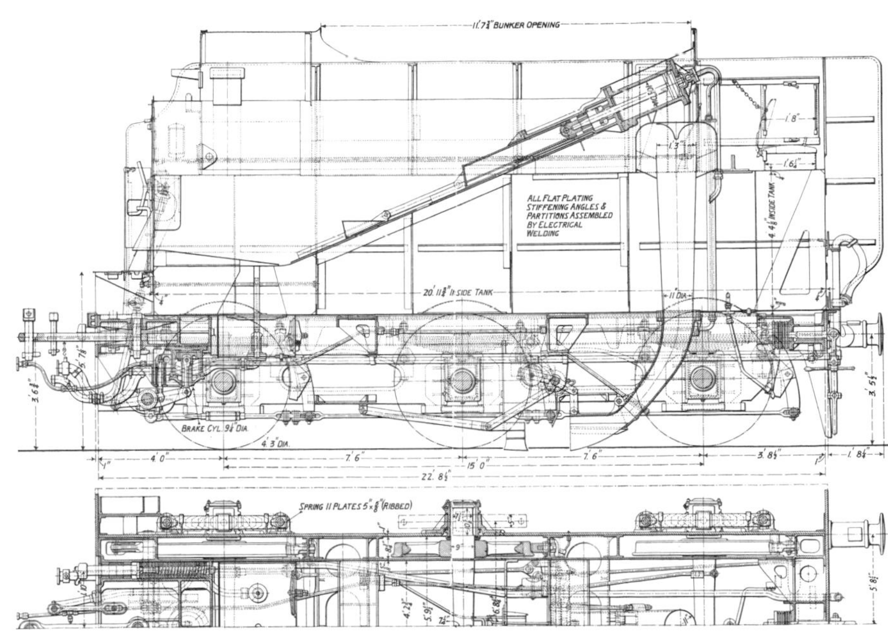

Below left *LMS: one of the 'Princess-Coronation' Class of 'Pacifics', not streamlined externally, but very thoroughly streamlined internally—No 6230,* Duchess of Buccleuch (British Railways).

Top right *LMS: the 'Coronation Scot' train and its engine, en route for the USA, being loaded up at Southampton* (British Railways).

Above right *LMS: major contributions to immaculate riding of the Stanier 4-6-2—the bogie with spring control.*

Right *LMS: Stanier 'Duchess' Class 4-6-2s—a boon to the fireman is a tender with steam-operated coal pusher.*

Top *LNER: the world record breaker—No 4468,* Mallard *(having Kylchap blastpipe)—just before leaving Barkston on the southbound run on which the maximum speed of 126 mph was attained. The ex-North Eastern Railway dynamometer (now in the National Railway Museum at York) is marshalled immediately behind the tender* (H.M. Hoather).

Above *LNER: the 'Pacific' engine,* Mallard, *bearing the commemorative plaque on the boiler side* (British Railways).

It was nothing unusual for the Westinghouse brake testing team when they were called out for another set of tests on Sunday, June 3 1938 but, when they arrived at Kings Cross, they were interested to find that the dynamometer car was coupled immediately behind the tender, and those who took notice of such things saw that the engine was not one that had been previously used, No 4468 *Mallard*. Furthermore, the driver and fireman spoke with, broad Yorkshire accents, instead of the Cockney speech of Kings Cross Top Shed. It was not until they had actually left that their railway hosts 'came clean' and confessed that the brake tests were merely a cloak for the real purpose of the journey—an attempt on the world speed record! How *Mallard* was driven, almost to destruction, to attain the maximum speed of 126 mph is a matter of history. As with *Silver Fox*, two years earlier, the big-end of the inside cylinder failed, and *Mallard*'s part of the day's proceedings had to be concluded at Peterborough. When the press were gathered at Kings Cross to greet the conquering hero it needed all the diplomacy of those concerned to explain why the train was hauled by an Ivatt large-boilered 'Atlantic'. But the record was secured, to stand for all time on behalf of the steam locomotive.

Seven months later, also on a Sunday, it was the turn of the LMS to break records, though of a different kind. During 1938, 10 more 'Pacific' engines of the 'Coronation' Class had been built at Crewe, five streamlined, but in Midland red with gold lines, and five non-streamlined, and it was one of these latter that was subjected to a very severe heavy load test from Crewe to Glasgow and back on February 26 1939. A train of 20 coaches was made up, including the dynamometer car, making a load of 610 tons behind the tender and this was taken, without assistance and at astonishingly high speed, over the severe gradients of the North Country. Some of the magnificent feats of hill climbing, at high speed, are shown graphically in the accompanying diagrams (below); but, in answer to the natural question as to how far the science of locomotive engineering had advanced by the year 1939, one stage of the performance may be compared with a record-breaking London and North Western occasion 26 years earlier. Both represent the climax of heavy-load engine working between Carnforth and Shap Summit just prior to the First and Second World Wars. Both were tests on which the load hauled in relation to the nominal tractive effort of the locomotives was the same.

Engine no	**1159**	**6234**
Engine name	**Ralph Brocklebank**	**Duchess of Abercorn**
Class	Claughton	Princess-Coronation
Date	4 Nov 1913	26 Feb 1939
Load (trailing tons)	360	610
Engine & tender weight (tons)	116	162.6
Nominal tractive effort (lb)	24,000	40,000
Nominal tractive effort (tons)	10.7	17.8
Ratio: Load/engine (weight)	3.1	3.74
Ratio: Load/nominal (te)	33.6	34.2
Average speeds (mph)		
Carnforth-Oxenholme	65.5	67.3
Oxenholme-Tebay	47.7*	53.0
Tebay-Shap Summit	50.8	46.7
Max indicated horse-power	1,669	3,209
IHP per ton of te	156	180

* Includes check of 18 mph on Grayrigg bank.

Both were outstanding efforts for the period at which they were made and, so far as the load hauled by the Stanier 'Pacific' engine, not to be repeated in ordinary traffic.

O.V.S. Bulleid left Kings Cross in October 1937 to become Chief Mechanical Engineer of the Southern Railway, at a time when the high command at Waterloo had come to regard the steam locomotive as little more than an outdated nuisance, to be endured only until electrification could be extended to the whole line. On the LNER it had been the neon-lights display, and Bulleid at once began to work for the restoration of its prestige in his new surroundings. The time when he could introduce external streamlining, air smoothing, or whatever one liked to call it, was still some years away; but in the generally disappointing performance of the 'Lord Nelson' Class 4-6-0s he found a situation requiring immediate analysis and attention. Powerful engines of their day, and always free-running they were capricious steamers. It is true

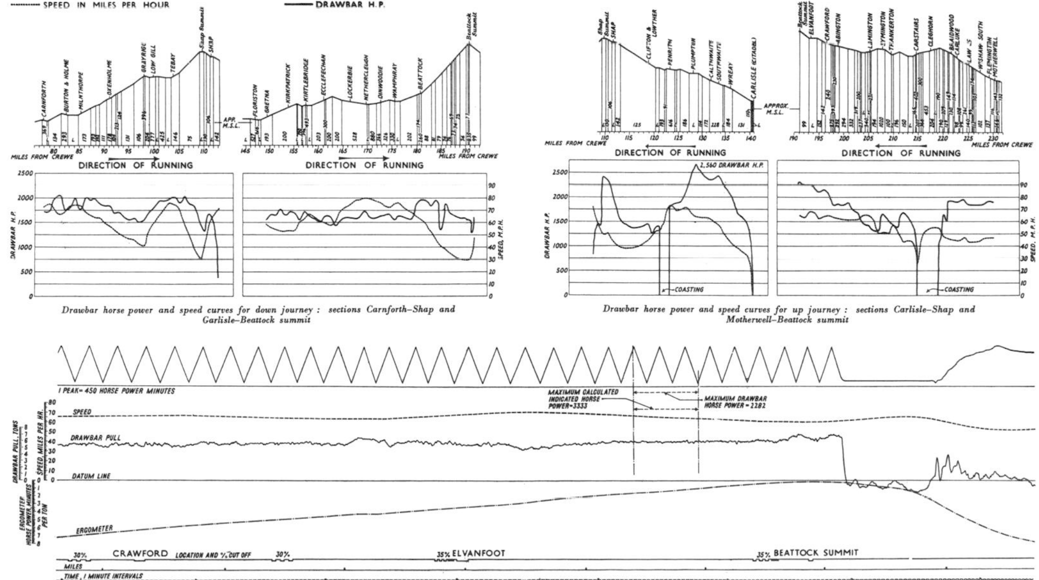

Drawbar horse power and speed curves for down journey: sections Carnforth–Shap and Garlisle–Beattock summit

Drawbar horse power and speed curves for up journey: sections Carlisle–Shap and Motherwell–Beattock summit

Dynamometer car chart between Crawford and Beattock summit

EAST ANGLIAN
2859
L N E R

863
SOUTHERN

D
12
5

4

Opposite page, top to bottom

LNER: in the autumn of 1937 a new luxury train was put on between Liverpool St and Norwich. It was not sharply timed, but two of the 'Sandringham' Class 4-6-0s were streamlined, in the same style as the 'A4' 'Pacifics', and were named specially East Anglian *and* City of London (British Railways).

Internal streamlining on the Southern: 'Lord Nelson' Class 4-6-0, No 863, Lord Rodney, *incorporating the first Bulleid modifications* (British Railways).

Southern Railway: the Bulleid modifications finalised on No 850, Lord Nelson, *here seen on an outward-bound Continental boat express near Hildenborough* (E.R. Wetherset).

Southern Railway: the Continental boat express approaching Tonbridge, hauled by 'Lord Nelson' Class 4-6-0, No 859, Lord Hood (British Railways).

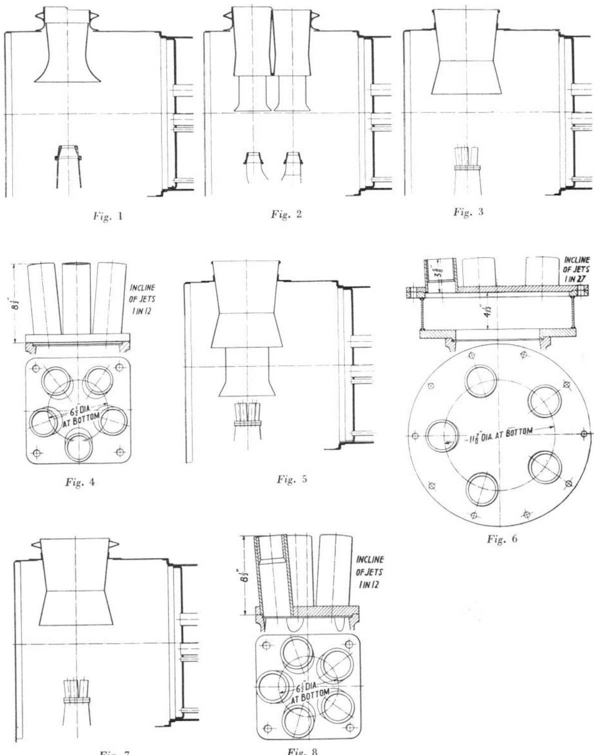

Above *Southern Railway: stages in the improvement of the 'Lord Nelson' Class front end—Figs 7 & 8 represent the final version.*

they had to cope at times with Yorkshire, Welsh, and Kentish coal; but those were the conditions for which they had been designed in the first place. Before he retired Maunsell had begun experimenting with them, but Bulleid soon determined that the trouble lay at the front-end. He fitted them with multiple-jet blastpipe and large diameter chimneys, and completely re-designed the cylinders and piston valves, using the principles of internal streamlining which had been so successfully developed on the Gresley locomotives. The result was an absolute transformation.

Some of the finest work done by these rebuilt engines was on the Bournemouth Pullman trains, which regularly loaded up to 500 tons, or more. The hillclimbing was of such quality as to render unnecessary any display of the speed capabilities of which these engines possessed in such full measure. It was very unfortunate that war came when it did in 1939 because at that time the rebuilt engines were only just getting into their stride, and their prowess might well have tempted the operating department to some notable acceleration.

And so we come to a milestone in the history of the British locomotive, when the initiative and enterprise of the Great Western in developing the basic machine to new heights of achievement in the later 1920s had been taken up and extended many times over by the north-going lines in the 1930s. Then, at the very end of the period under review, came the remarkable revival of major steam practice on the Southern. It is an interesting reflection at this stage that the contentment of the Swindon authorities with the state of development attained in the 'Castle' and 'King' 4-6-0s led to the Great Western being overtaken in many aspects of locomotive practice by the other three major companies, by 1939.

A cause of regret is that no means of establishing comparative quantitative results was then available. Assessment could be made by analysts experienced in the recording of locomotive performance; but, significant as are many of the inferences drawn, they are not the same as the hard facts of sustained examination on a stationary testing plant. We were to learn much in post-war years from the work done at Swindon and Rugby.

7. Great Western: through war to the finale

In the winter of 1939–40 an outward appearance of easy contentment seemed to rest over the locomotive department at Swindon. Despite the spectacular advances in practice on the LMS and LNER, the annual statistical returns for the Grouped railways published in *The Railway Gazette* showed the Great Western still to be in the lead so far as the general economy of the CME's department was concerned, as the tables opposite show. But while the Board had every reason to be satisfied with such a showing, the plain fact remained that not a single new design of locomotive for heavy main line duty had been introduced since 1927, when the production of the 'King' Class 4-6-0s had proved of world-wide interest. The 'Grange' and 'Manor' Classes of mixed traffic 4-6-0 were no more than variations on the basic design of Churchward's 'Saint' Class, and the 'Manor' was not a particularly successful one at that. Collett, of course, was ageing and had in any case come to look with some disdain upon the latest productions of Crewe and Doncaster.

Construction of 'Castle' and 'Hall' Class 4-6-0s continued at first, as replacement of older engines became necessary, but beneath the surface quite an amount of new thinking was in progress at Swindon by the men who would have to take over when Collett did eventually retire. A very important, though at first quite unobstrusive activity, concerned the practice of locomotive testing. It can be traced in the first place to the 'splendid isolation' that had been fostered by the top management of the locomotive Department at Swindon following Stanier's departure for the LMS. Collett looked with the greatest disfavour upon the Institution of Locomotive Engineers, which he was once heard to apostrophise as 'a lot of blue pencil commercial travellers'. Swindon men were strongly dissuaded from joining; but the Divisional Locomotive, Carriage and

Wagon Superintendent at Old Oak Common was expected to join, attend meetings, and generally keep his ear to the ground for news of impending activities in other directions. Thus it became known that the LMS and the LNER were getting together on the subject of a stationary locomotive testing plant.

Steam locomotive maintenance and running costs, 1938

	GWR	LMS	LNER	Southern
Repairs and partial renewals				
per engine	£484	£530	£568	£512
per engine mile	4.33d	4.39d	5.30d	4.78d
Running expenses excluding fuel				
per train mile	19.89d	20.76d	21.23d	21.82d
per engine	£1517	£1728	£1514	£1677
Wages connected with loco running				
per train mile	12.28d	11.81d	12.41d	11.94d
per engine	£937	£981	£943	£918
Coal				
per train mile	6.65d	7.70d	7.64d	8.78d
per engine	£507	£639	£581	£675
Water				
per train mile	0.34d	0.52d	0.56d	0.50d
per engine	£26	£43	£43	£38
Lubricants				
per train mile	0.15d	0.17d	0.15d	0.17d
per engine	£12	£14	£12	£13
Stock of engines	3630	7613	6518	1816

d = original penny (240 to the £)

In 1934 Sir Nigel Gresley had sent his great 2-8-2 express engine, the *Cock o' the North*, to France for testing on the Vitry plant, as though to highlight the absence of a modern plant in Great Britain; and in discussions with Stanier, who would have been well enough aware of the limitations of the Churchward plant at Swindon, the idea was formed that perhaps the Great Western would join with the two northern companies in jointly sponsoring the construction of a thoroughly modern plant capable of absorbing the maximum output of the largest modern locomotives. The Southern was left out of consideration, because R.E.L. Maunsell was still in office and no appreciable development in steam locomotive practice was then contemplated.

After Stanier had left Swindon for the LMS, a proposal from the Traffic Department for a high speed service from Paddington to Birmingham came at a time when the differences between the actual point-to-point running times made by many of the heaviest and fastest trains, and those laid down in the working timetables, were causing some concern to the Chief Civil Engineer, who questioned whether some of the permanent speed restrictions were being exceeded. Then, as on other occasions, the organisation of the CME's department of the Great Western Railway, including responsibility for locomotive running, proved invaluable.

A senior draughtsman concerned with locomotive testing, C.T. Roberts, was deputed to prepare charts showing the actual speeds regularly run in maintaining the fastest schedules between Paddington and Exeter, and Paddington and Birmingham, following a series of observations on the footplate. As a result, and from careful examination of the graphs drawn, Roberts came to the conclusion that, in fulfilling the most severe of their assignments, drivers were working their engines so as to require a roughly constant rate of evaporation in the boiler. If, on the other hand, they had maintained the point-to point times laid down in the working timetable, the demands upon the boiler would have been quite markedly fluctuating. It was felt that engine-

Above left *A famous 'Castle', about the time of nationalisation, with no evidence of ownership on the tender—No 5069,* Isambard Kingdom Brunel (M.W. Earley).

Left *The climax of pre-war performance: the* King George V *hauling a 15-coach load on the Cornish Riviera Express, near Aldermaston* (M.W. Earley).

Right *One of the celebrated Dean Goods 0-6-0s allocated for war service* (British Railways).

Above *No 5914,* Ripon Hall, *had the wartime style of painting for all passenger engines—plain green with no lining* (British Railways).

Left *A popular branch line and local train tank engine—0-4-2, No 4800* (British Railways).

Below *The first Hawksworth design: the modified 'Hall' Class of 1944, at first unnamed. This is engine No 6959, later* Peatling Hall (British Railways).

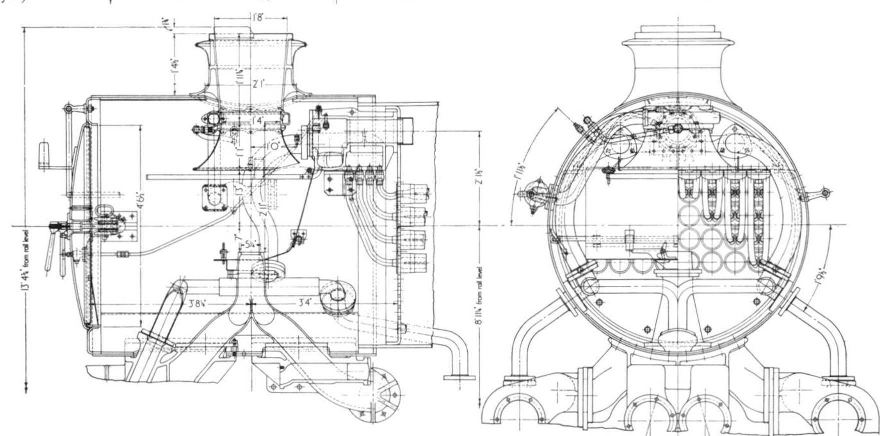

GWR: 'Castle' Class with 3-row superheater—layout of smokebox (British Railways).

GWR: 'King' Class—first application of 4-row superheater on engine No 6022, King Edward III (British Railways).

testing procedure should in future be based on constant rates of evaporation, and authority was given for the stationary testing plant at Swindon to be thoroughly modernised to enable the evaporation rates for the standard express passenger locomotives to be established.

Work was well advanced when the first approach to Collett was made by Stanier and Sir Nigel Gresley, regarding possible GWR participation in a new joint stationary testing plant. With tongue in cheek, one fears, representatives of the LMS and LNER were invited to Swindon and taken to see the old Churchward plant. Shades of that one-time maximum absorption of 500 horsepower(!)—for there was the 2-cylinder 4-6-0, No 2931, *Arlington Court*, blazing away, all out, at about 70 mph and developing something like 1,200 indicated horsepower. It was explained to the visitors that the modernised plant could absorb at least 2,000 horsepower. Quite clearly the LMS and the LNER had got to go it alone.

Although the work that Roberts and those associated with him had done bore no immediate fruit so far as the development of Great Western locomotive practice was concerned—in fact rather the reverse, because it fostered a rather defeatist attitude at Swindon towards further acceleration of train services—in testing practice the seeds were well and truly sown. During the war years, as opportunity presented itself, the principles of testing at constant rates of evaporation were developed by the young men who had been associated with Roberts, and in due course the full flowering of the system was to make one of the most important of Swindon's contributions to the final phase of steam traction under the nationalised British Railways.

At midsummer 1941, having reached the age of 70, Collett retired. Although his term of office as Chief Mechanical Engineer included such notable events as the introduction of the 'Castle' and 'King' Class, he himself was not primarily an engine designer. He was essentially a 'works' man, and his conduct of the CME's department over 20 years was aptly described in a biographical note published in *The Railway Gazette* at the time of his retirement '. . . as soundly progressive rather than revolutionary'. Undoubtedly the most important of his innovations was the system of optical lining up of locomotive frames and cylinders, permitting construction to much finer limits of accuracy, and subsequent economy in maintenance costs.

His successor, previously Principal Assistant to the CME, was F.W. Hawksworth, a man with a lifetime of service on the Great Western Railway, much of it in the headquarters drawing office at Swindon. As an expert engine designer he was the perfect counterpart and junior partner to Collett, though while Stanier was still at Swindon, and Principal Assistant, he had felt that Hawksworth would have benefited from a further spell in the works. The posts of Chief Draughtsman and Locomotive Works Manager were falling vacant at about the same time. Although nominally assistant to G.H. Burrows, Hawksworth was virtually running the drawing office, but Stanier recommended that, as the most likely successor eventually as CME, he should go to the works. Collett, however, brushed the suggestion to one side, saying that he could not spare him from the drawing office. As a young draughtsman, Hawksworth had made the general arrangement drawing of *The Great Bear* and, as Chief Draughtsman, he supervised the design of the 'Kings' in 1926–7.

It was remarkable that, as soon as he was required to build new locomotives as part of the resumed replacement programme at the end of the war, he made a fundamental change in the design of the standard 2-cylinder 4-6-0 type. Churchward's basic engine design was American in concept, with the cylinders, valve chests and smokebox saddle contained in a pair of identical castings bolted together on the centreline of the locomotive. So far as the steam circuit was concerned, it had the great advantage of having no external joints, but it involved a considerable complication so far as the main frames were concerned. The American locomotives from which Churchward originally took the idea had bar frames, whereas he wished to retain the traditional British plate frames, as giving greater flexibility on curves. But a plate frame in its normal form could not have been accommodated at the front end and Churchward had devised an ingenious though complicated compromise, using a bar frame at the front end, passing beneath the cylinder casting and then splayed out at the rear end for ease of attachment to the plate frame that carried the bearings for the coupled wheels. A very large number of locomotives had been built using this arrangement of framing; for in addition to the 4-6-0s of the 'Saint', 'Hall', 'Grange' and 'Manor' Classes there were several hundred 2-6-0s of the '43XX' Class and its successors, the '28XX' Class heavy goods 2-8-0s, not to mention the many 2-6-2, 2-8-0 and 2-8-2 tank engines, all of Swindon standard design.

The new Chief Mechanical Engineer had not been long in office before the locomotive drawing office was launched into a period of activity in new design, greater than had been experienced for very many years. The 'Modified Hall', or '6959' Class was very far from a simple modification. Although in outward appearance it looked almost the same, nearly everything about it was new. The use of plate frames throughout involved a complete redesign of the front end. The cylinders were cast separately from the saddle and bolted to the frames on each side with a fabricated stiffener between the frames. This stiffener was carried up to form the saddle for the smokebox and within it were fitted the exhaust pipes from the cylinders to the blastpipe. The Churchward bar-framed bogie was at last discarded in favour of a plate-framed design, and the time-honoured No 1 standard boiler was modified to have a new type of superheater, giving a higher degree of superheat. So many innovations were embodied in this new design that one looks back rather wistfully as to how Great Western locomotive practice might have developed had not the stultifying effect of nationalisation descended upon us so soon after the war.

Little by little we learned of the great project of Hawksworth's new express passenger locomotive

One of the cross-breed 'Duke-dog' 4-4-0s introduced in 1936, carrying the British Railways number and insignia, after nationalisation (E.D. Bruton).

Above *Oil firing: one of the heavy freight 2-8-0s stationed at Llanelly, No 2872, converted to oil firing in 1946* (British Railways).

Right *First of the Hawksworth 'County' Class 4-6-0s, No 1000, before naming, as introduced in 1945. This engine was the only one of the class originally to have a double chimney* (British Railways).

Right *One of the new Hawksworth 4-6-0s, No 1015,* County of Leicester, *working the northbound 'Devonian' express, Kingswear to Bradford, near Teignmouth* (E.D. Bruton).

Below *A later, as yet unnamed, engine of the 'County' Class, No 1007 positioned on the stationary testing plant in Swindon Works* (British Railways).

Top *First of the 'Hall' Class to be converted to oil firing, No 5955,* Garth Hall. *Later engines of the class similarly altered had their numbers changed to the '39XX' series to distinguish them* (British Railways).

Above *The first 'Castle' Class 4-6-0 to be converted—No 5091,* Cleeve Abbey—*showing the smaller type of tender first attached* (British Railways).

for post-war traffic, which was most unfortunately stillborn. Nothing was published about it, and Hawksworth himself shut up like an oyster when anyone ever suggested there had ever been such a proposal; but at one time, within the shrouded walls of the Swindon drawing office, it was at one time a very live issue. The two draughtsmen principally concerned, who both rose to high office elsewhere in after years, told me that they had the sketchiest instructions from the then-Chief Draughtsman, F.C. Mattingley. A 'Pacific' was to be designed, carrying a boiler pressure of 280 lb per square inch, and having 6 foot 3 inch coupled wheels, but otherwise using as many standard features as possible. The young men of the drawing office were thrilled beyond measure. If the 'King' front-end was retained, the new engine would have a tractive effort of no less than 47,000 lb, by far the greatest of any British passenger locomotive. Not unmindful of Stanier's work on the LMS in pre-war days, principal attention was first directed to the boiler and to the front-end. Surprisingly, however, the drawing office saw nothing of Hawksworth at this time, and the only directive they had was in no more than the merest outline from Mattingly.

Quite a lot of work was done on the boiler, which began to look very 'un-Swindon' and more like that of an LMS non-streamlined 'Duchess', with a regulator in the dome—yes, a domed boiler on a GWR express locomotive! The degree of superheat designed for was far higher than anything previously used at Swindon, and was a feature that Hawksworth himself was known to favour. Simultaneously another senior draughtsman was making a very thorough redesign of the 'King' front end, completely streamlining all the ports and steam passages internally in the Chapelon style. All this was in progress while war was still raging, even though the ultimate issue was no longer in doubt. It would have been a magnificent engine, but then, as cryptically as it had begun, work was stopped. Apparently higher authority even than the Great Western top management would not sanction work on what was to be a purely express passenger locomotive in wartime. As will be told in a later chapter, Bulleid succeeded in 'bending the rules' by calling his 'Merchant Navy' Class 'Pacific' a mixed traffic

Top *Later engines of the 'Castle' Class which were converted had larger tenders attached. This engine, No 5083,* Bath Abbey, *like No 5091, still carried the sliding screen for the cab window fitted as a wartime ARP screen* (British Railways).
Above *Progenitor of all Great Western 4-cylinder 4-6-0s—No 4000,* North Star, *with 'Castle' type boiler—just after nationalisation* (Kenneth H. Leech).

engine, and by having the first published photograph of it at work on a goods train. Those who were closest to Hawksworth knew that he was very upset at having his 'Pacific' vetoed, while Bulleid had got away with it.

The 'Modified Halls', the '6959' Class, first of which took the road in the autumn of 1944, were very successful. They steamed well, ran freely, and soon became popular with shed and works staff from the detail design of the new superheaters. These included the elimination of the flat metal-to-metal joints by which the elements were attached to the header in the old standard Swindon superheater. The radical change in the front-end design seems to have been accepted without comment. It would have been very interesting to have comparative maintenance costs, on a long term basis, between the Churchward and the Hawksworth designs. Despite the undoubted advantage of having all elements of the steam circuit within the two castings bolted together on the centre line of the locomotive, the joint between the plate and bar sections of the main frame must have been an inherent source of weakness, and the need to stay the buffer beam with diagonal rods on those types having a leading pony truck was further evidence of some undesirable flexibility at the leading end. Nevertheless it must not be forgotten that the original design had served the Great Western well for 40 years, and it was only the action of a man who had been familiar enough with it throughout its life, in changing it as soon as he succeeded to the highest executive office in the Locomotive Department, that makes one probe a little deeper into its basic features.

It would seem that hopes of building the 'Pacific' had not entirely faded when the end of the war came because, when a further batch of mixed traffic 4-6-0s was authorised in 1945, the opportunity was taken to try out, in a new and more powerful variety, two features that had been included in the original proposals for the 'Pacific', namely a boiler pressure of 280 lb per square inch, and 6 feet 3 inch coupled wheels. It was at first intended to use the 'Castle' boiler, strengthened to take the higher pressure; but the weight came out too heavy, and the actual design was based on that of the Stanier '8F' 2-8-0,

Engine class	'Castle'	LMS '8F'	10XX
Length of barrel	14 feet 10 inches	12 feet $3\frac{9}{16}$ inches	12 feet $7\frac{3}{16}$ inches
Diameters (outside): maximum	5 feet 9 inches	5 feet $8\frac{3}{8}$ inches	5 feet $8\frac{3}{8}$ inches
minimum	5 feet $1\frac{15}{16}$ inches	5 feet	5 feet
Heating surfaces (square feet)			
Tubes	1,885.62	1,479.0	1,545.0
Firebox	163.8	171.0	169.0
Superheater	262.62	245.0	254.0
Combined	2,312.0	1,895.0	1,968.0
Grate area (square feet)	29.36	28.65	28.84
Boiler pressure (psi)	225	225	280

which Swindon had been building for the Ministry of Supply for general use on the British railways during the war, and for which all the necessary tools and presses were available. The boiler proportions are shown above.

The '10XX' Class, named after 'Counties', had the same 'engine' layout as the '6959' Class 'Halls', and with the higher boiler pressure had a nominal tractive effort of 32,580 lb, nearly 1,000 lb, more than a 'Castle'. The first 20 engines of the class were distributed rather indiscriminately, with six each at Old Oak Common and Bristol (Bath Road), four at Newton Abbot, two at Stafford Road (Wolverhampton) and one each at Exeter and Plymouth, and in the straitened circumstances that prevailed just at the end of the war there was apparently no opportunity to brief the running inspectors as to the potentialities and limitations of the new engines. In consequence they had a somewhat mixed reception from the men. Some, seeing that they carried a boiler pressure of 280 lb per square inch, thought they would be a 'super-King', tried to drive them accordingly, and were surprised when they quickly ran short of steam! At Bristol they worked turn and turn about with 'Castles', but their best and really brilliant work was done north of Wolverhampton, where they ran very heavy trains with conspicuous success. They also did very well in Cornwall. When pulled up to relatively short cut-offs, and the regulator was opened wide, if not necessarily full open, they imparted a pronounced fore and aft surging motion to the leading coaches in a train. The Churchward 'Saints' had always done this, though to a lesser degree, and for passenger comfort it was better for the 'Counties' to be worked with a cut-off of around 25 to 30 per cent. It made no difference to the efficiency of the engine working.

Having got the first 20 'Counties' into traffic, Swindon works switched at once on to a new batch of 'Castles', incorporating Hawksworth's precepts of boiler design. The new engines, known officially

Experiments with higher degrees of superheating: engine No 5049, Earl of Plymouth, *with 4-row superheater, on the 5.55 pm Paddington to South Wales express near Cholsey (the author is on the footplate)* (M.W. Earley).

One of the 'Grange' Class of 5 foot 8 inch 4-6-0s, No 6838, Goodmoor Grange, *climbing Hemerdon bank, South Devon, with the Penzance–Wolverhampton express* (M.W. Earley).

as the '5098' Class had three-row superheaters of similar design to those on the 'Modified Hall' Class. The first two, engines 5098 and 5099, had the standard Swindon sight feed lubricator, but the later ones—numbered 7000 to 7007—had mechanical lubricators. To provide comparison in a complete range of superheating one of the existing 'Castles', No 5049, *Earl of Plymouth*, was rebuilt with a four-row apparatus, and it was in the comparative tests carried out shortly after the war that the new principles inaugurated by C.T. Roberts were brought to fruition. The three varieties of superheater were then:

'Castle' boilers

Class	**'4073'**	**'5098'**	**'5049'**
Small tubes			
Number	197	170	138
Outside diameter (inches)	2	2	2
Flues			
Number	14	21	28
Outside diameter (inches)	5⅛	5⅛	5⅛
Elements			
Number	84	84	112
Outside diameter (inches)	1	1¼	1¼
Heating surfaces (square feet)			
Tubes	1,858	1,800	1,670
Firebox	163	164	163
Super heater	263	313	393
Total	2,284	2,277	2,226
Grate area (square feet)	29.4	29.4	29.4

At the end of the war, S.O. E11 had succeeded Roberts as engineer in charge of locomotive testing, still reporting to the chief draughtsman in charge of the locomotive section of the drawing office, and he was developing the precision methods of engine testing inaugurated by Roberts. These were evident in some results from the comparative tests carried out after the war between a standard 'Castle', the first of the '5098' Class, and the 4-row superheater engine No 5049. The performance of No 5098 showed work of the highest standard attained by these engines, and were related to the rates of firing and steam production. In British Railways days it was agreed with the Trade Unions that the maximum firing rate that was to be required of a single fireman was an average of 3,000 lb of coal per hour. The firing rate from the viewpoint of scientific analysis is usually related to the grate area of the locomotive, and the results established from engine No 5098 were as follows:

Steam rate	**Coal rate**	
lb per hr	lb per hr	lb per square feet of grate area per hour
6,000	595	20.2
8,000	795	27.0
10,000	1,020	34.7
12,000	1,255	42.7
14,000	1,505	51.2
16,000	1,779	60.5
18,000	2,075	70.7
20,000	2,404	82.0
22,000	2,777	94.0
24,000	3,228	109.7

The coal consumption per drawbar horsepower hour is generally quoted as a yardstick of thermal efficiency, but these tests showed how it varied with the speed, this being a constant speed run for an hour or more on the Swindon stationary testing plant.

Level track: firing 57 lb/square feet/grate area/hour

Load behind tender (tons, tare)	Speed (mph)	Coal per train mile (lb)	Coal per dhp hour (lb)
254	71	25	3.5
326	64.5	27.5	3.17
399	60.5	29.5	2.95
472	58.5	30.25	2.8
544	55	32.5	2.7

It is then interesting to see what was required to sustain a steady speed of 65 mph on level track with varying loads, thus:

Load behind tender (tons, tare)	Coal per square feet of grate area per hour (lb)	Coal per dhp hour (lb)
254	49.5	3.6
326	49.5	3.2
399	56	3.0
472	67	2.95
544	77	2.95

Firing at a rate 3,228 lb per hour, to provide steam at a rate of 24,000 lb per hour, would, in BR days have been considered just a little more than could be expected from an average fireman, but it is impressive to see what engine No 5098 produced in the way of performance on level track when steamed up to this standard. It is also interesting to see how the thermal efficiency deteriorated (as represented by the coal per dhp hour) as the speed rose, even though the loads were lightened appropriately.

24,000 lb per hour: level track

Load behind tender (tons, tare)	Speed (mph)	Coal per train mile (lb)	Coal per dhp hour (lb)
254	86.5	37.5	4.3
326	82	39.2	3.8
399	78.75	41.8	3.5
472	73.75	45.0	3.2
544	69.5	45.0	3.1

So far as the lightest of the above loads is concerned, as long ago as October 1929, I personally logged a run on the 'Cheltenham Flyer' when, because of a slight check in the early stages, we were nearly a minute late passing Steventon; but by that time the driver was stepping up the performance to some purpose, and with a load exactly equal to the lowest in the foregoing tables, 254 tons tare, the 14.5 miles from Didcot to Tilehurst, on level track, were covered at an average of 85 mph. With Reading passed 2 minutes early on the schedule then operating, the effort was naturally eased down. At that time the engine was, of course, one of the medium superheat units, No 5003, *Lulworth Castle*. Between Didcot and Tilehurst this great spurt would have involved a steam consumption very little less than 24,000 lb per hour.

In planning the first post-war passenger train schedules, three levels of performance from the 'Castle' Class engines were used as follows:

	Steam rate (lb per hour)	Coal rate (lb per hour)
Basic	16,000	1,779
Recovery	18,000	2,075
High	20,000	2,404

The steam and coal rates were averages usually considered to apply over 97 per cent of the total running time. The timetables were arranged to suit the basic performance, leaving the higher steam rates to be used in recovering lost time. Not long after the actual tests were completed, I had the privilege of some footplate runs on engine No 5098, *Clifford Castle*, on the long and varied double-home turns between Newton Abbot and Shrewsbury, via the Severn Tunnel, and I found her a very satisfying engine. The longest run I made can be summarised thus:

Engine 5098: Newton Abbot–Shrewsbury

Load: 421 tons tare, 460 tons full	
Length of journey	216.5 miles
Booked time, including 10 stops	367 minutes
Left Newton Abbot	3 minutes late
Arrived Shrewsbury	6½ minutes late
Actual time, including stops	370½ minutes
Booked running time	312 minutes
Actual running time	319 minutes
Net running time	295 minutes
Net average speed	44 mph
Water consumption	38 gallons per mile
Coal consumption (estimated)	40–42 lb per mile
Coal per square feet of grate area per hour of running time	56 lb
Maximum estimated dhp at 61 mph	1,450
Maximum speed on trip	84 mph

While the fitting of a four-row superheater to the 'Castle' class engine No 5049 did not seem to make

One of the 'Grange' Class, shortly after nationalisation, in the new style—No 6873, Caradoc Grange (Kenneth H. Leech).

One of the heavy mineral 2-8-2 tanks, converted from the 2-8-0 type, in the new painting style of British Railways (Kenneth H. Leech).

First of the new pannier tank 0-6-0s, with domeless taper boilers—No 9400—photographed when newly out of Swindon in the severe weather of the 1946–7 winter (British Railways).

One of the large mixed-traffic 2-8-0s, No 4707, on a heavy Saturday relief express train at Whiteball summit (Kenneth H. Leech).

A 'County' Class 4-6-0, No 1014, County of Glamorgan, *on the 1.15 pm express Paddington to Weston-super-Mare, near Twyford (the author is on the footplate)* (M.W. Earley).

a great deal of difference to the performance, and the engine remained the only one of its kind, it was far otherwise with the 'King' Class engine No 6022 which was similarly altered in 1947. Hawksworth was aware of the deterioration in performance that resulted when, because of poor coal, it was not possible to maintain boiler pressure up to sizzling point, and the following table shows how the boiler and superheater of engine No 6022 were modified.

	Standard 'King'	**Engine 6022**
Type	Single: Jumper Top	Single: Jumper Top
Blastpipe diameter (inches)	5½	5¼
Increase in area with jumper raised	38.25 per cent	41.9 per cent
Heating surfaces (square feet)		
Tubes	1,655.5	1,114.0
Firebox	193.5	194.5
Flues	352.0	704.0
Total evaporation	2,201	2,012.5
Superheater		
No of elements	16	32
Heating surface (square feet)	289	489

While not showing any appreciable advantage over a standard 'King', in good working conditions the high superheat engine showed a definite advantage in adversity. In dynamometer car trials between Paddington and Plymouth in uniformly good conditions, with high grade Welsh coal, the overall results are shown opposite.

The changes to the standard designs that had prevailed on the Great Western Railway for so many years, initiated by Hawksworth, were carried to a much further extent in later years, as will be described in later chapters of this book.

It was in the confused economic situation of the 1945–6 winter, following the return with a very large majority of a Labour Government in the General Election of 1945, that supplies of locomotive coal became critical on the GWR; and this was no more than a mild foretaste of what was to follow, nationally, within a year. The best grades were being exported, and in South Wales in particular, above all places, one had the ludicrous position of very many locomotives being fired with low grade American coal! The Great Western management of that time was not one to take such a situation lying down, and Hawksworth was authorised to convert 10 heavy mineral 2-8-0s, and 8 tank engines of the 2-8-0 '4200' Class, all engaged in South Wales, to oil firing. Oil fuelling plants were erected at Llanelly and Severn Tunnel Junction. The converted engines, at first working entirely west of Severn Tunnel Junction, were very successful, and this conception of a scheme of limited application led to a second one being launched. In 1938 the rapidly increasing cost of locomotive coal had led the GWR to consider the abolition of steam haulage at all points west of Taunton, and a distinguished firm of consulting engineers was commissioned to estimate the cost of a complete changeover to electric traction. It did not prove financially attractive; but in 1946 the cost of hauling Welsh coal to the West of England led to a similar project with oil firing.

With the idea of eventually making Cornwall an all-oil fired area, conversion began, experimentally, of certain express and mixed traffic engines of the 'Castle' and 'Hall' Classes. At first, when they were under close observation from headquarters at Swindon they were run on the Paddington–Bristol route, but in the summer of 1947 some of them were transferred to Laira shed, Plymouth, and began regular working to and from Penzance. One diagram, that involved haulage of the 'Cornish Riviera Express' in both directions included two return trips from Plymouth to Penzance in the day, a total mileage of 320, double manned. Both 'Castle' and 'Hall' Class engines were very successful, and

Coal consumption

Engine no	Superheater	lb/train mile	lb/dhp hour	lb/square feet of grate area per hour
6001	Standard	42.28	3.33	59.6
6022	4 - Row	41.23	3.10	57.7

steamed with complete consistency. Unfortunately, the news of this carefully planned limited application of oil firing and its success came to the ears of someone in Governmental authority just at the time when the fuel crisis of the 1946–7 winter broke out over the heads of the Labour Government. Lease-lend had ended and we became desperately short of coal. The Great Western project was hailed as a national inspiration. Finance was made available for converting a large number of locomotives on other railways, and the erection of oil fuelling plants was put in hand at many centres in Great Britain. Only when some £3 million of public money had been spent did another government department point out that we did not possess the foreign exchange to buy the necessary oil! Many of the fuelling plants were never used at all, and the Great Western plan went down in the general *débâcle.*

Before the GWR ceased to exist, two further new locomotive designs sponsored by Hawksworth, but originating in different and diverse circumstances, need to be described. The first was a variant of the powerful and extremely popular '57XX' Class of 0-6-0 pannier tank, of which there was already no fewer than 853 in service. More were needed in 1947, and it was proposed to build to the existing design. But apparently representations were made, it is said by certain directors, that it was not quite the thing to have empty stock trains hauled into Paddington by engines having a very large dome; something more modern was desirable. The view was passed down to Swindon, and a new shunting tank engine with a domeless boiler was duly designed. The engine portion was exactly the same as a '57XX' with 17½ inch by 24 inch cylinders, 4 ft 7½ inch wheels and carrying a boiler pressure of 200 lb per square inch, but the No 10 standard taper boiler, as used on the Collett '22XX' 0-6-0 tender engines, increased the total engine weight from 49 to 55.3 tons, and this took the Route Restriction colour from blue up to red, and so made the route availability of the new engines considerably less than that of the '57XX' Class to the embarrassment and annoyance of the Running Superintendent. A pilot batch of 10 was built at Swindon in 1947 and, after nationalisation, orders for another 200 were placed with outside contractors.

The '94XX' Class, as they were known, were excellent engines in themselves, but they were not so handy for shunting as the domed-boilered '57XX' Class. The latter had a relatively narrow cab, with all the controls of regulator and brake valve readily

A 'King' at Kings Cross, in 1948—No 6018, King Henry VI, *undergoing clearance tests before the British Railways Interchange Trials. The engine is still in the GWR style of painting* (C.C.B. Herbert).

at hand for a driver looking outside the cab. The taper-sided firebox of the '94XX' Class needed a wider cab and, when leaning out, drivers found to their consternation that they could not reach the brake valve. This was subsequently rectified by fitting a second pivoted handle to provide a remote control for the brake valve. When, under nationalisation, certain regional boundaries were changed and the West of England main line of the former LMS came under Western Region management as far north as Kings Norton, a batch of the '94XX' 0-6-0 tanks was transferred to Bromsgrove, for banking on the Lickey Incline. The Churchward setting of the Stephenson link motion was ideal in the laborious low speed conditions in which the bank engines did all their work, and there is a memorable photograph of a *posse* of four of them banking a massive train of oil-tank wagons.

The last Great Western steam locomotive design was not actually built until 1949. But Hawksworth was still in the chair, though nominally subservient to the boffins of the Railway Executive. There is good reason to believe, however, that the '15XX' 0-6-0 tank engine was largely inspired by Captain Hugh Vivian (Chairman of the Locomotive Committee of the Board in Great Western days) but, as a locomotive man himself and Chairman of Beyer, Peacock & Co, still taking much interest in Swindon affairs. I had been writing to him on some point concerning Beyer-Garratt locomotives, and almost as a postscript to his letter he wrote: 'I am glad that at last we've got a GWR engine with outside Walschaerts valve gear.' Actually the '15XX' was a variant of the '94XX' with the same boiler, but with outside cylinders and outside valve gear. The intention was to have a shunting engine available for 24-hour continuous service, to which all necessary attention could be given from the 6-foot. There was no need to get over a pit to do ordinary day-to-day maintenance work. The '15XX' class, however, came too late to have any influence for the future, and only 10 were built. In any case, the LMS had already shown how much more economically diesel-electric shunting locomotive could do the same job.

One of the latest examples of the very numerous 0-6-0 pannier tank engines, one of a batch of 10 built in 1947 with condensing apparatus for working through the London Underground tunnels to Smithfield goods station (British Railways).

8. Upheaval on the LNER

This chapter, more so perhaps than any other in the entire three-volume span of this work, is concerned far more with personalities than with engineering. It covers a sadly negative period, all the more depressing to students of locomotive history in view of the enterprise and exhilaration of what had gone before. There is no doubt that the sudden death of Sir Nigel Gresley, in April 1941, from a heart attack, took the top management of the LNER by surprise, and unprepared, though friends who knew him well were concerned to see how stout and unhealthy-looking he had become, and he had not yet reached the age of 65. Whether, like Collett on the GWR, he would have been prepared to go on to 70 is a moot point; certainly since Bulleid left for the Southern in October 1937 he had taken no apparent steps to provide for the succession. Bulleid's position as Assistant to the Chief Mechanical Engineer had been awarded to D.R. Edge, a 'Carriage and Wagon' man, most of whose previous experience had been on the Great Central section, and not to the remotest degree a 'replacement' for Bulleid. Gresley had retained his small headquarters staff at Kings Cross with B. Spencer dealing with locomotives and N. Newsome, carriages and wagons.

Able as these two were, they were no more than intermediate in status, and by far the most senior man in the CME's department was Edward Thompson, Mechanical Engineer, Doncaster. He was then 60 years of age. Prior to the grouping in 1923 he had moved about considerably, having been at different times on the Great Northern, Midland, and North Eastern Railways, not to mention a spell with Beyer, Peacock & Co. His first major appointment on the LNER was in 1930, as Mechanical Engineer, Stratford, from which he went to Darlington in a similar capacity in 1933, and finally to Doncaster in 1938. The last mentioned post, with responsibility for the Western Section of the Southern Area (GN & GC lines), was the one he held at the time of Sir Nigel Gresley's death. It was apparently in some hesitation that the Board considered appointing Thompson as Chief Mechanical Engineer, on the grounds of his age. The next in line was A.H. Peppercorn, Mechanical Engineer, Darlington; but he was primarily a running man, and there had been thoughts earlier if Gresley, like Collett on the GWR, had been willing to stay on till he was 70, one or other of the two 'up and coming' young men, J.F. Harrison (then at Gorton) or R.A. Smeddle, from Darlington, might be ready to take the most senior office. But no doubt imagining that, in the midst of the war, Thompson would act as a good caretaker, continuing his reputation as a careful maintenance man for his remaining five years, the Board put him in as CME, though divesting him of the responsibility for electrical engineering which Sir Nigel Gresley had. Little can Sir Ronald Matthews and his Board have foreseen the hornets' nest that would soon be stirred up!

Four years later I was to hear from Thompson's own lips of the situation he precipitated at the interview in which he was appointed Chief Mechanical Engineer. Sir Ronald Matthews, underlining the very difficult conditions in which they were working in wartime, said he felt sure the CME would appreciate there was no need to spend time designing new locomotives. Gresley had left them the finest stud in the country, and they would carry on. And then Thompson astounded him by replying: 'My

LNER: diagram of converted 2-8-2 (Class 'P2') to 'Pacific' type Class 'A2/2' (Railway Gazette).

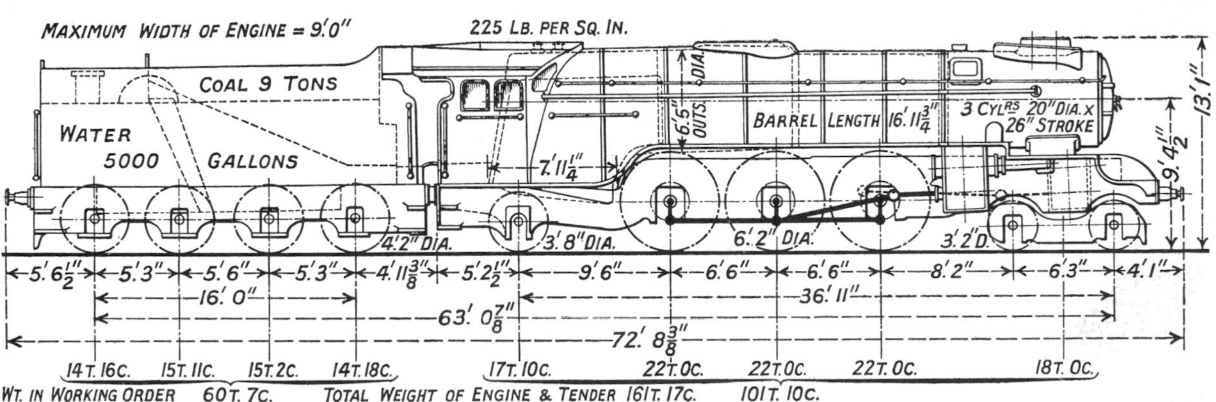

This page, top to bottom

Wartime grime on the LNER: an unidentified 'V2' 2-6-2 ('Green Arrow' Class) on a down expresss near Hatfield (M.W. Earley).

Changes under E. Thompson: one of the 'Hunt' Class (formerly with three cylinders) rebuilt, with two cylinders inside, in 1942—No 365 The Morpeth (British Railways).

The Thompson 'B1' 4-6-0: one of a post-war batch built by the North British Locomotive Company in 1946—No 1040, Roedeer (North British Locomotive Company).

One of the 'orphans of the storm': engine No 508, Duke of Rothesay, *one of the four engines authorised as 2-6-2s but built with the ungainly wheel spacing adopted for the Thompson 'Pacifics'* (British Railways).

Opposite page, top to bottom

Memories of the pre-war LNER style: one of the earlier 3-cylinder 4-6-0s of the 'Sandringham' Class, originally Burnham Thorpe, *as renamed not long before the Second World War—No 2805,* Lincolnshire Regiment (British Railways).

Thompson's rebuild of the pioneer Gresley 'Pacific' No 4470, Great Northern—*not an attractive looking locomotive* (British Railways).

One of the 'K4' 3-cylinder 2-6-0s specially built for the West Highland line, No 1997, Mac Cailin Mor, *as rebuilt with two cylinders, and forming the prototype of the new standard Class 'K1'* (British Railways).

Thompson's rebuild of a 'K3' 2-6-0, No 206, with only two cylinders and a higher boiler pressure. This engine was intended to be the prototype for a new Class 'K5', but actually it was the only one so treated (British Railways).

2805
L N E R

GREAT NORTHERN
4470
N E

1997
L N E R

206
N E

appointment is at your disposal, Chairman . . .' and he went on to explain by how much he disagreed, and how necessary it was for changes to be initiated and entirely new standards set up. He told Sir Ronald that while Sir Nigel Gresley was 'the greatest engine designer we ever had, he made one mistake . . .' and he enlarged upon the shortcomings of the conjugated valve gear.

The Chairman was in a difficult position. Not an engineer himself he was not able to judge the force of Thompson's contentions, but he was won over by a characteristically heroic gesture: 'Set up an independent enquiry and I'll stand or fall by its findings'. Sir Ronald Matthews was obviously impressed by the deep sincerity of Thompson's feelings, and he asked who should make the enquiry. Thompson first asked Bulleid to do it, who somewhat naturally refused, because the whole exercise seemed an indictment of an engineer to whom Bulleid had always been unswerving loyal. Sir William Stanier, appreciating the difficulties Thompson was in, agreed to do it, and sent E.S. Cox to Doncaster. The report, without actually condemning the conjugated valve gear, went to the stage of saying that he would not use it himself; and that apparently was good enough for Thompson to begin his depredations.

As the conjugated valve gear was at the centre of the hornets' nest stirred up by Thompson on the LNER in the middle of the Second World War, it is important to appreciate just what all the fuss was about. The drive to the valve spindle of the inside cylinder was derived from a combination of levers connected to the valve spindles of the directly-driven valve gear of the outside cylinders. It was an extremely simple geometrical mechanism and the derived motion came through the interaction of levers involving five pin joints. The derived motion on the 4-cylinder engines of the Great Western and the LMS came through three pin joints. There was nothing theoretically wrong with the conjugated gear on the Gresley 3-cylinder locomotives; it was the standard of construction in main works on the LNER that was the cause of most of the trouble with it. To obviate inaccuracy in the erection of locomotives, particularly at Doncaster where most of the largest engines were erected and maintained, generous clearances had to be given in the pin joints of the valve gear—not only in the derived motion for the Gresley 3-cylinder engines, but in the Walschaerts gear generally. It was necessary also on the connecting and coupling rods, giving rise to what was known as the 'Gresley ring', in their goings and comings.

However, 'clanking' rods, though sometimes resulting in uncomfortable riding on the footplate, could be endured; the accumulated slack in the five pin joints of the derived valve gear, on the other hand, brought deep trouble. It led to the valve spindle overrunning and delaying the point of cut-off of the steam in the middle cylinder, which meant that cylinder was doing far more than its proper share of the work, and imposing excessive loads on the middle connecting rods, and big-end. This weakness in the machinery of the Gresley 'Pacifics' had been well enough known in pre-war years; but the occasions on which the engines had to give up their trains because of an over-heated middle big end are remembered best not from the failure of the train engine, but by the gallant efforts of the crews to retrieve the situation with the 'Atlantic' provided at a moment's notice in substitution. The most serious failure of all was, of course, that with the 'A4' engine No 4468, *Mallard*, following the attainment of the world record speed with steam of 126 mph. Nevertheless, the outward manifestations of Thompson's precepts did not become apparent for some little time, though within the LNER the stresses began to build up. The Running Superintendents in the Southern, North Eastern and Scottish Areas were independent officers responsible directly to the respective divisional general managers, and they naturally took unkindly to the high handed way in which Thompson sometimes acted with

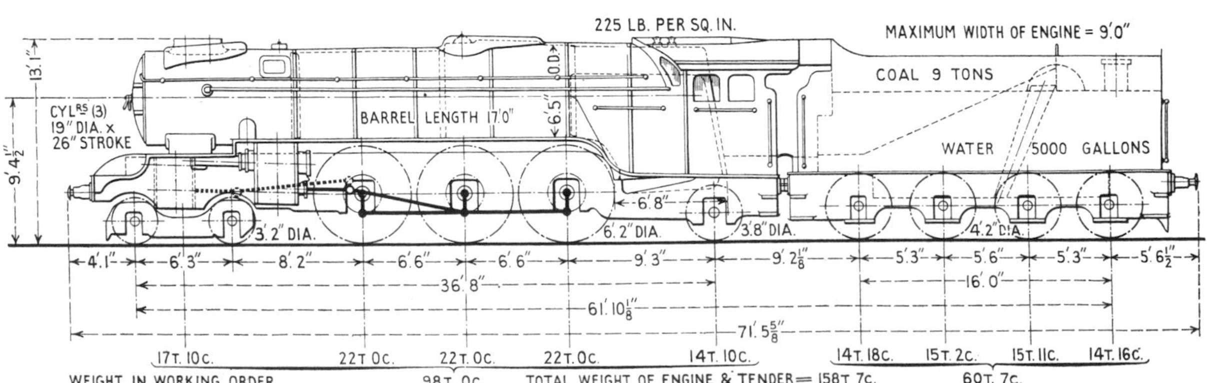

individual locomotives in their charge.

In the Chief Mechanical Engineer's department there was a complete reorganisation of personnel. Headquarters was transferred from Kings Cross to Doncaster, and while Edge was retained as Assistant, in matters of design Thompson dealt with the Chief Draughtsman, E. Windle. Gresley's personal assistants went into the wilderness—Spencer, indeed, went out of railway service altogether for a time. Peppercorn combined the duties of Mechanical Engineer, Doncaster, with those of Deputy CME, though he exercised no influence so far as design work was concerned. J.F. Harrison was Mechanical Engineer, Gorton, and R.A. Smeddle, in the similar appointment at Darlington. In the meantime construction to orders placed before Gresley's death went ahead, with the completion during 1943 of further examples of the large 2-6-2 mixed traffic engine, Class 'V2', and of the 2-8-0 heavy freight type, Class '02', both with three cylinders and derived valve gear for the middle cylinder.

As related in Chapter 1 of this book, Gresley had designed a smaller 2-6-2 tender engine which was intended to be a replacement engine for the many older classes which were nearing the end of their life-span. Only two of these engines, Class 'V4', had been built at the time of Gresley's death, and his successor did not wish to perpetuate the design, which included the derived valve gear for the middle cylinder. Instead, to meet the need for a medium powered mixed-traffic engine, Thompson produced, in the 'B1' 4-6-0, what was undoubtedly his best design.

It was a logical, realistic, and handsome synthesis of existing components, involving no new patterns, tooling or other items of capital expenditure, thus:

Component	**Previous standard use**
Boiler	'Sandringham' Class 4-6-0
Cylinders, motion	'K2' 2-6-0 (modified to provide long travel valves)
Coupled wheels	'V2' 2-6-2
Bogie	'Sandringham' Class

With 20 inch by 26 inch cylinders, 6 foot 2 inch coupled wheels and carrying a boiler pressure of 225 lb per square inch, the nominal tractive effort was

Right *Austerity running in 1945: the 'Flying Scotsman' leaving York, hauled by a dirty and out-of-condition 'A4' 'Pacific', No 4482,* Golden Eagle *(the author is on the footplate)* (W. Hubert Foster).

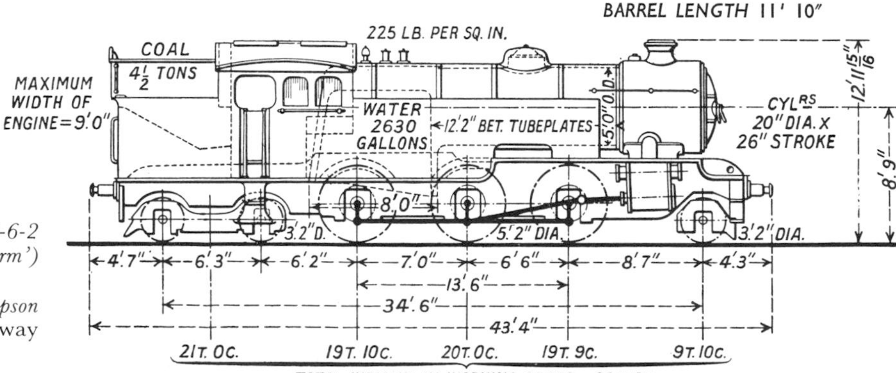

Left *LNER: diagram of Thompson 4-6-2 Class 'A2/1' ('Orphans of the storm')* (Railway Gazette).

Right *LNER: diagram of Thompson 'L1' Class 2-6-4 tank* (Railway Gazette).

Top *Prototype of the new standard 'L1' Class 2-6-4 tank engine, introduced by Thompson in 1946* (British Railways).
Above *LNER: one of the former Great Central Railway 2-8-0 heavy mineral engines, No 6292, rebuilt by Thompson with a new standard boiler* (British Railways).

26,878 lb. The 3-cylinder 'Sandringham' Class 4-6-0 was designed primarily for the Great Eastern Line at a time when restrictions on weight precluded the use of heavier engines than the Holden 4-6-0s of the '1500' 'B12' Class. The 'Sandringhams', having a maximum axle load of 18.35 tons, were accepted because of the reduced hammer blow effect from the 3-cylinder layout. The 'B1', although having a maximum axle load of 17.75 tons, had a high route availability because the hammer blow effect was much reduced below what had been customary in 2-cylinder locomotives of such capacity. In earlier years it had been the usual practice to balance two-thirds of the reciprocating parts by weights cast into the driving wheels, and it was these weights that contributed largely to the hammer blow effect. On the 'B1s' only 35 per cent was balanced. The 'B1', introduced at the end of 1942, proved an excellent medium-power motive power unit, though harsh and uncomfortable to ride; it received general commendation in the railway world as a good practical job in the conditions of wartime.

Thompson's next essay in locomotive design, however, left many of us veritably speechless! When I was invited to his home in Doncaster in the winter of 1945/6 he told me how much he had admired the Great Western engine layout on the 4-cylinder locomotives, in which the equal length of connecting rod for the inside and outside cylinders made it so much easier to get uniformity of valve events, which he always emphasised could not be done with the Gresley 3-cylinder layout. But the way he chose to demonstrate this particular predilection was unbelievably harsh. The story was put about that the great 'P2' 2-8-2 engines of the *Cock o' the North* Class, because of their long wheelbase, rode badly on the curving stages of the Edinburgh–Aberdeen main line, for which they had been designed, and that their maintenance costs were high. I would not go so far as to suggest that this was a trumped up charge to justify their drastic rebuilding, but I will say that in my footplate experience on several of

Post-war efforts to revive earlier elegance—the pioneer Gresley streamlined 'Pacific', Silver Link, *once more in Garter Blue with stainless steel lettering, but with the side valences not replaced* (British Railways).

them they rode easily and elegantly round the sharpest curves, and never gave any impression of binding, or of spreading the road. Anyway, in the late autumn of 1942, Thompson took No 2005, *Thane of Fife*, out of traffic, and at Doncaster the most horrible mutilation began. The front-end streamlining was stripped off; the spliced on front portion of the main frames removed and, by the removal of the leading pair of coupled wheels, space was made for an entirely new front end, supported by a leading bogie.

To follow out his ideas of equal length connecting rods, the inside cylinder was pushed as far forward as possible, and the outside cylinders moved rearwards. The inside cylinder, of course, had a separate set of valve gear, but the whole locomotive as rebuilt looked a thorough misfit. Everything about it looked wrong, particularly the inordinate length between the bogie and the leading pair of coupled wheels. As a wartime expedient to try out a new engine layout, it might just have passed as an ugly makeshift, involving a minimum of new parts; but after 'running in' between Doncaster and Leeds, and incurring a number of 'hot boxes', it was returned to Scotland early in 1943 and stationed at Dundee to resume its former duties. The Running Department in Scotland, Gresley to a man, were not amused. The 'P2s' had been designed specially for the Aberdeen road, and with 8-coupled wheels and an adhesion weight of 79 tons to match a tractive effort of 43,452 lb, they had proved remarkably effective. Now the tractive effort had been reduced to 40,318 lb and the adhesion weight to 66 tons and, as I expected when I saw the dimensions of the rebuilt engine, it was to prove very touchy on wet rails. The boiler proportions were also changed. The comparative dimensions were:

Class	**'P2'**	**'A2'**
Type	**2-8-2**	**4-6-2**
Cylinders (number of)	3	3
diameter × stroke (inches)	21 × 26	20 × 26
Boiler pressure (psi)	220	225
Heating surfaces (square feet)		
Tubes	1,122.8	1,004.5
Superheater flues	1,354.2	1,211.57
Firebox	237	237
Superheater elements	776.5	679.67
Total	3,490.5	3,132.74
Tractive effort (lb)	43,452	40,318
Adhesion weight (ton)	79	66

When it became apparent that the rebuilt 2005 was not merely a rather ugly guinea-pig for a new idea but the shape of things to come, the heather was soon on fire. The remaining five 'P2' engines were summoned to Doncaster for mutilation and, in 1944, completion of the last four of the final batch of 25 'V2' 2-6-2s was held up, and they eventually emerged as 4-6-2s in the same form as the rebuilt 'P2s', but with 19 inch by 26 inch cylinders, and a rather shorter boiler. Thompson had by then become thoroughly nettled at the criticism his policy was receiving in the railway and technical press, and he referred to the modified 'V2s', or 'A2/1' engines, Nos 3696-9, as 'the orphans of the storm'!

The situation on the LNER with the current theme of denigrating everything Gresley had done—at any rate so far as official utterances from Doncaster headquarters were concerned—could have been regarded as a rather sour transient phase, had it not been echoed in the railway press by certain

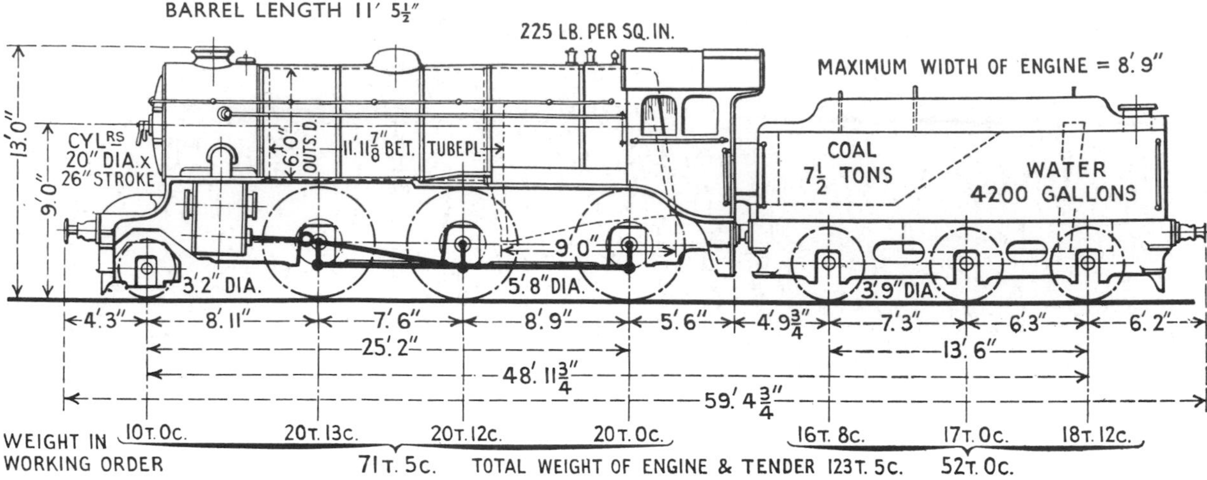

Above *LNER: diagram of Thompson rebuilt 2-6-0 'K3' with two cylinders, as Class 'K5'* (Railway Gazette).

Opposite page, top to bottom

An ex-LNER 2-6-0 Class 'K4' now preserved—The Great Marquess—*here seen on its original duties on the West Highland line, climbing the first bank out of Fort William on the southbound run* (E.D. Bruton).

The Gresley 'P2' Class 2-8-2 designed for the Edinburgh–Aberdeen route—No 2002, Earl Marischal, *as running in 1940–3* (British Railways).

Peppercorn's version of the Class 'A2' 'Pacific'—first of the new type, introduced in 1947 and named after the Chief Mechanical Engineer (British Railways).

Named after a great ally: the streamlined 'Pacific' No 4496, formerly Golden Shuttle, *renamed* Dwight D. Eisenhower. *This is now preserved, in the USA* (British Railways).

self-appointed 'political agents' of the new regime, who not only repeated the parrot cry against the derived valve gear for the middle cylinder, but added some depredations of their own about the unsuitability of the Gresley swing-link pony truck, 'like the same designer's bogie', which it was averred did not give sufficient side control for steady riding. How certain editors failed to put the 'blue pencil' through such nonsense, it is hard to imagine, especially when, subsequently, the 'orphans of the storm' acquired a particularly bad reputation for wild and unsafe riding at high speed!' The sad thing about it is that the Gresley 'Pacifics', his 'P2' 2-8-2s, and the 'V2' 2-6-2s were all beautifully smooth and elegant riding locomotives, even at the highest speeds.

In the early summer of 1945 I made a number of footplate runs on LNER locomotives, collecting data for articles commissioned by one of the leading engineering journals. Except in Scotland, where the Running Superintendent took a particular interest in my travels, no prior arrangements were made. I just presented my pass to the drivers concerned and climbed aboard. In this particular odyssey I rode four 'V2' 2-6-2s; two 'A4' streamlined 'Pacifics'; a new Thompson 'B1' 4-6-0; an ex-Great Eastern 4-6-0; an 'A3' 'Pacific', and one of the Thompson 'Pacifics' rebuilt from a Gresley 2-8-2 of the 'P2' Class. With one exception the results were a complete negation of all that had been preached since Thompson took office. One of the 'V2s' was run down and badly off her beat; but this did not deter the driver, and he flailed her along merrily and kept time from Aberdeen to Edinburgh. A second 'V2' was in good condition mechanically, but so hamstrung with bad coal as to need rear-end banking on the severe gradients of the Waverley route. The third 'V2' was in good shape and turned in an excellent performance, while the fourth was really quite exceptional in her thermodynamic behaviour, giving immaculate running on a very short cut-off. The Gresley 'Pacifics' were all good, and the old Great Eastern 4-6-0 so comfortable that I wished she could have continued from Ipswich to March instead of the new 'B1' that actually took over, and which I stigmatised at the time as a 'vicious, kicking little brute'! Useful motive power units though they were, the 'B1s' were rough and uncomfortable at the best of times.

Then there was the Thompson 'A2' 'Pacific', the *Wolf of Badenoch*, which we had on the down 'Aberdonian' from Ediburgh to Aberdeen on a wet summer morning. I wrote a long article for *The Railway Magazine* on this trip, and in consideration for my hosts who had given me the privilege of a

2002
L N E R

A. H. PEPPERCORN
525
L N E R

DWIGHT D. EISENHOWER
4496
L N E R

footplate pass, I must now confess that I did not tell the whole story. With a very heavy train the engine slipped at the slightest provocation and, while the drivers were nursing the engine gingerly up the many steep gradients on this route, I thought back wistfully on how *Cock o' the North* and *Earl Marischal*, in their original 2-8-2 state, had torn purposefully into these gradients and with similar loads climbed them at 30 mph or more, where we were struggling to make 20 mph. In the damp air, too, we were the victims of a piece of bad detail designer, because an outside steam pipe had bolted connections on two faces at right angles—to the main frame, and to the valve chest. Leakage was inevitable, and we travelled with a veil of steam drifting back to the cab. On arrival at Aberdeen we found that some of the bolts securing this pipe to the main frame had worked loose, and the nuts were missing. I was not impressed with the Thompson 'A2'.

Although he was not directly responsible for locomotive running, Thompson had heard of my round of footplate journeys, and it was then that he invited me to visit him in Doncaster, and to stay as guest at his home. I was in something of a cleft-stick. Privately I was opposed to the principles underlying all his work so far, though in my writings I tried to maintain a façade of impartiality. The public relations people in London were anxious that I should go, but were not so pleased afterwards when he made available to me, for publication, a good deal of information that had been confidential until then. They felt they should have handled it through the Press Office. But it was typical of the way Thompson rode rough-shod over fellow officers on the railway! Much of what we discussed at his own fireside concerned his views on the shortcomings of the Gresley locomotives; but what he did vouchsafe to me, to the annoyance of the Press Office in London, was his plan for the complete standardisation of the locomotive stock of the LNER.

Left *A well-known Gresley 'Pacific', the* Diamond Jubilee, *originally one of the 180 lb series, but here seen rebuilt with 220 lb boiler and working a Leeds express, shortly after nationalisation* (E.D. Bruton).

Below *One of the 'Football Club' series of 3-cylinder 4-6-0 'Sandringham' Class engines, in BR style of painting—No 61657,* Doncaster Rovers (British Railways).

Right *LNER: diagram of Thompson rebuilt '04' GCR 2-8-0 as Class '01'* (Railway Gazette).

Below right *Peppercorn 'A1' Class 'Pacific' named after a famous 19th century Great Northern engineer,* Patrick Stirling. *This is No 60119 in BR painting style* (British Railways).

The new standard types were to be 10 in number as follows:

1) 4-6-2 'A1' (Express Passenger). Prototype rebuilt from original series of Gresley 'Pacifics'.

2) 'A2' (Heavy Passenger and Freight). Prototype rebuilt from 2-8-2 'P2' Class.

3) 4-6-0 'B1' (General utility type). New design with standard components.

4) 2-6-0 'K1' (Mixed Traffic). Prototype rebuilt from Class 'K4' with standard components.

5) 2-8-0 '01' (Mineral). Prototype rebuilt from Great Central Robinson 2-8-0.

6) 0-6-0 'J11' (Freight). Prototype rebuilt from Great Central 0-6-0.

7) 2-6-4T 'L1' (Mixed Traffic). New design with standard components.

8) 0-8-0T 'Q1' (Heavy shunting tank). Prototype rebuilt from GCR 0-8-0 tender engine.

9) 0-6-0T 'J50' (Medium shunting engine). Prototype rebuilt from ex-GNR Gresley 0-6-0T.

10 Light shunting engine. To be designed.

It can well be imagined with what attention, and surprise that I listened as he unfolded this programme; surprise at the relatively large number of old engines that were to be rebuilt as prototypes for the new standards, and a secret horror that some of the original Gresley 'Pacifics' were evidently to be rebuilt on similar lines to the unfortunate 'P2s'. Relatively few non-standard types were to be maintained. The 'Sandringham' 4-6-0s were to be converted to 2-cylinders, to become Class 'B2'; similarly the Gresley 'K3' Moguls were to become 'K5' with only 2 cylinders. I was told that an experimental rebuilding was in hand for the 4-4-0s of the 'D49' Class. The large stud of ex-Great Central '04' Class of 2-8-0s was to be rebuilt to Class '01' and, apart from the 'Pacifics', the only other engine that would be maintained were the Gresley 'V2' and the 2-6-2 tanks of Classes 'V1' and 'V3'. Everything else was apparently marked down for the 'chop'. It was an extraordinary programme for a man whose likelihood of remaining Chief Mechanical Engineer did not extend to more than a few years. At his suggestion I wrote a monograph on the standardisation work he had put in train, for publication by the LNER, but he retired at the end of June 1946, before even the draughting of the monograph was finished.

Perhaps the most disappointing and tactless act in his short and stormy career as CME was his choice of the pioneer Gresley 'Pacific', the *Great Northern*, for rebuilding as what he intended to be the proto-

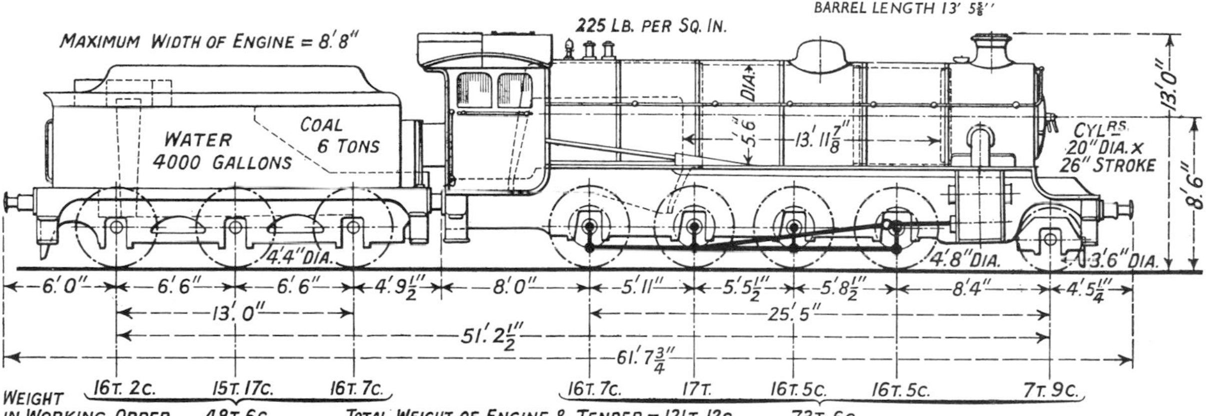

Thompson 'Pacifics'

Class	**'A2'**	**'A2/1'**	**'A2/2'**	**'A1'**
Coupled wheel diameter (feet/inches)	6 2	6 2	6 2	6 8
Cylinders				
Diameter (inches)	19	19	20	19
Stroke (inches)	26	26	26	26
Boiler pressure psi	250	225	225	250
Heating surfaces (square feet)				
Tubes and flues	2,216.07	2,216.07	2,216.07	2,345.1
Firebox	245.3	215	237	231.2
Superheater	679.67	679.67	679.67	748.9
Total	3,141.04	3,110.74	3,132.74	3,325.2
Grate area (square feet)	50	41.25	50	41.25
Nominal tractive effort (lb)	40,430	36,387	40,318	37,397
Number of engines in class	15	4	6	1

type of his new express passenger 'Pacific' Class. What a splendid engine for future preservation the *Great Northern* would have been, carrying the old GNR livery in which it first appeared, in 1922. As it was, it was rebuilt with new cylinders, three independent sets of valve gear and the ugly wheel spacing to which Thompson had accustomed us in the rebuilt 'P2s' and the 'orphans of the storm'. As if to obliterate all traces of its historic lineage, the engine was painted in Royal blue, lined out in the style of the Great Eastern, and had 'NE' on the tender.

Thompson was very proud of this engine. He sent me photographs of it and offered to arrange footplate trips; but when I was able to take up this offer, with the engine working the down 'Aberdonian' from Kings Cross to Grantham, the inspector who rode with me was very lukewarm in his support of the prevailing regime. He was particularly sorry that no further 'V4' 2-6-2s had been built, which he considered would have been far better than the 'B1' 4-6-0s. In view of the rather strained situation that had developed on the LNER, the very full account of the journey which I wrote was not published in *The Railway Magazine* until some 18 months later. The engine worked very smoothly and produced plenty of horsepower on occasions; but with the slow wartime schedule, and a load of no more than 440 tons, nothing special was required. On the good track of the Great Northern main line the action of the engine at speed was much more comfortable than that of the rebuilt 'P2', *Wolf of Badenoch*, in Scotland.

In 1946 construction of a new batch of 'A2' 'Pacifics' was authorised. These differed both from the rebuilt 'P2s' and from the 'orphans of the storm' in the cylinder and boiler dimensions, but also in that the steam collector, sometimes referred to as the 'Banjo Dome', used on the later Gresley engines

An attractive picture of one of the 'B1' 4-6-0s—No 61039, Steinbok*—working 'light engine' into York station* (E.D. Bruton).

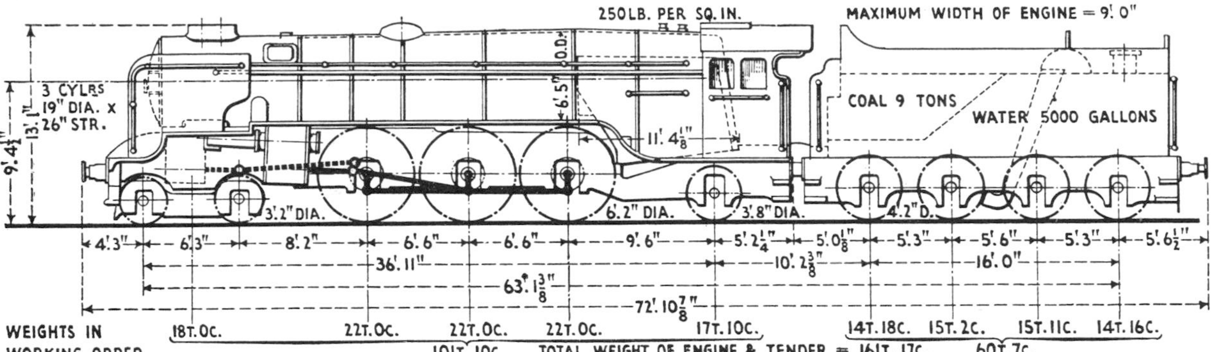

LNER: diagram of the new standard 'A2' 'Pacific', by Thompson (Railway Gazette).

was abandoned. The small deflecting shields on either side of the chimney on the earlier 'A2s' were replaced by large shields extending down to the running plate. Basic dimensions of the three varieties of 'A2' 'Pacific' are shown in the accompanying table (above left). The first of the new engines, No 500, the 2,000th built at Doncaster, was named *Edward Thompson*. In the renumbering scheme which was applied to the entire locomotive stock, the six rebuilt 'P2' engines became 501-6, and the four 'orphans' 507-510. The new engines of the 1946 batch, apart from No 500, were 511 to 524.

With Thompson's retirement the programme of standardisation that he had drawn up slackened somewhat, and only the 'B1', 'K1' and 'L1' Classes were built in any quantity. A number of the '04' ex-Great Central 2-8-0s were converted to the new '01', but generally speaking the running department preferred them in their original form. The leading dimensions of the three standard 2-cylinder classes were as follows:

LNER standard 2-cylinder classes

Class	B1	K1	L1
Type	4-6-0	2-6-0	2-6-4T
Coupled wheel diameter (feet/inches)	6 2	5 2	5 2
Cylinders			
Diameter (inches)	20	20	20
Stroke (inches)	26	26	26
Boiler pressure (psi)	225	225	225
Heating surfaces (square feet)			
Tubes & flues	1,508	1,240	1,198
Firebox	168	168	138.5
Superheater	344	300	284
Total	2,020	1,708	1,620.5
Grate area (square feet)	27.9	27.9	24.74
Nominal tractive (lb)	26,878	32,081	32,081

For a time in 1953, certain ex-LNER 'A1' 'Pacifics' were working over the West Coast main line between Glasgow and Crewe. One of them, No 60152, Holyrood, *is seen here on the morning Birmingham–Glasgow express just north of Lancaster* (the late Ian S. Pearsall).

One of the 'K1' Class standard 2-6-0s of ex-LNER design ordered from the North British Locomotive Company in 1949, after nationalisation, in BR style of painting (North British Locomotive Company).

In July 1946, Thompson was succeeded as Chief Mechanical Engineer by A.H. Peppercorn, but at that time all was agog with the daunting prospects of nationalisation. Nevertheless with the likely vesting still some 18 months ahead, and with authorisation for 15 more 'A2' 'Pacifics' and for 49 of the new 'A1' Class, Peppercorn had to consider whether to build these of the Thompson type or to make modifications. As a running man himself, and a very loyal follower of Sir Nigel Gresley, he was no doubt aware of the many criticisms made of the Thompson designs. Windle, the Chief Draughtsman at Doncaster, was a dry old character, and from talks I had with him I gathered that not infrequently he had his tongue in his cheek. I could well believe the story that he had begun redesigning the 'Pacifics' even before Thompson retired! The weakness, as could be imagined from a mere sideways look at them, lay in the long spacing between the bogie and the leading pair of coupled wheels, resulting in undue flexing of the frames and constant troubles from the outside pipe connection to the valve chests. The advantages from having all three connecting rods of equal length were minimal compared to the troubles it caused elsewhere.

On his appointment as CME, Peppercorn immediately brought Spencer back to his former post as technical assistant, and with J.F. Harrison as Assistant CME, the Gresley tradition was in a fair way to strong revival at Doncaster, except that in future the conjugated motion for the valves of the middle cylinder on the big engines was not restored in new designs. In laying out the revised front end design for the 'A1' and 'A2' Pacifics, Windle was able to retain the divided drive, but the outside cylinders were brought forward to a conventional position, with longer connecting rods, and the wheel spacing between the rear pair of bogie wheels, and leading coupled wheels reduced from 8 feet 2 inches to 5 feet 7 inches, on the 'A2s', and to 5 feet 9 inches on the 'A1s'. Peppercorn's 'Pacifics' in consequence had a neat, compact appearance that had been completely lacking in their immediate predecessors. The boilers on both varieties were the same as those of the Thompson 'A2', except that the Gresley 'Banjo Dome' was restored.

The new engines had all the dimensional requirements of a very fast and powerful unit, having the apparent advantage over the Gresley 'A4' streamliners of 10 inch diameter piston valves, against 9 inch and that the cut-off of 75 per cent, in full gear against 65 would give them extra power in getting away with a load. But although certain of their admirers among LNER locomotive men considered that the 'A1s' in particular were the finest express passenger engines that ever ran the road in Great Britain, it is a matter of history that they did not quite make it, and never superseded the Gresley 'A4s' on the most arduous duties of post-war years.

In the first place, admittedly with the advantage

One of the Peppercorn Class 'A2' 'Pacifics'—(ex LNER) No 60527, Sun Chariot*—hauling an express fish train from Aberdeen up the steep gradient leading to the Forth Bridge* (E.D. Bruton).

of hindsight, I think it was a mistake to put grates with an area of 50 square feet on to both 'A1s' and 'A2s'. I realise that when they were on the drawing boards of Doncaster the LNER was still under the lingering influence and recollection of the colossal loads of wartime. I remember so well a Running Superintendent making a comparison thus wise: '. . . the Gresleys are the greyhounds of the service, but if you have to take 600 tons on a dirty night give me a Peppercorn every time.' The fallacy in that argument was that 600-ton loads were getting few and far between, and with the thin fires normally used it was often a case of firing coal simply to keep those 50 square foot grates covered. Furthermore, as scheduled speeds were smartened up towards pre-war, if not necessarily streamline standards, it was found that many of the Peppercorn 'Pacifics' were addicted to bad riding. Some of those I rode travelled to a continuous yawing action, that became progressively uncomfortable as speed rose, while others 'hunted' violently at times. They had a bogie inherited from Thompson days. It was satisfactory on a small 4-6-0 locomotive, but had inadequate side control for a huge engine like a Peppercorn 'Pacific'. Except on the fastest main line duties south of Newcastle, where their coal consumption showed up badly against the 'A4s', the Peppercorns were well appreciated engines and, on the Aberdeen route, as soon as enough 'A2s' were available, the Thompsons were taken off. It was ironic, in view of the arguments advanced for the rebuilding of the 'P2s', that in their modified form they returned such a poor performance.

Mechanically, the Peppercorns were excellent engines, and had a fine record of trouble-free mileage. This was particularly the case with the five 'A1s', Nos 60153-7, fitted with roller bearings throughout. From the viewpoint of history it is a pity that no precise details of their performance came to be taken on one or another of the stationary testing plants in British Railways days. The 'A1s' were not built in time to represent the Eastern and North Eastern Regions in the Interchange Trials of 1948, while, in 1955, when the Western Region was testing 'Pacifics' against the re-draughted 'King' Class 4-6-0s on the Paddington–Plymouth run, and an 'A1' was requested for trial, conditions could not be agreed between the two Regions. Perhaps it was just as well, because the bad riding of the 'A1s' had not then been cured, and serious trouble could well have arisen if any attempt had been made to drive them really fast on some of the curvaceous stretches of the West of England main line between Reading and Taunton. The only time I have been really scared on the footplate of a steam locomotive was on one of these engines working a Birmingham–Glasgow express over the Caledonian line between Carlisle and Beattock. Some notes on their later work is contained in a subsequent chapter of this book.

9. Bulleid on the Southern

When Sir Herbert Walker chose O.V.S. Bulleid to succeed Maunsell as Chief Mechanical Engineer of the Southern Railway in the summer of 1937 one can well imagine that neither he nor anyone else at Waterloo foresaw what the startling sequel would be. Walker himself was in his 70th year and was due to retire in mid-October. He had been one of the foremost advocates of electrification and, but for the war, one can be sure that his successors would have pushed ahead with the extensions to Dover and Thanet, and then to Bournemouth. The role of the Chief Mechanical Engineer was generally seen as that of maintaining steam traction on the rapidly contracting non-electrified lines, ultimately envisaged as little more than the West of England main line beyond Basingstoke, and the country branches. There was even talk of the former line being handed over to the Great Western! Bulleid's appointment took effect from November 1 1937 and, by that time, Walker had been succeeded by Gilbert S. Szlumper, son of a former Chief Engineer of the London and South Western Railway, and the Southern.

Although Bulleid's previous status had, for the previous 14 years, been no more than that of 'Assistant to . . .' he had all that time been the close confidant and often ebullient friend of Sir Nigel Gresley, and those who knew him best were well enough aware that he was an engineer of a most original turn of mind. If those who recommended him to the Southern imagined that they were appointing a quiet caretaker to preside over the final obsequies of steam traction, they were in for some surprises. Nothing was further from Bulleid's mind. His own self-set parameters of performance for a super-express passenger locomotive, which he himself said were dictated by operating requirements, were so startlingly in advance of anything currently being worked on the Southern Railway as to suggest that for once it was the locomotive department and not the traffic that was trying to set the pace. In a paper presented to the Institution of Mechanical Engineers in December 1945, which he modestly called 'Some Notes on the *Merchant Navy* Class locomotives, Southern Railway', Bulleid opened thus: 'In designing these engines, passenger trains of 550-600 tons were envisaged, with average start-to-stop speeds of a mile a minute on short runs (for example to Dover) and 70 mph on longer runs (to Exeter) with a maximum of 90-95 mph. The ever-increasing proportion of express goods trains also made it desirable to have general-purpose machines.'

This paper was written four years after the first of these engines had been put into traffic, and the preliminary work on the design had begun well before the outbreak of war. It is nevertheless a moot point as to whether the Operating Department ever contemplated the regular running of passenger trains as heavy as 600 tons. With standard main line stock, it would have meant 18 or 19 coaches, which was far greater than could be accommodated at Waterloo, or Victoria on the South Eastern side, and which would involve an intolerable nuisance to passengers and operating staff alike. Furthermore, a few rough calculations suggest that a locomotive of far greater tractive power than the 35,000 to 40,000 lb indicated

The Bulleid influence beginning: engine No 863, Lord Rodney, *(on right) with large diameter chimney, in conjunction with multiple jet blast pipe, in contrast to the original design on left, represented by No 854,* Howard of Effingham (C.R.L. Coles).

The modified 'Nelson', No 863, Lord Rodney, *on the Continental boat express, near Bromley (Kent) in 1939* (H.C. Casserley).

would be needed to get such a load to Exeter at an average speed of 70 mph. Bulleid in his paper indicates that initially he had set out to provide 'Silver Jubilee' standards of speed on the Southern, but with loads of 550 to 600 tons. The 'Silver Jubilee' and 'Coronation' averages between Kings Cross and Newcastle were only 67 mph. No, one feels that at the outset Bulleid was rather flying his kite.

It was first proposed that this super-locomotive should be a 4-8-2. Bulleid would, of course, have known of Gresley's project for a 4-8-2 enlargement of the standard 'A3' Pacific, and would have delighted in being the first to produce a British 4-8-2. But it was turned down by the Civil Engineer, and the amended proposal of a 2-8-2 was so hemmed around with restrictions and conditions that no real progress had been made by the time war came in September 1939, other than first sketches on the drawing boards. With his experience of the Gresley 'V2s', and his knowledge of their spectacular running on trains like the Yorkshire Pullman, Bulleid was convinced that 6 foot 2 inch coupled wheels would be large enough, and to ensure continuity of work on the project in wartime it could be described officially as a mixed traffic engine that would be invaluable in hauling gargantuan loads of freight. The problem of weight reduction was constantly with him, but he solved it with a use of electric welding that was unprecedented in British locomotive construction. In particular he designed the first British all-welded boiler and thereby saved a notable amount of weight by avoiding the use of rivets and the extra metal used in lap joints.

In the constructional work put into the new engines, which were, of course, of the 'Pacific' type, Bulleid revealed himself as a master engineering designer, far in advance of most of his contemporaries in the techniques he used, and in the care, skill and humanity with which he carried his workforce with him. The same, perhaps, could not be said of his regard for his technical assistants, who were often kicked around, to some extent! The boilers for 10 locomotives were built by the North British Locomotive Company. In placing the contract, care

The final arrangement of the modified and very successful 'Lord Nelson' Class 4-6-0, shown here by No 851, Sir Francis Drake, *on a wartime Bournemouth express near Hook* (M.W. Earley).

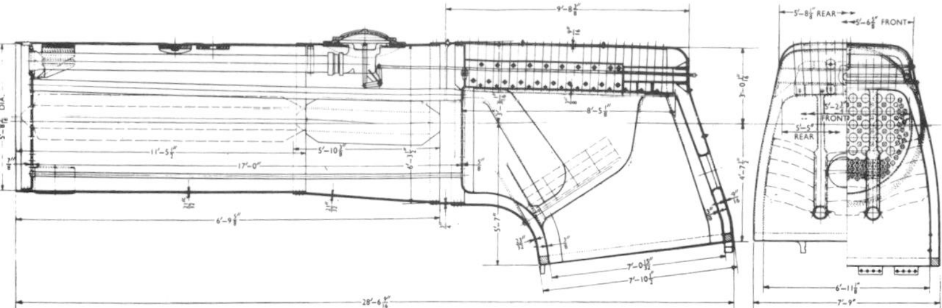

Left *Boiler and firebox of SR 'Merchant Navy' Class 4-6-2 showing thermic siphons in firebox* (British Railways).

had to be taken to convince the Ministry of Supply that they were urgently needed for handling the wartime traffic on the Southern, and although this signified Government approval at a critical time in the war, constructional work at Eastleigh was cloaked in some secrecy, not from any strategic reasons but to be able to spring a public relations surprise when the mighty new 'war weapon' took the road. The boiler, as shown in the accompanying drawing, was an appropriately large one, designed for free steaming on inferior fuel. The firebox contained two thermic syphons, but Bulleid was narrowly beaten by his old chief in being the first to use them on a British locomotive. Gresley had used one on one of his new 'V4' 2-6-2 engines, completed at Doncaster earlier in 1941.

Having designed what eventually proved to be a magnificent boiler and firebox, once jokingly described as being so good that it would steam on garden refuse(!) Bulleid then went a long way towards ruining the whole engine with an unbelievably complicated collection of innovations at the front end. The cylinder, piston valve and smokebox design was admirable, and altogether conducive to a very fast, and free running locomotive. The cross-sectional drawing herewith shows the very large piston valves and the short direct steam passages, while the 5-nozzle multiple jet blastpipe, of the type that had proved so successful in the re-draughting of Maunsell's 'Lord Nelson' Class 4-6-0s, was a further guarantee of free steaming with no risk of an impeded exhaust. To minimise weight and avoid the need for making more than the very minimum of patterns, the majority of the parts were welded steel fabrications, including the triple arrangement of the ashpans. So far as other features of the front-end were concerned, it is fitting that Bulleid should give his own explanation, as in the paper presented to the Institution of Mechanical Engineers in December 1945.

'As to lubrication,' he said, 'it was felt that the steam locomotive had reached a stage of development in which it was desirable to enclose as much of the motion as possible, so that continuous flood lubrication could be adopted. The parts are less accessible if enclosed, but if the results desired, namely, no attention between general repairs, reduced wear, and freedom from heating, were achieved, this would not matter.

'The problem is complicated by the relative movement of the frame to the crank axle and especially so in the case of an engine with an inside crank axle. In the engine in question, not only was it decided to enclose the three sets of valve motion but also the middle connecting rod, crosshead, slide bar and crankpin. Moreover the three sets of valve gear had to be located between the frames. This meant that the inside piston rod and the three valve guides had to be taken through the leading end of the casing.

Below *Southern: first steps towards improving the 'Lord Nelson' 4-6-0s—No 857,* Lord Howe, *rebuilt with large diameter round-topped boiler in the Gresley style* (the late W.J. Reynolds).

Right *Detail of the unusual form of piston valve on 'Merchant Navy' Class 4-6-2.*

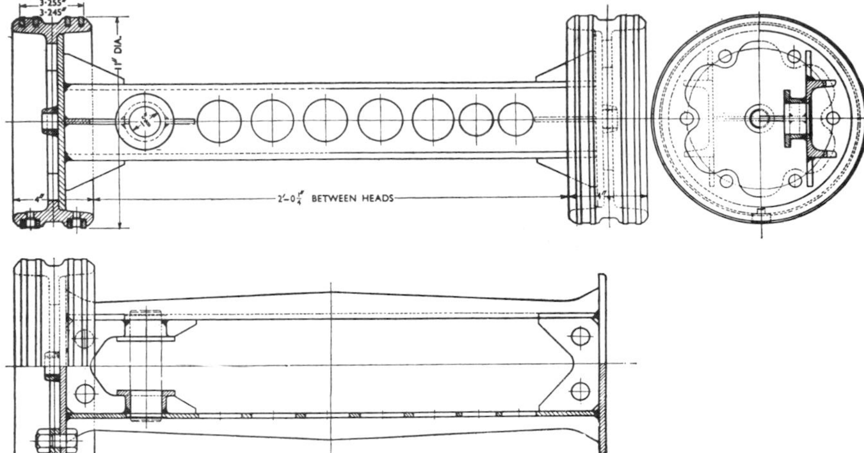

'Flood lubrication was adopted as being simpler when oscillatory movements are involved. Two reversible gear pumps of normal design (chain-driven from the valve crankshaft) draw oil from the sump and force it through distributing pipes from which it is discharged over the moving parts.

'As the middle big-ends tend to throw oil off during the upper half-revolution, it was fitted with a tundish which collects the oil during the lower half-revolution and retains it during the upper. The forked type of big-end is used, as with this design the brasses are well supported and the oil ways are more conveniently arranged. The brass back, too, forms a useful oil holder.

'The method adopted to prevent oil escaping when the crank axle passes through the casing is shown in Fig 6 [an accompanying line drawing]. At first, trouble occurred due to the pumps becoming choked with fluff from cleaning cloths, and so on. Leakage of oil from the sump was also considerable at first, but this loss has been reduced, and the consumption is now reasonable. The special oil for the enclosed system is of the non-emulsifying mineral type, with corrosion and oxidation inhibitors.

'The special conditions were such that no existing valve motion could be accommodated satisfactorily in the very restricted space available. Moreover, it was desirable to keep down the unsprung weight of the driving crank axle; then, too, should it be necessary to remove the driving axle, as little of the sump as possible should be disturbed.

'The new valve gear used on these engines was therefore invented, each piston valve being operated by an independent set of motion. The three sets of gear are operated by a three-throw secondary crankshaft. Each throw of this secondary crankshaft oscillates its quadrant link by a vertical connecting rod pinned to an arm extended backwards from the link; at the same time, it reciprocates the foot of the combination lever by a horizontal link pinned to the big end of the vertical connecting rod. The quadrant link operates the upper end of the combination lever in the usual manner.

Below *Multiple jet blastpipes on earlier Southern locomotives: ex-LSWR 'N15' Class 4-6-0, No 755,* The Red Knight, *(assimilated to 'King Arthur' Class) in wartime plain black livery* (British Railways).

RADLEY
930
SOUTHERN

35022

Opposite page, top to bottom

A 'Schools' Class 3-cylinder 4-4-0, No 930, Radley, *fitted with multiple jet blastpipe and large chimney* (British Railways).

One of the earliest air-smoothed 'Pacifics' of the 'Merchant Navy' Class, with original numbering—21C8—and named Orient Line, *running at 72 mph near Hook with an up West of England express (the author is on the footplate)* (M.W. Earley).

Southern Region: a 'Merchant Navy' Class 4-6-2, No 35022, Holland America Line, *just after nationalisation* (British Railways).

Bulleid 'Pacific' No 21C15, Rotterdam Lloyd, *on a popular post-war express, the 'Bournemouth Belle'* (M.W. Earley).

This page, top to bottom

The inward bound 'Night Ferry' train, with French-type sleeping car, passing Shorncliffe, hauled by 'Battle of Britain' Class 'Pacific', No 34074, then unnamed (Reverend A.C. Cawston).

A striking view of a 'Battle of Britain' 4-6-2, on an up Continental boat express among the white cliffs of the Folkestone Warren. The engine carries the original type of numbering '21C157' but the tender is lettered 'British Railways'. The engine is named Biggin Hill (Reverend A.C. Cawston).

One of the 'West Country' series of smaller Bulleid 'Pacifics' on a Channel Islands boat train from Weymouth, at Worting Junction, near Basingstoke—engine No 34020, Seaton (Derek Cross).

One of the smaller Bulleid 'Pacifics', No 34086, 219 Squadron *('Battle of Britain' Class) on the outward bound 'Golden Arrow' Continental express, near Hildenborough* (Derek Cross).

'The combined motion is conveyed, through a plunger working in a guide, by the valve rods to the valve-operating rocker shaft. Provision has been made for the frame to rise 2 inches, and fall 1½ inches relative to the crank axle and for this axle to move sideways as much as a ¼ inch from its mid-position. By locating a lay shaft 4 feet from the crank shaft centre, the maximum rise of the frame meant a lengthening of the hypotenuse by 0.04 inch, a negligible amount in a chain 11.8 feet long, consisting of 118 links. The lay shaft in turn drives the 3-throw crankshaft by a second chain. As the chain wheels are equal in diameter, the three-throw crankshaft is driven truly in phase with the crank axle.

'The power required to overcome the frictional resistance of 11-inches, piston valve not under steam pressure and cold, was found experimentally to be 3 hp at 300 rpm. As there was no data on the behaviour of chains under locomotive conditions nor on the maximum load the chain might have to transmit, nor on the affect of a snatch, a chain 2 inches wide was fitted. This chain will transmit 75 hp at a chain speed of 130 feet per minute.

'The weight of the toothed wheel secured to the axle is 125 lb, and half the weight of the chain is 30 lb, a total of 155 lb. Three eccentrics plus the portion of the eccentric rods carried by the axle would have weighed 1,281 lb, so the new drive reduces the unsprung axle weight by 1,126 lb.

'A point that was considered was the effect of slackness in the chain. Assuming a sag of as much as 3 inches, the design of the rocker chain is such that most of the sag under load is absorbed by the rise of the rockers up the teeth. Only the small remainder affects the valve events, which will be delayed. This can be corrected by altering the cut-off. The chain drive has behaved well, and no chains have broken to date.' The basic dimensions of these remarkable locomotives were:

Cylinders (3)	
Diameter (inches)	18
Stroke (inches)	24
Valve gear, (3 sets)	
Bulleid type	
Piston valve diameter (inches)	11
Steam lap (inches)	1⅝
Valve travel (inches)	6¼
Coupled wheel diameter (feet/inches)	6 2
Boiler pressure (psi)	280
Heating surfaces (square feet)	
Small tubes	1,241.6
Superheater flues	934.3
Firebox	275.0 (including syphons)
Total evaporative	2,450.9
Superheater	
Number of elements	40
Heating surface	822
Total heating surface (square feet)	3,272.9
Grate area (square feet)	48.5
Tractive effort (lb)	37,500
Total engine weight (tons)	94.75
Adhesion weight (tons)	63

An interesting feature that no doubt had the whole-hearted approval of the Civil Engineer, was that no part of the reciprocating weight was balanced. The

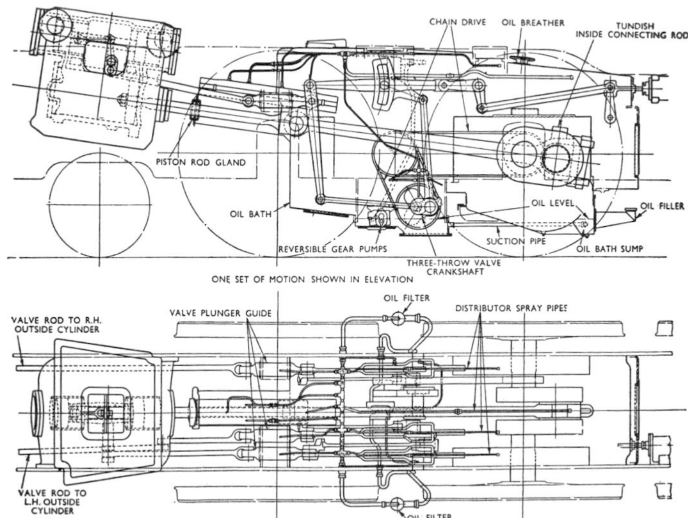

Left *'Merchant Navy' Class 4-6-2: lay-out of valve gear, oil bath and inside cylinder* (British Railways).

Right *Southern Railway: finalised design of multiple jet blastpipe and large chimney for 'Lord Nelson' Class locomotives* (British Railways).

Far right *Smokebox and inside-cylinder valve chest of 'Merchant Navy' 4-6-2* (British Railways).

Right *High level view of one of the Bulleid 'Q1' Class Austerity 0-6-0s showing its unusual construction, on a coal train near Selling, Kent* (the late Ian S. Pearsall).

Below *The 'Night Ferry' with no fewer than seven of the very heavy French-type sleeping cars and seven other vehicles which sometimes needed double-heading, as seen here with an 'L1' 4-4-0 No 31753 piloting a 'Battle of Britain' 'Pacific'* (Derek Cross).

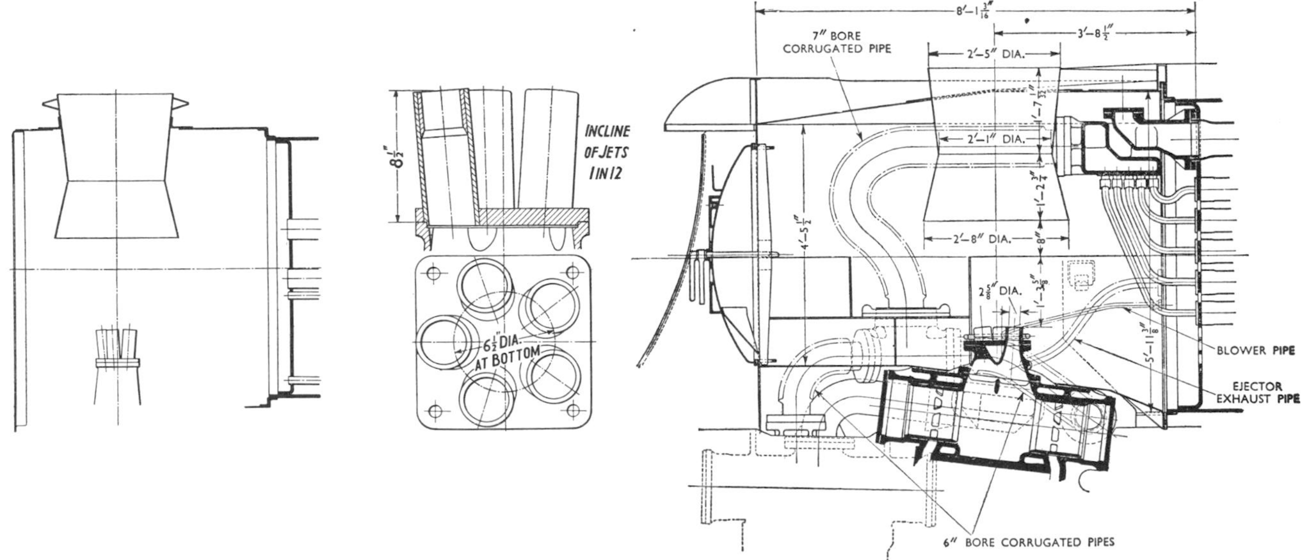

Left *In the post-war years, despite the introduction of the 'Pacifics', older engines were still called on for very heavy work. One of the Urie 'Arthurs', dating from 1922, No 747,* Elaine, *on a 16-coach Bournemouth express in 1945 (the author is on the footplate)* (M.W. Earley).

Below left *This photograph of Bulleid 'Pacific' No 34073,* 249 Squadron, *on a Kent Coast express, shows clearly the large-diameter column of exhaust steam issuing from the multiple jet blastpipe and its associated large chimney* (Reverend A.C. Cawston).

Opposite page, top to bottom

One of the multiple-jet 'Schools', No 30919, Harrow, *on a Ramsgate–Victoria express near St Mary Cray Junction* (Derek Cross).

4-6-0, locomotive No 30851, Sir Francis Drake, *showing the final BR form of the 'Lord Nelson' Class* (British Railways).

Hard pulling on the Kent Coast line: an express from Ramsgate, climbing the Sole Street bank, hauled by a multiple jet 'Schools' 4-4-0, No 30938, St Olaves (Derek Cross).

cylinders were small for so large an engine with an exceptionally short stroke of 24 inches. Despite the absence of any reciprocating balance, in general the engines rode well.

As if to emphasise that the engines were new in every respect, Bulleid devised a new system of numbering for them, somewhat on the continental style, 21C, instead of the usual 2C1 for a Pacific, and the first engine to be steamed, in February 1941 was 21C-1. True to his original ideas on capacity, the engine was set to haul a trial train of 20 coaches from Eastleigh to Bournemouth and back on February 22. But her first bow to the public in general, and her official naming, came on March 10 1941 when Lieutenant Colonel J.T.C. Moore-Brabazon (later Lord Brabazon of Tara) named her *Channel Packet*, and the 'Merchant Navy' Class was duly launched. Lieutenant Colonel Moore-Brabazon was then Minister of Transport and, in all the attendant publicity given to the occasion, it was emphasised that the engines were intended for passenger and heavy goods services.

As might have been expected with so revolutionary a design of valve gear, there were many teething troubles, and until the summer of 1942 the 10 engines of the class were almost entirely employed in freight service. Bulleid himself seems to have been completely unabashed, and indeed delighted to diagnose and solve successive problems as they arose. When the locomotives began to take up passenger working, principally between Waterloo and Exeter, advantage was taken of their increased haulage capacity to load some of the few express trains regularly to 16 or 17 coaches, but of course running at speeds far below the very exacting levels Bulleid had set himself at the start. Nevertheless the Southern main line had suffered less than most from the incessant heavy pounding of wartime, in extenuated conditions of maintenance, and drivers were inclined to turn the blind eye to the official maximum speed limit of 75 mph. In logs published in *The Railway Magazine* occasional spurts to nearly 90 mph were to be noted.

At their best the 'Merchant Navy' Class loco-

478

30851

motives were brilliant, though admittedly never showing much likelihood of reaching the 600-ton 70 mph average speed norm. In their regular workings engines were changed at Salisbury, giving round trips of 168 miles to and from Waterloo, or 176 to and from Exeter. When more of the class were available, they worked between Waterloo and Bournemouth. That they were heavy coal burners became apparent at an early stage in their history. When Bulleid was questioned on this he said he was glad, because it showed they were doing a lot of hard work. The tenders were of relatively small capacity, however, and carried no more than 5 tons of coal. One of their greatest disadvantages, particularly in bad weather, was their liability to slipping, which often resulted in very slow starts, or poor ascents of severe gradients. As mileage since overhaul increased, and wear developed in the various component parts of the valve gear, the timing would go adrift and give poor performance, and a high-mileage run-down 'Merchant Navy' could be a rather fearsome locomotive to ride.

In the discussion at the Institution of Mechanical Engineers on Bulleid's paper, one speaker said he was glad to see that a steam reverser had been fitted. I do not think many of the drivers who had to handle them would agree with him. Probably Bulleid's familiarity with the hand-operated screw reversers on the Gresley locomotives made him determined to give the Southern men something easier to handle. On certain older engines the Southern had the Stirling type of steam reverser, which had a good dead-beat action; but something new was devised for the 'Merchant Navy' Class, and it turned out to be the most erratic fiddling thing imaginable. Most drivers with whom I rode on the footplate made a single adjustment soon after starting, and then left it alone for the rest of the journey, making all adjustments for variations of power entirely on the regulator.

To the great disappointment of the theorists who believed that the only way to drive a modern locomotive was with a fully opened regulator and the shortest possible cut-off, such methods were impracticable on the 'Merchant Navy' Class. One could rarely be sure what the actual cut-off was, but anything shorter than about 25 per cent set up severe vibration. Much of the hardest and fastest work with those engines was with little more than 100 lb per square inch pressure in the steam chests. As will be told later, in reference to the stationary plant trials of one of these engines at Rugby, this method of working seemed to have little effect on the overall efficiency. For the record, the fine names given to the first 20 of the 'Merchant Navy' Class were as follows:

Engine no	Name	Date built
21C-1	*Channel Packet*	1941
21C-2	*Union Castle*	1941
21C-3	*Royal Mail*	1941
21C-4	*Cunard White Star*	1941
21C-5	*Canadian Pacific*	1941
21C-6	*Peninsular and Oriental SN Co*	1941
21C-7	*Aberdeen Commonwealth*	1942
21C-8	*Orient Line*	1942
21C-9	*Shaw Savill*	1942
21C-10	*Blue Star*	1942
21C-11	*General Steam Navigation*	1944
21C-12	*United States Lines*	1944
21C-13	*Blue Funnel*	1945
21C-14	*Nederland Line*	1945
21C-15	*Rotterdam Lloyd*	1945
21C-16	*Elders Fyffes*	1945
21C-17	*Belgian Marine*	1945
21C-18	*British India Line*	1945
21C-19	*French Line CGT*	1945
21C-20	*Bibby Line*	1945

Diagram of 'Q1' 'Austerity' 0-6-0 goods engine (British Railways).

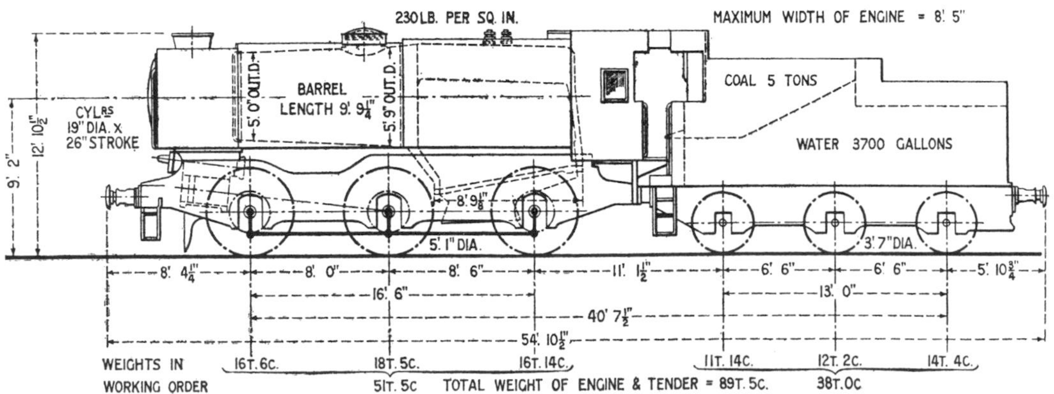

One of the final batch of 'West Country' 'Pacifics', No 34100, Appledore, *on an outward bound Continental boat train just east of Tonbridge* (Derek Cross).

Construction of 40 0-6-0 tender engines was authorised by the Government in 1941. The Civil Engineer advised Bulleid that he could accept a locomotive not exceeding 54 tons in all-up weight with a route availability covering 93 per cent of the entire system, and having a tender weight not exceeding 39½ tons. The Maunsell 'Q' Class built in 1938 would have met the case, but Bulleid felt that he could build a much more powerful and generally useful locomotive by reconsidering the whole project from first principles. Like Churchward on the Great Western, some 40 years earlier, he felt that where weight was limited the first consideration was the boiler. In a talk to the enginemen at Feltham in 1942 he said: 'The locomotive is a coal-burning machine, and given reasonable design and an average fireman it may be said that the work done depends on the coal consumed. In other words, the boiler should be the largest that can be fitted so that the engine can do as much work as possible. The evaporative capacity of a boiler is dependent on the grate area and the firebox heating surface and volume. A large volume is needed to ensure that the gases have time to burn, as the flame is extinguished as soon as it enters the tubes. A large heating surface is necessary to ensure that the maximum heat is transferred to the water. The largest firebox, as regards width at the top and allowing proper vision from the cab, which we can fit inside the Southern loading gauge is that of the 'Lord Nelson' Class. I therefore copied this firebox design in shortened form with a grate area of 27 square feet. This meant that I could save time and material by using the same press blocks to make the plates.'

Preliminary design of the boiler showed that it would weigh 21¼ tons, thus leaving 32¾ tons for the rest of the locomotive. The wheels were of the lightweight type used on the 'Merchant Navy' Class; the frame, robust in itself, was lightened wherever possible by welded joints and fabricated members instead of castings while, as Bulleid himself said, the running plate and wheel splashers were survivors of earlier practice and obstruct access to an engine with inside cylinders. The cab was fabricated from thin sheet, and everything made easy of access for the driver and fireman. Never, it was said, had such an austere and undressed engine previously taken the road in Great Britain and, in the spirit of the hour, one sensed that Bulleid had taken some impish delight in sending cold shivers down the spines of the traditionalists. The 'Q1' had the same sized cylinders and wheel diameter as Maunsell's 'Q' Class but, with a higher boiler pressure of 230 against 200 lb per square inch, and a much larger firebox, it was a much more powerful locomotive, beyond the tractive effort superiority of 30,000 against 26,157 lb.

The stark ugliness of the 'Q1' led to a good deal of criticism from those who had fixed ideas as to what a British locomotive should look like. One commentator, who was shown a photograph, was frankly disbelieving, and said: 'Has such a horror really been built?' But the 'Q1s', 40 strong, did excellent work, and in this present age, when sentiments towards the appearance of locomotives have changed so radically as to bring admiration as fervent as that lavished on the Great Western 'Kings' to their diesel-hydraulic successors, one of the 'Q1s' has been preserved and is in service on the Bluebell Railway.

The end of the war brought the introduction of the smaller version of the 'Merchant Navy' Class, the 'West Country'—smaller all round, with a maximum axle load of 18¾ tons, against 21; cylinders 16¾ inches diameter against 18 inches and a proportionately smaller boiler and firebox. The tractive effort was 31,000 lb, and it was intended that these smaller engines would operate on secondary lines where the 'Merchant Navy' Class was precluded by weight. It proved capable of just as exceptionally fine performance as the larger

'Pacifics' and, it must be added, equally subject to the running difficulties experienced when mileage began to mount up. But what is perhaps most extraordinary, in retrospect, is the vast investment made in these smaller engines. It seemed as though the avowed policy of the Southern Railway to extend its electrified network was being cast aside, and available money for capital investment expended on steam. It was not as though the building of many more Bulleid 'Pacifics' in 1945 and after was accompanied by the large scale scrapping of older engines in the medium power category, as the LMS had done in the 1930s.

Between June 1945 and October 1947, no fewer than 70 of the smaller 'Pacifics' were built while, after nationalisation in January 1948, another 40 were added, together with 10 more of the larger 'Merchant Navy' Class. By May 1950 the Southern Railway had 150 'Pacifics' on the road, not far short of the LNER total, and nearly three times as many as the LMS! At that time steam operation remained on the Waterloo–Exeter route, and the various extensions in Devon and Cornwall; from Waterloo to Bournemouth and Weymouth, and the boat train route to Dover, and the North Kent line to Ramsgate which latter was already electrified as far as Chatham. The route mileage, including the various alternative ways to Dover, used by relief trains at peak times, was about 615 and of this the 104 miles west of Exeter, to Plymouth and to Ilfracombe was very lightly used. How the Board of the Southern Railway in its last years was persuaded to authorise such a vast programme of steam locomotive building is indeed a mystery. So far as the running department was concerned it would seem there were times when they were at their wits' end to know how to use so many 'Pacifics', and one frequently saw these hauling the lightest and slowest of local trains.

This is not to denigrate either the design or the performances capabilities of these smaller Bulleid 'Pacifics'. They were capable of an astonishing output of power, as will be shown in a later chapter dealing with the Interchange Trials organised by the Railway Executive in the first months after nationalisation. It is true they could be fiddling and frustrating engines if one attempted to drive them in anything approaching copy-book style; but, on the other hand, they were easy on the fireman's side, and steamed very freely. In my own footplate experience of them, which extended from Dover through to Ilfracombe in the west, on both 'West Country' and 'Merchant Navy' Classes, I found that the worst black marks I had to chalk up against them were for slipping.

I have vivid memories of a 'Merchant Navy' trying to get the Night Ferry train under way from

Above *Eight coaches was the maximum load to be taken single-handed over the tremendous gradients of the Somerset and Dorset Line. Here a Bulleid is piloted by an ex-SDJR 2-8-0* (Ivo Peters).

Left *'West Country' 'Pacifics' on the Somerset and Dorset Line: No 34040,* Crewkerne, *approaching Midsomer Norton in zero degrees Centigrade weather* (Ivo Peters).

the start at Dover Marine. The driver was a most capable man, but as carefully as he 'pumped' the regulator, it seemed that nothing would stop the engine slipping, and it was not until we got inside Shakespeare's Cliff Tunnel that the engine found her feet. I have a note that the first three-quarters of a mile from the start took 6½ minutes. No driver with whom I travelled, either on a 'Merchant Navy' or a 'West Country' attempted to run with anything like a full regulator opening. Even when working quite hard the steam chest pressures were around 120 to 140 lb per square inch, while the boiler pressure see-sawed up and down between 200 and the full 280 lb per square inch.

Neither did any driver attempt to adjust the power output by intermediate adjustment of the steam reverser. It was usually set at a point indicated on the scale at about 25 per cent cut-off; but I always remember the words of an old locomotive man whose life's work and richly varied experience belonged to many generations before the Bulleid 'Pacifics'. Some young friends were talking to him about the cut-offs used in working various types, and he smiled, and shook his head, saying: 'Don't believe that thing [the pointer on the reverser scale] it's the biggest liar on the engine.' I thought of this one evening when I was riding a 'West Country' from Cannon Street down to Folkestone. It was a lively, though not exactly rough rider, and I waited until we were through the most intense parts of the suburban area before I crossed over to the left-hand side of the cab to note the setting of the reverser. Not long after the actual trip, in an article describing it, I wrote: 'The steam reverser was not of very great help in trying to assess the working, for after the driver's adjustment immediately on the east side of London Bridge, the pointer was cheerfully indicating mid-gear; and so it remained all the way up to Knockholt!' Actually, in deference to my Southern hosts, I somewhat whitewashed the situation. The pointer showed that the reverser was some little way into *backward gear*!

No one took any notice of what the gear showed on a Bulleid 'Pacific'; one just fiddled about until the engine *felt* right, set it, and left it alone for the rest of the trip. The most serious trouble that occurred with these extraordinarily willing engines was with the totally enclosed valve motion, and worse still with the inside connecting rod and its somewhat sensitive big-end. There was often leakage from the oil bath, which aggravated the natural tendency of these engines to slip, and Bulleid's own remedy for dealing with irregularities in the valve timing by adjusting the cut-off was nullified by the awkwardness in adjusting the reverser anyway. But some of the worst failures came from a collapse of the inside big-end. Totally enclosed one could not hear it when it was knocking badly, nor smell it when it was heating, and as one driver put it to me once: '. . . the first thing you know anything's wrong is when the big-end packs up, and the conn rod punches a hole in the bottom of the oil bath!' It was recurrent troubles of this kind that led British Railways later to rebuild the engines with an orthodox type of valve gear.

Troubles apart, however, Bulleid will forever be remembered as the man who, by his novel and imaginative engine designing, pulled the Southern Railway out of what might have become a progressively worsening mediocrity in steam, despite the brilliance of the 'Schools' Class 4-4-0s. He put the locomotive department once more on the crest of a wave, so that when the time came for the British Railways Interchange Trials, the Southern men, with Bulleid 'Pacifics', set out with over-brimming confidence, ready to 'knock spots' off all rivals. And so far as actual running was concerned they very nearly did! Of course Bulleid's involvement with the Southern was by no means finished when the 'West County' 'Pacifics' took the road, and there is much to be told in a future chapter.

Bulleid 'Pacifics' in the West Country: engine No 34033, Chard, *running through Seaton Junction at full speed with an Ilfracombe–London express* (Derek Cross).

10. LMS: wartime pointers to the future

As the moment of the actual declaration of war approached, at the first week-end in September 1939, events moved fast among the senior officers of the LMS locomotive department. R.A. Riddles, then Mechanical and Electrical Engineer, Scotland, was seconded to the Ministry of Supply, as Director of Transportation Equipment. R.C. Bond, whose work as Superintending Engineer of the joint LMS-LNER testing station at Rugby, would be suspended forthwith, was sent to Glasgow to replace Riddles, with the title of Acting Mechanical and Electrical Engineer, Scotland. At that critical moment C.E. Fairburn was in charge of the CME's department because Stanier was in mid-Atlantic returning as quickly as the *Queen Mary* could bring him from his abortive visit to New York, to read a paper on 'Lightweight Rolling Stock' to the summer meeting of the Institution of Mechanical Engineers, which was cancelled. Steam locomotive work on the LMS fell almost entirely into the hands of H.G. Ivatt, Principal Assistant for Locomotives, because Stanier himself became quickly involved with special wartime duties of high national importance.

Riddles' appointment, of course, included the provision of locomotives for work behind what was at first expected to be the main battle line of the British Expeditionary Force in Northern France, and it was no surprise to learn that the Stanier '8F' 2-8-0 had been chosen to fulfil the role so stoutly played by the Great Central Robinson 2-8-0 (LNER Class '04) in the First World War. Orders were placed for 240 of the LMS '8F', with various modifications to suit Continental operating conditions; but although the contractors built the first of them in the record time of five months from receipt of order, it was ironic, though in the long run fortunate, that they were not ready before the Nazi onslaught that eventually led to Dunkirk. Otherwise they would undoubtedly have been lost. In the event none of them left British shores until much later in the war. The changes from the standard LMS design were interesting, though some, incorporated no doubt at French request, seemed rather questionable elaborations on locomotives intended for the rough and tumble conditions in the proximity of a battle-front. In the initial stages of the war, however, Anglo-French strategy was based on the *defence* of the Maginot Line, in presumably fairly static conditions! The inclusion of the Flaman type self-recording speed indicators, and brushes for working in conjunction with the French automatic train control apparatus, seemed of doubtful necessity.

The more practical changes in detail design involved the substitution of materials in more ready supply for the high tensile alloy steels used in some of the major components. For example, ordinary mild steel was used for the main frames, instead of the high tensile steel in the LMS locomotives. This necessitated an increase in thickness from 1 inch to $1\frac{1}{16}$ inch. On the LMS locomotives the coupling and connecting rods were of manganese molybdenum steel, and for these mild steel was substituted. To offset the increase in weight that would have resulted from this change the connecting rods were shortened by 5 inches and the piston rods lengthened by the same amount. In the motion work, solid pins and plain bushes replaced the needle roller bearings used on the standard LMS locomotives. Steam brakes were fitted for the engine and tender, and as Continental stock was expected to be hauled, Westinghouse brake equipment for the trains. The amount by which the overall weight of the locomotive was increased by use of thicker frames and other modifications was not stated at the time of completion of the first engine. It was numbered 300 in the LMS style on the smokebox door, and lettered 'WD'.

The streamlined 'Pacific' No 6244, King George VI, *built at Crewe 1940, one of the last engines to be painted LMS red before the adoption of austerity black* (British Railways).

The LMS '8F' as adapted for overseas service in 1940, showing air compressor and other fittings for the Westinghouse brake (North British Locomotive Company).

For service at home, construction of new locomotives, entirely of existing designs, was at first very much slowed down by the switching of so much of the works capacity at Crewe, Derby, Horwich and elsewhere on to war production. In 1940 Derby turned out no more than one new 2-6-4 tank, and eight '4F' 0-6-0s, while Crewe produced just five new streamlined 'Pacifics'. The year 1941 saw nine new 2-6-4 tanks, and two '4F' 0-6-0s from Derby, with 14 '8F' 2-8-0s from Crewe. 1942 was much the same; eight 2-6-4 tanks from Derby and 18 2-8-0s from Crewe. R.C. Bond was brought down from Glasgow to take on the job of Works Superintendent at Crewe in May 1941. The output target with which he was presented was: 1) not less than 40 locomotive repairs per week; 2) four Mark V Cruiser Tanks per week; and 3) new locomotives at three per fortnight, in that order or priority. Actually, as previously mentioned, Crewe built only 14 new locomotives in the whole of the year 1941. In the meantime the scrapping of old engines had been reduced to an almost minimal extent, and one old type, the maintenance of which was considered to be of major importance for the wartime traffic was the ex-London and North Western 'G1' Class heavy 0-8-0 freighter. In the early autumn of 1942 tank construction was moved away from Crewe, and emphasis restored to locomotives, so that in 1943 the output from the works began to look more like its normal self. It was the same at Derby.

It had been in 1935 that a taper boiler had been designed for the complete renewal of the ill-fated super-high pressure 4-6-0 *Fury*, to produce a new engine of 'Royal Scot' capacity in No 6170, *British Legion*. After some slight alterations to the original draughting this proved a very successful engine, setting standards of performance on London–Manchester expresses up to the very highest set by the original 'Royal Scots'. The new boiler was very much in the Great Western tradition brought to the LMS by Sir William Stanier; in addition to the tapered barrel it had a circular, drumhead type of smokebox resting on a saddle casting that incorporated the inside cylinder and its associated valve chest. This was being found superior to the Derby type of built-up smokebox, in direct comparison between the Stanier '5X' Jubilee Class 3-cylinder 4-6-0s and their Derby counterparts of the 'Baby Scot' Class. In 1942, when there was time to consider passenger locomotive development, and the boilers of the 'Royal Scot' were nearing the time for renewal, it was natural to think of rebuildings on the lines of the *British Legion*.

The weight of this engine, however, and that of the original 'Royal Scots' precluded their use on the

Stanier '8F' standard 2-8-0 built to War Department order by Beyer, Peacock & Co, in 1940, and originally numbered 400. It was later taken into LMS stock, and lent to the Great Western Railway for wartime freight service (British Railways).

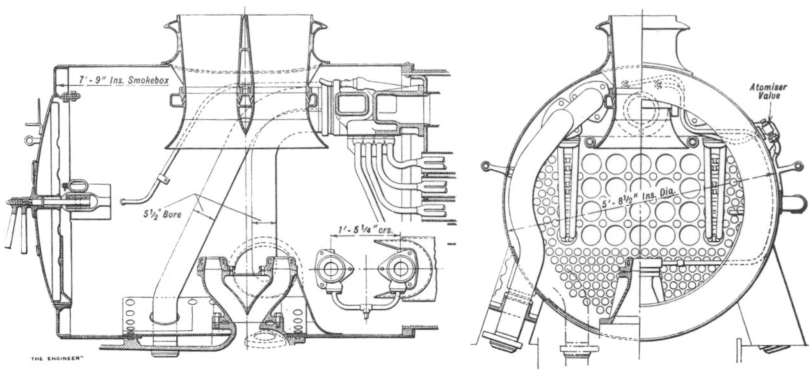

Left *LMSR: section of smokebox, showing twin-orifice blastpipe and double chimney on converted 'Royal Scot' Class 4-6-0* (British Railways).

Below *A converted 'Scot', No 6133,* The Green Howards, *in the post-war livery* (British Railways).

Midland Division and since, with the availability of more 'Pacifics', some could be spared from the Western Division, some re-thinking around the 'British Legion' design was undertaken to reduce weight. A new boiler of 'Royal Scot' capacity, but shorter in the barrel, was designed so that it could be used as a replacement, not only for 'Royal Scots' but for the Jubilee Class '5X' 4-6-0s and for the 'Baby Scots'. This was designated type '2A', and its dimensions as compared to that on *British Legion* were as follows:

New standard taper boilers

Type	**On engine 6170**	**2A**
Heating surfaces, tubes		
Small (number)	180	198
Small outside diameter (inches)	1⅞	1¾
Flues (number)	28	28
Flues outside diameter (inches)	5⅛	5⅛
Heating surfaces (square feet)		
Tubes	1,793	1,667
Firebox	195	195
Superheater	348	348
Total	2,336	2,210
Distance between tube plates (feet/inches)	14 3	13 0
Grate area	31.25	31.25

The '2A' boiler was first fitted to two 'Jubilee' Class '5X' 4-6-0s—No 5735 *Comet* and 5736 *Phoenix*—and was accomapnied by a twin-orifice blastpipe and double-chimney. The '5X' Class engines had 17 inch diameter cylinders, and these were not changed, although the nominal tractive effort was increased by the use of a boiler pressure of 250 lb per square inch, against the previous 225. The increase was from 26,610 to 29,590 lb. The larger boiler increased the total weight of the locomotive from 79.55 to 82 tons, and this was acceptable for use on the main lines of the Midland Division. The rebuilt engines proved very successful, and design work went ahead for rebuilding the 'Royal Scots' with the same type of boiler.

While in the case of the two '5X' 4-6-0s it had been simply a case of putting a larger boiler on to an existing locomotive, with the 'Royal Scots' the process of rebuilding was such as to cover all essential features. They had new frames, new cylinders and new bogies, in addition to the '2A' boiler. They may have been sufficient non-significant bits and pieces such as the cabs, name and smokebox number plates to satisfy the accountants that it *was* a rebuild, but from the basic engineering viewpoint the so-called 'Converted Scots' were absolutely new engines. Nine of them were replaced in 1943, and because of this the original engines will be reckoned as among the shortest lived of express passenger engines of the old companies, with the first of them withdrawn after no more than 16 years. Towards the end it was reported that they showed a tendency to crack their frames, which rather surprised the CME's department. The 'Jubilees' which had an almost identical design of frame were largely immune from this trouble, though of course their normal duties did not involve anything like such hard pounding as was frequently meted out to the 'Royal Scots'.

There is no doubt that a great deal of care and hard work was put into the redesign of these engines. Stanier himself had been seconded to the Ministry of Production in 1942, for full time duties as one of a team of scientific advisers, and management of the CME's department rested upon his deputy C.E. Fairburn. As mentioned in an earlier chapter of this book, however, Fairburn was an electrical engineer and left all matters concerning steam locomotives to Ivatt, while in design E.S. Cox was playing an increasingly important part. The first of the 'Scots' to be renewed was No 6103, *Royal Scots Fusilier*, and the official photograph showed it turned out in dull unlined black, though curiously enough with the smokebox smartly polished. I was interested that No 6103 should have been the first to be renewed because it was with this engine in its original condition that I had one of the hardest runs I ever experienced with one of them; when relentless pounding and expert firing enabled the sharp timing of the southbound 'Midday Scot' to be more than kept over the mountain section between Carlisle and Lancaster on a day of exceptionally severe storms and gale force side winds.

Three of the new engines, the pioneer 6103, and Nos 6108 and 6109 were sent at once to Leeds (Whitehall Junction shed) to join the reboilered 'Jubilees', 5735 and 5736. Leeds had a few double-home turns to and from Glasgow St Enoch, and while the timings on the Midland part of the line had been much decelerated from pre-war levels, those in Scotland were still surprisingly brisk, and needless to say the loads were very heavy. The new engines were a welcome addition to the stock and soon began to show off their paces. Although nothing in the way of full dress trials could be conducted in wartime, observers from the CME's department were out and about, and in 1944 it was

Below *Another historic survivor of the Stanier '8F' Class, now in service on the Severn Valley Railway, was Engine No 8233, originally WD307, built by the North British Locomotive Company in 1940* (courtesy of Severn Valley Railways).

Bottom *The first post-war LMS express locomotive livery (lined black with maroon edging), on engine No 6134,* The Cheshire Regiment *('Royal Scot' Class)* (British Railways).

M 4748
M
4748
BRITISH
RAILWAYS

44756
44756
BRITISH
RAILWAYS

4767
L M S

44686

Opposite page, top to bottom

Variations on the standard 'Black Five' 4-6-0: a) *roller bearings throughout, Caprotti valve gear—engine No 4748 (introduced in 1948);* b) *roller bearings throughout, Caprotti valve gear, twin orifice blastpipe, double chimney—engine No 44756 (introduced in 1948);* c) *roller bearings, Stephenson link motion twin-orifice blastpipe, double chimney—engine No 4767 (introduced in 1948);* and d) *modified version of Caprotti valve gear, with outside drive and high raised running plate—engine No 44686 (introduced in 1951)* (all British Railways).

This page, top to bottom

First of the 'Royal Scots' to be renewed with taperboiler, new cylinders and front end—No 6103, Royal Scots Fusilier, *rebuilt at Crewe in 1943* (British Railways).

The record-breaker of 1936, once again with a domeless boiler, and resplendent in LNWR black—4-6-2, No 46201, Princess Elizabeth (British Railways).

Memories of the London and North Western Railway in experimental British Railways liveries—the lined black of Old Crewe on a converted 'Scot', No 46112, Sherwood Forester (British Railways).

Another converted 'Scot' in the experimental light green of early BR days, No 46139, The Welch Regiment (British Railways).

arranged for a set of indicator trials to be made. Engine No 6138, *London Irish Rifleman*, one of the nine renewed that year, emerged new from the works fitted with the necessary shelter round the front end, and as soon as it was thoroughly run in, arrangements were made for indicator diagrams to be taken while the engine was working ordinary service trains on the West Coast main line. I was in correspondence with Mr Ivatt at the time, and he told me how pleased they were with the results of the tests, and sent me a set of typical indicator diagrams. These showed that the engine had at times been working with the point of steam cut-off as nearly as 5 per cent of the piston stroke, and I eagerly awaited the opportunity of making the footplate journeys that Mr Ivatt had agreed to arrange for me.

The diagrams taken off engine No 6138 gave the following results:

Cut-off per cent	**Speed mph**	**Indicated horsepower**
5	62	925
10	60	1,070
15	60	1,520
18	62	1,670
22	56	1,700
26	52	1,820
32	44	1,840
38	30	1,670
46	22	1,440
Full gear	5	420

The horsepower developed at the cut-offs less than 15 per cent certainly pose some questions, and examination of the original diagrams show that nearly as much steam was passing through the cylinders at 5 per cent as when the cut-off was indicated as 10 per cent. These tests involved the taking of no other quantities, such as coal and water consumption; but the general impression given was very gratifying and, by the end of 1945, 29 out of the 70 engines of the original class had been renewed.

On my first footplate journey, with engine No 6117, *Welsh Guardsman*, I saw for myself continuous working for long periods with 10 per cent cut-off and, when driven thus, to average 55 to 60 mph on slightly rising gradients, hauling a gross trailing load of 450 tons. On the lengthy ascent from Settle Junction to Blea Moor, where the gradient is continuously at 1 in 100, the cut-off was first of all 22, and then 30 per cent and this latter sustained a fine speed of 36 mph. The equivalent drawbar horsepower was about 1,420, and I estimated that the indicated horsepower would be about 1,750. North of Carlisle the load was reduced to 320 tons, and for much of the *uphill* running a cut-off of 10 per cent sufficed. The following analysis of the engine working gives an overall impression of a journey in which a late start from Leeds was converted into a punctual arrival in Glasgow. The details of working need to be studied in conjunction with the indicator records taken with engine No 6138. For most of the time steam was on, in conjunction with these very short cut-offs, the regulator was wide, if not always completely full open.

	Leeds to Carlisle (miles)	**Carlisle to Glasgow (miles)**
Full gear	1.1	0.3
30 per cent cut-off	5.0	Nil
22 per cent cut-off	11.9	3.9
15 per cent cut-off	30.8	30.7
10 per cent cut-off	38.6	50.9
Steam off, coasting	25.6	29.6
Total	113.0	115.4

It is only necessary to repeat that the loads on the two sections were 450 and 320 tons respectively. At the same time, in view of such extensive use of relatively short cut-offs, I was a little surprised that the coal consumption was not lower. It is, of course, not possible for a single observer to get an accurate estimate, but from a careful check on the water

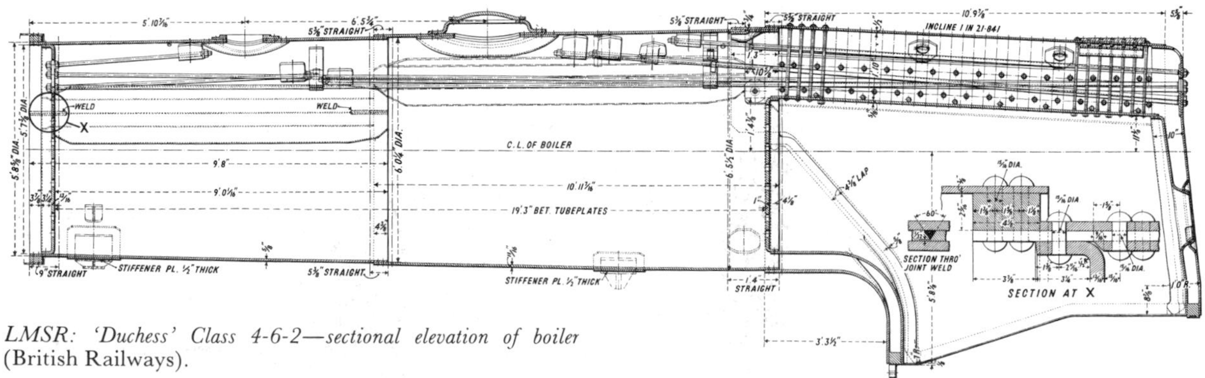

LMSR: 'Duchess' Class 4-6-2—sectional elevation of boiler (British Railways).

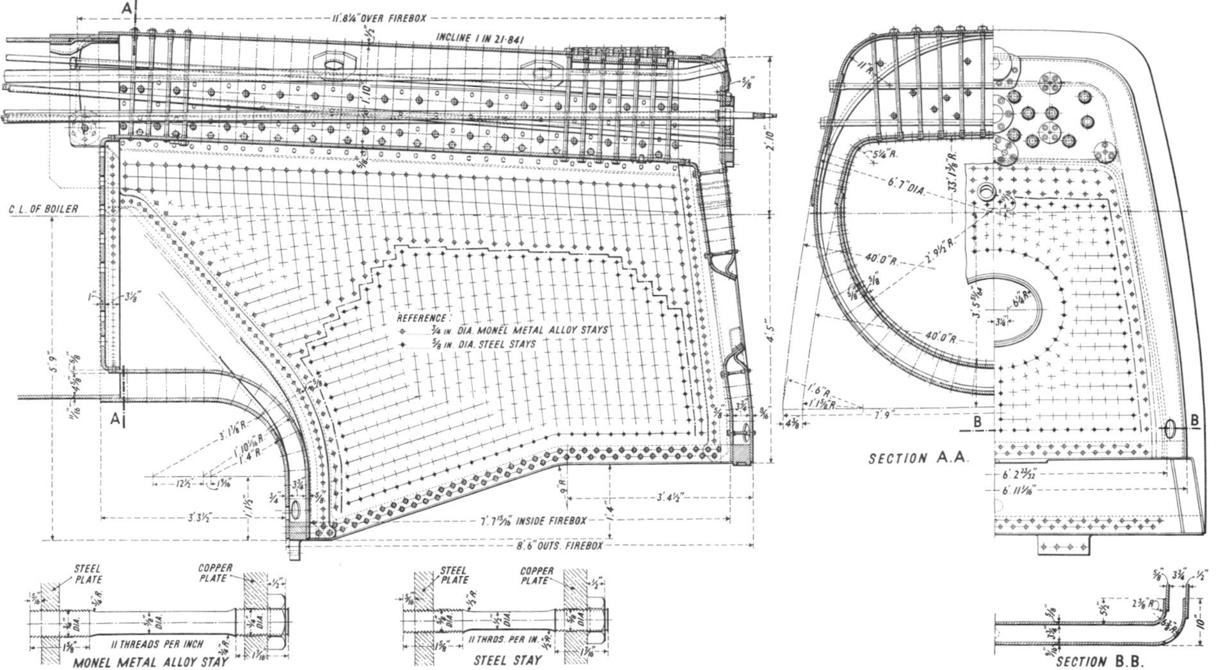

Above *LMSR 'Duchess' Class 4-6-2: detail of firebox and combustion chamber* (British Railways).

Right *One of the last two Stanier 'Pacifics' to be built with roller bearings throughout—No 6256,* Sir William A. Stanier, FRS, *built at Crewe 1947* (British Railways).

Below *Ivatt Class '4' 2-6-0, No 43012, working a local train on the Somerset and Dorset line near Chilcompton.*

consumption, and comparison with subsequent published test reports on these engines, I do not think it was less than about 52–53 lb per train mile. One came to the conclusion that these new engines provided yet another case of where the percentage of cut-off indicated on the reverser scale does not provide a reliable *relative* guide to the vigour or otherwise with which a locomotive is being worked. On the renewed 'Scots', at 10 per cent cut-off, it became obvious that the steam intake to the cylinders was much larger than it would be with a similar reverser setting on some other 4-6-0 locomotives of comparable nominal tractive power.

Although giving a good thermodynamic performance, the new engines had not been long in traffic before they were giving trouble in other respects. They became discredited in the eyes of the footplate men because, after about four to six months in traffic since repair, they became very rough. They seemed subject to severe rolling at the back end, and it needed steam to be shut off completely before it could be damped out. The original 'Scots' were hard riding engines, but any rolling was quickly damped out, and did not appear dangerous. In the new engines the suspension had been altered, presumably to forestall any recurrence of the trouble with cracked frames, but the change had evidently introduced troubles of its own. A great deal of attention was given to this problem, and E.S. Cox himself devoted much time to it, riding on a number of locomotives in varying states of repair, or disrepair. But although from the maintenance point of view the new engines proved superior to the old, the class as a whole never lived up to its early promise as a motive power unit. When J.F. Harrison transferred from the Eastern Region of British Railways to become Chief Mechanical Engineer of the London Midland he always insisted that the 'Scots' were their best engines. This may well have been so from an overall costing point of view; but I doubt if many of the footplate men would have agreed with him.

In the meantime there had been important changes in top personnel on the LMS. In October 1943 S.J. Symes, who had been personal assistant to the CME when Stanier was appointed in 1932, and who became Chief Stores Superintendent in 1935, was due for retirement. He was essentially a locomotive man; before the grouping he had been Chief Draughtsman of the Midland Railway, and until Fairburn's appointment as Deputy CME in 1937 he had usually acted as CME during Stanier's absences overseas. To replace him the LMS secured the release of R.A. Riddles from his second wartime appointment of Director General of Royal Engineer Equipment. The task of Stores Superintendent might have seemed, outwardly, a humdrum occupation after the vital tasks of direct engineering participation; but on the LMS, particularly in wartime, it was regarded as a key position and already, in the case of W.K. Wallace, the stepping stone to Chief Civil Engineer of the company. Stanier retired early in 1944 and was succeeded naturally by Fairburn, but there were no further changes in the department at the time. Ivatt remained as Principal Assistant for Locomotives, and working in close collaboration with R.C. Bond (Works Superintendent at Crewe), he was busy perfecting new details designed to cope with the changing conditions of maintenance at the principal running sheds.

Wartime experience on the LMS with American-built 2-8-0s that were used in Great Britain before D-Day gave first-hand experience with rocking grates, self-emptying ashpans, and self-cleaning smokeboxes, and during the war experiments had been made to see how these features could advantageously be applied to the standard LMS locomotives. Designs were worked out for rocking grates, self-emptying ashpans, and self-cleaning smokeboxes which could be applied not only to all new locomotives of standard design, but which could be added to older locomotives of the same classes as the opportunity presented itself. Difficulties of a kind that were to loom up after nationalisation were fore-

Left *A Stanier 'Jubilee' Class 3-cylinder 4-6-0 in the lined black (LNW) livery of early BR days—No 45700,* Amethyst (British Railways).

Right *LMSR: diagram showing arrangement of self cleaning smokebox* (British Railways).

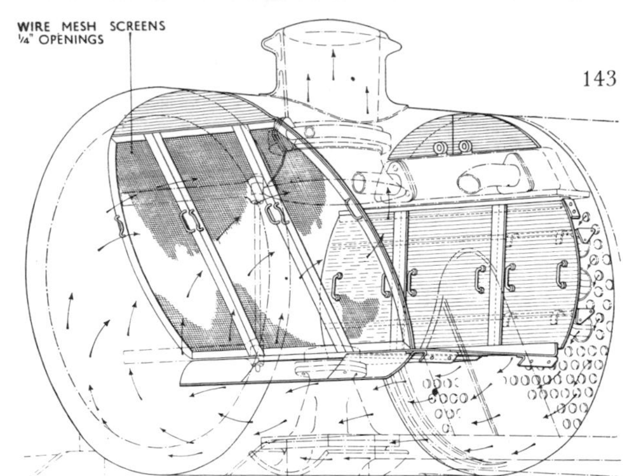

Below *A 'Jubilee' Class 3-cylinder 4-6-0, No 45729,* **Furious,** *climbing the 'Long Drag' to Blea Moor (14 miles at 1 in 100), near Stainforth, with a Scottish-bound excursion* (Derek Cross).

shadowed about the end of the war when the LMS adopted apparatus constituting a self-cleaning smokebox. Engineers on other railways felt that a considerably sharper blast would be necessary to overcome the resistance to the flow of gases when they had to pass under the diaphragm, and that the diaphragm itself would be an obstruction to tube cleaning. Experience on the LMS convinced Ivatt and his men that this would not be so, and instead one had the great advantage of a locomotive that would run from one boiler wash-out day to the next without the need for once opening the smokebox door. The accompanying perspective drawing shows the direction of the exhaust gases beneath the diaphragm plate and then upwards through the wire mesh screen. A further drawing shows the layout of the rocking grate and self-emptying ashpan.

In the meantime LMS' influence on the motive power scene on the British railways as a whole received a powerful shot-in-the-arm in 1943 when the wartime Railway Executive Committee placed orders with non-LMS workshops for a further 245 of the Stanier '8F' 2-8-0. Of these 80 were built at Swindon, and loaned to the Great Western Railway;

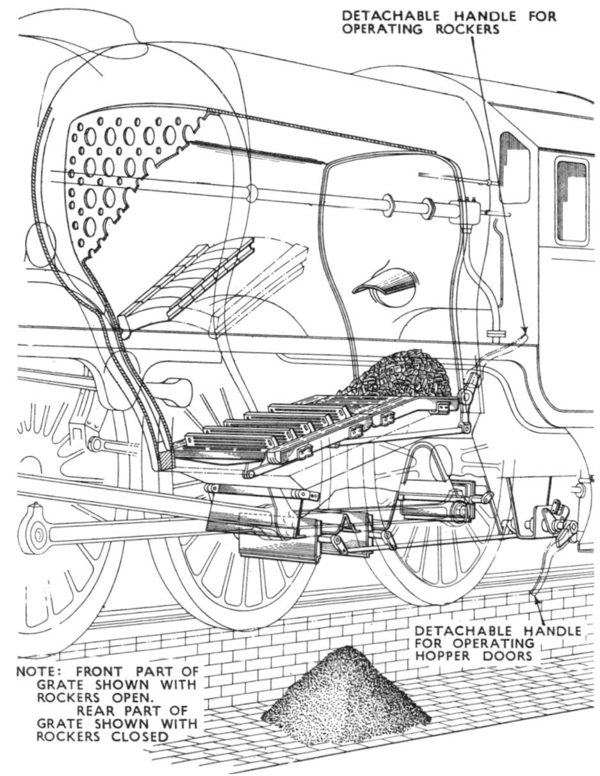

Right *LMSR: diagram of rocking grate and self emptying ashpan* (British Railways).

another 60 were built by the LNER (30 each at Darlington and Doncaster) and loaned to the LNER, and the remaining 105 at the Southern shops of Ashford, Brighton and Eastleigh, and all allocated to the LMS. The Works at Crewe and Horwich recommenced building engines of this class on their own account in 1943. Ultimately the class numbered 719 locomotives. This total included many returned from war service overseas. Of the 240 ordered by the Ministry of Supply in 1939 the records available show that 46 never returned. Although essentially a heavy freight type their excellent front end made them free running despite coupled wheels of no more than 4 feet 8½ inches and I shall not forget the occasion before the war when one of them was put on to my usual evening train from Euston and, with a load of 215 tons, sustained a speed of over 60 mph up the 1 in 337 from Wembley. It was only when I alighted at Bushey, the first stop, that I discovered the engine was a 2-8-0 and not the usual 'Black Five' 4-6-0.

In the autumn of 1945, uncertainty came to the Chief Mechanical Engineer's department from the sudden death of Mr Fairburn, at the relatively early age of 58. That it caught the high management of the LMS unprepared was evident from the time that elapsed before a successor was appointed. Fairburn's original appointment to the LMS, in 1934, had been at the strong instigation of Sir Harold Hartley and he immediately began to seek around for another of the highest academic attainment, such as Fairburn had possessed. Some of his fellow Vice Presidents, however, thought otherwise, and there was deep divergence of view. Riddles, of course, would have been a strong candidate for the post, but in the meantime Ivatt was designated as Acting Chief Mechanical Engineer. Then with the new year came the news that Sir Harold Hartley had resigned his Vice-Presidency of the LMS, and had joined the Board of BOAC. Ivatt's appointment as Chief Mechanical Engineer of the LMS followed, dating from February 1 1946, while at the same time Bond went from Crewe to become Mechanical engineer, Locomotive Works. Six months later he was appointed Deputy Chief Mechanical Engineer. E.S. Cox became assistant for locomotives with particular responsibility for design. The final LMS appointment, with great importance for the future, was that of R.A. Riddles as a Vice-President of the

LMSR: the Ivatt Class '2' 2-6-2 tank engine (British Railways).

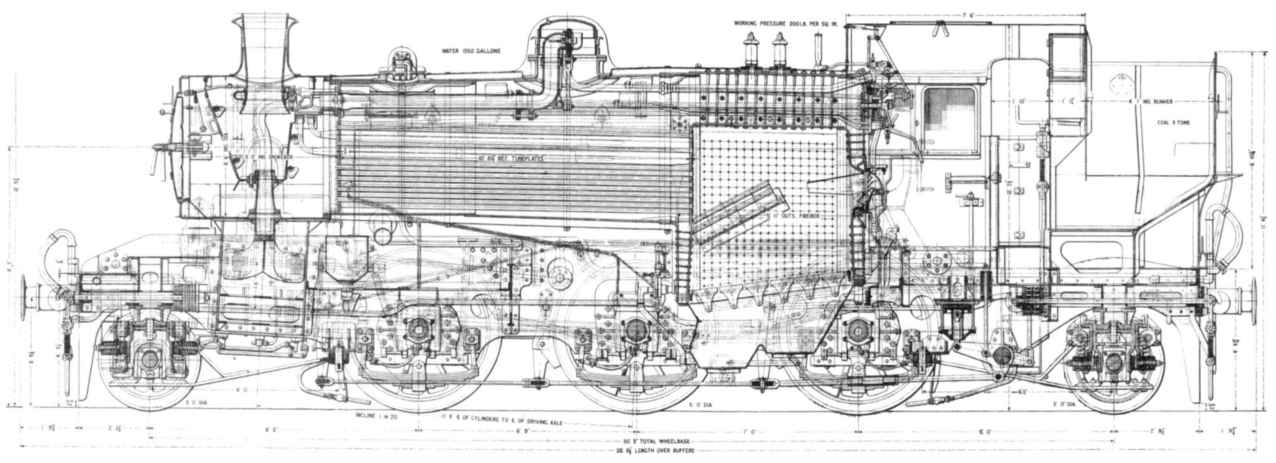

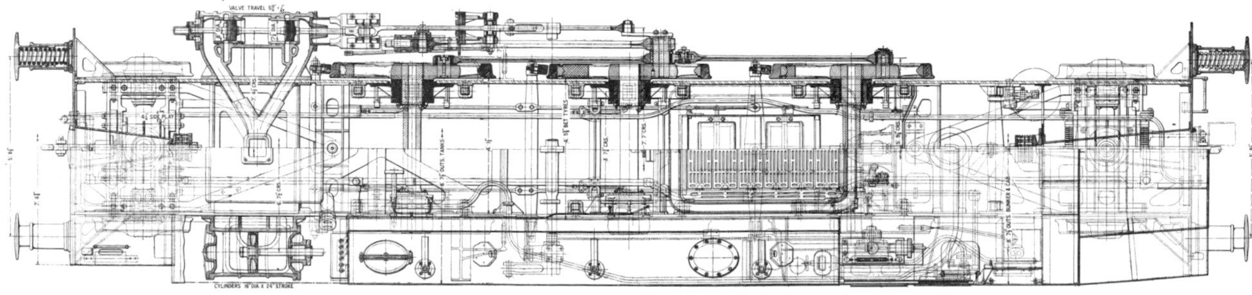

Right *The last Midland compound 4-4-0 to remain in traffic—engine No 41168 which was not withdrawn until July 1961* (British Railways).

Below *While many of the 'Baby Scots' were rebuilt with the new standard taper boilers, many remained unchanged under national ownership, like No 45516 seen here on an up Liverpool and Manchester express near Tring* (E.D. Bruton).

Right *A 'Black-5' in the Fell country—No 44709 on a Morecambe to Glasgow express drawing to a stand at Tebay, prior to taking rear-end banking assistance up the Shap incline* (Derek Cross).

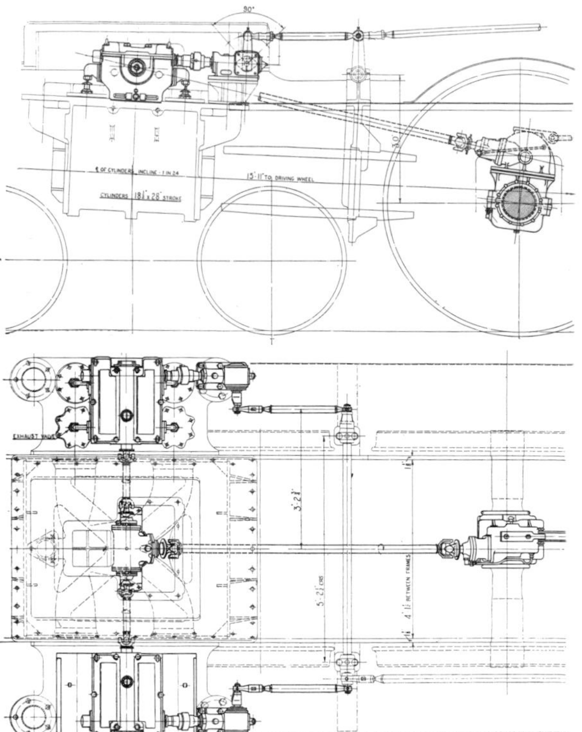

Left *The British Caprotti valve gear, with drive from inside the frames, as fitted to LMSR Class '5' mixed-traffic 4-6-0s of the 4738-57 series* (British Railways).

Opposite page, top to bottom

A Caprotti-valve 'Black-5' 4-6-0, No 44739, stopping at Tebay, prior to taking rear-end banking assistance up Shap, with a heavy express goods train (Derek Cross).

The pioneer LMS 'Pacific', No 46200, The Princess Royal, *(introduced in 1933) here seen in BR livery climbing Beattock bank with the morning Birmingham–Glasgow express* (Derek Cross).

One of the 'Ivatt' Class '2' 2-6-0s introduced just before nationalisation—engine No 46491 here seen leaving Penrith with the Keswick portion of 'The Lakes Express' from London Euston (Derek Cross).

company, with responsibility for all engineering work.

The last years of the LMS were full of activity in locomotive design. In this chapter I am concerned only with steam, but it is important to give advanced notice, as it were, that these last two years saw also the completion, under the LMS imprint, of the first British main line diesel-electric locomotive, an achievement that was ultimately of immense benefit to the motive power situation on the nationalised British Railways. On the other side, E.S. Cox had forecast that steam traction would be with us at least until the early 1960s—a remarkably accurate forecast to make in the 1940s—and that he recommended everything should be done to improve efficiency, not only in terms of coal consumption but in greater availability, longer mileages between visits to works for overhaul. In view of the politico-economic climate that developed after the General Election of 1945, his more ambitious proposals were not pursued; these included a large 4-6-4 for express passenger work, and a 4-8-4 for mixed traffic. In the meantime, T.F. Coleman, still in office as Chief Locomotive Draughtsman at Derby headquarters, produced a design for a 2-6-2, of Class '7' capacity which seems to have been inspired by the success of Sir Nigel Gresley's 'V2' class on the LNER despite the Thompson denigrations of it. This proposal was also dropped, and the only entirely new designs were a 2-6-0 of Class '4' capacity, and the still smaller 2-6-0 and 2-6-2 tank of Class '2'. The Class '4' included bad proportioning of the draughting arrangements, and it was a troublesome and poor steaming engine at first. The Class '2' 2-6-0 was of relatively small capacity—too small to commend it to certain areas outside the LMS after nationalisation.

Ivatt's more important work on steam concerned the equipping of new batches of existing standard designs with improved details. One feature that was shown to yield an almost spectacular increase in mileage run between repairs was the fitting of manganese steel liners on axleboxes and hornblocks. On the 'Black Five' 4-6-0 locomotives, the majority of which ran around 60,000 miles between 'General Repair' and first 'Intermediate Repair', those fitted with manganese steel liners ran more than 100,000 miles, while between the first and second classified repair the mileage from such engines went up from about 55,000 to 77,000 miles. The 'Duchess' Class 'Pacifics' were the finest of all Stanier's locomotives, but to the last two that were built in 1947, Ivatt incorporated all the latest features of LMS development. They had roller bearing axleboxes with manganese steel liners throughout, a re-designed back-end and a cast steel trailing truck, and of course a rocking grate and hopper ashpan. The first of the two, No 6256 was named *Sir William A. Stanier FRS*, and the second, *City of Salford.* These two engines were without much doubt the finest of all British steam express locomotives. They may have had their near-equals, but not their superiors.

I had the privilege of an engine pass to ride No 6256 about a year after construction, on the up 'Midday Scot' from Glasgow to Carlisle. At the beginning of 1949 schedules were not very fast, and

44739

46200

46491

Anglo-Scottish service on the Midland: the southbound 'Thames-Clyde Express', Glasgow to St Pancras, passing Dore & Totley South Junction, near Sheffield, hauled by 'Jubilee' Class 4-6-0, No 45573, Newfoundland (E.D. Bruton).

we were allowed 82 minutes for the 73.5 miles from Carstairs to Carlisle with a load of no more than 385 tons; it was easily done on a minimum of coal and water, but what interested me particularly was the riding. After a year of intensive usage, and already some 70,000 miles 'under the bonnet', as motorists would say, with plenty of fast running at 75 to 80 mph the riding was at all times perfect. What these engines could do in the way of power output when really put to it is dealt with in a later chapter. In 1947 authorisation was given for the building of many more general utility 4-6-0s in the 'Black Five' series, and that 30 of these should include various features that were then experimental, as follows: 10 engines, Nos 4738-4747, would have plain bearings and the British Caprotti valve gear; 10 engines, Nos 4748-4757, would have roller bearings and the British Caprotti valve gear; nine engines, Nos 4758-4766, would have roller bearings and the standard Walschaerts valve gear; and one engine, No 4767, would have roller bearings, and outside Stephenson Link motion. In addition to the above, many more of the standard type were to be built, though all new ones having manganese steel liners on the axleboxes and horn guides.

It is not often that devices calculated to save in day-to-day maintenance, and to reduce fuel consumption, can be incorporated in an otherwise standard locomotive design without some increase in prime cost or weight; and the Timken roller-bearing axles on the Class '5' 4-6-0s provided a case in point. The driving axles, with their special housings for the roller races, constitute a massive ensemble and, to provide adequate clearance from the front of the ashpan, it was necessary to increase the coupled wheelbase by 4 inches, the distance between the driving and trailing pair of wheels being increased from 8 feet to 8 feet 4 inches. This in turn, meant longer frames, and in consequence the total weight of the engines with roller bearings was 75 tons 6 cwt, against 72 tons 2 cwt, for a standard engine. All but 3 cwt of this increase was added to the adhesion weight, which became 57 tons 6 cwt, with a maximum axle load of 19½ tons against the previous 18¼ tons. It remained to be seen whether this increase in weight was justified by the performance of the locomotive concerned.

In theory, poppet valve gears, which provide such snappy opening and closing of the valves themselves, and which permit independent adjustment of the cut-off, would appear to be a very attractive proposition. In America remarkable results were obtained on individual test runs with a Pennsylvania K4 Pacific equipped with the Franklin gear, so much so that the gear was adopted for the 6100 Class 4-4-4-4s. But in this country, despite much careful experimenting, the results have not appeared conclusive.

In this new series of experiments, Caprotti valve gear, of the latest British design, was tested against one of the best layouts of Walschaerts gear in this country. One has no hesitation in writing the previous sentence, for when locomotives with driving wheels no larger than 6 feet in diameter regularly attained speeds of over 80 mph and sometimes exceed even 90 mph one may be very sure that the valve gear design was exceedingly good. The new Caprotti engines included some interesting changes in design, and the lowering of the running plate and the fitting of sizeable splashers imparted a very neat external appearance. Big-diameter outside steam pipes at the front end were taken more or less for granted in those days.

In the new engines the general layout was carefully arranged to give quick access to all parts likely to need attention. With the valve gear, the cambox was arranged to slide out on to a temporary platform

The final BR style for the largest ex-LMS locomotives: the Stanier 'Duchess' Class 'Pacific', No 46245, City of London, *in the restored livery of LMS red* (British Railways).

so that the valves could be inspected. Generally this use of poppet valve gear differed from most others previously tried in this country in that the standard engine was re-designed where necessary to suit the valve gear, rather than the reverse. Thus the valve gear incorporated all those features which the wide experience of the manufacturers had shown desirable, without imposing the restrictions that were sometimes necessary when poppet valve gear had been applied, with all the appearance of a 'last hope', to some existing locomotive of doubtful capacity. Thus the valve gear was given a real chance. The reversing gear in the cab was so arranged that the same number of turns was required to work the gear from full forward to full reverse as with the standard piston valve gear, so as to avoid any confusion on the part of the drivers.

The comparison between Class '5' engines fitted with the Walschaerts and Caprotti gear was naturally not confined solely to coal consumption and repair charges. It was possible that one or other of the alternative arrangements under investigation might show enhanced power per unit of weight, which called for special consideration. This possibility would have concerned to no less extent the third valve gear under observation, the Stephenson Link Motion on engine No 4767. From examination it seemed that the layout of the gear on that engine closely resembled that of the Great Western 'Hall', particularly on the shortness of the eccentric rods. This feature tends to accentuate the characteristic of the gear, whereby the lead increases as the cut-off is shortened. On the Great Western engines the lead, which was adequate for fast running when the cut-off is 20 to 25 per cent was reduced to nothing at all at about 40 to 50 per cent, and with the gear still further forward the lead became negative. This setting had the effect of giving enhanced power at slow speeds, very rapid acceleration, and a capacity for hard slogging on heavy gradients which Walschaert engines with a constant lead of $\frac{3}{16}$ inch to ¼ inch do not possess.

The trial of Stephenson Link Motion on so excellent an engine as the Stanier was therefore something of an event. The fitting of the gear outside the frames was decided upon for two reasons: to have it in a similar position to the Walschaerts, so that comparative costs for maintenance should be on the fairest basis; to avoid the use of the heavy eccentrics which long valve travel would otherwise require. On the score of maintenance alone the case for putting valve gear, Stephenson or Walschaerts, outside was not by any means clear cut. With outside gear if a big end was to be taken down, the motion had also to be partly dismantled, with consequent re-assembly afterwards, whereas in a similar case inside motion need not be touched.

Subsequent history seems to have shown that the results did not favour the Caprotti gear. I have never seen any official statements to this effect, but no more locomotives were built with it. My own experience travelling as a passenger behind the Caprotti Class '5' engines, and one trip from Leeds to Carlisle on the footplate suggested that those engines were singularly lacking in plain 'guts' in getting away with a load and in climbing a gradient. They ran very freely on the faster stretches of line, but sometimes the loss of time on the adverse sections was more than could be recovered afterwards. My trip on the footplate, with the 'Thames–Forth Express', on one of the Caprotti engines fitted with roller bearings, was very disappointing. The engine steamed well enough but seemed quite unable to produce any appreciable power from the cylinders, and with a not-immoderately heavy load of 300 tons gross behind we lost quite a lot of time, particularly between Settle Junction and Blea Moor.

11. Non-steam developments on all four main line railways

Despite the rapid extension of the Southern Railway electrified system in the 1930s there were train workings even within its confines where steam traction had to be maintained. The Continental boat train service between Victoria and Newhaven Harbour was one of these. The wide variation in passenger loading from season to season, and the need to include vehicles in the trains on which the sealed containers for registered luggage could be conveyed, had made it impracticable to operate the service with fixed formation multiple-unit electric trains. Before the war the Earle-Marsh 'Atlantic' engines of the former London Brighton and South Coast Railway were used, and two of them were re-allocated to the duty when the service was first restored after the Second World War. They were subsequently replaced by two 'Schools' Class until the time came for the new electric locomotives, CC1 and CC2, to take over. The design for these latter had been prepared in outline before the war, and although they were not the first non-steam main line locomotives to be produced since Sir Vincent Raven's 4-6-4 electric locomotive for the North Eastern Railway in 1922, they were the first to enter regular revenue earning service.

Locomotive No CC-1 was completed at Ashford works in 1941. It was a joint project carried through by Bulleid and the Electrical Engineer, Alfred Raworth. The electrical equipment was produced by English Electric Ltd, and incorporated in the body the running gear designed by Bulleid. The specification provided for a mixed traffic locomotive with a maximum service speed of 75 mph because, in addition to the boat trains to and from Newhaven, there was also a considerable freight traffic via this route to the Continent, successors to the celebrated *Grande Vitesse* express goods trains of Stroudley's day on the London Brighton and South Coast Railway. The nominal tractive effort specified was 40,000 lb, sufficient to haul freight trains of up to 1,000 tons. The first of these locomotives was carried on two six-wheeled bogies, and each of the six axles was driven by a separate electric motor, through single reduction spur gearing. One of the problems that presented itself in the design stage arose from the standard Southern Railway system of current collection, from a third rail. Although four collector shoes were provided on each side of the locomotive it was foreseen that, in passing over points and crossings where there were gaps in the conductor rails, there could be moments when none of the collector shoes might be in contact with the conductor rail. On the standard multiple unit electric trains of the Southern Railway the distance between the motored bogies ensured that at least one collector shoe was in contact when passing such localities.

The method of solving this problem was ingenious. The motors on each bogie were supplied with current through a booster set, consisting of a 600-volt motor coupled to a generator working at the same voltage. Between the motor and the generator, on the common shafting, was mounted a heavy fly wheel, and this stored enough energy to keep the booster set running when the locomotive was passing over gaps in the conductor rails, and ensured the continuity of the current supply to the traction motors. Compared to the electric locomotives

Southern Railway: diagram of electric locomotive, CC-1 (British Railways).

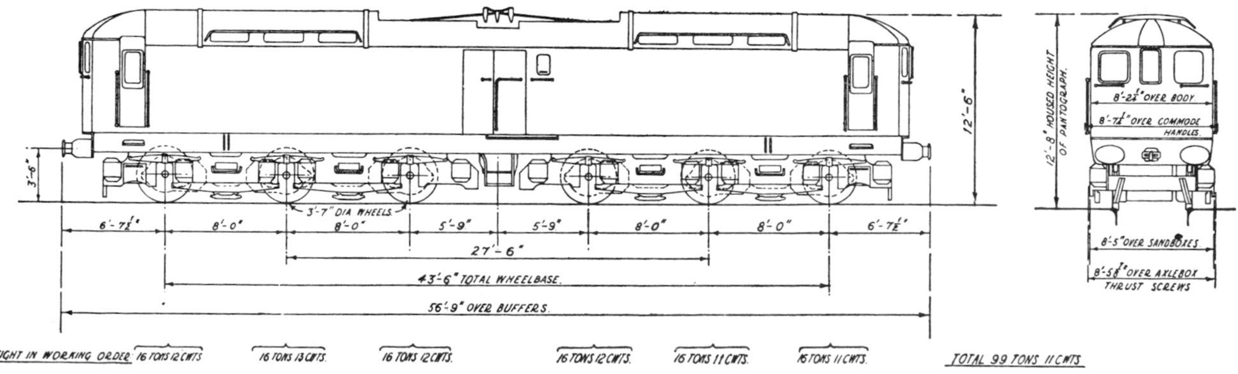

Manchester–Sheffield–Wath electrification: a heavy freight train hauled by Bo + Bo electric locomotive, No 26032 (British Railways).

introduced later on British Railways, CC-1 and CC-2 were rather heavy, weighing 99½ tons in working order. It was intended to provide for current collection in certain freight sidings from overhead wires and, to work in such localities, the locomotives were fitted with a pantograph on the roof. It is curious that, when CC-1 was first introduced and official descriptions of it issued to the technical press, there were several references to the 'ingenious' methods of maintaining current supply to the traction motors when passing over gaps in the conductor rails; but in no published description was there any reference to how it was done! One can hardly imagine the details were withheld for reasons of wartime security.

The accompanying line diagram shows the overall size and wheel spacing of the locomotive and, to meet the special conditions, Bulleid designed a new type of bogie without a bolster. The usual centre was replaced by four quadrants, of which two were placed over the bogie frames, and two were in line with the outermost axles of each bogie. The bogies were kept in line with the centre line of the locomotive by means of spring gear. It is interesting to recall that the wheels were of the Box-pox type used on Bulleid's steam 'Pacific' locomotives. The amount of equipment mounted on the bogies, and the lack of space that resulted, led to an unusual and somewhat complicated, arrangement for braking. Although the Westinghouse air brake was standard on the multiple unit electric trains of the Southern Region, all the locomotive-hauled stock had vacuum brakes, and this applied to the Newhaven boat trains. So a vacuum exhauster, electrically-driven, had to be installed in the locomotive; but for braking the locomotive itself, because of the lack of space on the bogies Westinghouse air brakes were installed, requiring much smaller cylinders.

Locomotives CC-1 and CC-2 were originally designed for one-man operation and this, requiring the provision of a deadman's handle, as on multiple unit electric trains, introduced a further complication. The normal locomotive brake was 'straight air', and was used when shunting, running light-engine, or hauling unbraked freight trains, and provided for direct application of compressed air up to a maximum pressure of 60 lb per square inch, from the driver's brake valve to the brake cylinders. But to enable the deadman's handle to fulfil its function, in the event of incapacitation of the driver, the automatic air brake had also to be installed on the locomotive. When working vacuum-fitted passenger trains, the automatic vacuum brake apparatus was linked, for simultaneous and proportioned operation with the straight air brake on the locomotive, the driver being able to operate the dissimilar brakes on locomotive and train by actuating a single brake valve handle.

In 1943 a very comprehensive series of tests was conducted, to determine the braking characteristics in six different conditions of service, with: 1) 80-wagon empty freight train, unbraked and loose-coupled; 2) 1,000-ton (about 75 wagons) loaded freight train, unbraked and loose-coupled; 3) 80-wagon empty freight train, with up to 15 wagons at the head of the train, vacuum braked and close coupled, with the rest of the train unbraked and loose-coupled; 4) 1,000-ton (about 75 wagons) loaded freight train with up to 15 wagons at the head of the train, vacuum braked and close-coupled, with the rest of the train unbraked and loose coupled; 5) 16-coach passenger train, vacuum braked and close-coupled; and 6) 40-vehicle fast freight train, vacuum braked and close-coupled.

Some of my close colleagues at Westinghouse were personally involved in much of the testing, and from their unofficial comments one gathered that a 'high old time' was had with some of the loose coupled trains. The paper subsequently presented to the Institution of Locomotive Engineers in May 1944 includes the following paragraph:

'The freight train trials included observations recorded on the 25-ton brake vans, fitted with hand brakes which, however, were not applied during the trials, in order to obtain uniform and comparable results. The vans formed an excellent means of recording locomotive braking performance. The approaching crescendo of sound from the impacting buffers ahead of an uncontrolled van gave a feeling of apprehension until the observer had become familiar with the personal probabilities likely to result. As a measure of shock intensity the tumbler instrument was most useful, obviating vague descriptions such as "heavy", "medium" and "light" shocks. A shock throwing over 15 tumblers would have caused damage to rolling stock if continued, and injury to staff if taken unawares; but a shock not sufficient to throw over two tumblers was considered almost ideal, although on such occasions some shock effect could be experienced on the locomotive. It was ascertained that, for practical purposes, shocks throwing over more than nine tumblers were undesirable.' Reflecting upon these tests, 40 years later, it is remarkable to recall the inconvenience, not to mention danger, to personnel that was not only tolerated but taken as a normal 'way of life' on railways, when the loose-coupled unbraked freight train was the principal source of revenue on many of the British railways.

I may add that the principal observer on that tail-end brake van was the senior vacuum brake engineer of Westinghouse, the late A.G. Brackenbury, who had also been present in the LNER dynamometer car in July 1938, when the world record speed with steam traction, 126 mph, by the Gresley Pacific engine *Mallard* was attained. In 1943 despite a few broken ribs(!) he stuck doggedly to this hazardous task of shock observation.

It was some years later when I had a footplate pass to ride CC-1 on the outward-bound Newhaven boat train (under nationalisation it had been renumbered 20001). In the early hours of the same morning it had worked a 65-wagon freight train from Polegate (junction of the Eastbourne branch) to Norwood Junction sidings. Although, as stated earlier, the locomotives had been designed for one-man operation, their use in composite links with steam locomotives made it desirable to have two-man crews so a change could be readily made from electric to steam if need be. In 1949, when I rode No 20001, the Newhaven 'Continental' was not a very exacting train to work. Leaving Victoria at 9.05 it had to be fitted into the busy Brighton electric timetable, and from East Croydon to follow the 9.00 semi-fast from London Bridge; and, with this train making passenger stops at Three Bridges and Haywards Heath, the 41.1 miles from Victoria to our divergence from the Brighton main line at Keymer Junction were allowed no less than 58 minutes and we took the full 70 minutes scheduled to pass Lewes, 50.2 miles. There had been one or two spurts up to 70 mph, but with a load of no more than 350 tons it was a very easy task for a locomotive designed in the Bulleid style to take 750 tons.

Before the outbreak of the Second World War the London and North Eastern Railway had embarked upon the great task of electrifying the former Great Central main line across the Pennines, with lengthy ascents from Sheffield and Manchester to the summit point at the east portal of the notorious Woodhead Tunnel. It was hard going enough even with the moderate loads of most of the passenger trains; but the freight traffic was extremely heavy, particularly the westbound coal workings from the major concentration point of the great mechanised marshalling yard at Wath-on-Dearne. The line from Wath up to Penistone was also included in the electrification scheme. The purely freight line from Wombwell Main Junction to West Silkstone Junction is exceptionally severe and includes the Wentworth Incline, 2 miles of 1 in 40 ascent, where it used to need four 2-8-0 engines of the Great Central '04' Class to lift a loaded coal train of 1,000 tons up the gradient at a speed of about 6 mph. It was there also that the one and only LNER 6-cylinder Beyer-Garratt 2-8-0 + 0-8-2 banking engine was employed.

Although the outbreak of war in 1939 had halted work on the electrification scheme as a whole, design work proceeded with the electric locomotives, and the first of these was completed early in 1941, so that trials could be conducted on a short section of line equipped with a 1,500 volt dc catenary system. Like the Southern CC-1, the pioneer LNER electric locomotive was designed for mixed traffic, but of a very different kind. The mineral trains required not only great power for hauling 1,000-ton loaded coal trains on severe gradients, but equally important for the control of them when descending the same gradients, regenerative braking equipment was included, because, as on the Southern, one was dealing with the bugbear of loose-coupled unbraked wagons.

The overall dimensions of the new locomotive of the Bo + Bo type can be appreciated from the accompanying line diagram. The line was being electrified on the 1,500 volt dc system with overhead wire current collection. There were four force-ventilated nose-suspended traction motors each having a maximum one-hour rating of 467 horsepower, giving a total of 1,868 for the locomotive, but the normal one-hour rating at a speed of 26 mph was 1,740, giving a total tractive effort at that speed

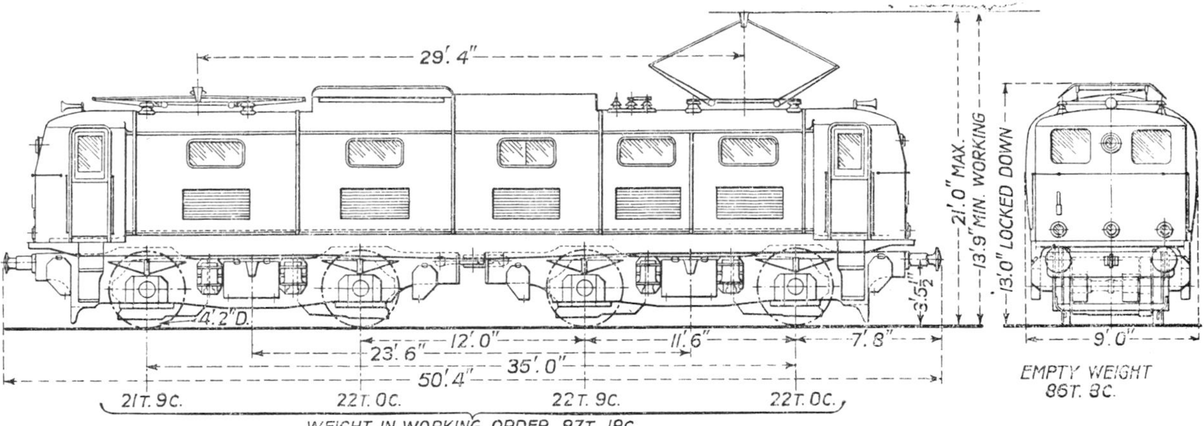

LNER: diagram of locomotive for Manchester–Sheffield–Wath electrification (British Railways).

of 25,000 lb. The maximum starting tractive effort was 45,000 lb, for which the total locomotive weight of 87.9 tons provided ample adhesion. Reference to the diagram shows the lengthy bogie wheelbase of 11 feet 6 inches, with 4 foot 2 inch diameter wheels; but the locomotive was designed to negotiate 5-chain curves. The weight of the locomotive was not transferred to the bogies through the central pivots, but through four side bearers on each bogie supported by helical springs. The centres were for pivoting only, but were given a small amount of spring-controlled side play.

The neat body exterior encased five compartments in addition to the driving cabins at each end, and a corridor down one side gave access to them all. The five compartments were: train heating boiler room, high tension control compartment, resistance chamber, and two auxiliary equipment spaces. The driving cabs had control consoles extending across the full width of the locomotive, with the driver himself positioned on the left-hand side. As will be seen from the diagram, there were pantographs at each end of the locomotive. As a mixed traffic unit, provision had to be made for vacuum braking of passenger stock. At that time Westinghouse had not yet developed its electrically-driven vacuum exhauster, and on this locomotive the exhauster was of the Northey-Boyce type. As on the Southern CC-1, the locomotive brakes were Westinghouse, the self-lapping driver's brake valve of which applied simultaneously the air brakes on the locomotive and the vacuum brakes on the train. Only one locomotive was built in 1941, No 6701, while work on the electrification project between Manchester, Sheffield and Wath was at standstill, for the duration of the war; but some very satisfactory acceleration and running trials were carried out on the Manchester, South Junction and Altrincham line, which had been equipped on the 1,500 volt dc system, some years previously.

In the closing stages of the war the retreating German forces destroyed or removed a vast amount of rolling stock and fixed equipment of the Netherlands State Railways and, although magnificent efforts after the war had restored many electric services, by the end of 1946 the engineers of the NSR, having the same system of electrification as that currently being installed by the LNER, paid a

The Western Region Gas Turbine locomotive, No 18000, built by Brown-Boveri in Switzerland, emerging from Sonning Cutting with a London–Cheltenham express (M.W. Earley).

Left *Manchester–Sheffield–Wath electrification: a westbound mixed freight near Bullhouse, on the climb towards Woodhead Tunnel—locomotive No 26029* (Eric Oldham).

Left *Manchester–Sheffield–Wath electrification: a heavy coal train near Bullhouse, hauled by Bo + Bo locomotive, No 26002* (Eric Oldham).

Below *Manchester–Sheffield–Wath electrification: westbound coal train approaching Dunford Bridge, eastern end of Woodhead Tunnel, hauled by locomotive No 26019* (E.D. Bruton).

Below right *Another picture of the Brown-Boveri gas turbine locomotive, No 18000, on a Western Region Cheltenham to Paddington express near Twyford* (M.W. Earley).

visit to England to discuss the design of No 6701, before proceeding further with their own post-war plans. They were impressed and interested to learn that authorisation for 84 of the same design had been given. As a result of this visit it was arranged that the LNER locomotive, by that time renumbered 6000, should be temporarily transferred to the Dutch railways for extended trials in main line service, which could not then be conducted in England. The locomotive was therefore shipped by the Harwich–Zeebrugge train ferry, and put into regular passenger service in Holland, running 400 miles a day on trains between Eindhoven and Utrecht. The maximum permitted speed was then 65 mph, but No 6000 was also used in freight service, hauling loads of 1,000 tons. These trains were fully braked, and it was found that on level track the maximum permitted speed of 40 mph was reached in 5 minutes from rest. These tests, while creating much interest among Dutch railways engineers, were most valuable to the LNER as giving experience in regular service that was not obtainable then on their own lines.

By the time the LNER electric locomotive No 6000 was running trials in Holland, another major non-steam project was under way, that of the Great Western Railway experiment into gas turbine propulsion. This was not quite such a revolutionary step as might be imagined, for although the 2,500 horsepower express passenger locomotive ordered from the Swiss firm of Brown Boveri & Co at the end of 1946 was only the second in the whole world to use the gas turbine system of propulsion, the pioneer locomotive ordered from that firm by the Swiss Federal Railways in 1939 had proved extremely reliable in operation. It had been intended for use on branch lines where the traffic density was insufficient to justify electrification. Such importance was attached to the development that, in spite of the extreme difficulty in obtaining fuel oil during the war, the Federal Government released some of its exiguous supply to enable the gas turbine locomotive to be put into regular passenger service, and by June 1944 it had run some 32,000 miles in a year of regular working, with completely satisfactory results. In the knowledge of this performance F.W. Hawksworth recommended to the Board of the GWR the purchase of a similar but larger locomotive, for trials in comparison with the standard steam locomotives.

In a different age, Great Western locomotive history was repeating itself because, some 40 years earlier, on the recommendation of G.J. Churchward, locomotives of an outstanding Continental type had been purchased for trial and comparison. Historians may also smile that even in its very last years the Great Western was running to its tradition, inaugurated with the broad gauge, of doing things differently from everyone else; that while the LNER and the Southern were concerned with new electric locomotives, and the LMS was deeply involved with diesels the Great Western should have espoused the gas turbine. Before referring to the principles of operation involved it is important that the end-

product, in terms of operating economics, should be appreciated. In the years just after the end of the Second World War the thermal efficiency of the gas turbine, at the drawbar of the locomotive fell roughly half-way between that of steam and diesel-electrics. The relative percentages were 6-8; 15 to 16, and 26 to 28. The gas turbine, when developed to production line standards, was expected to be considerably cheaper in first cost than a diesel electric, and it would use a lower and thus cheaper grade of fuel oil. There was also expected to be a very large saving in lubricating oil. On steam locomotives the cost of this could be reckoned at about 10 per cent of the fuel costs, while on diesel-electrics (from American experience) it could be anything from 20 to 30 per cent. Against this the gas turbine locomotive operating on the Swiss Federal Railways was returning a lubricating oil cost of less than one per cent of the fuel cost.

The principles of the gas turbine locomotive may be followed by reference to the accompanying diagram. This actually refers to the Swiss locomotive but the first GWR unit, No 18000, was the same, though slightly larger: 2,500 horsepower against 2,200. The power unit was supported in the locomotive frame by three-point elastic suspension. The air entered the compressor 'C' through the inlet '7' and flows via the outlet pipe '8' to the air-heater 'D'; thence it passed to the combustion chamber 'A'. The air required for combustion entered this chamber through the swirl vanes '1', and that supplied in excess of combustion requirements through the slits '2'. The initial air became heated by the combustion of oil that issued from the burner '3', and the purpose of the excess air was to reduce the temperature of the resultant gases to a value suitable for the turbine blading. The gases then passed on, at a temperature of 850–1,100 degrees Fahrenheit, from the combustion chamber to the gas turbine 'B'. There they expanded, giving up heat for the production of mechanical work, and afterwards flowing via the exhaust passage '5' to the air heater 'D', where they parted with heat to the compressed combustion air. This was afterwards discharged into the atmosphere through the slits '6' in the roof of the locomotive. The outlet pipe '8' was fitted with several expansion joints '9', to accommodate the different rates of expansion of the turbine set and the air heater.

The gas-turbine locomotive supplied to the GWR, No 18000 had the following initial specification:

Continuous net output of the gas turbine unit	2,500 hp
Tractive effort at the wheel rim a) when starting b) continuously	33,000 lb from 0 to 20 mph 13,000 to 60 mph and 8,800 lb at 90 mph
Maximum continuous speed	90 mph
Weight in working order	113 tons
Adhesion weight	75 tons
Length overall	65 feet 6 inches
Fuel	Furnace fuel oil
Trailing load corresponding to tractive effort of 13,000 lb at 60 mph	850 tons
Maximum trailing load in fast freight service	1,200 tons

Fuel supply: enough for non-stop runs of 250 miles

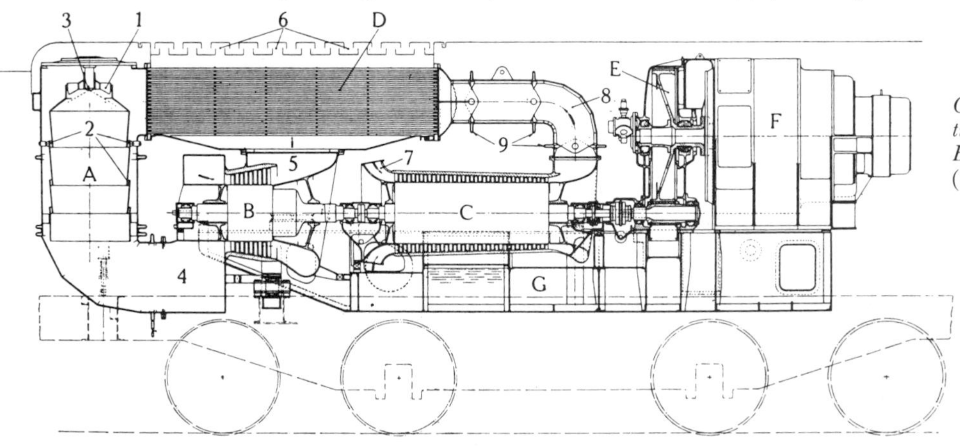

Fig. 162. Section of the gas-turbine set of the locomotive.
A. Combustion chamber. B. Gas-turbine. C. Compressor. D. Air-heater. E. Gear. F. Generator. G. Bedplate of unit.

GWR: section of the gas-turbine unit of the Brown-Boveri locomotive, No 18000 (British Railways).

Right *The Metropolitan-Vickers Gas Turbine locomotive, No 18100, approaching Bath, with the down 'Merchant Venturer' express—Paddington to Bristol.*

Below *The Brown-Boveri Gas Turbine No 18000, on a down West of England express, passing Cowley Bridge Junction, Exeter* (British Railways).

Bottom *The pioneer British diesel-electric main line locomotive, LMS No 10000, built in 1947, on loan to Southern Region, and here seen working the 'Bournemouth Belle' 12-car Pullman train at Winchfield, Hants* (M.W. Earley).

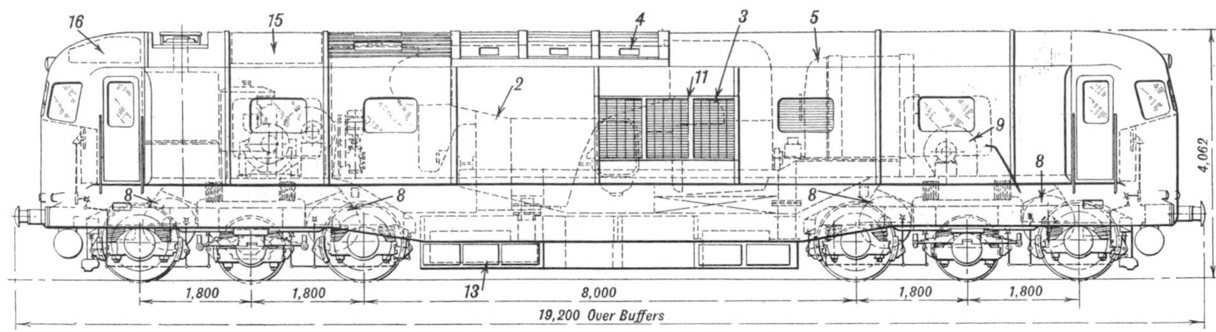

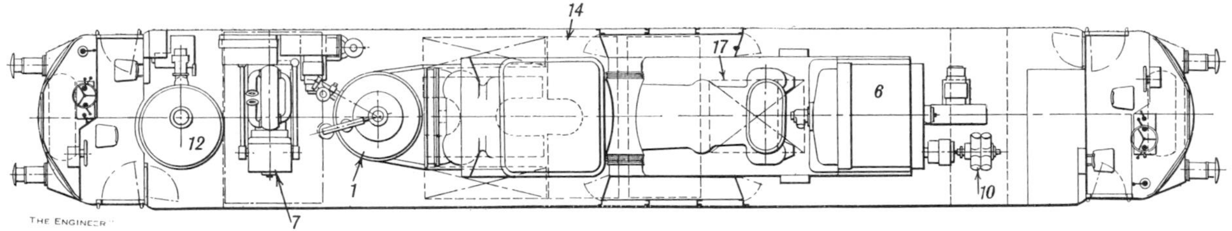

1. Combustion Chamber
2. Gas Turbine
3. Air Compressor
4. Air Preheater
5. Reduction Gear
6. Main Generator
7. Diesel Generator Set for Auxiliaries
8. Traction Motors
9. Fan for Traction Motors
10. Compressor and Vacuum Pump
11. Lubricating Oil Radiators
12. Train Heating Boiler
13. Storage Battery
14. Heavy Fuel Oil Tanks
15. Water Tank for Boiler
16. Light Fuel Oil Tank
17. Lubricating Oil Tank

GWR: diagram of the Brown-Boveri gas turbine locomotive, No 18000 (British Railways).

When the locomotive was in regular service on the Western Region of British Railways, I had many runs as a passenger behind it, and the performance so far as weight haulage and speed was always very good, equal to a 'King' Class 4-6-0 steam locomotive. In wintry conditions, however, the train heating boiler was ineffective and, by the time the journey's end was neared, the coaching stock was icy cold. It was just tolerable on the Paddington–Bristol runs, but when the locomotive was in the Plymouth link, things were pretty grim for the passengers. Another characteristic of No 18000 was the smell—a sickening aroma of hot oil that pervaded the atmosphere in the first three or four coaches of the train. The enginemen soon had a nickname for the newcomer; it became known as *Kerosene Castle!* The accompanying diagram (above) shows the general layout of the locomotive as built. To translate the metric dimensions on the drawing issued by Brown-Boveri, the bogie wheelbase was 11 feet 10 inches, the driving wheel diameter 48.6 inches, and the length over buffers 63 feet. It was only the outer axles of each bogie that were driven, by series type dc motors completely suspended, to reduce the unsprung weight to a minimum. It will be seen from the diagram that the actual weight came out rather heavier than the original estimate, 115 tons, against 113.

To gain as wide an experience as possible with this novel type of locomotive the Great Western Railway, on the recommendations of Mr Hawksworth, ordered a second gas turbine locomotive from the Metropolitan-Vickers Electrical Company. It was at first intended that this locomotive should be powered by a gas-turbine of a similar type designed by the builders (in conjunction with the Ministry of Aircraft Production) for use in aircraft jet engines, and also supplied to the Admiralty; but, as the project developed, realisation that the application of such a plant to railway purposes would involve some loss of thermal efficiency if used without waste heat recovery, led to a change of design. Instead there was incorporated a new type of gas turbine which Metropolitan-Vickers were developing for high-performance railway locomotives. The new plant dispensed with a heat exchanger and used a considerably higher compression ratio than the one originally proposed. The result was that it proved possible to provide a power unit with a higher rated tractive effort without any appreciable increase in total locomotive weight. As will be seen from the accompanying drawing (right), a special feature was the single shaft arrangement, in which the turbine unit was coupled directly to the compressor and, via gears, to the generators.

The power unit was carried on three supports and mounted centrally in the body of the locomotive. Each main generator supplied current to two axle-mounted traction motors which drove the road axles through torsionally resilient single-reduction spur gears. All six axles of the locomotive were motor driven. The output of the turbine, at 7,000 revs per minute, is 3,500 horsepower and, allowing for auxiliary demands and transmission losses, the power available at the rails was originally 2,700 hp. It is interesting to recall that the layout provided that this output varied only slightly over the entire speed range between 20 and 75 mph. The maximum designed speed was 90 mph. When first put into regular service in 1952 between Bristol and Paddington this Metro-Vick gas turbine locomotive gave evidence of tractive power considerably in advance of any steam locomotives then operating on the Western Region. I had many runs behind it, and the climbing of the 1 in 100 gradient through the Box Tunnel was very impressive. A year later, however, when I had the privilege of a footplate pass, a regulating device had been applied to limit the maximum output, and the performance of the locomotive was much reduced. When I climbed aboard at Bath on the up journey there was a senior engineer of Metropolitan-Vickers also riding, and he expressed surprise that I should have been given a pass. Apparently he made strong representations to British Railways, and I was subsequently asked to suppress all details of the locomotive working in anything I subsequently wrote. The performance was certainly not very creditable to the designer.

It was on the LMS that the true pointer towards the future development of British railway motive power came to be seen in the introduction, late in 1947, of the first diesel-electric main line locomotive, No 10000, and shortly afterwards the sister engine No 10001. They were the products of a close and whole-hearted co-operation between H. G. Ivatt, and his staff, and the English Electric Company. In his book *A Lifetime with Locomotives*, the late R.C. Bond, then Deputy CME of the LMS, put the situation succinctly: 'We knew far more than any contractor about locomotive design from the railway point of view. The English Electric Company knew far more than we could hope to know about the design of diesel engines and electric transmissions. The locomotives would give us the experience in daily service needed to assess the potential benefits of diesel traction under British conditions. They would at the same time provide private manufacturers with a 'shop window', as it has been called, enabling them to compete more effectively in what was clearly becoming an important world market.' The combined operation produced two splendid locomotives that gave excellent service for nearly 20 years.

The power rating of the new locomotives was chosen with some deliberation. Diesels work at their most efficient when under full power, or near to it, and in contrast to the gas-turbine locomotives then under construction for the Great Western, both of 2,500 hp and more, the LMS diesels were designed with engines having a rated horsepower of 1,600. This would enable them to work singly on the

Diagram of the Metropolitan-Vickers gas turbine locomotive No 18100 (Western Region) (British Railways).

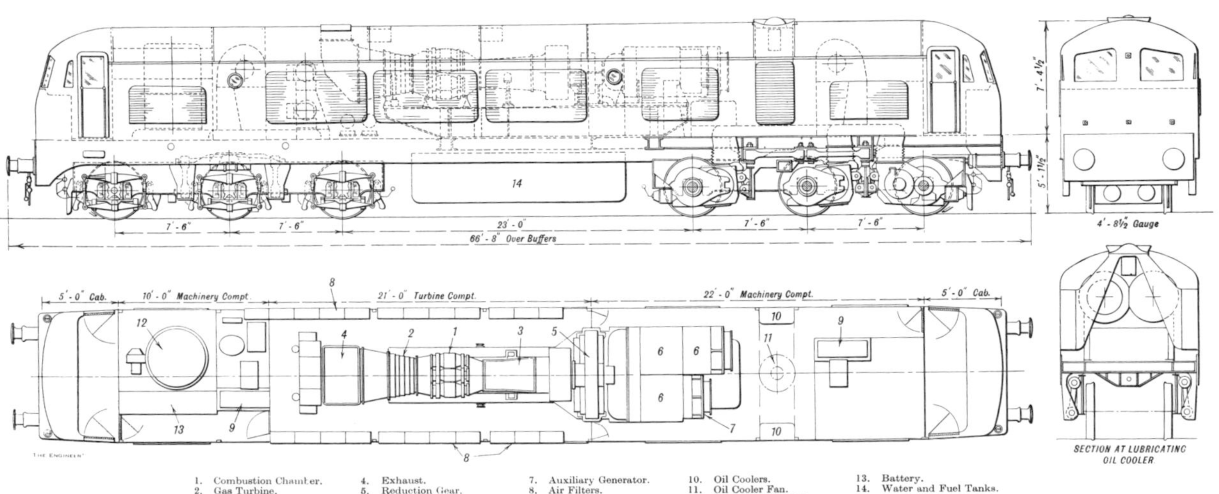

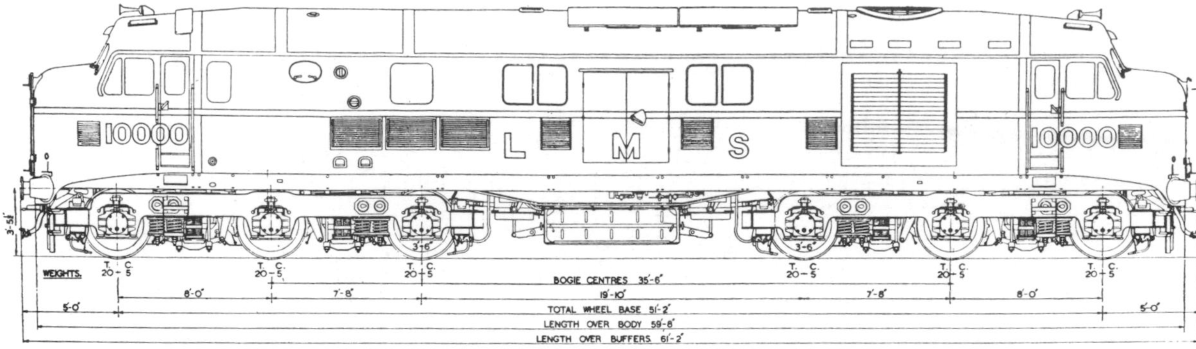

LMS: diagram of the first British main line diesel-electric locomotive, No 10000, built in 1947 (British Railways).

express train services of the Midland Division, with loads not greatly exceeding 350 tons, and on fitted freight trains. On the West Coast main line, where maximum pre-war passenger workings had demanded outputs of about 2,500 drawbar horsepower from the Stanier 'Pacific' engines, it was proposed, in comparative trials, to couple the two new diesels in multiple units (operated by one driver). In the years 1947-8 there were not many express trains on that route requiring a *continuous* output of anything like 2,500 hp and in service I personally noted several cases of loads of around 500 tons, worked singly by one or other of the two diesels. The engine actually fitted was a 16-cylinder V-type, four cycle turbo-charged unit, having a 12-hour British Standards Institution rating of 1,600 hp at the maximum speed of 740 revs per minute. It was a standard and well tried English Electric product, and gave no trouble from the very start.

The power equipment could be divided into four main groups, namely the power unit consisting of the diesel engine and the main generator; the traction motors, with their gears and gear cases; the control equipment, and the auxiliary apparatus. Of the first, the main generator was directly coupled to the engine crankshaft. It was of the direct current type, self ventilated, while the engine had 16 cylinders 10 inches diameter by 12 inches stroke. The aluminium-alloy pistons had three compression and two scraper rings, with a fully floating gudgeon pin. The traction motors were mounted on the bogies but, while it was considered essential for good riding to have these of the bolster type, the usual layout for such bogies could not be adopted because there would be no room to accommodate a traction motor on the central axle of each bogie. The engineers of the LMS, under the active personal direction of Mr Ivatt, designed a novel arrangement in which the weight was carried on the axes of the bolsters themselves, at four points through sliding surfaces. With this arrangement the centre pivot was required to deal only with location and traction forces. This arrangement resulted in a beautifully riding 'vehicle'. With the exception of the master controllers, one of which was mounted in each cab, all the other control equipment was housed in a single dust tight main control cubicle in the generator compartment.

The accompanying drawing (above) shows the overall dimensions of the locomotive. By later standards the all-up weight of 121.5 tons would be considered heavy for a machine developing no more than 1,600 horsepower; but there is no doubt that the

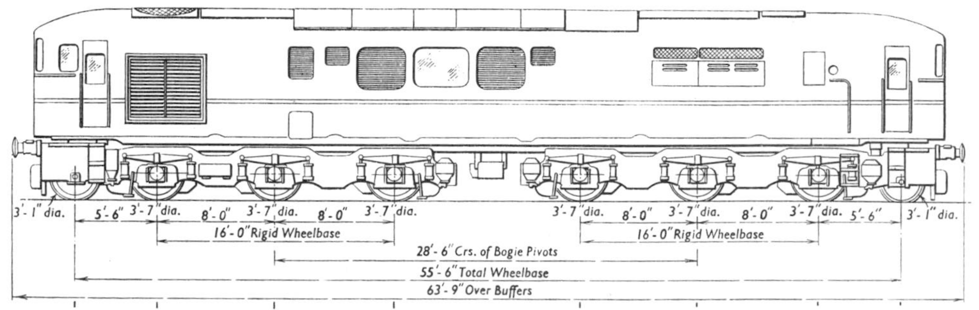

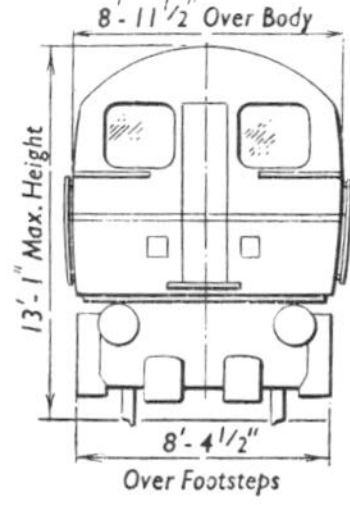

Southern Region: diagram of diesel-electric locomotive (1,750 hp) (British Railways).

The Southern Region diesel-electric locomotive, No 10201, passing Winchfield, with the down 'Bournemouth Belle' (M.W. Earley).

designers 'played safe' as it were, and produced a locomotive that proved very reliable, and a valuable forerunner of subsequent units that proved extremely useful at a time when the diesel programme was being driven forward at a speed that experienced locomotive men felt was injudicious, to take the most charitable view of it! This is not to say that no haste was involved in the construction of the first diesel-electric locomotive, No 10000. The year was 1947, and Ivatt and his men were most anxious that the project, entirely LMS in its origin and fulfilment, should be finished in time to be recognised as a purely LMS job with, of course, generous acknowledgement of the co-operation of English Electric. So there was a great race at the finish to get No 10000 completed before the end of the year and have the initials LMS on the sides. It was a close finish. In the first week of December 1947, No 10000 was driven out of the paint shop at Derby by Ivatt himself, and no more than a week later it was at Euston for inspection by the Board. Sir William Stanier was there too, to witness the unveiling, by the Chairman of the LMS Board, of the nameplate of Ivatt's latest steam 'Pacific', *Sir William A. Stanier FRS.* As to No 10000, the letters 'LMS' were in stainless steel, riveted to the body sides. The second diesel-electric No 10001, was completed early in 1948, but significantly without the initials 'LMS'.

Details of some notable runs by these two locomotives, and also with the other non-steam units referred to earlier in this chapter, are included in Chapter 15 of this book. Also included are full details of tests carried out by British Railways on the Southern Region diesel-electric locomotives introduced in 1951. These latter were, so far as the machinery was concerned, generally similar to Nos 10000-1 of the LMS, but had the 1-C-C-1 wheel arrangement, with engines rated at 1,750 hp.

The third Southern Region diesel-electric locomotive, No 10202, transferred to the London Midland Region, and here seen on the up 'Royal Scot' near Acton Bridge, Cheshire (T. Lewis).

12. Scientific testing: rival systems

With the approach of nationalisation following the British General Election of 1945, it seemed inevitable that there would be much comparing of existing locomotive designs, and in so doing the differing precepts of testing on the Group railways of 1923 and after, and their equipment for doing so, began to come under careful scrutiny, even before the vesting date for nationalisation itself. At the outset the Southern had lain rather outside this field of argument. Until Bulleid's appointment as Chief Mechanical Engineer in 1937 steam traction had been at something of a discount and such tests were confined to the occasional indicating of a specific design. No dynamometer car was available. On the Great Western, the fillip that testing practice received in the 1930s has been described in Chapter 7, and despite the war much thought and practical work was devoted to the developing of what eventually blossomed out as the Controlled Road system of testing. Against this both the LNER and the LMS, in totally different ways, seemed inclined towards testing at constant speed.

In March 1943 T. Robson, who was then in charge of the Darlington dynamometer car of the LNER, read a paper before the Institution of Locomotive Engineers on 'The Counter Pressure Brake Method of Testing Locomotives'. In his preamble he said: 'Although this country was the birthplace of the steam locomotive, other countries are far ahead of us both in testing equipment and outlook on experimental work. There were facilities for counter pressure testing in Russia, France, Poland and Germany. In Russia a special track was provided free from other traffic, and this, in the Author's opinion, is the best possible arrangement and will give the most practical results.' In the 1930s Robson had been sent by Sir Nigel Gresley to France to study the methods in use there for counter pressure testing. The principle involves the hauling of one or more locomotives which are steamed *in backward gear* to provide a load for the locomotive on test, and by regulating the backward power applied to these 'brake' locomotives the speed could be controlled within fine limits, irrespective of the gradients of the line. Robson was fortunate in having the splendid near-level length from Darlington southwards for 44 miles to York, and his tests were made over this section. The counterpressure locomotive was a tough old Worsdell Class 'S' 4-6-0, No 761, one of the later batch built in 1906, and illustrated in its pristine condition in Volume 1 of this book. As specially adapted for test purposes, it is shown in the accompanying diagram.

Live steam from the boiler was admitted to a cavity in the blast pipe, and from there drawn into the cylinders while the exhaust ports were open. Water from the boiler was admitted to the cylinders. At first the LNER followed French practice in passing water into the steam chests, but when the amount of power being absorbed reached about 600 horsepower the metallic packing was melted out of the piston and tail-rod glands, and then the water injection was led direct to the cylinders, as shown in the diagram. In any case the old engine was being flailed, contrariwise as it were, to a far greater extent than she probably had to work normally in her prime, and when the rate of absorption began to approach the 900 horsepower mark the driving axle-boxes began to heat badly. But the substitution of large solid bronze boxes with large bearing surfaces and a specially generous supply of oil feeds enabled them to stand up to this rather murderous treat-

North Eastern Railway: Class 'S' 4-6-0 adapted for counter-pressure testing. A: Water injector valve. B: Branch pipe to L and R cylinders. C: Water inlet to cylinders. D: Live steam to blast-pipe (Institute Mechanical Engineers).

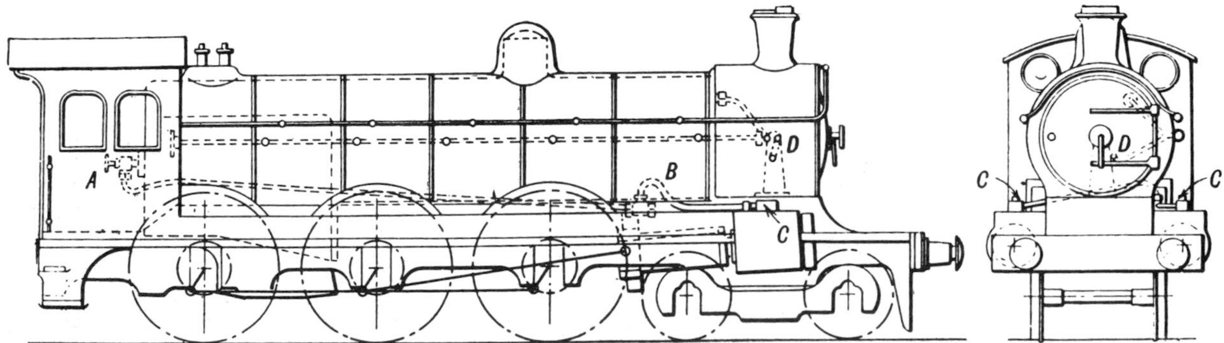

Right *Great Western Railway: a stationary testing plant at Swindon, in 1904, while under construction. A Dean Goods 0-6-0 being used to test the rollers* (British Railways).

Below *Dynamometer car tests on one of the earliest 'Castle' Class engines, in 1924, No 4074,* Caldicot Castle, *which made three return trips from Swindon to Plymouth and back* (British Railways).

Bottom *The Interchange Trials of 1925: the GWR 4-6-0, No 4079, and the LNER 4-6-2, No 4475, alongside each other at Kings Cross shed* (the late W.J. Reynolds).

ment. It was reported that, as modified, the locomotive satisfactorily absorbed 1,500 horsepower over a distance of 16 miles, with the regulator full open and the reverser position varying between 50 and 60 per cent cut-off, *in backward gear*! It should be added that the reversing wheel was fitted with a special slow pitch screw so as to permit a very fine adjustment to maintain the constant speed required on tests.

To secure the overall survey of the performance of a locomotive, tests had to be carried out at a wide range of speeds, and in using such a busy main line as that between Darlington and York, prior arrangement had to be made with the Operating Department to ensure that a clear road was obtained and, what was of course more important, that once embarked on a constant speed, no other traffic was delayed. Generally speaking it was not usually possible to make more than one return trip from Darlington to York and back in a day, especially when working at the lower speeds. Mr Robson referred somewhat wistfully to the degree of priority given to road testing of locomotives in other countries. In Russia, for example, in Imperial days, a test run using a counter-pressure brake locomotive was given priority equal to that accorded to the Czar's train; everything else had to give way. On the LNER the test train was there on sufferance; but perhaps the density of traffic on the Imperial Russian railways was not so intense, or so fast, as that between Darlington and York.

Up to the time of railway nationalisation the LMS also had strongly favoured the principle of testing at constant speed, and a major research project had been authorised for the building of a Mobile Locomotive Testing Plant, designed by Dr H.I. Andrews. Not all sections of the British railways were so ideally suited to constant speed as the Darlington–York line of the LNER, or the Great Western main line between Paddington and Swindon, and as both the LMS and the LNER then considered that constant speed was one of the *desiderata* for obtaining reliable measurement of fuel consumption, evaporation and so on, the former company gave consideration to means of maintaining constant speed other than with a counter pressure locomotive. The latter would be difficult to adjust on a sharply undulating road. Although the LMS and the LNER were jointly committed to the construction of a new stationary testing plant at Rugby, it was felt that this would not necessarily be a complete substitute for road testing. The Mobile Locomotive Testing Plant, designed by Dr Andrews, was to be complementary to this, and it was actually completed first, in 1947.

It embodied rheostatic braking, and the key to success lay in the automatic control of the electric loading on the main generators. It was essential that fluctuations in drawbar pull due to a change in

The London and North Western dynamometer car, built in 1908, showing instrument table (foreground) on which high power outputs of the 'Claughton' Class engines were recorded (British Railways).

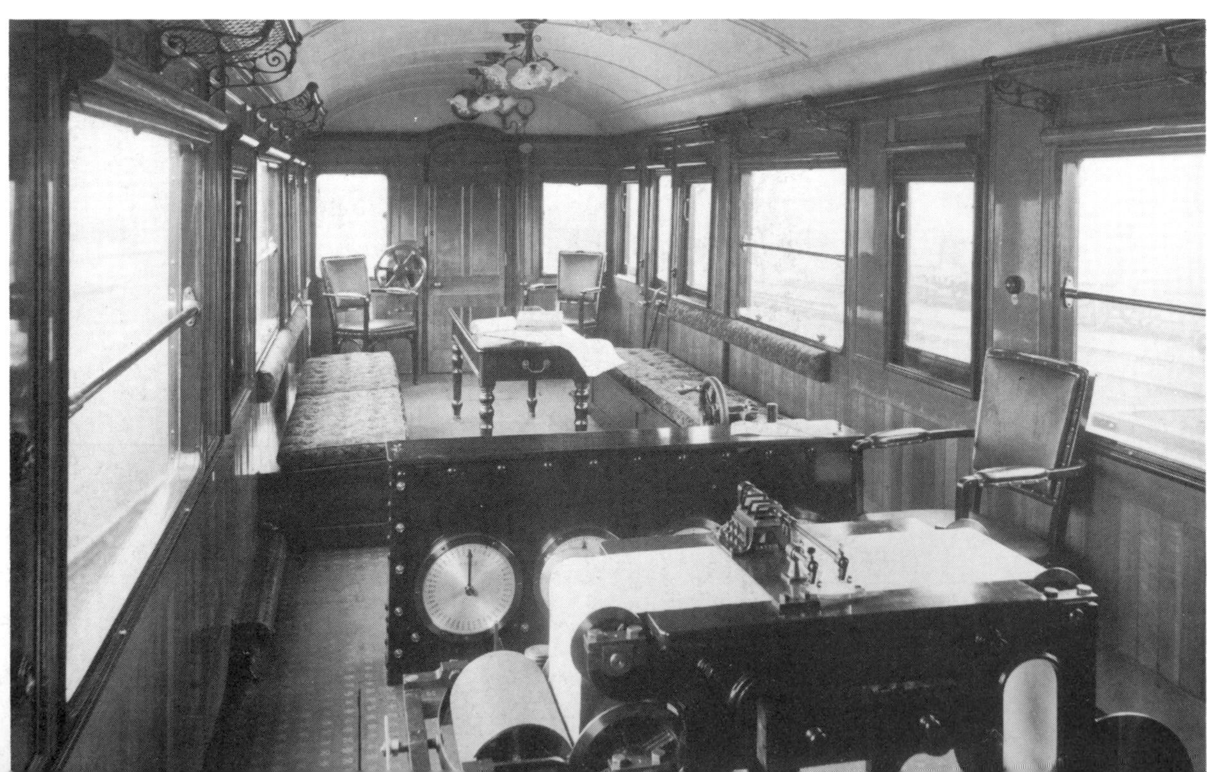

gradient, or from other causes should be compensated for immediately, and a very high degree of sensitivity to such changes had to be built into the equipment. It was done by relating the voltage on a speedometer-generator on the dynamometer car to a voltage preset to represent the stipulated test speed. The small differences, immediately they occurred, were amplified and transmitted to mercury arc rectifiers for the regulation of main generator loading. It might be thought that this very sensitivity would have led to severe 'hunting', with the speed see-sawing up and down; but remarkable accuracy was obtained from the outset, with speed maintained to within 0.1 mph either side of the stipulated constant value. It was a measure of the precision with which the performance of electrical apparatus may be computed beforehand.

That was not all. The electrical wizardry built into the controls would permit the running characteristics of one route, gradients, permanent speed restrictions and so on to be reproduced over another. This, it was suggested, would be valuable in gauging the road performance of a locomotive over a route where, because of structural clearances or axle loading restrictions, it was not permitted to run. It might be thought that such would be no more than an academic exercise, except that the prospects of better running with larger locomotives could be equated to the cost of improving the line to permit their use. A more practical advantage of being able to simulate the running characteristics of one line and apply them on another would have been that tests could have been conducted over a route with a low traffic density, with the physical characteristics of a much busier one superimposed upon it. This would have thus saved the embarrassment of increasing line occupation with the running of test specials. So far as constant speed control was concerned, it meant that the entire length of hilly routes could be used for test purposes, instead of merely the uphill sections.

The Midland Railway did most of their engine testing between Derby and Manchester, a route with a profile like the gable of a house, and, in former days, the test work ended when the summit was reached, at Peak Forest. With the mobile testing plant, if the pre-arranged speed of the test was 30 mph—a typical uphill speed on that route in steam days—the constant speed feature could hold the speed accurately to 30 mph going downhill, while still making maximum demands upon the steaming ability of the locomotive. The only trouble was that 30 mph was not exactly a representative speed to test the performance of an express passenger locomotive and, engines of the Midland Railway, and those of similar design built since grouping, in 1923, were subsequently found to be deficient in performance when the speeds were worked up to over 70 mph.

Head-on aspects of the 1925 Interchange Trial rivals (the late W.J. Reynolds).

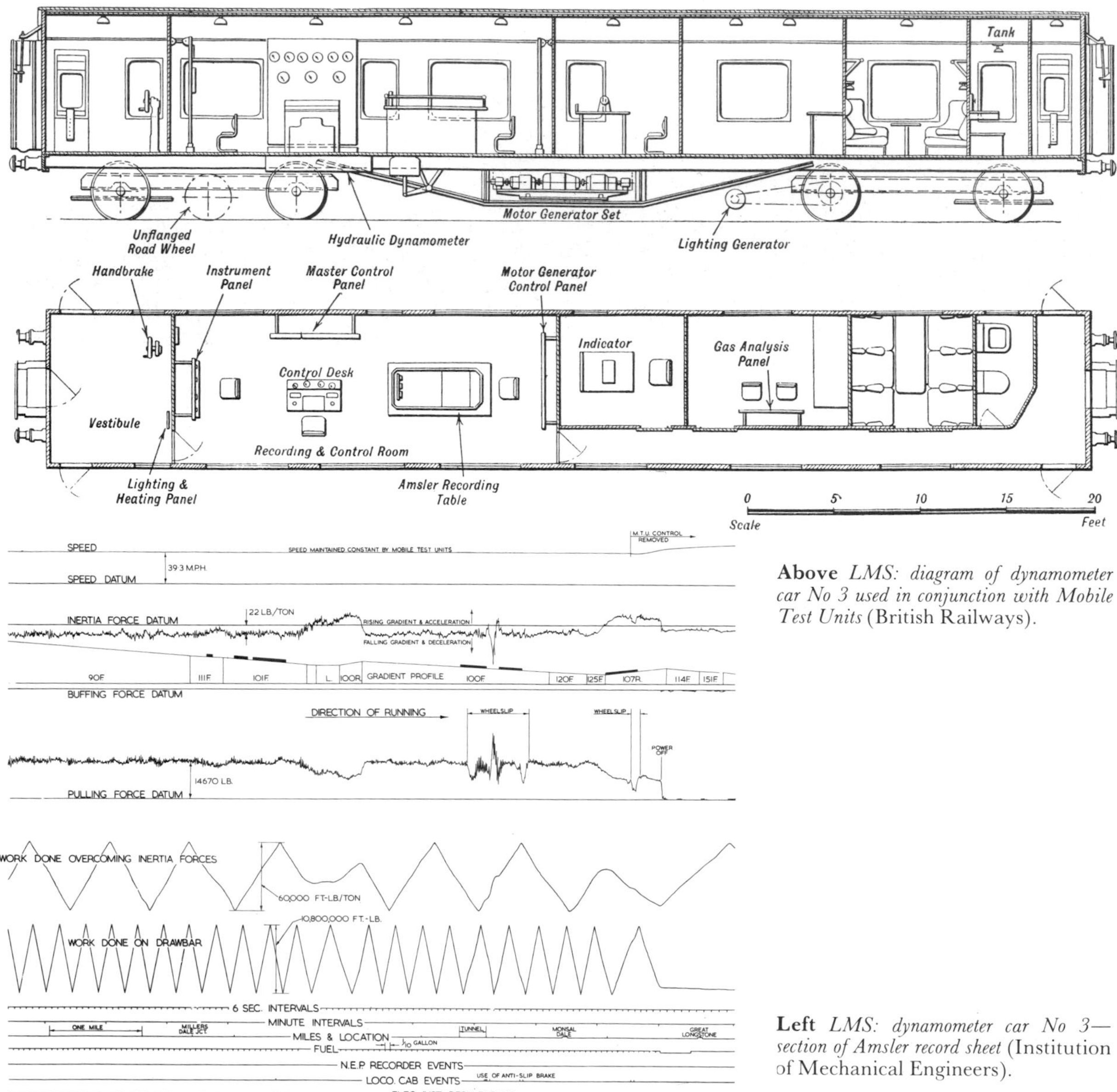

Above *LMS: diagram of dynamometer car No 3 used in conjunction with Mobile Test Units* (British Railways).

Left *LMS: dynamometer car No 3—section of Amsler record sheet* (Institution of Mechanical Engineers).

The accompanying diagram (top) shows the arrangement of the new LMS Dynamometer car designed for use in conjunction with the Mobile Testing Plant. I had the privilege of travelling in this car not long after nationalisation, when it was being used for some exploratory tests on one of the ex-Southern 'Merchant Navy' Class 4-6-2s that had been fitted experimentally with a mechanical stoker. It was one of a series of tests made between Clapham Junction and Salisbury, using the constant speed technique for as much of the journey as practicable. The train left from one of the Windsor line platforms at Clapham Junction, and followed the 'Riverside' line as far as Point Pleasant Junction, and from there took the spur on to the Putney Bridge–Wimbledon line, used jointly by Southern Region and the electric trains of the London Transport 'District Line'. The test train passed on to the Southern main line at Wimbledon. A 'path' had been arranged following immediately

1926: a 'Castle' tested between Euston and Carlisle—GWR No 5000, Launceston Castle, *entering Crewe, with the 10.30 am Liverpool and Manchester express. An unidentified LNWR 'Precedent' Class 2-4-0 is on the left* (courtesy of E.S. Cox).

after the passage of the 'Atlantic Coast Express' when the line would be clear to provide an uninterrupted test run at a constant speed of 50 mph as far west as Andover Junction. Beyond that station a temporary speed restriction for permanent way repairs compelled a reduction to 20 mph. The test train consisted of the new dynamometer car and two mobile test units—three vehicles in all.

Referring to the drawing showing the dynamometer car layout, the three key positions in the Recording and Control Room were those of the engineers at the Instrument Panel, at the Amsler Recording Table, and at the Control Desk, the last mentioned being the man in overall supervisory charge of the whole exercise. On the Instrument Panels the various dials related to the thermodynamic performance of the locomotive: boiler pressure, steam chest pressure, temperatures and so on. The instruments were not self-recording so that the man concerned had to keep a continuous log of the various quantities. On the Amsler table a graphic record was kept of speed, drawbar pull, drawbar horsepower, and of the work done, and the measures taken to ensure complete accuracy were certainly impressive. So also were the methods used to record the indicated horsepower. With this system of testing it was considered essential to maintain a constant value of this and, on the trip I made, the stipulated working conditions on the locomotive were a steam chest pressure of 200 lb per square inch and a cut-off of 20 per cent. The value of '200' was chosen to allow for fluctuation in the boiler pressure below the rated value of 280 lb per square inch, though actually the test conditions demanded on this run bore little relation to the way the 'Merchant Navy' Class was handled in normal traffic.

There is no doubt that these engines were among the most erratic that have ever run on British Railways and, in subsequent tests on the new stationary plant at Rugby and on the Settle and Carlisle line, they proved extremely difficult to control to any degree of operational stability; and my impression of the London–Salisbury test run was that extreme scientific methods were trying to be imposed on a machine which just did not react to them. On the return journey the test requirements were again a steam chest pressure of 200 lb per square inch with a cut-off of no less than 30 per cent. This would have been considered very heavy working in ordinary service. With the 500-ton 'Bournemouth-Belle' all-Pullman train steam chest pressures of around 130 lb per square inch, were enough to keep time, with cut-offs of about 25 per cent. I was not altogether surprised that the boiler failed to stand up to this severe requirement, and the test had to be abandoned. No official results were published of the Mobile Test Plant results with the 'Merchant Navy' Class. Tests that gave more consistent and reliable results were made on the London Midland Region, with one of the Stanier 'Black Five' 4-6-0s, running from Derby to Willesden Junction and back via Leicester and Rugby.

Six round trips were made, to cover all the desired combinations of speed and cut-off. Here again, however, theory seemed to override normal practice. All tests were made with the regulator of the locomotive fully open. I would not be so dogmatic as to state that in ordinary practice these excellent locomotives were *never* worked in this manner; but certainly full regulator working would be very exceptional. One would have thought that if it was desired to establish the economics of these engines driving, on test, the customary style would have given more realistic results. The cut-offs used

Left Launceston Castle *at Durran Hill shed, Carlisle, being coaled ready for the southbound dynamometer car test run to Crewe* (courtesy of E.S. Cox).

Below *Dynamometer car test run with an LMS 'Black-5' 4-6-0, using the former Lancashire and Yorkshire Railway dynamometer car* (British Railways).

Right *'Full-dress' trials with the Great Western 'Kings'. A striking view of engine No 6005,* King George II, *showing the shelter built round the front end to shield men taking indicator diagrams and other measurements* (British Railways).

Below right *The new LMS dynamometer car, used in conjunction with trials using the Mobile Testing Units* (British Railways).

ranged from 10 per cent to 30 per cent, in steps of 5 per cent, then to 60 per cent in steps of 10 per cent and finally to full gear. The speeds covered every 10 mph up to 60 mph but not every speed at each cut-off. An interesting and comprehensive series of test results was obtained with engine No 44764 of this class, and it was revealed that at cut-offs below 20 per cent, even using full regulator, the performance was poor. Working in 15 per cent the maximum drawbar horsepower attained was less than 500 at 60 mph, while in 10 per cent only 300 was attained. The corresponding figures for 20 and 25 per cent cut-off, at 60 mph were 750 and 900, showing clearly why drivers, as practical men, rarely worked these engines at less than 25 per cent and with less than a full regulator opening.

Against the highly theoretic approach to locomotive testing, postulated by Dr Andrews and some, though not all of the staff of the Chief Mechanical Engineer's department of the LMS, the Great Western Railway, at Swindon, was adopting a totally different philosophy. Needless to say, as the time for nationalisation approached, there was intense rivalry, as in every other facet of locomotive engineering. But partisanship apart, the Great Western approach to testing was immeasurably the more practical of the two. It was based upon constant steaming rates rather than constant speed, and had the immense advantage that it enabled test results to be translated immediately into practical timetabling applications. It was not, of course, until after nationalisation that the rival philosophies of locomotive testing procedure came into head-on collision; but then, it did not take the practically minded senior locomotive engineers of the Railway Executive long to decide which was the better, and ordain that in future it should be the basis of the standard procedure. Although 100 per cent LMS in

their earlier affiliation, they decided in favour of the Great Western system.

It was generally agreed by all parties that the laboratory-like testing of locomotives, which of necessity had to be conducted at constant speed, should be supplemented by road testing. Otherwise, the resistance offered to a train in passing through the atmosphere at speed could not be assessed. In pre-war years a highly scientific approach to the measurement of air resistance had been made by F.C. Johansen, using methods used in the aircraft industry and evaluating the effects of side and head-winds of varying strength upon scale models positioned in a wind tunnel. It had long been felt that the formulae evolved by earlier experimenters for train resistance had been rendered obsolete by the modern trends towards the air-smoothing of the exterior of passenger rolling stock, and by the improvements in bearing design and lubrication. The formulae evolved by Johansen became generally accepted as a means for making reasonably accurate estimates of the horsepower being developed by locomotives when the conditions were stable, for a few miles at the least, and no dynamometer car was available to make direct measurements. But while air resistance, and the resistance or assistance to motion offered by head, cross, or favourable winds provides the major uncertainty when one tries to reproduce the stability of laboratory conditions, by making road tests at scientifically regulated constant speeds, it is clear that laboratory and road tests at the same speed and the same cut-off could produce considerably varying results.

In any case constant speed running on all but a minimal number of routes in Great Britain is so exceptional as to be quite unrepresentative of ordinary service requirements either for passenger or freight traffic. Brief reference has been made in

A forward look into the indicator shelter on engine No 6005, showing special test fittings and the confined space in which the operators had to work (British Railways).

earlier chapters to the studies made by the testing section of the Locomotive Drawing Office of the Great Western Railway, at Swindon, towards means of effecting a close reconciliation between results obtained on the stationary testing plant in Swindon Works and those from dynamometer car runs, sometimes made with service trains, and always involving all the fluctuation in speed that such runs involve. It is the latter, of course, which represent the basic requirement of railway service and, while a locomotive running in the rarefied atmosphere of a stationary test plant might return a highly gratifying value of thermal efficiency, the day to day variations in coal consumption in working the same set of trains, with identical loads, that had been revealed in earlier, much publicised dynamometer car test exercises, are enough to show up the uncertainties that daily working imposes on locomotive performance.

The inconsistencies that can arise in dynamometer car test runs with service trains, and which no doubt led Charles Roberts and his colleagues to seek means of reconciliation in the 1930s, are no more clearly revealed than by a close examination of one of the earliest runs with the Swindon car, with the famous engine No 171, *Albion*, when in its first 4-6-0 condition, and which was more than once quoted as an example of high locomotive performance. Details extracted from a published chart of the run were as follows:

Speed (mph)	**Gradient rising**	**Cut-off (per cent)**	**Drawbar (horse-power)**	**Drawbar pull (tons)**
63	1 in 1,320	18	800	2.14
58	1 in 754	20	900	2.6
60	1 in 834	23	1,100	3.06

One can imagine that Churchward, as was his wont, put his rule on the chart, and was well satisfied by such a pull as 3 tons at 60 mph; but it is not until one looks a little further into those figures that they become quite inexplicable. The load behind the tender was given as 337 tons tare, probably around 355 tons with passenger and luggage and, taking account of the relative small effects of gravity on those slight gradients, the rolling resistance of the coaches works out at 12, 13½, and no less than 17 lb per ton in the three cases—obviously quite irreconcilable. From the chart it would appear that conditions were quite stable at the time the measurements were taken, so that one cannot assume that any acceleration, or deceleration, was having an effect. The most charitable view that one can take is that a heavy adverse wind had sprung up by the time the train was approaching Shrivenham. For the record, the Johansen formula for train resistance gives a value of 11.5 lb per ton at 60 mph.

In 1928 in a series of dynamometer car trials on the LNER on service trains between Doncaster and Kings Cross, one of the Gresley Pacific engines involved, conveying the same loads and making the same speed on six successive days, showed coal consumptions varying between 34.95 and 40.65 lb per mile; but the coal related to the work, in pounds per drawbar horsepower hour, showed an even greater variation, between a maximum of 3.44 lb and a minimum of 2.89 lb—a 19 per cent variation—and the variations did not correspond with the actual consumption. For example, the highest actual figure of 40.65 lb was recorded on a day when the rate per drawbar horsepower was one of the lowest, 2.99 lb. In other words, while the overall results for the week were very satisfactory, on the finer points of performance there were inconsistencies, even though the same engine, the same grade of hard Yorkshire coal, and the same engine crew were involved throughout.

On the Great Western Railway the theory had been advanced that locomotives will run at maximum efficiency if the rate of evaporation in the boiler is maintained as nearly constant as possible throughout a run. Such conditions would be easy enough to sustain on a stationary test plant, with all facilities for stabilised performance at hand. But, although the close analysis of the details of many hard runs seemed to show that when a maximum effort was called for, drivers were tending to work their engines in a manner corresponding to such conditions, something more precise than the judgment of an experienced engineman, with a Running Inspector at his elbow, was needed to secure exact reconciliation of stationary plant results in a road test. For it was by that time believed that, if the rate of steam feed through the cylinders was constant, the test plant results would be exactly reproduced on the road, no matter how widely the speed varied in the course of the journey. The problem came of devising some apparatus that would give the driver an exact and constant indication to enable the necessary adjustments to the cut-off to be made on a road test, and equally on the test plant.

Such an instrument was made at Swindon by using the blast pipe tip as an orifice meter, which would indicate the rate of flow by the difference in pressure across it. Simple enough as it is in theory, in applying this principle to a locomotive, several points had to be borne in mind, seeing that one had to convey an indication of what was happening at the tip of the blastpipe first of all to the driver, and then also to observers in the dynamometer car.

Since the giving of an accurate indication to the driver was the fundamental necessity for successful working of the entire system of testing, it requires special reference. The arrangement designed at Swindon is shown in principle and practical detail in the accompanying diagram. Air at very low velocity was allowed to filter into a pipe (from the reservoir at the right-hand end of the 'basic' diagram) which at the opposite end was open to the exhaust steam just below the blastpipe. The rate of air infiltration was controlled and indicated with sufficient accuracy by passing the air through a needle valve and a bubble jar. Air pressure in the pipe line attained the pressure of steam below the orifice, and any excess air filtered away in the exhaust steam. The difference in levels of the mercury in the manometer gauge was in some measure proportional to the steam rate and, before commencing any test, a pointer was fixed to the gauge showing the level of the mercury that must be maintained.

Tests made from Swindon confirmed what had been believed, and hoped, that if the steam rate was maintained constant, even though the speed might vary considerably, the performance characteristics of the locomotive, coal and water consumption, and indicated horsepower were the same as those measured in a constant speed test on the stationary plant at the same steam rate. With the theory proved completely valid by the tests out on the line, refinements were embodied, particularly in the method of recording coal consumption. Instead of the rough and ready weighing of a locomotive tender before and after a run, the coal was made up into bags containing one hundredweight each and, when a test at a constant steam rate was in progress, these were brought forward from the tender by two men riding in the tender, and the contents emptied on to the shovelling plate as the fireman needed them. The time when each new bag was brought forward was logged, and subsequently plotted; when constant steam rate working was in progress the rate of coal usage was also completely uniform. The system of testing, for which S. O. Ell was responsible, was known as the Controlled Road System. Purely Great Western in origin, it was

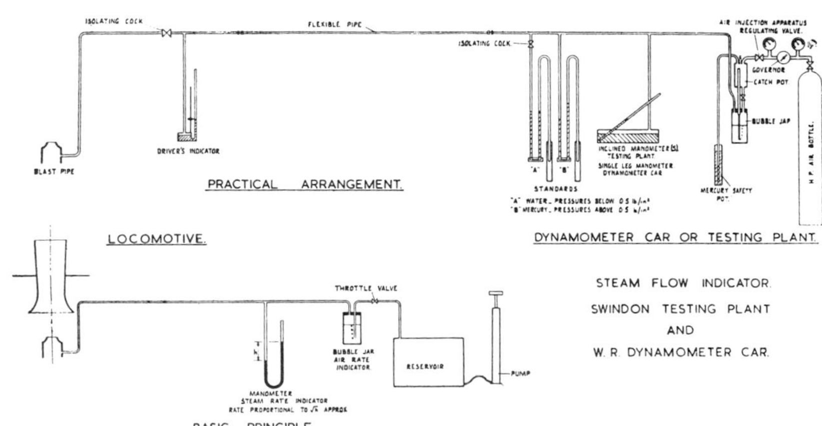

Western Region: diagram of steam flow indicator, designed for monitoring controlled road tests (British Railways).

subsequently adopted as the standard system of road testing on British Railways.

Although it is taking the story a few years ahead of the time of its acceptance as a British standard, some details of an actual run will serve to show how the system worked out in practice. The test in question was with a 4-cylinder 4-6-0 of the 'King' Class, fitted with a high degree super-heater, and the run was from Stoke Gifford yard, near the site of the present Bristol Parkway station, to Scours Lane yard, just to the west of Reading. The load was one of 23 bogie passenger coaches (781 tons) and, to maintain standard express passenger train speed, a steam rate of 28,700 lb per hour was required. The test began when acceleration from rest had just attained 40 mph and the indicated horsepower was 1,900. After that with the IHP remaining almost constant just below the 2,000 mark, the speed varied from a sustained 47 mph climbing a 1 in 300 gradient, to 81, 57 and then 77 mph before a reduction to 15 mph for a temporary speed restriction. Subsequently, speed was vigorously worked up to a maximum of 69 mph before the test ended. The locomotive was steamed with the regulator full open for the whole time, including the period of severe speed restriction. Deceleration was effected entirely by the brakes, and the cut-off which had been 23 per cent at 77 mph was progressively lengthened to 65 per cent by the time speed had

A more accurate method of measuring coal consumption on test runs was obtained by use of a special coal-weighing tender, here seen attached to 'Black-5' 4-6-0, No 45081, on a Glasgow to Morecambe express, passing Carnforth (Derek Cross).

been reduced to the stipulated 15 mph. With the same constant steam rate continuing this heavy train was afterwards accelerated from 15 to 60 mph in 6 miles of level track.

The development of the Controlled Road System of testing, its application on the Settle and Carlisle, and the Carlisle and Hurlford sections, is noted in Chapter 17 of this book, together with some tabulated comparative results obtained with a variety of locomotives. In the trials conducted in the North of England and in Scotland, the Mobile Test Units designed by Dr Andrews were used on some of the maximum load runs to avoid the need for making up trains of excessive length composed of ordinary coaching stock, which would have been inconvenient to accommodate in some of the sidings.

Dynamometer car test run of a different kind. Testing the effectiveness of the audible cab signalling equipment in October 1947. The car was used primarily to provide an accurate record of the speed which was 96½ mph. The engine is No 5056, Earl of Powis *('Castle' Class)* (M.W. Earley).

13. The British Railways Interchange Trials of 1948

The nationalisation of British Railways in January 1948, and the setting up, at 222 Marylebone Road, London, of a small but highly authoritative section under the Member of the Railway Executive responsible for Mechanical and Electrical Engineering that should, in the future, direct policy, nationwide, on locomotive construction and maintenance, and equally on design, at one stroke terminated any thoughts that the practice of the former independent railways would continue. The fact that the newly appointed Chief Officer (Locomotive Works), R.C. Bond, and the Executive Officer (Design), E.S. Cox, like the Member himself, R.A. Riddles, both came from the LMS might have suggested that, in the future, LMS ideas were likely to predominate, did not prove wholly well founded. Indeed, whatever may have been discussed by the new triumvirate 'behind locked doors', there was outwardly an evident desire to examine the existing motive power as objectively as possible. One major point had been decided for them: the new power, for some years, would have to be steam. A Government White Paper on capital investment had deferred the prospects of large-scale electrification; foreign exchange was not available to purchase the large quantities of oil that would be needed for large-scale diesel traction, even if sufficient experience had been available to decide on suitable types—which it certainly was not.

With the utmost energy and enthusiasm, a two-pronged drive towards future practice was at once initiated. Cox began formulating plans for an entirely new range of steam locomotives, while concurrently plans were laid for a series of Inter-change Trials, which, to quote the Foreword to the report subsequently issued '. . . were initiated primarily as a means of producing, in as short a time as possible, indications of the most desirable features to incorporate in the design of future steam locomotives and they were not intended to be a contest between locomotives of similar types, which it was appreciated, had been designed to fulfil the requirements of their particular Region.

'From the outset it was realised that these indications would be of a very broad nature as the trials were carried out under the normal operating conditions obtained at the time of each test run and without any special preparation of the locomotives. It was agreed that the locomotives used should be taken direct from traffic having run between 15,000 and 20,000 miles since last general repair and there was consequently some variation in mechanical condition, particularly in the case of freight locomotives. It was also realised that, in the existing circumstances, inequalities which are liable to be experienced in any variable speed testing on the track would be present. Traffic delays and temporary speed restrictions may be mentioned as examples of these inequalities and, whilst the traffic delays tended to cancel out over a number of tests, the number and siting of temporary speed restrictions affected some locomotives more than others.'

In fact, without taking into account anything of the personalities involved on the test trains, and their attitudes to it, the stage was set for the most inconsequential, and unrepresentative series of competitive trials ever to be held on the railways of Great Britain. It would be unkind to those who planned it with the best and most altruistic of motives to suggest that taken all round it was a colossal waste of time and money; but for the pur-

1948 Interchange Trials: the Bulleid 'Pacific' No 35019, French Line-CGT, *at Paddington ready to take the 1.30 pm to Plymouth, on a preliminary run* (C.C.B. Herbert).

Above left *Replacement for an early casualty in the preliminary runs—the GWR 'Hall' Class 4-6-0, No 4920,* Dumbleton Hall, *going hard east of Reading, having been substituted for the celebrated* Mallard *on April 27 1948* (M.W. Earley).

Above *Eastern Region: the GWR 4-6-0, No 6018,* King Henry VI, *at Wakefield, having worked a Leeds and Bradford express down from Kings Cross* (Overend Press Agency).

Left *Western Region: ex-LMS converted 'Scot' 4-6-0, No 46162,* Queen's Westminster Rifleman, *turning on to the Berks & Hants line at Reading with the 1.30 pm Paddington–Plymouth express* (M.W. Earley).

pose for which it was originally ordained it very nearly was. But in another, and unexpected sense it was invaluable. Few of the locomotive engineers in middle levels of responsibility relished the prospects of nationalisation. They had grown up developing a sense of intense loyalty to their respective railways, whether it was at Doncaster and Darlington, at Swindon, at Ashford, Brighton and Eastleigh, or at Crewe and Derby. The whole business promised naught except distasteful uncertainties, even on the LMS where some of their own bosses were now taking supreme command. But with the setting up of the *ad hoc* committee to plan and carry through the Interchange Trials, and eventually to report on them, the first months of nationalisation became a joyous and exciting exercise, after the restraints and miseries of the war years, and it brought together, on ground with which they were already very familiar, men of all four of the old companies.

That committee, which could in many respects be regarded as the spearhead of subsequent and very profitable inter-Regional cooperation, consisted of C. S. Cocks, of the Southern, who had the intimidating task of fathering the detailed design of the Bulleid 'Pacifics', but who had not lost any of his sense of humour in the process; Sam Ell, of the Great Western, nurtured in the Swindon drawing office, and inheritor and perfecter of the precepts of modern testing first postulated by Charles Roberts; R.G. Jarvis, of the LMS, an all-round enthusiast, who in his eventual retirement went to live within sight and sound of the Festiniog Railway, and finally there was Bert Spencer, veteran of them all but still young in spirit, with a mighty bank of experience behind him in the many years he had as personal locomotive assistant to Sir Nigel Gresley, and on whose drawing board at Kings Cross the first proposals for the *Cock o' the North, Silver Link* and *Green Arrow* took shape. It was a galaxy of talent happily integrated under Spencer's chairmanship, and from this seed the spirit of inter-Regional co-operation in locomotive engineering germinated. I shall always remember the remark made by a member of the Swindon dynamometer car test team whom I met at Plymouth when they were in the course of trials with the LMS 'Black Five' 4-6-0. He simply said: 'We're having a grand time!'

In his book on the British Standard steam locomotives published in 1966, E.S. Cox has written: 'Eighteen years have passed since then and for those who were not interested in the trials at the time it may briefly be recalled that the best all-round running performances were achieved by the LMS 'Rebuilt Scots' and the Bulleid Pacifics. The latter were, however, much inferior in efficiency to any of the others, and this was not due to the enterprising manner in which they were driven, but to inbuilt design characteristics. The lowest consumptions in lb per dbhp/hour were attained by the LNER 'A4' Pacifics, which, however, almost alone among the contestants, suffered mechanical breakdown on three occasions, due to hot inside big-ends. The Stanier 'Pacific' came second as regards low specific coal consumption, but was driven throughout in a very unenterprising manner, so that its running performance was far below the potential which other records have proved this class capable of attaining. Of the mixed traffic engines the LNER 'B1' performed better than anticipated and the LM Class '5' rather worse, but both displayed a similar and satisfactory efficiency.'

Put in perhaps less tactful language, the road performance of the Stanier engines was one of the major disappointments of the whole exercise. The choice of a driver for the 'Duchess' Class 'Pacific' was very unfortunate, while those who handled the 'Black Five' seemed to be bent upon coal dodging rather than the maintenance of the running times of their trains. Those who handled the Bulleid 'Pacifics', on the other hand, were inspired by the exhortations of their shedmaster at Nine Elms, the inimitable J. Pelham Maitland, and duly set out in colloquial terms, to 'knock spots off' everyone else! That they used a lot of coal in the process went without saying, as all who knew the Bulleid 'Pacifics' in their hey-day will appreciate; but they exhilarated the enthusiasts who travelled behind them, and who gloried in the knowledge that the Southern had stepped into the very forefront of express locomotive running. But there was another side to it, even allowing for the vagaries of performance turned in by individual drivers. Turning again to the writings of E.S. Cox, he inveighed:

'The benefits and shortcomings of these tests from the point of view of Riddles and his men lay in other directions. They did confirm what had already been gathered from experience on the LMS, that a properly designed steam locomotive would work satisfactorily anywhere from Land's End to John O'Groats on appropriate duties. They showed that the simplest and most straightforward designs were at no disadvantage compared with the more complex. They indicated that capacity to boil water was as essential as ever it was, and that with modern cylinders and valve events, choice of number of cylinders, other than as demanded by loading gauge, was of little importance, and that relatively small wheels were no bar to high speed.

'With the benefit of wisdom after the event,' he continued, 'it can now be seen, however, that we were misled in certain directions by the essentially artificial characteristics of all such trials. For example, employment of the most experienced drivers of whom the regions were possessed, masked the true facts of adhesion. We concluded that

Below *Western Region: the 8.30 am Plymouth to Paddington, on a preliminary run worked by ex-LMS converted 'Scot' 4-6-0, No 46162,* Queen's Westminster Rifleman, *in Sonning cutting* (M.W. Earley).

Right *London Midland Region: the 10.15 am express to Manchester, leaving St Pancras, hauled by ex-LNER 'B1' Class 4-6-0, No 61251,* Oliver Bury, *with the Horwich dynamometer car* (C.C.B. Herbert).

uncompensated 4-6-2 engines could be almost as sure-footed as 4-6-0s, not realising that it was the supreme expertise of individual drivers who coaxed seemingly reliable adhesion out of the various "Pacifics" even when on mountainous routes. In the hands of "run of the mill" drivers and with indifferent weight adjustment on individual axles, such engines could become most uncertain starters. The end coupled locomotives, on the other hand, sat down at the back end the more firmly on the track, the greater the drawbar pull, and the "Pacifics" could only match their adhesion reliability in the hands of all comers when their axle weights were compensated throughout as was the case abroad. The sure-footedness of the Western "Kings" during the trials was thus a true indication, but that of the various "Pacifics" was not fully representative of what they could be like under day-to-day conditions.'

This rather extraordinary 'confession' made 18 years after the conclusion of the Interchange Trials rather underlines the suggestion that the ex-LMS triumvirate had, prior to nationalisation, less experience with 'Pacifics' than some of the other railways. And it was not only with 'run of the mill' drivers that 'Pacifics' were apt to 'sit up and dance'! On the down 'Flying Scotsman', for example, when I was on the footplate of a Gresley 'A4', a very experienced Gateshead driver had the greatest difficulty in starting from Berwick-on-Tweed and on a wet rail slipped continuously all the way up the 1 in 190 gradient to Burnmouth. Then again, even on the LMS, when I was riding a 'Princess Royal' on the morning Birmingham–Glasgow express, even on a dry rail we slipped so badly on Beattock bank as to take no less than 31½ minutes to climb the 10 miles to summit. As for the Bulleid 'Pacifics', even in my own footplate experience it only seemed to need a shower of hail to make them almost unmanageable. In later years, when some of them were put on to the severely graded Somerset and Dorset line, their load classification had to be made the same as that of the LMS 'Black Five' 4-6-0s.

While the Interchange Trials were still in progress, active consideration was being given at BR Headquarters on new standard designs, and it is remarkable that no fewer than four new 'Pacifics' were proposed, of which the largest was to be a development of the existing LMS 'Duchess' Class. The other three were entirely new, as follows; using the former LMS power classification: Class '6', Express passenger; Class '6', Mixed traffic and Class '5', Mixed traffic. The first and last were intended for work previously done by the rebuilt 'Scots' and the 'Black Five' 4-6-0s respectively, while the Class '6' mixed traffic was something intermediate. The theoretical advantage of a 'Pacific' over a 4-6-0 for the same work was considered to lie in the more economical combustion rates that would be possible on the larger firegrates of the Pacific. On the average rate of work on duties allocated to Class '5' locomotives it was argued that the larger grates would have shown savings 'almost exactly equated by the capital charges on the increased cost of the Pacific over the 4-6-0', to quote E. S. Cox. The design team of the Railway Executive were encouraged to persevere with their ideas for a medium powered 'Pacific' by the remarkable running performances of the Bulleid 'West Country' 'Pacifics' in the Interchange Trials, which impressed the professionals and thrilled their supporters in the ranks of the amateur enthusiasts, albeit at the expense of heavy coal consumption.

At the time the trials took place, train schedules on the principal express routes had only just begun to recover from the worst of the wartime decelera-

tions, and even though the loads were heavy, the tasks set to the largest express locomotives were considerably easier than those on the same routes prior to the outbreak of war in 1939. The table below shows the differences.

They were not the fastest in operation before the war but the most comparable in time of day and service. There was, for example, a Grantham to Kings Cross run in 100 minutes, and on the LMS there were faster trains on 'XL' limit timings between Crewe and Euston; but the times quoted were those of the up 'Flying Scotsman' on its winter schedule, and of the down 'Royal Scot'. In extenuation of the easier schedules, account must also be taken of the ravages of war on track, and the fact that many of the drivers had not been in top link work when schedules were at their tightest. The Southern men on the 'Merchant Navy' Class engines were enterprising to a degree, though not to the same extent as their colleagues on the 'West Country' 4-6-2s in the mixed traffic engine trials that followed. Cox mentions particularly the work of the rebuilt 'Scots' which though returning very poor work at times was brilliant at others. It is, however, significant that the driver concerned, F. Brooker of Camden Shed, was an old hand with a distinguished prewar record, and the spells of poor running could very likely be attributed to the bad riding of the engines, on track suffering from arrears of maintenance. It has already been mentioned in Chapter 10 how the rebuilt 'Scots' were troubled by persistent rolling on occasions. While the LMS

Railway	Route	Distance (miles)	Comparative times in minutes	
			August 1939	May 1948
GWR	Exeter–Taunton	30.8	35	38
	Taunton–Westbury	47.1	50	55
	Westbury–Paddington	95.6	95	113
Southern	Waterloo–Salisbury	83.8	86	103*
	Salisbury–Sidmouth Junction	75.8	85	90
LMS	Euston–Rugby	82.6	80	93
	Rugby–Crewe	75.5	76	90
	Crewe–Carlisle	141.1	154	183
LNER	Kings Cross–Peterborough	76.4	83	90
	Peterborough–Grantham	29.1	36	38
	Grantham–Kings Cross	105.5	105½	122

* 95 minutes in up direction

Left *Eastern Region: dynamometer test run, Kings Cross to Leeds, worked by Bulleid 'Pacific' No 35017,* Belgian Marine, *('Merchant Navy' Class) near Potters Bar* (M.W. Earley).

Right *Western Region: the ex-LNER 'B1' 4-6-0, No 61251,* Oliver Bury, *at Taunton with the Wolverhampton–Penzance express, and the ex-GWR dynamometer car* (J.C. Collins).

choice of a driver for the rebuilt 'Scots' was fortunate that for the 'Duchess' Class 'Pacific' was not so, and that engine, the *City of Bradford* turned in the most unrepresentative performance of any in all the trials.

To those with vivid memories of the dashing and spectacular work of Great Western locomotives in the Interchange Trials of 1925 the performance of the 'King', and still more that of the 'Hall' in the mixed traffic engine series was a great disappointment. It was bad enough that Great Western locomotives were not permitted to run anywhere on the London Midland or the Southern Regions, but the actual running showed little of the sparkle that had come to characterise the work of Swindon-built locomotives, not infrequently even in the war years. At the time much was made of the fact that they were compelled to use hard Yorkshire, instead of Welsh, coal; but this was not a very sound argument, and it tended to obscure what I have always felt was the true reason for the rather pedestrian running of both engines. The high management of the Great Western Railway was deeply antagonistic to nationalisation as a whole, and these sentiments were passed down, if not necessarily as far as individual drivers and firemen then certainly to divisional officers. The Old Oak driver chosen to work the 'King', both to Plymouth and to Leeds, was a 'safe' man who, with unfamiliar coal, set out to keep the leisurely schedules, and no more. I was a passenger on his last trip from Leeds to Kings Cross, and it was adequate and punctual but no more. The same crew took the 'Hall' from Marylebone to Manchester, with equally dull results.

Down in the West Country a ridiculous situation was allowed to develop. The train chosen for the test run was the Wolverhampton–Penzance service, not long restored after its suspension during the war years. The normal working was for Newton Abbot and Wolverhampton sheds to provide the power on alternate days, though the locomotives working through were remanned in each direction at Bristol. West of Newton Abbot engines were also changed at Plymouth. The enginemen at Stafford Road shed, Wolverhampton, worked no lodging turns and, whereas certain duties on the north to west route via the Severn Tunnel were worked on this basis by Newton Abbot and Shrewsbury men on alternate days, the Wolverhampton–West of England service had always involved a crew-change at Bristol. For the 1948 Interchange Trials a complete change in the engine working was made. The Wolverhampton-Penzance express was to change engines at Bristol, and the competing engines from all regions to work thence to Plymouth. From the locomotive point of view it was a logical enough step. The Wolverhampton men could work out and home as usual, but with the same engine in both directions, while the Bristol–Plymouth run gave the engines on trial a heavy load run with the full train to Newton Abbot, and then after detaching the Torquay and Paignton portion, a reduced load to take over the mountainous South Devon line.

It was an excellent arrangement for everyone except the host region! It was decreed that the enginemen involved should work from Bristol, and until then the men at Bath Road shed had never worked *any* lodging turns. Suspicious of nationalisation in any case they saw this as a possible thin end of the wedge, and the large express passenger 'link', which worked variously to every direction of

Locomotive	Route (region)	Coal per train mile (lb)	Coal per dhp hour (lb)	Coal (lb per square foot grate per hour)
WR 'King'	Western	48.82	3.74	67.5
	Eastern	47.25	3.39	64.9
ER 'A4'	Western	42.45	3.19	47.8
	Eastern	39.08	2.92	44.1
	London Midland	41.25	3.00	46.7
	Southern	45.57	3.20	52.3
LMR 'Duchess'	Western	41.67	3.24	38.5
	Eastern	44.05	3.04	41.6
	London–Midland	44.09	3.07	42.7
	Southern	42.74	3.17	42.0
LMR 'Rebuilt Scot'	Western	42.76	3.64	62.6
	Eastern	46.66	3.26	67.4
	London–Midland	41.42	3.37	62.0
	Southern	44.39	3.24	68.3
SR 'Merchant Navy'	Western	48.02	3.61	45.9
	Eastern	49.41	3.73	47.9
	London–Midland	50.66	3.57	48.0
	Southern	50.85	3.52	50.8

the compass from Bristol, but always on a 'single-home' basis, refused *en bloc* to work the train. It would have been easy enough to allocate the duty to Plymouth men, who knew the road, and worked many lodging turns, but instead volunteers were called for, and the only one who came forward was a relatively inexperienced man, who had in any case to learn the difficult road from Newton Abbot to Plymouth. Not surprisingly his performance, on what would have been a tough assignment for the top link Laira men was indifferent; but in the official report the blame was laid on the coal! When later in the year 1949 there was a re-run, with Welsh coal, the test trains were worked by a Plymouth driver of outstanding ability, with an almost sensational improvement in the performance, again, officially, attributed to the coal!

The results of the trials of the express passenger engines in 1948, all fired with South Kirkby coal, are shown above:

In appraising the coal results from the ex-LNER 'A4' 'Pacifics', which were on average the lowest of all in the express passenger class, it must be recorded that they alone of all the locomotives

Mallard, *of 126 mph fame, on the 1.30 pm Paddington–Plymouth express, passing through Sonning cutting* (M.W. Earley).

classes engaged in the trials suffered three complete failures on the road, and had to be removed from their trains. In the original proposals for the tests, submitted to The Railway Executive on March 24 1948, the LNER representative in the express passenger group was to have been of the latest 3-cylinder 4-6-2 type, otherwise a Peppercorn 'A2'. The first of the new 'A1' Class was not completed at Doncaster until August 1948. Whether it was felt that the 6 foot 2 inch coupled wheels of the 'A2' were too small, or whether the engines of this class were not felt to have been sufficiently tried out in traffic one cannot say, but in the end the Gresley 'A4' was substituted. Although this class had fallen somewhat from the pinnacle of fame it occupied on the outbreak of war, it had survived the attempted denigrations of the Thompson era fairly well, though the Gresley 'Pacific' stud as a whole was not in the best of condition after the war. The celebrated *Mallard* was not one of the best, and there was concern at Running Shed level when high authority decreed that she should represent the Eastern and North Eastern Region. Concern was justified when she failed at Savernake with a hot middle big-end on her first preliminary return trip from Plymouth, before even the trials proper had started.

Another of the double-chimneyed 'A4s', *Seagull*, was substituted, for the Paddington–Plymouth tests, and 60034, *Lord Faringdon*, for the Euston–Carlisle, and Kings Cross–Leeds tests, and came through without mishap. Then for the last phase, *Seagull* took up the running again, and on her first pre-test run with the 'Atlantic Coast Express' got no farther than Andover, where she failed with the same trouble. On the following day *Mallard* appeared. She got to Exeter, and back to Waterloo on the following day; then on June 8 she made an excellent test run, with some particularly fine running between Salisbury and Sidmouth Junction. On the return journey, however, she got no farther home than Salisbury, where she had to come off the train once again with the same trouble. *Seagull* had been repaired in time to finish the last two days of tests on the Southern, without further incident.

Except in respect of the Bulleid 'Pacifics' of both varieties, which were still relatively new, the Interchange Trials of 1948 revealed little in the way of engine performance that was not already known collectively to the men who formed the testing committees, but it was the running of the Bulleid 'West Country' 'Pacifics' in particular, and their enthusiastic drivers and firemen that bemused the design team of The Railway Executive into believing the rightness of their thinking on the imagined superiority of 'Pacifics' over 4-6-0s, for the intermediate classes of passenger and mixed traffic duties. Cox later admitted, with the advantage of hindsight, how wrong they had been, but not before the singularly ineffective Class '6' standard 'Pacific' had been built, fortunately in no great numbers.

Another regrettable outcome of the trials was the failure to show up the merits of the Swindon setting of the Stephenson link motion, as applied to a mixed traffic locomotive. One is aware that in the modern situation any locomotive with an inside valve gear would be unacceptable; but the LMS had shown its appreciation of the modern potentialities of the link

Great Central Line: an express from Marylebone arriving at Manchester (London Road, now Piccadilly) hauled by ex-GWR 4-6-0, No 6990, Witherslack Hall, *with the ex-LNER dynamometer car* (British Railways).

motion by building one engine of the 'Black Five' 4-6-0 Class with that gear outside; and in due course that locomotive, still happily preserved in working order, gained the reputation of being one of the strongest engines of the whole class. Unfortunately, between them the two drivers who handled the GWR 4-6-0 No 6990, *Witherslack Hall*, in the 1948 Interchange Trials did not seem to have it in them to bring out those merits, the one through lack of enterprise and the other by sheer inexperience.

The Western Region authorities complained that their locomotives had been penalised by having to use Yorkshire, instead of Welsh, coal and by way of appeasement a further series of trials was run later in 1948 using South Wales Abergorki coal, which had characteristics generally the opposite of those of the Yorkshire 'hards' used in the main series of trials. The Welsh coal had a high fixed carbon and low volatile matter content; it was very friable and dusty and burned with a short flame. Its calorific value was 15,100 BThU per lb against the 14,400 BThU per lb of the South Kirkby coal. The comparative results for both the 'King' and the 'Hall' Class engines are shown in the accompanying table, though in the case of the latter engine it was not a straight comparison. In the tests with Welsh coal the engine concerned was worked by a top-link Laira (Plymouth) driver of first class ability.

The slightly higher calorific value of the Welsh coal could be considered to have favourably influenced the consumption, in the proportion of 15,100 to 14,400; but that would not account for the enormous difference between the performance of the 'Hall' Class engines 6990 and 6961. On his first westbound journey, the 'volunteer' driver on the former engine used no less than 54.68 lb of coal per train mile, compared to 38.6 lb by the Laira driver on No 6961.

Western Region: trial comparisons

'King' Class

Date	April 1948	November 1948
Engine no	6018	6001
Coal (type)	South Kirkby	Abergorki
Consumption		
lb/train mile	48.82	42.28
lb/dhp hour	3.74	3.33
lb/square feet of grate/hr (running time)	67.5	59.6

'Hall' Class

Date	June/ July 1948	November/ December 1948
Engine no	6990	6961
Coal (type)	South Kirkby	Abergorki
Consumption		
lb/train mile	46.91	36.24
lb/dhp hour	4.11	3.22
lb/square feet of grate/hr (running time)	74.5	58.0

Above left *Great Central Line: ex-GWR 4-6-0, No 6990,* Witherslack Hall, *on a dynamometer car test run from Manchester, entering Marylebone* (H.G. Tidey).

Above *One of the War Department 'Austerity' 2-8-0s, of which Nos 63169 and 77000 were tested in the 1948 Interchange trials* (North British Locomotive Company).

Many of the locomotives involved in the Interchange Trials were subsequently subjected to much more comprehensive and scientific tests on one or other of the stationary plants, accompanied by controlled road testing in the Great Western style. The results of these later trials are collated and discussed in Chapter 17. Two classes that were not so dealt with, and which produced some spectacular examples of high power output in the Interchange Trials, were the rebuilt 'Scots' of the former LMS, and the Bulleid 'West Country' 'Pacifics'. So far as the former class was concerned, there is no doubt that F. Brooker, of Camden shed, was an extremely able, indeed dedicated driver, and in view of the performances that he achieved in 1948, it is interesting to recall that in 1955 some special tests made at Rugby, at the request of the motive power department, that the maximum indicated horsepower to be expected with a single fireman lay a little below 1400 in the speed range 35 to 65 mph. The figures for the 1948 Interchange Trials relate to the drawbar and not the indicated horsepower, in each corrected to its equivalent value for level track.

LMS Class '6P' 4-6-0 'Rebuilt Scot': DHP records

Route	Number of readings	Average edhp	Maximum edhp
Paddington–Plymouth	13	1,546	1,685
Kings Cross–Leeds	6	1,290	1,395
Euston–Carlisle	8	1,193	1,442
Waterloo–Exeter	8	1,518	1,782

The maximum value of all, 1,742 edhp was registered east of Crewkerne while climbing a 1 in 200 gradient at 57½ mph. The actual drawbar pull was then 4.5 tons (5.19 tons corrected for gradient) with the engine working in 30 per cent cut-off, with the main valve of the regulator one quarter open.

The Bulleid 'West Country' 'Pacifics' had a nominal tractive effort of 31,000 lb, and on this basis could be grouped with the Great Western 'Castles', the Southern 'Lord Nelsons', the 'Royal Scots' and with the Gresley non-streamlined 'Pacifics' of the LNER. Rarely, one imagines, have any of these famous classes produced running to touch many of the achievements of these Southern 4-6-2s in the 1948 Interchange Trials. Three different drivers from Nine Elms shed were involved, but it was on the Great Central, Great Western and Highland Lines that they so excelled. In particular it was Driver Swain and Fireman Hooker, perhaps the most far travelled crew in all the trials, who set

The War Department 'Austerity' 2-10-0 specially named North British. *Mr R.A. Riddles (left) and A. Black of the North British Locomotive Company are standing in front of the engine.*

the standard by their astonishing work over the Great Central line early in June, including the highest equivalent drawbar horsepower attained by *any* locomotive—large express engines included—in the whole series of trials, 2,010.

The work over the Midland line, though entirely adequate, was less extravagantly exciting, but when Swain and Hooker got up to Perth and set off up the Highland line, some of one's reactions to the reports of it verged upon sheer disbelief. Incidentally this redoubtable pair had already worked the 'Merchant Navy' Class 4-6-2 in the trials between Euston and Carlisle, and they took the 'West Country' up to Perth working as pilot to LMS engines on ordinary service trains. Hooker can justifiably claim to be the only man who ever has shovelled his way over the entire distance from Euston to Inverness.

Southern 'West Country' 'Pacifics': dhp records

Route	Number of readings	Average edhp	Maximum edhp
Marylebone–Manchester	7	1,747	2,010
St Pancras–Manchester	14	1,154	1,370
Bristol–Plymouth	11	1,460	1,715
Perth–Inverness	11	1,597	1,950

The above tables summarise the details of horsepower records contained in the official report published by The Railway Executive in 1949. One of the most noteworthy performances recorded in the report came in the first ascent of the lengthy incline between Struan and Dalnaspidal on the Highland line on July 13 1948 when an output of 1,115 horsepower at the drawbar, 1,530 to 1,540 equivalent, was sustained for 10 miles on a 1 in 70 gradient, at a speed of 36¼ mph. The engine was being worked in 25 per cent cut-off with regulator opened wide enough to give a steam chest pressure of 240 lb per square inch. The mechanical failures to which the Bulleid 'Pacifics' were so frequently susceptible were entirely absent on all the engines involved in the Interchange Trials.

Southern Region: the up 'Atlantic Coast Express' near Hook, worked by ex-LMS converted 'Scot' 4-6-0, No 46154, The Hussar, *fitted with 8-wheeler tender specially for the tests* (M.W. Earley).

14. The new British standard steam locomotives

In his book on the British Standard Steam Locomotives, E.S. Cox states that plans for a new range of designs for general use were in active preparation early in 1948, even before the Interchange Trials were completed. It rather suggested that certain minds had been made up in advance, though when R.A. Riddles addressed the Institution of Locomotive Engineers, on his installation as President in November 1950, he spoke of the difficult task they had undertaken. In the meantime railway enthusiasts, without appreciating many of the underlying reasons, had been delighted that construction had continued of pre-nationalisation types in both 1949 and 1950, including many more Bulleid 'West Country' 'Pacifics', Great Western 'Castles' and 'Halls', and the Peppercorn 'A1' Class 'Pacifics' on the LNER. But it is singular that in its issue of December 1 1950, *The Engineer* carried, on the very 'leader' page that had commented upon Riddles's presidential address, another leader entitled 'The Time Factor', which opened thus:

'Amongst common popular errors not the least common is the underrating or neglect of the time factor in human affairs. The reformer cannot understand why arbitration takes so long. The socialist is but little interested in results that cannot be achieved in his lifetime. Five-year plans seem to indicate the limit of his vision. All these blame someone for delays. The Reformer attributes them to the stupidity or malevolence of mankind; the progressive accuses the manufacturer of supineness or devotion to self-interest; the socialist asserts that vested interests and traditionalism set up, wilfully, barriers to the progress of civilisation. None of them recognises that there is a law of inertia that is applied as surely to human affairs as physical inertia applied to a motor-bus or an Atlantic liner . . .' and I could add, equally, to a railway locomotive! More than three years were to elapse after Vesting Day before the first of the new British Standard locomotives took the rails.

In November 1950, Riddles had given some broad indications as to what was forthcoming, and to the dismay of many industrialists it became clear that reliance for a major part of the motive power of Great Britain was to be placed on steam, for some time to come. He put it picturesquely that they were going to buy the form of locomotive that gave them the most tractive effort per pound sterling. The then-high costs of diesel-electrics and gas-turbine electrics in relation to tractive effort, quite apart from the cost of imported fuel for them, made them unattractive for general adoption, quite apart from

An attractive picture of the 'flagship' of the British standard fleet—the Class 'BR7' 'Pacific', No 70000, Britannia, *photographed here outside the one-time official LNWR residences which are at Crewe* (British Railways).

Above *The smaller, and very successful, version of the standard mixed traffic 4-6-0 Class 'BR4', built at Swindon* (British Railways).

Opposite page, top to bottom

A BR standard type derived from the ex-GWR 2-6-2 passenger tank engine—the '82000' Class, built at Swindon (British Railways).

The 'BR3' mixed traffic 2-6-0, a very un-Great Western looking design, built at Swindon (British Railways).

The BR standard Class '5' mixed traffic 4-6-0 of which the first batch was built at Derby (British Railways).

Below *'Britannia' Class: Smokebox arrangement* (British Railways).

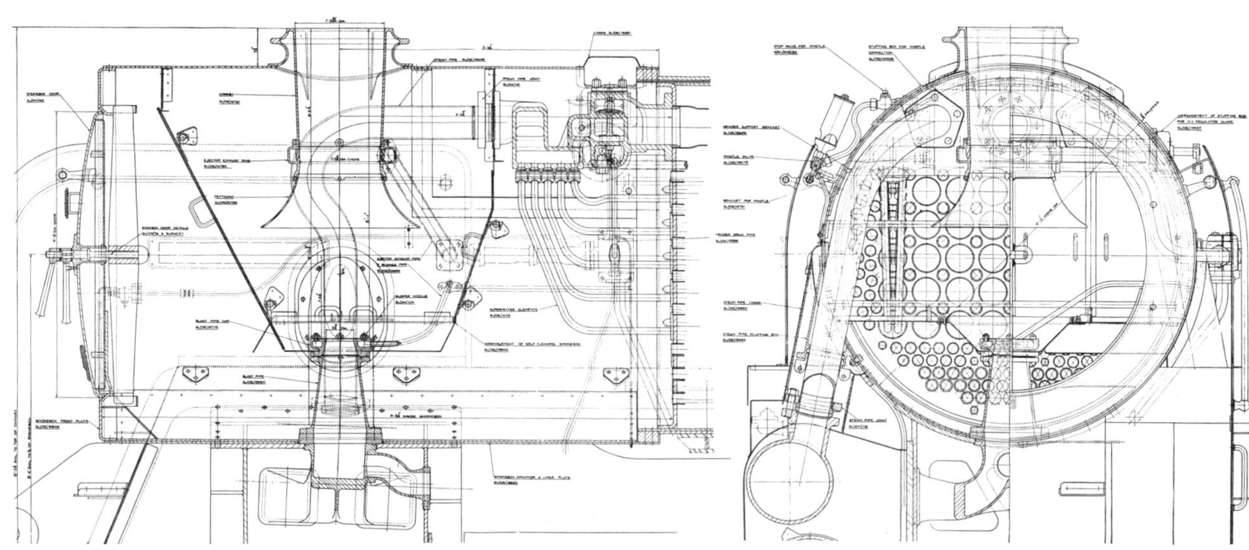

82000
82000

77001

73000
73000

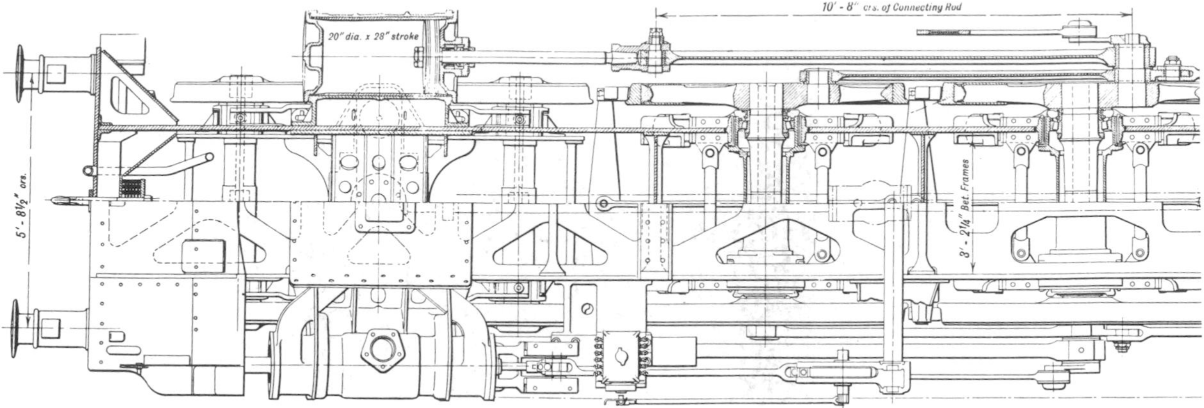

'Britannia' Class: plan of forward part, showing arrangement of framing, and welded attachment to horn guides (British Railways).

the very big question of what their life was likely to be in railway service.

Amid the euphoria surrounding the widespread introduction of diesels in America, there were disturbing reports that all was not quite as well as the more ardent publicists would have us then believe. But, in the general policy he and his staff were adopting, Riddles made it plain that he did not rule out the eventual adoption of other forms of motive power; but he emphasised that comparison should be made with steam locomotives of the most advanced design, and not those of 15 to 20 years ago. In so saying he was virtually ruling out, as obsolete, everything except the Stanier-Ivatt designs on the LMS and the Bulleid 'Pacifics'.

There is no doubt that the running performances of the 'West Country' Class in the Interchange Trials created a profound impression, not only among their most ardent enthusiast supporters but also at No 222 Marylebone Road. That their more exotically novel features could not be accepted for a new standard locomotive was realised from the outset; but the broad concept of a 'Pacific' with a large firegrate, exceptionally free steaming boiler, and a front end that would develop power seemingly out of all proportion to its physical size, appeared to be ideal for a more-than-medium sized mixed traffic engine.

In referring to the new locomotives it should be mentioned that the former LMS power classification '5X' (adopted originally for the ex-LNW large boilered 'Claughton' Class 4-6-0s, as intermediate in power between the Class '5' of the original engines and the Class '6' of the 'Royal Scots') was abandoned, and engines previously classed '5X' became Class '6', with the previous Class, '6' advancing to '7'; and likewise the Class '7' 'Pacifics' of the LMS became Class '8'. The Bulleid 'West Country' 'Pacifics', now BR Class '7', had a nominal tractive effort of 31,000 lb, and the new standard Class '7' mixed traffic 'Pacific', also with 6

The 'BR4' standard 2-6-4 tank, was based upon the Stanier design of the LMS, and first examples were built at Brighton (British Railways).

The 'BR4' mixed traffic 2-6-0, '76000' Class, closely derived from the ex-LMS '3000' Class introduced just before nationalisation. Construction was at Horwich and Doncaster Works (British Railways).

foot 2 inch coupled wheels was planned to have a tractive effort of 32,150 lb.

Although the new standard 'Pacific' was designed with the idea of equalling performances of which the Bulleid had proved so remarkably capable in the Interchange Trials, there was little, understandably, in the design that was followed. The 'West Country' and the larger 'Merchant Navy' Class were a complete negation of all the principles that The Railway Executive had set itself, in making all the working parts readily accessible for attention and maintenance from the six foot; and while the principles behind the Bulleid, in encasing the motion in an oil bath, with a specially designed valve gear was to ensure perfect lubrication, and absence outside of anything likely to give trouble, in actual practice the design had not been developed to the stage when it *was* trouble free. Although the individual locomotives involved in the Interchange Trials all did extremely well, their behaviour was unfortunately not typical of the designs as a whole. Before discussing the design of the new locomotives in any detail, it is interesting to see alongside each other the basic dimensions of the 'West Country' and the 'BR7' 'Pacific':

Mixed Traffic 'Pacifics'

Class	**West Country**	**BR7**
Heating surfaces (square feet)		
Tubes	1,869	2,264
Firebox	253	210
Superheater	545	677
Total	2,667	3,151
Grate area (square feet)	38.25	42
Boiler pressure (psi)	280	250
Tractive effort (lb)	31,000	32,150
Weights (in working order) (tons)		
Bogie	15.5	17.1
Coupled wheels	18.75	20.25
Coupled wheels	18.75	20.25
Coupled wheels	18.75	20.25
Trailing truck	14.25	16.15

The engine layout was entirely different. The Bulleid had three cylinders, $16\frac{3}{8}$ inches diameter by 24 inches stroke, with the Bulleid chain driven valve gear; the '7MT' had two cylinders, 20 inches diameter by 28 inches stroke, with conventional Walschaerts valve gear.

Before leaving the Bulleid 'West Country' 'Pacific', and the undoubted influence it had towards the BR locomotives, I must add that the performances in the Interchange Trials were unrepresentative in another respect. These engines were normally driven with a relatively narrow regulator opening, so that one could, with some justification, question the provision of so high a boiler pressure as 280 lb per square inch. In the trial runs on the Great Central line, and also on the Highland, in both of which Driver Swain of Nine Elms shed was at the regulator, the values of steam chest pressure quoted in the official report indicate that in most of the cases of high drawbar horsepower the regulator was wide, if not necessarily full open. On the Highland line, in particular, steam chest pressures up to 245 lb per square inch, were recorded and undoubtedly contributed to the high power output achieved. The locomotives used in the tests on the Great Central line and on the Highland were not the same, but both responded admirably to the technique in handling used by Driver Swain, and the firing of Bert Hooker.

By March 1949 the requirement of the new range of standard locomotives had been finalised, and production design was launched, with the work divided between the main drawing offices of the four one-time independent railways. At first, work was initiated on only six out of the 13 types considered to fulfil the immediate needs of British Railways. These six, and the design offices to which they were allocated were as follows:

Ref no	**Type**	**Power class**	**Running numbers from**	**Drawing Office responsible**
1	4-6-2	7	70000	Derby
2	4-6-2	6	72000	Derby
3	4-6-0	5	73000	Doncaster
4	4-6-0	4	75000	Brighton
5	2-6-0	3	77000	Swindon
6	2-6-2T	3	82000	Swindon

To complete the immediate picture, four additional designs that were ready adaptations of existing ones were subsequently undertaken, thus:

7	2-6-0	4	76000	Doncaster
8	2-6-4T	4	80000	Brighton
9	2-6-0	2	78000	Derby
10	2-6-2T	2	84000	Derby

The five types, references 3, 7, 8, 9 and 10, were thinly disguised variations of existing LMS standards, while references 5 and 6 used an adaptation of the Swindon standard No 2 boiler, as fitted to the '51XX' and '56XX' Great Western tank engines. Reference 4, the new Class '4' 4-6-0, was in effect a tender engine version of the LMS standard 2-6-4 tank, with a somewhat longer boiler barrel, and was thus closely related to reference 8. Great care was taken to design a uniform and distinctive external style for the whole series, and this led to the new Class '5' 4-6-0, and the new Class '4' 2-6-4 tank looking somewhat different from their LMS progenitors whereas, of course, they were virtually identical in their usefulness.

Initially, of course, interest in the new range was centred almost entirely upon the 7MT Pacific, as being the only really new design; and inevitably the introduction of the class was attended by a good deal of publicity 'ballyhoo', with the nameplate *Britannia* unveiled by the Minister of Transport, the Right Honourable Alfred Barnes, at a ceremony at Marylebone Station on January 30 1951, witnessed by a galaxy of 'top brass', and the national press in full strength. It was an imaginative stroke to name the first of the new engines *Britannia*, and the new 7MT Pacifics became the 'Britannia' Class. On the face of it they were a simple, straightforward 2-cylinder design, with everything outside and readily accessible, designed to take on, with reduced maintenance charges, lower coal consumption and longer mileage between classified repairs, the work of the regional 4-6-0s of the 'Castle', 'Lord Nelson' and rebuilt 'Scot' Classes, and equally that of the

The light branch line Class '2' 2-6-0 derived from the similar LMS design (British Railways).

An interesting variant on the BR standard Class '5' 4-6-0, fitted with Caprotti valve gear, built at Derby (British Railways).

Bulleid 'West Country' 'Pacifics' and the Gresley 'V2' Class 2-6-2s. It was, of course, appreciated at the outset that the take-over would be no more than gradual, though it was then thought that steam traction would have to carry on for some considerable time, and with many units of the regional classes mentioned already having a high total mileage to their credit, the activities of the new standard locomotives would be progressingly increased.

But, in designing what was to be simple straightforward 2-cylinder locomotive, certain features relatively new in British Railways practice were introduced and gave considerable trouble in the early stages. There was first of all the regulator. Opinion and preferences had been varied among the private railway companies as to the best form of regulator to use. The Southern, and the LMS had used the simple sliding grid type, in the dome, while until the introduction of the so-called 'Banjo Dome' the LNER had used the Lockyer double-beat pattern. The GWR had remained faithful to the Churchward type designed nearly 50 years previously. Because many regulators did not work very freely, and often required some strength from the driver to operate them, BR adopted the proprietary multiple poppet valve type marketed by the Superheater Company Ltd, but for some reason mounted it on the saturated rather than the super-

'Britannia' Class: longitudinal section through firebox, showing connection between cab and tender front (British Railways).

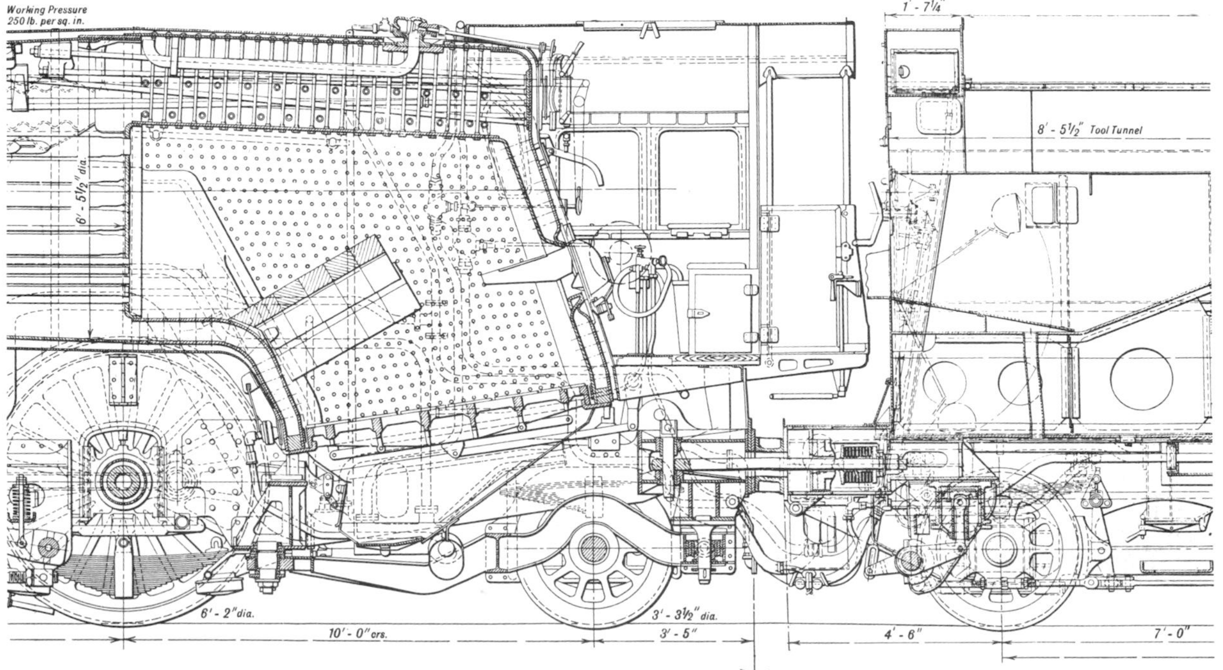

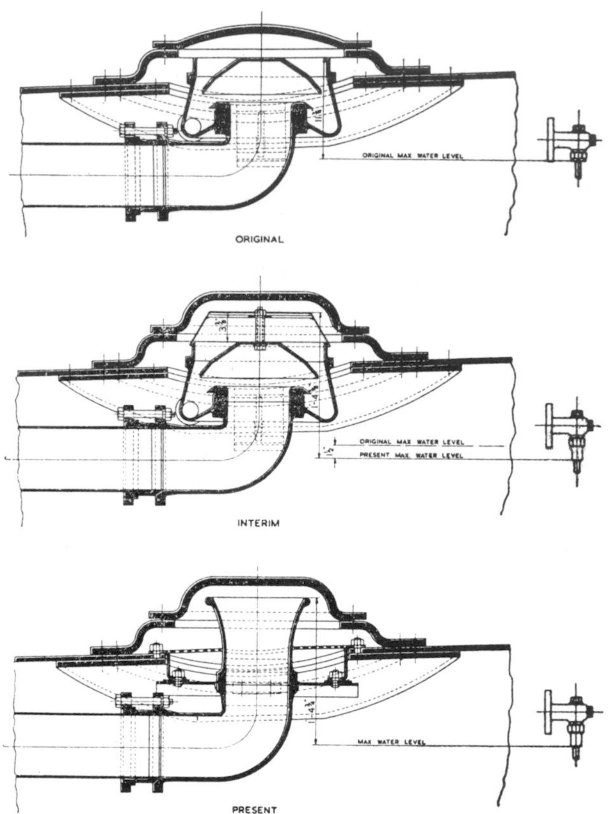

heated side of the superheater itself. The accompanying diagram shows the more usual arrangement. But the Superheater Company also marketed what was called a steam drier. This also BR decided to adopt, and it was mounted in the steam dome, on the new 'Pacific' engines. The general arrangement of these engines, as originally built, is reproduced herewith.

Engine No 70000 was turned out new from Crewe works on January 2 1951, and after running in was put on to a dynamometer car test run from Crewe to Carlisle with a train of empty stock weighing 442 tons behind the tender. The booked time for the 141.1 miles, non-stop, was 174 minutes, and it is reported that a late start of 8 minutes was recovered, and Carlisle reached punctually. The load was 22 tons above the maximum permitted in ordinary service to a Class '7' engine on these timings, but with only the crew of the dynamometer car, and no luggage the total load behind the tender could not have been much over 445 tons; and on hearing of the times made, with a net time of about 164 minutes, I must admit I was reminded of an occasion in the early days of the *First* World War

Left *'Britannia' Class: successive stages in design of steam collector* (British Railways).

Below *The Class '2' 2-6-2 tank engine, '84000' Class* (British Railways).

when the LNWR 4-cylinder 4-6-0 *Sir Gilbert Claughton* working the Glasgow portion of the 10 am from Euston, with a gross load of 440 tons, ran from Crewe to Carlisle in 157½ minutes.

Of course it was necessary to try out the capacity of the *Britannia* by going very hard from Carnforth up to Shap Summit, and this 31.4 miles was climbed impressively in 35 minutes 5 seconds. The final stage of 7 minutes 5 seconds for the last 5.5 miles up from Tebay, with full regulator and cut-off finally advanced to 50 per cent was achieved by a slight mortgaging of the capacity of the boiler. It was not to be expected that such usage of steam could be met for any appreciable time. The minimum speed on the 1 in 75 gradient to Shap Summit was 36 mph. Except between Carnforth and the summit, however, it would seem that the engine was working under fairly easy steam. Cox rode on the footplate on this inaugural, though quite private, occasion and on the return trip to Crewe next day Riddles himself drove the engine, with Bond also on the footplate.

The triumvirate had every reason to be pleased with this debut though, in his autobiography, Bond is not very enthusiastic about footplace conditions. He wrote: 'Though the *Britannias* rode very well, they were not particularly comfortable on the footplate. They were noisy and very dusty. Unduly stiff springing of the trailing truck made them very hard riding at the back end. The cab floor extended back to the tender front which no doubt made firing easier. But the absence of the usual fall-plate between engine and tender allowed strong air currents to swirl round the cab, which was draughty and laden with coal dust. Conditions were later much improved, first by canvas screens fitted between engine and tender, and later by reversion to the conventional fall-plate arrangement.'

One did not look for comfort in the armchair sense when riding on the footplate of steam locomotives; neither one would expect it to be a 'white-collar' job. But there are degrees in everything, and writing personally for a moment I think I could claim, by the year 1951, to have had my fair share of rough, dirty and wild riding engines. I need only mention Great Northern 'Atlantics', ex-LNER 'B1' 4-6-0s, and run down 'King Arthurs'! I do not think, however, I had previously struck anything quite like the *Britannias*. As vehicles they rode steadily, but they were harsh, unfriendly things with a noisy wracking vibration that could become very tiring on a run of 1½ to 2 hours. I have ridden most of the way from Edinburgh to Kings Cross (393 miles), through the night from Crewe to Perth (290 miles), and whole way from Paddington to Penzance (305 miles) in one continuous run, but I never remember being so wearied, or so heartily sick of locomotives than after the run from Liverpool Street

One of the BR standard Class '4' 4-6-0s under construction at Swindon Works (British Railways).

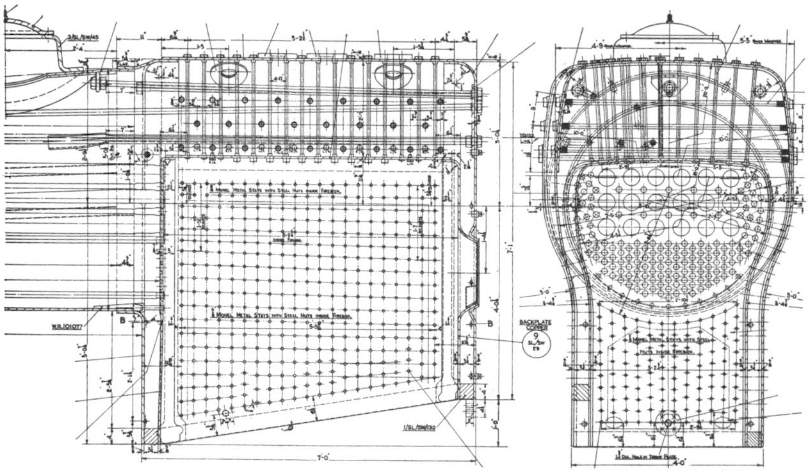

Top *The standard locomotives in service: 'Britannia' Class 4-6-2, No 70004,* William Shakespeare, *pulling away from Folkestone Junction sidings with an inward bound Continental boat express* (M.W. Earley).

Above *'Britannias' on the Western Region: 4-6-2, No 70027,* Rising Star, *on the up 'Red Dragon' east of Reading* (M.W. Earley).

Left *BR Class '3' 2-6-2 tank engine—arrangement of firebox directly derived from Swindon practice* (British Railways).

Right *London Midland Region: the up day Irish Mail passing Conway, hauled by 4-6-2, No 70050,* Firth of Clyde (Derek Cross).

Below *The 'Clans' at work in the North: engine No 72001,* Clan Cameron, *making heavy weather of the Shap incline with a Liverpool–Glasgow express* (Derek Cross).

Bottom *Engine No 72002,* Clan Campbell, *taking water at the troughs south of Tebay with a Glasgow–Manchester express* (Derek Cross).

Top *Just north of the border: engine No 72009,* Clan Stewart, *taking the former Caledonian line at Gretna Junction, with an express from Crewe to Perth* (Derek Cross).

Above *A Class 'BR4' 4-6-0, No 75012, hauling an express from Workington to Manchester, at Morecambe South Junction* (the late Ian S. Pearsall).

to Norwich on *Britannia* herself in the summer of 1951. Some, I found, were better than others, but they never became favourites of mine for footplate riding. Unfortunately, to get the data I needed for technical articles that were much in demand at the time, I had to ride quite a lot of them from that first summer onwards.

Of the first batch of 25 *Britannias* built in 1951, although a few of them were tried experimentally on the Southern including the exhibition engine No 70004, *William Shakespeare*, which had spent most of the summer on display at the Festival of Britain exhibition at Battersea, a total of 15—Nos 70000–70014—were allocated to the Eastern Region for service on the Great Eastern Line, while Nos 70015–70024, distinguished with names of old broad gauge express engines, went to the Western Region. At first these 10 were divided between Old Oak Common, Newton Abbot and Plymouth (Laira). The Great Eastern men at Stratford and Norwich, who previously had no larger engines than the 3-cylinder 'Sandringham' Class 4-6-0s, and the Thompson 'B1' Class, gave them a warm welcome, despite sustaining the first of several alarming failures. Engine No 70000, after acquitting herself with distinction on the Crewe–Carlisle dynamometer car trials in January 1951, was sent to Stratford to take up what was to be her regular work, and then trouble struck.

Cox has written: 'On the rainy Sunday of February 2nd 1951, Bond and I, hastily summoned by 'phone, found ourselves viewing the bits and pieces of a fragmented right-hand piston head and cylinder cover. Twelve days later the left-hand head disintegrated, and it took only further periods of nine and six days respectively before the left-hand back cylinder relief valve blew out and disappeared into the blue, and the cylinder cover on the same side fractured.' Although in his book Cox was writing of the incidents 15 years after they happened,

Top *Scottish Region: a CTAC Tour special passing Gretna Junction, hauled by a 'BR5' standard 4-6-0, No 73109* (Derek Cross).

Above *Another 'BR5' 4-6-0, No 73075, on a southbound 'Tours' special, at Mossband water troughs just south of Gretna* (Derek Cross).

there was no attempt to cover them up at the time; when Cox read his paper to the Institution of Locomotive Engineers, in March 1951, Riddles, from the Chair, told members of the trouble, and how they were sure it could only be caused by *water* in the cylinders. It was quickly traced to the steam drier device fitted in the dome. The idea was that steam drawn up into the dome was caused to swirl round, by a system of fixed spiral vanes, so that small particles of water, shaken outwards by the centrifugal action, could flow back into the boiler through an outlet orifice in the bottom of the steam drier. It was thought that water passing direct to the cylinders could have been caused in light steaming conditions, or when the engine was coasting, by the water level in the boiler being above its maximum level visible in the gauge glass, and passing directly into the outlet orifice of the drier, or even to surge up and over the top of the main steam inlet. The immediate remedy was to lower the maximum water level and, by substituting a dome cover of greater height, enable the level of the main steam intake to be raised. But the ultimate answer was to discard the steam drier altogether.

By mid-May 1951 the performance of the 'Britannias' had settled down to the extent that a party of us were invited to travel to Rugby to see No 70005, *John Milton*, running on the new stationary test plant. Two extra coaches and the Horwich dynamometer car were put on to the 10.30 am train from Euston which did not normally stop at Rugby; but one of the 'Britannia' locomotives, No 70009, *Alfred the Great*, was put on specially, and detached there with the three additional vehicles, which it duly propelled from the station into the test plant sidings. The full results from the comprehensive series of tests carried out on engine No 70005, followed by Controlled Road Tests on the Settle and Carlisle line, are discussed later, in Chapter 17 of this book; but on the return journey to Euston, on which I was privileged to ride in the dynamometer car, some interesting work was performed by engine No 70009. The car and the coaches for the visitors were attached to a train booked to cover the 82.6 miles in 94 minutes, but a late start of 9 minutes gave plenty of incentive to run harder than usual, with a heavy train weighing 485 tons behind the tender. The circumstances became particularly interesting when, because of indifferent coal, difficulty was found in maintaining steam pressure, and south of Bletchley it dropped from 220 to 190 lb per square inch. By lengthening the cut-off to no less than 35 per cent, speed was well maintained and, despite an engineering slack near Weedon, the 80.2 miles from Rugby to passing South Hampstead was covered in 78 minutes. There was ample time to make a slightly early arrival in Euston, had we not been stopped by signal for 3 minutes outside.

In September and October 1951, I rode a total of 645 miles on the footplate of six different locomotives of the 'Britannia Class, to such diverse destinations as Norwich, Penzance and Dover. All the locomotives concerned performed well, particularly No 70019, *Lightning*, on the up 'Cornish Riviera Express' between Penzance and Plymouth and No 70022, *Tornado*, between Newton Abbot and Bristol. The Festival of Britain exhibition engine No 70004, *William Shakespeare*, with no more than a moderate load of 395 tons on the outward bound 'Golden Arrow' Pullman boat train, made a rather shaky start out of London, and throughout the long adverse stretch to the crest of the North Downs at Knockholt the engine was not steaming well.

The boiler pressure varied between 170 and 190 lb per square inch, instead of 250, and despite the use of cut-offs between 30 and 40 per cent we could not manage a better average than 35 mph over the 15.8 miles from Wandsworth Road to Knockholt. It was not until the downhill stretch from Sevenoaks to Tonbridge was reached, and taken under easy steam, that full boiler pressure was attained. All engines of the class ran freely when opportunity offered. The best example was an attained maximum of 80 mph on dead level track between Bridgwater and Bristol, with a load of 350 tons behind the tender. The working conditions were, cut-off 25 per cent, steam chest pressure 215 lb square inch. No driver with whom I rode in 1951 worked at less than 20 per cent cut-off, but most preferred 25. The harsh and noisy riding was present in varying degrees in all six engines, but those on the Norwich run were perhaps the worst and most tiring in their personal effect.

On the strength of these experiences I wrote a leading article in *The Engineer* entitled 'Britannia Locomotive Prowess'. After referring to the inevitable comparisons that would be made between the new engines and established favourites on some routes I continued:

'More interesting perhaps than the comparisons between the "Britannias" and their predecessors are the comparisons to be made between the work of the new engines themselves over different routes. Previously, in those arguments of a strongly partisan character that occur so frequently among railway enthusiasts, discussions upon the relative difficulty of express trains schedules had little solid basis of fact, as the coal consumption of, say, a Great Eastern engine in hauling the Hook of Holland boat train down to Parkeston Quay each night was no criterion when comparing that duty with that of a Churchward 4-6-0 of the Great Western in working a two-hour express from Paddington to Bristol. Even now, with "Britannia" Class engines operating on both these routes, one has to make allowance for different qualities of coal, and different degrees of skill in driving and firing. But at least the basic machine is now the same, and is moreover one expressly designed to suit the widest possible variety of coal, and to be generally acceptable and welcome to the vast majority of footplate men.'

That article had scarcely appeared when we learned of the serious mishap of the engine, *William Shakespeare*, when working the up 'Golden Arrow',

A 'BR9' 2-10-0, No 92078, on a lengthy train of coal empties, 60 wagons, near Watford Junction (British Railways).

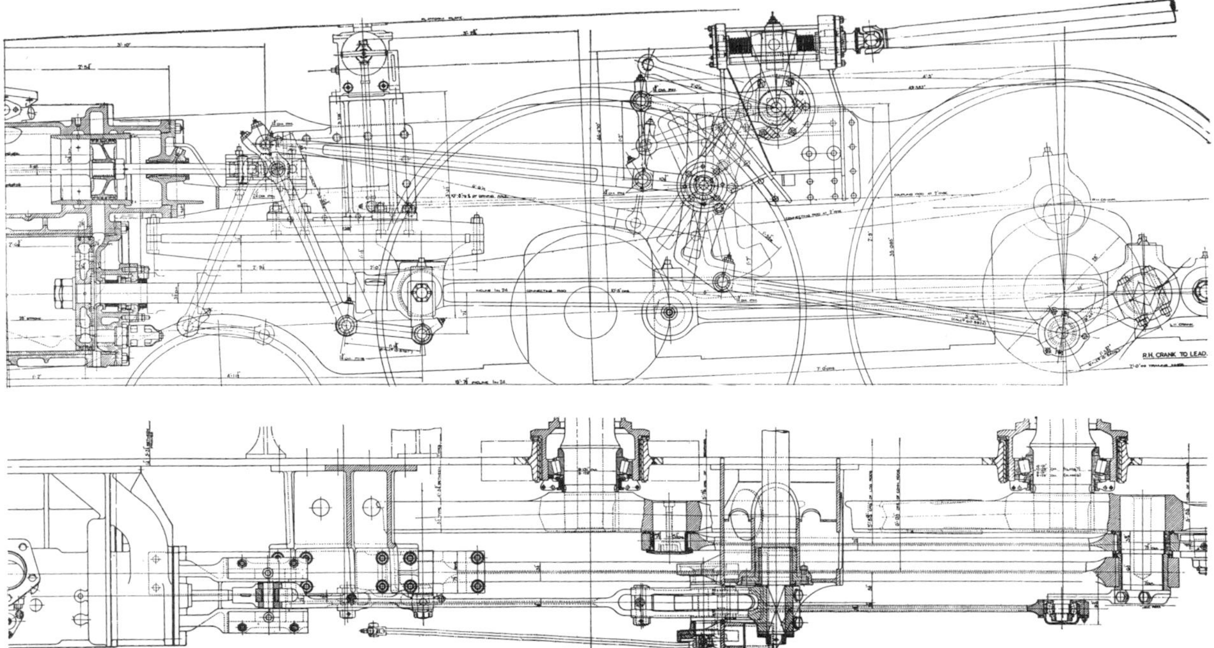

'Britannia' Class—arrangement of Walschaerts valve gear (British Railways).

and that *all* engines of the class had been temporarily withdrawn from service. With locomotives that had been so widely publicised it was only natural that extreme curiosity should have been felt as to the nature of the trouble. Rumours circulated orally, but the technical press maintained almost complete silence—a silence of understanding and sympathy in the face of an unexpected source of weakness. Actually the mishap with engine No 70004 was the culmination of a series of similar ones, but was the most serious and potentially dangerous. It was subsequently revealed that some three months earlier No 70014, *Iron Duke*, then working on the Southern, had failed with all its coupled wheels shifted on the axle, and that six other engines followed, with shifted wheels and bent side rods. These had been rectified, according to what was then believed, and the engine put back into traffic. In fact, on the day before I rode on No 70004, with an evening engagement at Hythe, I had alighted from the 5 pm from Cannon Street at Sandling Junction and witnessed No 70014 thundering up the bank from Folkestone with a London-bound boat train in most impressive style. It was the complete fracture of a coupling rod on No 70004, accompanying loose wheels while running at high speed, that led to Riddles's decision to take all the 'Britannias' out of traffic at once.

The LMS had some previous experience of bent coupling rods on the rebuilt 'Scots', and on the Midland compounds, but not with loose wheels. The difference in the case of the 'Britannias' lay in the use of roller bearings. The diameter was 9.130 inches on the leading and trailing coupled wheels and 10.130 inches on the driving. The bearings themselves were of the standard Timken tapered type, but from the accompanying drawing it will be appreciated that the section of the axle providing the wheel seat had to be a slightly smaller diameter. It will be seen also that the axles were hollow. Cox said that this had been done to save weight, but in originating the practice as long previously as 1922 on the Great Western Railway, it was done for a different purpose altogether. At Swindon they were experimenting with heat treating driving axles, and at first it improved the outside without penetrating to the heart. Stanier was then Works Manager, and some years ago when I was writing his biography he told how, by boring out the axles, it enabled the coolant in the heat treatment process to get to the inside and give a uniform improvement throughout the axle. It was first applied on the 'Abbey' series of 4-cylinder 4-6-0s in 1922; while it resulted in some weight reduction that was a bonus, rather than the prime cause of the innovation. On the 'Duchess' Class 'Pacifics' of the LMS the diameter of the wheel-seats on the coupled axles was 10½ inches. The first coupled, which included the built-up cranks for the inside cylinder drives, had a central hole 3 inches in diameter bored through; the second and third coupled had a 4½ inch diameter central hole. The 'Britannias' had a 4 inch diameter central hole through all their axles, which as previously explained, had to be slightly less in the wheel seat than in the roller bearing.

It was in the process of pressing the wheels on to the axles that the uncertainties arose, though they were unsuspected at first. It seemed that the limits of dimensions to which the wheels and their seats were machined were very close to the border line of safety, and some engines of the class seemed able to take any amount of severe pounding without showing the slightest sign of falling victim to the kind of failure first experienced with *Iron Duke*, and then still more seriously with *William Shakespeare*.

Engine No 70005, *John Milton*, for example, was sent new to Rugby testing station, and subjected to the most severe pounding that anyone could imagine; then it went to the Settle and Carlisle line for Controlled Road Tests of the utmost severity. Yet it showed not the slightest sign of the wheels coming loose, or distress of any kind. But this engine, like all others of the class, was withdrawn until the remedy was found. Sensing that the 4 inch central hole in the axles was too large, especially on the 9 inch diameter axles of the leading and trailing wheels, it was decided to plug the axle for the length of the wheel fit and, to safeguard against buckling of the coupling rods, if an engine went into a severe slip, the elegant fluted section was replaced by a simple rectangular cross-section rod which, it was calculated, would take twice the load of the original design before taking a permanent set.

With these modifications completed, the 'Britannias' were put back into traffic, and established a general reputation as good, though not exceptional, engines. They were most appreciated on the Great Eastern line by crews who had never previously had such powerful engines. These were capable of transitory outputs of power that with moderate train loads made light of the sharp intermediate gradients.

It was on routes where they were a British Railways alternative to the indigenous classes that they were not so well received, particularly in their harsh and noisy riding and the tendency to slip. With uncompensated axle loading, engines of the 'Pacific' type are inevitably more liable to slipping then 4-6-0s, and on the Western Region there were sad tales of 'Britannias' in dire trouble on the steep gradients of Box and the Severn Tunnels. But one of the most extraordinary cases to come to my notice, vividly indeed because I was on the footplate, was on the Great Eastern, in the course of an intensive three days' running with these engines in 1953. It was one of the five built in 1952 with roller bearings only on the coupled axles, Engine No 70039. Working a 12-coach train on the 12.41 pm up from Ipswich and running at 72 mph past Kelvedon, the engine suddenly went into a violent slip and, although the driver shut the regulator at once, slipping continued for a while. After a normal spell it began again on the rise from Chelmsford, but then, still more remarkably, when we were under very easy steam *downhill*. It continued for nearly two minutes, between Harold Wood and Gidea Park, and again between Stratford and Bow Junction. The engine was afterwards 'stopped' for examination, but no one could tell me afterwards what caused it.

There is much more to be told of the 'Britannias' and their maximum performance later in this book, but for the moment I must pass on to the other two 12-wheeled locomotives of the standard range: the Class 6MT 'Pacific', named after Highland clans, and the remarkable '9F' 2-10-0, intended to be a heavy freighter, but actually proving to be a very versatile mixed traffic unit.

On paper the 'Clan' looked something of a mystery. Why should it have been necessary to have such a large and heavy engine, 137.6 tons, in working order, for a tractive effort of no more than 27,250 lb? It was only fractionally more powerful than the new standard Class '5' 4-6-0, with 26,120 lb of tractive effort. It seemed to be the outcome of the argument Bond put forward that a large grate, and the corresponding lower rate of combustion would induce economies in working that would outweigh the higher capital cost; but whatever theoretical arguments were put forward, the 'Clans' proved generally disappointing engines in traffic. Although another 15 were originally authorised after the construction of the first 10, in 1951, the orders for the subsequent batches were afterwards cancelled. The 10 engines of this class were allocated to Scottish Region, though some of them worked south from Glasgow to Manchester for a time. Being 'Pacifics' they tended to become loaded to far more than Class '6' capacity, and lost time in consequence. They had the same riding characteristics as the 'Britannias', harsh and noisy.

The original proposal for a large new freight engine took the form of a 2-8-2 with the 'Britannia' type of boiler, and 5 foot 3 inch coupled wheels. With a slightly reduced size of cylinders, as in the 'Clan', the tractive effort was no more than 35,912 lb. Riddles himself was not satisfied with this proposal. The existing standard 2-8-0s of the Great

Right *The heavy freight 2-10-0 Class '9F' '92000' series: No 92250 was actually the last of the class to be built at Crewe Works* (British Railways).

Below *Class 'BR4' 2-6-0 in Scottish freight service—engine No 76091 on a train of coal empties travelling from Hurlford to Bank Junction* (Derek Cross).

Above *A 'BR9' 2-10-0 with a heavy load of permanent way materials, climbing the 1 in 100 gradient through Kirkby Stephen on the Settle and Carlisle line* (Ivo Peters).

Right *The last steam locomotive to be built at Doncaster Plant: the standard Class '4' 2-6-0, No 76114, in 1957* (British Railways).

Western, LMS, and LNE Railways had tractive efforts of 35,280, 32,438 and 35,518 lb respectively, with adhesion weights of 67, 63 and 66, whereas the proposed new 2-8-2 would have only 67½ tons, with all the disadvantage, so far as adhesion was concerned, of a trailing truck under the firebox. During the war, under his direction the splendid 2-10-0 'Austerity' engine had been built for the War Department and he felt that the new BR engine should have 10 coupled wheels, and once assured that a wide firebox could be got in over 5 foot coupled wheels, the '9F', 2-10-0 went ahead. It was not possible to use the 'Britannia' boiler, and a new one had to be designed which was used only on the '9F'. In outward appearance it had some resemblance to that of the 'WD' 'Austerity' 2-10-0 because the barrel at the front end was slightly larger in diameter than the smokebox; but the proportions were generally different. The first batch of '9F' 2-10-0s were built at Crewe in 1954, only one year before the one that saw the launching of the modernisation plan for British Railways, which included the eventual replacement of all steam locomotives.

The '9F' was unquestionably the most distinctive and original of all the British standard steam locomotives, and with little doubt the most successful. On the other hand it is difficult to understand how authority for the construction of so many of these large and relatively expensive locomotives should have been given after the death knell of steam had been sounded. From the first deliveries of 32 in 1954, in successive years additions to the stock of 38, 45, 56, 62 brought the total up to 233 by the end of 1958, and with 15 in 1959, and final 3 in 1960, the grand total of 251 made the '9F' by far the most numerous of all the British Standard classes. Within eight years they had all been withdrawn. This is no place to try and unravel the mystery of how so many additional engines of the class should have been built when their usefulness was clearly to be confined to so few years. But as locomotives they were remarkable in their astonishing capacity for speed as well as their work in heavy freight haulage, some notes on their performances, including several maximum speeds of *90 miles per hour*, are given in a later chapter. There are also references to the experimental fitting of 10 of them with the Crosti boiler, three with a mechanical stoker, and one with the Giesl ejector and chimney.

To conclude this chapter there is a tabulated summary of the basic dimensions of the 11 standard classes built between 1951 and 1960.

British standard steam locomotives

Power class	**7**	**6**	**5**	**4**	**4**	**4**	**3**	**3**	**2**	**2**	**9**
Type	4-6-2	4-6-2	4-6-0	4-6-0	2-6-0	2-6-4T	2-6-0	2-6-2T	2-6-0	2-6-2T	2-10-0
Number series	70000	72000	73000	75000	76000	80000	77000	82000	78000	84000	92000
Coupled wheel diameter (feet/ inches)	6 2	6 2	6 2	5 8	5 3	5 8	5 3	5 3	5 0	5 0	5 0
Cylinder diameter (inches)	20	19½	19	18	17½	18	17½	17½	16½	16½	20
Stroke (inches)	28	28	28	28	26	28	26	26	24	24	28
Heating surfaces (square feet)											
Tubes	2,284	1,878	1,479	1,301	1,075	1,223	923.5	923.5	924	924	1,836
Firebox	210	195	171	143	131	143	118.4	118.4	101	101	179
Superheater	677	592	358	258	247	240	184.5	184.5	124	124	535
Total	3,151	2,665	2,008	1,702	1,453	1,606	1,296.5	1,296.5	1,149	1,149	2,550
Grate area (square feet)	42	36	28.7	26.7	23	26.7	20.35	20.35	17.5	17.5	40.2
Boiler pressure (psi)	250	225	225	225	225	225	200	200	200	200	250
Adhesion weight (tons)	60.75	56.9	58	51.5	50.5	53	48.5	48.7	40.5	41.2	77.5
Total engine weight (tons)	94	88.5	76	67.9	59.8	86.6	57.5	74	49.2	66.2	86.7
Nominal tractive effort (lb)	32,150	27,520	26,120	25,515	24,170	25,515	21,490	21,490	18,513	18,513	39,667
Total number built	55	10	172	80	115	155	20	45	65	30	251

15. Non-steam power on test

While the economic climate of the day at railway nationalisation, and for some years after, guided The Railway Executive in its policy of retaining steam traction and embarking upon a programme of standard locomotive building from 1951 onwards, the experimental non-steam locomotives inherited from the projects embarked upon by the private railways prior to nationalisation, were examined by dynamometer car, and stationary plant testing. The results obtained by the Locomotive Testing section of the CME's drawing office of the former Great Western Railway, at Swindon, covered the Brown-Boveri Gas Turbine locomotive No 18000, the introduction of which is referred to in Chapter 11 of this book, and the Southern Region diesel-electric locomotive No 10202 of 1,750 hp. This locomotive had the same excellent English Electric type of diesel engine as on the pioneer LMS diesel No 10000, but slightly uprated to give 1,750 instead of 1,600 hp. The Southern 10201 and 10202 had the wheel arrangement 1-C-C-1 and, together with the later and larger No 10203 (2,000 hp), could be considered the true prototypes of the very successful British Railways Class '40' diesels of the modernisation era.

The Swindon report covering the performance and efficiency tests on the Brown-Boveri Gas Turbine locomotive is dated November 1951. The attraction of the gas turbine as opposed to the diesel-electric type of locomotive lay in its potential economy in fuel costs. In the early 1950s the heavy oil used in the gas turbine was some 30 per cent cheaper than diesel oil; but actually the Western Region tests were as much concerned with examining the suitability of locomotive No 18000 for existing train service on the West of England main line, and comparing it to steam as in overall efficiency tests. The method adopted was an adaptation of the Controlled Road Testing System as developed at Swindon for steam locomotives. In this adaptation it was desirable for the locomotive to be worked for relatively long periods in selected controller notch positions, while records were taken of available effort and power at the drawbar with respect to speed and fuel oil consumption. After careful examination of train schedules and loading on the West of England main lines it was found possible to carry out the tests on ordinary service trains without interfering with the time schedules, and the following trains were chosen: the 3.30 pm Paddington to Plymouth and the 7.15 am Plymouth to Paddington.

They were interesting choices in the timetable of 1951. The first was actually faster than the Cornish Riviera, being allowed 148 minutes to its first stop, at Taunton, 142.7 miles. It slipped a coach at Heywood Road Junction, for Westbury, and after the 30.8 mile run from Taunton to Exeter, went on non-stop to Plymouth, with a load reduced by detaching the Torquay line portion. The up train was considerably slower. It attached the Torquay portion at Newton Abbot, and made stops at Teignmouth and Dawlish, while the final run up to Paddington, non-stop from Taunton, was allowed 160 minutes. So in its variety it provided a broad spectrum of haulage tasks. Two return trips with the dynamometer car were made. In the westbound direction the trailing load on both days was 395 tons, tare, to Heywood Road Junction, 359 tons to Exeter, and 239 tons to Plymouth. Returning the load was 228 tons to Newton Abbot on both days, 388 tons through to Paddington on the first day, while on the second there was one coach less between Newton Abbot and Exeter, 356 tons at first and then 386 tons for the rest of the journey. The loads on each section were not demanding, and were such that they could have been comfortably managed by 'Castle' Class steam locomotives.

An interesting feature of the working was the relatively high proportion of the distance over which the locomotive was not under power, thus:

Direction	**Down**	**Up**
Date	13.9.51	12.9.51
Distance, actual (miles)	225.2	225.2
Distance, under power (miles)	189.4	185.6
Total booked time (minutes)	270	300
Total booked running time (minutes)	259	275
Actual running time (minutes)	251.4	269
Overall time (including stops) (minutes)	264.4	296.3
Actual time under power (minutes)	204.0	213.4
Percentage time under power (minutes)	77.5	72.0

The records on the other two days were similar.

The major part of the working range of the locomotive was covered, except that the timetable demands and the loads conveyed did not extend the locomotive to the extent of using the ninth control notch for long enough to enable the characteristics in that working range to be obtained. It was remarkable nevertheless that in no more than 900 miles of travelling with ordinary service express

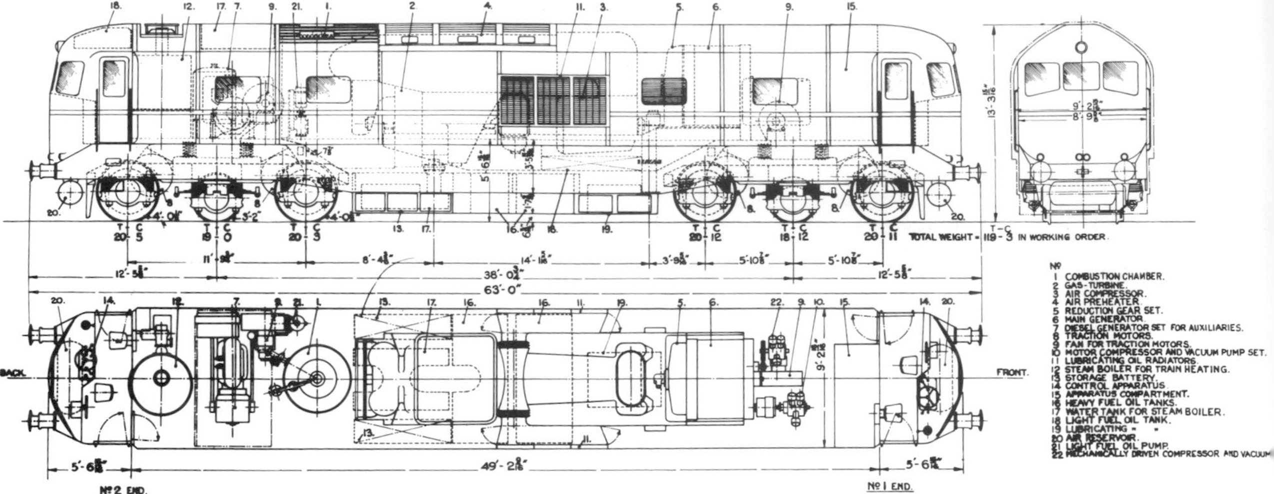

The Brown-Boveri gas turbine No 18000, on the Western Region—general arrangement diagram (British Railways).

passenger trains that the testing staff, with the aid of the Swindon dynamometer car, were able to collate enough performance data to present a very complete picture of the capabilities of this locomotive, and its overall economy.

Of course, the West of England main line of the former Great Western Railway includes a considerable variety of physical conditions, ranging from the dead level of the Brunellian main line between Paddington and Reading, to the exceptionally severe gradients of the South Devon line, with the 2 miles of 1 in 42 of the Hemerdon Incline the most trying. Between Reading and Exeter there are lengthy stretches of moderately severe gradients, but nearly all including such rapid fluctuations in the actual inclination as to preclude any steadily maintained speed. Yet the very variety of the physical conditions against which the locomotive was working provided an excellent test of the overall performance capability of the locomotive. While in constant running conditions, particularly at high power output, the gas turbine locomotive certainly had an overall thermal efficiency considerably higher than that of any steam locomotive, the practical engineers of the Western Region, while evaluating and confirming this high efficiency, nevertheless related the capacity of the locomotive to typical service trains, one having an overall timing considerably faster than the other, yet still involving quite a high proportion of the overall journey time when the locomotive was not under power.

Before discussing the actual results obtained it is important to recapitulate certain details of the data on which the design of this locomotive was based:

Nominal output of turbine	2,500 hp
Overall thermal efficiency at full load	16.9 per cent
Corresponding fuel consumption	0.87 lb/hp hour
Tractive effort	
During starting	31,500 lb up to about 21 mph
Continuously	12,400 lb at 64 mph
Continuously	8,400 lb at 90 mph
Maximum service speed	90 mph

As a result of the four test runs, the accompanying diagram (right) showing the relation of horsepower to speed was plotted for five notch positions of the controller, from 4 up to 8. To provide uniformity in presentation the horsepower registered by the drawbar pull in the dynamometer car was corrected to its equivalent value for level track. To explain this correction, if the train were running uphill, work additional to that registered on the drawbar of the dynamometer car would be needed to overcome the force of gravity on the locomotive; and the horsepower involved is added to that actually shown on the dynamometer car measuring instruments to arrive at the equivalent value. Similarly, if the train was running downhill, an appropriate amount would be deducted. Quoting the equivalent drawbar horsepower ensures that all values are strictly comparable, irrespective of whether the train is running uphill, downhill or on level track. With the results of scientific testing being published in official bulletins by British Railways, and discussion of them following, in several subsequent chapters of this book, it is emphasised now that in quoted values of drawbar horsepower, whether for steam, diesel, gas turbine or electric locomotives it will be the equivalent value, not the actual registered on the drawbar.

The graphs shown for the Brown-Boveri gas turbine locomotive are interesting as showing how closely they follow the characteristic form of a steam locomotive, with the maximum equivalent drawbar horsepower in any notch in the 30–35 mph speed range. When the same team of test engineers made a very thorough analysis of the performance of an ex-Great Western 4-cylinder 4-6-0 of the 'King', the characteristic curve of drawbar horsepower with a constant firing rate of 3,000 lb of coal per hour (the maximum for a single fireman) corresponded very closely to that of the gas turbine in notch 6, with a maximum in both cases at 35 mph of about 1,400 edhp. On the gas turbine it will be seen from the diagram that at 35 mph the fuel oil consumption rate was 1,800 lb per hour, and the consumption dropped rapidly as speed increased if the controller was kept in the same notch. So also did the drawbar horsepower to 1,050 at 60 mph and no more than 560 at 80 mph. At the latter speed the oil consumption had dropped to a little less than 1,300 lb per hour. If the value of 1,800 lb of fuel oil per hour was to be maintained, the controller would have needed advancing to the 7th notch, at 60 mph and the 8th at 70 mph. By contrast, on the 'King' Class 4-6-0, maintenance of a constant coal rate required a reduction of the point of cut-off in the cylinders from 30 per cent at 35 mph to 25 at 50 mph and 20 per cent at 70 mph.

A very interesting set of graphs from the gas turbine test is that in which the specified fuel oil consumption in lb per drawbar horsepower hour, is plotted against the actual power output, because it shows both the strength and the weakness of the gas turbine electric locomotive as a railway motive power unit. The lines plotted are those of constant speed and constant fuel oil consumption. On the

Gas turbine locomotive No 18000—graphs of drawbar horsepower characteristics (British Railways).

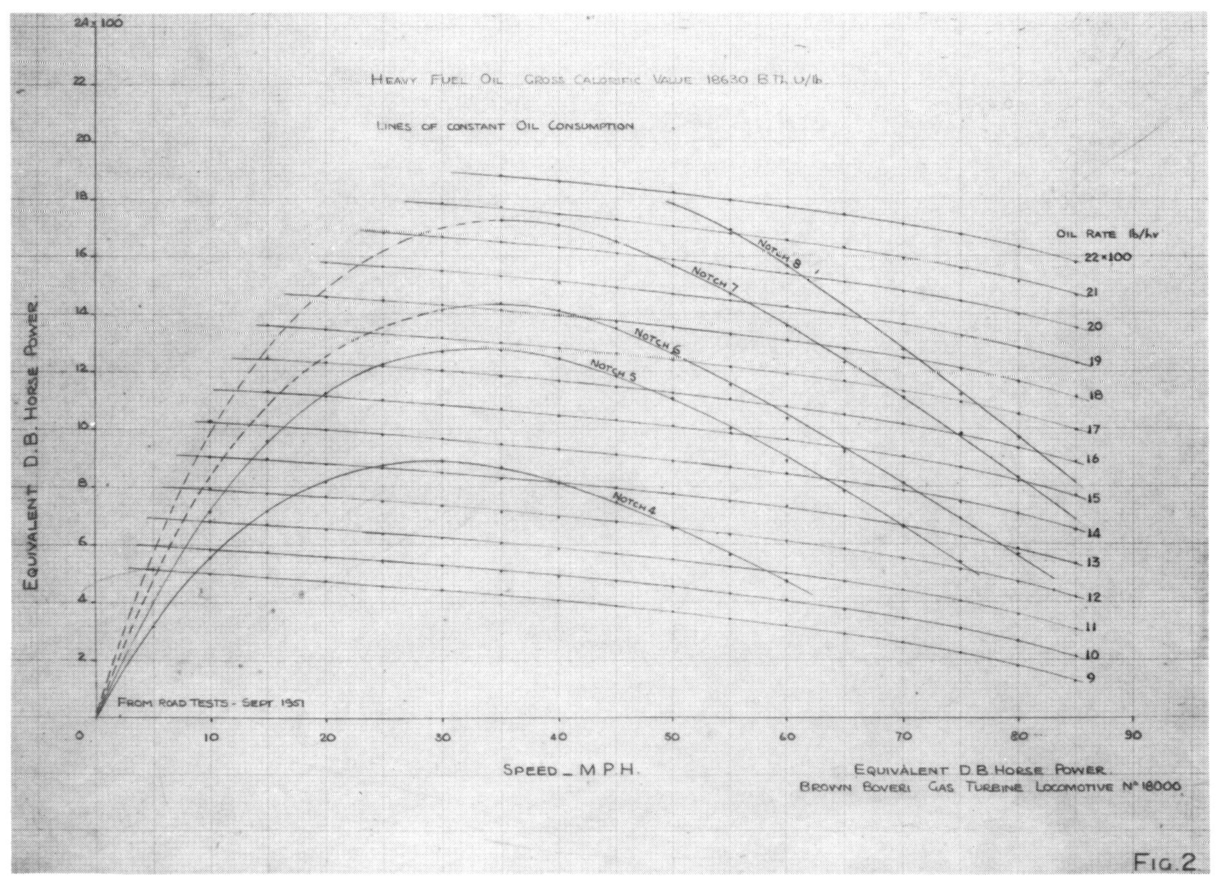

left-hand side of the diagram it will be seen that superimposed upon the uniform vertical scale of specific oil consumption is one of efficiency at the drawbar, and it will be noticed at once how the efficiency falls with decreasing demand for power. A few examples picked out from the diagram will emphasise this.

Speed (mph)	Oil rate (lb/hour)	edhp	Specific oil consumption (lb/dhp hour)	Efficiency at drawbar (per cent)
30	1,400	1,080	1.4	9.5
40	1,200	700	1.7	8.0
50	1,400	900	1.65	8.5
60	1,200	610	1.90	7.00
70	1,400	780	1.7	7.7
70	1,800	1,360	1.4	9.5
70	2,200	1,700	1.3	10

Even at the high output of 1,700 edhp at 70 mph the efficiency at the drawbar of no more than 10 per cent is a long way below the 16.9 per cent at full load aimed at in the design specification and, when it came to a summation of the results of the four days of test running, the figures, thermodynamically, seemed still more disappointing. For what was only the second gas turbine electric locomotive to be built anywhere in the world its record was not discouraging, for an entirely novel unit, and at the time of the 1951 tests between Paddington and Plymouth it had run a total of 46,000 miles in revenue earning service. Nevertheless the following overall test results virtually sounded its death-knell on British Railways.

A year prior to the test runs I had an opportunity of testing the running capacity of the locomotive while travelling as a passenger on the same two trains, and I found the performance impressive so

Gas turbine locomotive No 18000—graphs of oil consumption and overall efficiency related to drawbar horsepower (British Railways).

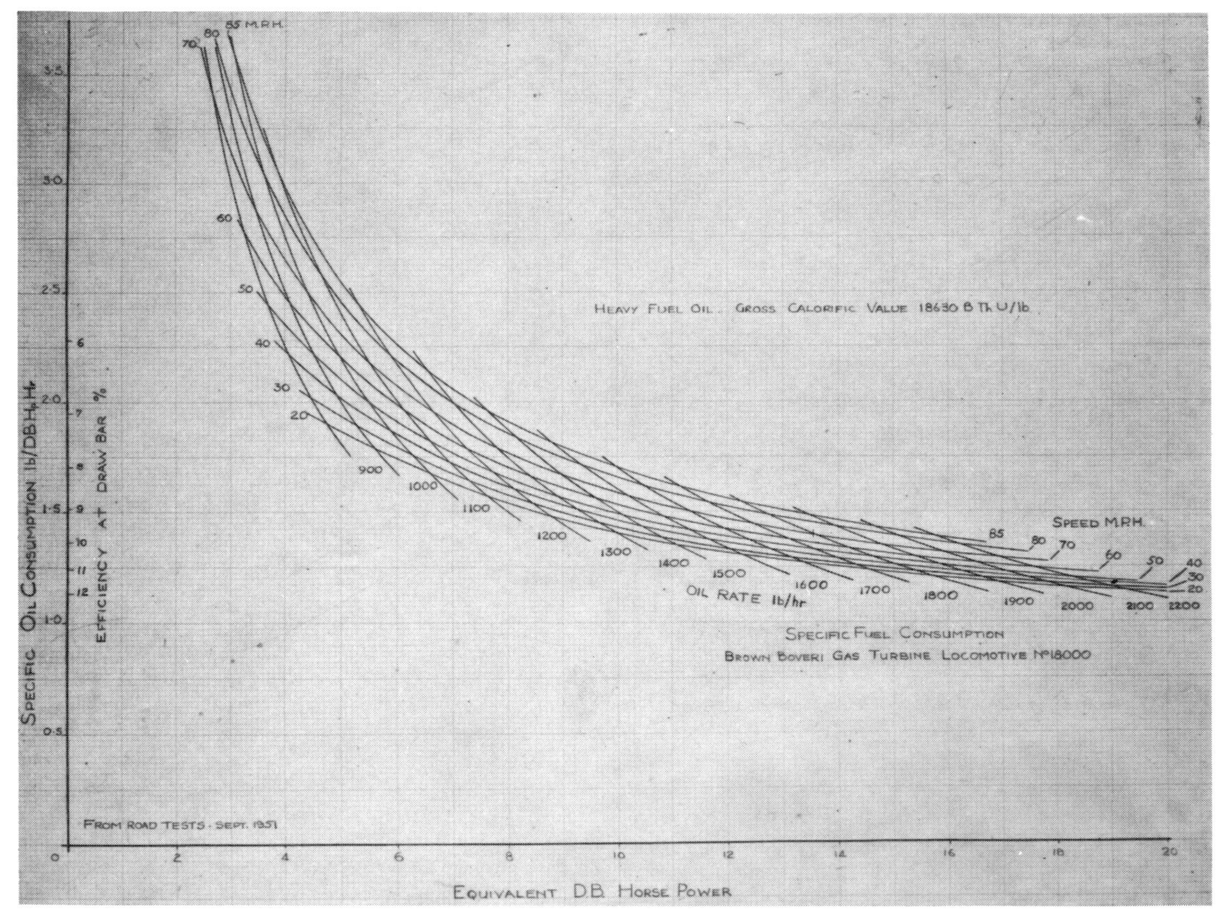

Brown-Boveri gas turbine electric loco No 18000

Tests between Paddington and Plymouth: September 1951

Date	11.9.51	13.9.51	12.9.51	14.9.51
Direction	Down	Down	Up	Up
Number of coaches and tare weight (tons)				
Paddington–Westbury	12-395	12-395	—	—
Westbury–Exeter	11-359	11-359	—	—
Exeter–Plymouth	7-239	7-239	—	—
Plymouth–Newton Abbot			7-228	7-227
Newton–Exeter			12-388	11-356
Exeter–Paddington			12-388	12-386
Average speed (mph)	53.6	53.7	50.2	49.4
Average dhp	721	831	736	729
Fuel (lb/dhp hour)	2.05	1.93	2.17	2.12
Efficiency: work done at drawbar per fuel oil used	6.66	7.09	6.25	6.39

far as speed was concerned; but, comparing the estimates of power output with the graphs in the Swindon report, it was evident that the locomotive was working under light power conditions, and thus in adverse circumstances so far as thermal efficiency counted. From Exeter on the east-bound journey, the load was one of only 10 coaches, 324 tons tare; and although we made a spectacular ascent to Whiteball tunnel, averaging 65 mph throughout on an average gradient of 1 in 270, comparison with the data in the test report shows that the locomotive was working in no more than the 6th notch, and at an efficiency, related to the drawbar of not more than about 8 per cent. The descent from Whiteball tunnel to Taunton was made entirely without power, with speed rising to 83½ mph on a steeply falling gradient. On the continuation run to Paddington, non-stop over 142.7 miles, the locomotive was worked at very light power. Allowing for incidental delays the net time was 150 minutes, an average of no more than 56.1 mph with a gross trailing load of 345 tons.

On the return journey, by the 3.30 pm train, the load was 384 tons tare from Paddington and 348 tons after detaching the Weymouth coach at Westbury. The 95.6 miles to this stop were covered in 98½ minutes, with relatively easy running throughout. With the reduced load the 47.1 miles to Taunton took 46 minutes. Speeds up to 82 mph were attained on the generally favourable sections of the line, and the initial section to the crest of the Mendip Range before Bruton, although smartly covered, probably required no more than the 6th notch of the controller. The climb to Whiteball tunnel, from a standing start at Taunton, was taken vigorously after a relatively slow immediate start from rest and, on entering the tunnel, after 3 miles rising at 1 in 90-86-80, the speed had not fallen below 48½ mph, from an initial 63 mph. On this journey the total running time for the 173.5 miles from Paddington to Exeter was 181¼ minutes, an average speed of 57.5 mph. The running, though a little better than service requirements, was comparable with average performance that would be expected from a 'Castle' Class steam 4-6-0 locomotive though, as previously explained, the demands of the service were far below the maximum capacity of the gas turbine locomotive.

Ever since the phenomenally rapid change from steam to diesel-electric traction began in North America, engineers in Great Britain sought authoritative data whereby the relative economic advantages of steam and diesel-electric locomotion could be compared on the fairest possible basis. It had often been felt that new diesel power had been compared with out-dated steam locomotives, while on other grounds there seemed to be evidence that the great metamorphosis in American railway motive power had been dictated by other than strict engineering or economic considerations. It was the more gratifying that in 1953, sometime before the great modernisation plan was launched, that British Railways published the first comprehensive test bulletin containing details of performance and efficiency tests on diesel-electric locomotives from which the fair comparison with up-to-date steam (that all railway engineers felt was so necessary) could be made. No testing establishment was being more ruthlessly objective in its methods than Swindon, and it was with the aid of the ex-Great Western dynamometer car and its experienced team of test engineers that the Southern Region diesel-electric locomotive was examined.

Though commonly referred to simply as 'diesels' these locomotives are basically direct current electric. They have all the traction characteristics of electric locomotives, but have their own 'private' generating station in the form of a diesel engine driving an electric dc generator. There were thus three distinct parts of the equipment, all of English Electric manufacture: the diesel engine, 16-cylinder V-type, turbo pressure charged; the main generator, running at 750 revs per minute, and the traction motors. One need not go into the specialist details of the electrical controls. The locomotive, which had an all-up weight of 135 tons, had a maximum tractive effort of 48,000 lb up to 8.75 mph and a continuous tractive effort of 21,700 lb at 24.5 mph.

Two sets of trials were conducted. The first series was on service trains between Waterloo and Exeter, a return trip of 343½ miles in a single day, by the 7.30 am eastbound train, returning at 1 pm from Waterloo. At the time one of the two diesel-electric locomotives was making two return trips daily between Waterloo and Exeter, while the second was working similarly between Waterloo and Weymouth.

The trains chosen for the dynamometer car tests were important, as in both directions a considerable number of intermediate stops had to be made. The longest distances scheduled to be made non-stop were 48.9 miles westbound (Yeovil Junction to Exeter) and 66.4 miles eastbound (Andover Junction to Waterloo). The stop-start nature of much of the running required by these schedules would not ordinarily be considered conducive to performance of high thermal efficiency overall, and the results are particularly interesting on this account.

The schedules were:

Westbound

Distance (miles)		Time (minutes)	Average speed (mph)
0.0	Waterloo	0	—
24.4	Woking	29	50.5
0.0		0	—
42.0	Andover Junction	45	56.0
0.0		0	—
17.4	Salisbury	21	49.7
0.0		0	—
28.4	Templecombe	34	50.2
0.0		0	—
6.1	Sherborne	11	33.2
0.0		0	—
4.4	Yeovil Junction	8	34.5
0.0		0	—
48.9	Exeter	56	52.3

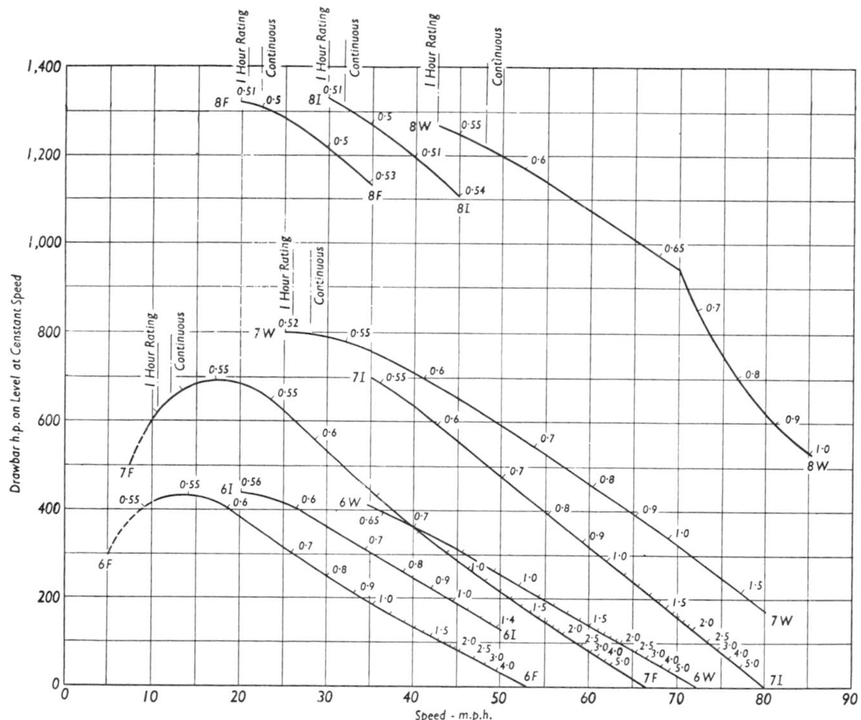

G C V fuel oil : 19,610 B.Th.U. per pound. Small figures on curves refer to specific fuel consumption in pounds per drawbar horsepower-hour, i.e. inclusive fuel consumption divided by drawbar horsepower. Large figures refer to controller notch position and field strength. F, full ; I, intermediate ; W, weak.

Southern Region: diagram of drawbar horsepower characteristics, locomotive No 10202 (British Railways).

Eastbound

Distance (miles)		Time (minutes)	Average speed (mph)
0.0	Exeter	0	—
12.2	Sidmouth Junction	16	45.8
0.0		0	—
14.8	Axminster	18	49.3
0.0		0	—
21.9	Yeovil Junction	25	52.5
0.0		0	—
4.6	Sherborne	7	39.4
0.0		0	—
6.1	Templecombe	10	36.6
0.0		0	—
6.8	Gillingham	9	45.3
0.0		0	—
21.6	Salisbury	25	51.8
0.0		0	—
17.4	Andover Junction	21	49.7
0.0		0	—
66.4	Waterloo	71	56.1

Moreover the line west of Andover Junction is a constant alternation of steep gradients, some of which have to be climbed immediately after a station stop. The route itself, and the duties required by the timetable, could well be considered as a symposium of British railway working in fast passenger train service. The results, as recorded in the Western Region dynamometer car, are shown in the accompanying table (right). A very careful check was kept on fuel oil consumption, as between time under power, when standing at stations, and when drifting and braking. This was important because the diesel engines had to be kept running and were using fuel all the time that the locomotive was not under power. The overall efficiencies recorded, varying between 17.6 and 19.6 per cent, represent a vast improvement over that of the gas turbine. The relative efficiencies, and comparable fuel costs for three different forms of railway motive power were quoted in a lecture to the Graduates Section of the Institution of Mechanical Engineers by Mr R.A. Riddles, in 1952, thus:

Loco type	Average train load (tons)	Unit cost of fuel	Thermal efficiency at drawbar	Cost of fuel (pence per unit)	(pence per dhp hour)
GWR 'Castle' Class	360	0.37d/lb	5.5	12.6	1.18
Brown-Boveri gas turbine	360	1.10d/lb	6.6	27.7	2.27
Southern diesel-electric	350	1.51d/lb	18.8	12.8	1.05

At the time Riddles was very much against the introduction of diesel locomotives as a replacement for steam, and it is important to emphasise that the above figures relate purely to running fuel costs. No account was taken of the difference in capital cost between the three forms of motive power, nor of the

Southern Region: tests of diesel-electric loco No 10202, Waterloo and Exeter

Direction	Down	Up	Down	Up
Date	28.4.52	29.4.52	30.4.52	1.5.52
Load:				
Waterloo–Templecombe (tons tare)	12-397	—	13-432	
Templecombe–Exeter (tons tare)	9-299	—	8-265	
Exeter–Salisbury (tons tare)	—	8-266	—	8-267
Salisbury–Waterloo (tons tare)	—	11-362	—	12-398
Average speed (running time) (mph)	50.2	49.4	54.0	52.1
Average drawbar horsepower	695	663	753	761
Oil:				
Average rate (lb per hour)	401	381	421	384
Rate under power (lb per hour)	477	472	508	486
Rate while drifting and braking (lb per hour)	48.5	51.7	49.7	48.6
Rate while standing at stations (lb per hour)	47.4	46.1	53.7	49.1
Pounds per dhp hour on total fuel used	0.700	0.732	0.69	0.659
Overall efficiency: per cent	18.6	17.6	18.7	19.6

greater availability of the diesel. Against the daily mileage of 687 then being worked in two diesel return trips between Waterloo and Exeter, a steam 4-6-0 of the ex-GWR 'Castle' Class would probably not work more than 325 miles in one day, represented by a single trip from Paddington to Plymouth, followed by a return trip from Exeter to Plymouth and back. Nevertheless the economic climate was not very favourtable to the diesels in the early 1950s and, at the time of publication of the bulletin on the tests of the Southern locomotive, the price of gas oil had risen from the 1.51 pence per pound quoted by Mr Riddles to 1.69 pence. A commentary in *The Engineer* in October 1953 included the following: 'Even with an overall efficiency of 18.8 per cent, the diesel showed no appreciable cash saving over steam, and on train services less favourable to the locomotive than those on which No 10202 was actually tested, this equality would probably disappear. In general utility service, with diagrams including a mixture of light and heavy duties, there is every suggestion that a modern steam locomotive would show lower fuel costs in present British conditions.'

A few weeks after the dynamometer car tests were concluded I had the privilege of riding in the cab of locomotive No 10202 on the 1 pm train from Waterloo as far as Salisbury, and was fortunate enough to strike an occasion when the load was considerably heavier than any in the test series: 14 coaches, with a tare weight of 466 tons. With a crowded passenger complement, the gross trailing was estimated at 500 tons. There was no locomotive inspector in the cab, and the crew were on their normal roster, which included duties mostly worked by steam. It would have been extremely interesting to have a full technical analysis of this run, for with the additional load the locomotive had to be driven at full power for the entire journey. There was, in fact, no time in hand to offset the effects of two checks, and the train arrived at Salisbury 8 minutes late. The following is an abbreviated log of the journey:

Distance (miles)		Schedule (minutes)	Actual time m s	Speeds (mph)
0.0	WATERLOO	0	0 00	—
3.9	CLAPHAM JUNCTION	7	7 10	—
7.3	Wimbledon		11 25	54½
9.8	Malden		14 09	60
13.3	*Hampton Court Junction*	18	17 36	65
17.1	Walton		21 03	60
19.1	Weybridge		23 02	68
—			sig stop	—
24.4	WOKING	29	32 30	—
6.6	*Milepost 31*		10 49	48
8.8	Farnborough		13 17	60
17.8	Hook		21 57	65
23.4	BASINGSTOKE		27 13	60
25.9	*Worting Junction*	29	29 51	53
34.8	Whitchurch		38 31	69
—			pw check	
42.0	ANDOVER JUNCTION	45	48 28	
2.8	*Milepost 69*		5 26	49½
6.3	Grateley		10 23	42½
11.8	Porton		16 02	73
16.2	*Tunnel Junction*	18½	19 44	76*
17.3	SALISBURY	21	21 57	—

* maximum before brake application

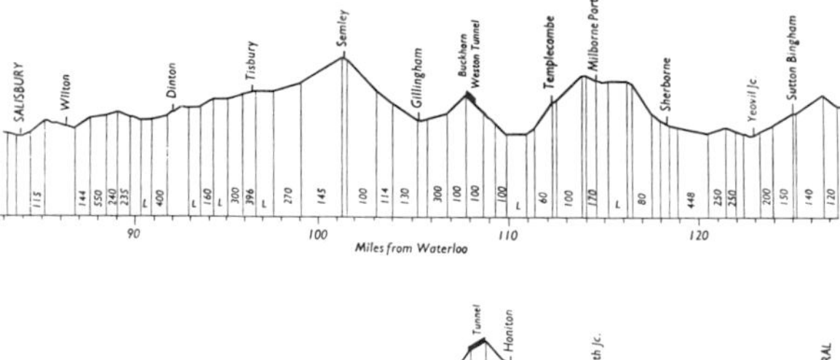

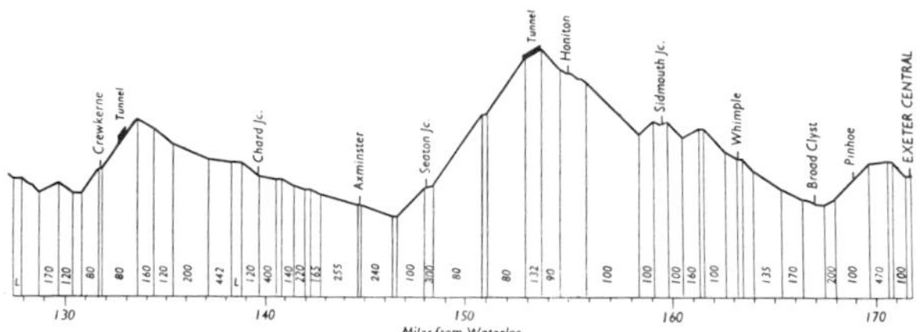

Southern Region: gradient profile of main line between Salisbury and Exeter (British Railways).

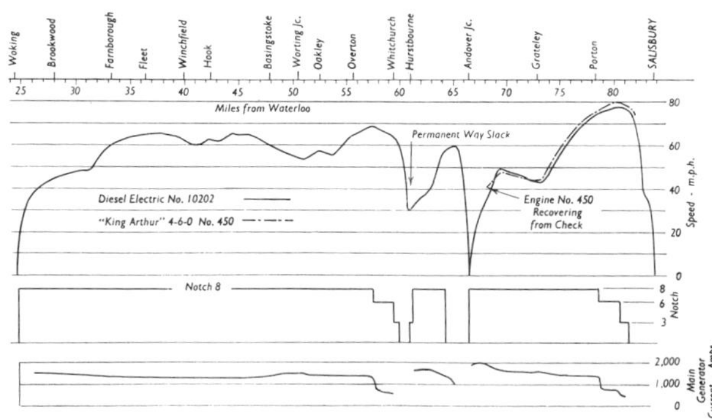

Southern Region: performance of Locomotive No 10202 Waterloo to Salisbury (The Engineer).

Without the checks we should just have kept time to Woking, and again to Andover; but there was a loss of a minute in the final section. Notch 8, the maximum, was used throughout to Weybridge, and again from Woking to Whitchurch. The equivalent drawbar horsepower registered in the earlier test series when working were as follows, together with the corresponding specific fuel consumption:

Speed (mph)	**Drawbar horsepower (Notch 8)**	**Fuel consumption per dhp hour**
45	1,250	0.55
50	1,200	0.58
55	1,140	0.61
60	1,075	0.625
65	1,005	0.64
70	945	0.67

On the final section, between Andover Junction and Salisbury, there was opportunity for making an interesting comparison with steam. A diagram of the running of the diesel west of Woking is shown in the accompanying chart (below left). The gradient is rising at about 1 in 300 from the start to Milepost 31; then there are slightly undulating gradients to Milepost 46, followed by a continuous rise at 1 in 249 to Milepost 52. Thence there are favourable gradients to Andover Junction. From the restart there is a stiff climb to Grateley, and it was here that the comparison with steam came to be made. On a prewar express, running non-stop from Waterloo to Salisbury, a 2-cylinder 4-6-0 of the 'King Arthur' Class, loaded to 450 gross trailing tons, was checked to 30 mph for permanent way repair work at Andover. The two trains, steam and diesel hauled, passed Red Posts Junction, 1.4 miles farther on, at the same speed of 40 mph; after which the times were as follows:

Distance (miles)		**Steam Actual time***	**Diesel Actual time***
		m s	**m s**
0.0	Red Posts Junction	0 00	0 00
1.4	Milepost 69	1 40	1 56
5.0	Grateley	6 18	6 53
7.9	Amesbury Junction	9 46	10 08
10.5	Porton	12 08	12 32
14.9	Tunnel Junction	15 48	16 14
16.0	SALISBURY	17 54	18 27

* from passing at 40 mph

Between Milepost 69 and the summit, just west of Grateley station, the gradient is 1 in 264 for 1¾ miles and then 1 in 165 for 3 miles. The lowest speeds were 43 mph (steam) and 43½ (diesel) and the maxima descending to Salisbury were 79 mph (steam) and 76 (diesel). The steam locomotive, with 450 tons, made slightly faster times, though the 'King Arthur' could not in 1952 be regarded as a modern locomotive. The British Railways classification was '5P'. It is interesting to recall that when the LMS introduced the first main line diesel-electric locomotive, No 10000, in 1947, of 1,600 hp it was considered to be roughly the equivalent of a Class '5MT' 4-6-0. The heavier load in the case of the Southern Region, No 10202, of 500 tons, against the 450 tons would slightly outweigh the superiority in times made by the 'King Arthur' hauling 450 tons, but the correspondence was nevertheless a close one.

A record exists of a very fast run from Andover to Waterloo by the diesel locomotive No 10202 with a considerably lighter load of 265 tons. Although there was not an observer in the cab on this occasion, it is evident from the speeds run that it was another 8-notch performance. It was made when certain accelerations were proposed and an experimental timing of 63 minutes for the 66.4 miles from Andover Junction was being worked to. The train passed Hampton Court Junction, 53.1 miles in 43 minutes 2 seconds from the dead start, having made a 'flying' average of 82.7 mph over the 36.5 miles from Overton to Weybridge. After this the locomotive was evidently eased down a little, though nevertheless completing the journey to Waterloo in 61 minutes 51 seconds despite two checks in the last 7 miles. A parallel to this fast run exists with steam because, in the 1930s when the 'Atlantic Coast Express' was being run exceptionally fast to make up lost time, the entire distance from Salisbury to Waterloo, 83.8 miles, was covered in 72¾ minutes. The 'Flying' average from Overton to Weybridge was almost exactly the same as that of the diesel, 82.0 mph, with a heavier train of 345 tons. The engine, again, was a 'King Arthur', the one that has now been preserved and restored to working order, No 777, *Sir Lamiel.*

In 1954 a further locomotive of the 1-C-C-1 type was built by the Southern Region at Ashford Works using, as in Nos 10201 and 10202, diesel engines and electric generators and motors of English Electric design and manufacture. This third locomotive, No 10203, was higher rated, with an engine of 2,000 hp capacity. It was thoroughly tested beween Waterloo and Exeter in 1955, and showed traction efficiencies of between 19 and 20 per cent. Details of the tests are discussed in some detail in the third volume of this series, in which the application of test results of economical train timing, as developed by the Swindon testing team, is described.

16. Later developments with steam

Bulleid was undoubtedly one of the most advanced thinkers whose products have enlivened the scene of locomotive engineering everywhere in the world. In the autumn of 1946 he was elected President of the Institution of Mechanical Engineers and, in his address delivered on October 18, having said that his very novel 'Merchant Navy' and 'West Country' 'Pacifics' were to be regarded not as final designs, but rather as stages in locomotive development, he riveted the attention of his audience, by continuing: 'A wide range of research work is in hand. The more interesting investigations are those being carried out into new modes of stay-to-plate fixing in fireboxes, to ensure speed and economy in manufacture and longer life in service by prevention of seepage and plate cracking; the effect of heat input and mechanical restraint upon welds in heat-sensitive steels, with the object of eliminating tyre slip in tyres applied by shrinking-on only and without fastenings of any known design.

'What sort of locomotive may we expect to see, if it is to meet most future requirements? It should be built so as to: 1) be able to run over the majority of the company's lines; 2) be capable of working all classes of trains up to speeds of 90 mph; 3) have its whole weight available for braking and the highest possible percentage thereof for adhesion; 4) be equally suitable for running in both directions without turning, with unobstructed look-out; 5) be ready for service at short notice; 6) be almost continuously available; 7) be suitable for complete 'common use'; 8) run not less than 100,000 miles between general overhaul with little or no attention at the running sheds; 9) cause minimum wear and tear to the track; and 10) use substantially less fuel and water per drawbar horsepower developed.

'It should incorporate a boiler from which stay and tube trouble has been eliminated; high steam pressure to enable reduced cylinder dimensions to be used, and a new design of cylinders with small clearance volume; feed water treatment by equipment on the locomotive itself; feed water heating by exhaust steam; all moving parts enclosed and continuously lubricated; all axle-boxes with roller bearings; and remote control with driving cabs at both ends.

'A new type of Southern engine has been designed, the construction of five of which has been authorised. It will incorporate the following features, and, it is hoped, will satisfy the desiderata given above. The locomotive is carried on two six-wheel bogies, the general design of which resembles those of the company's electric locomotives. These bogies have no centre pivot or bolster; the middle axle of each bogie is driven by a 3-cylinder single-expansion engine. The engine develops a torque, the uniformity of which is comparable with that of a nose-suspended electric traction motor, but has a higher speed range, and the unsprung weight is less . . .'

One could certainly not quarrel with any of the

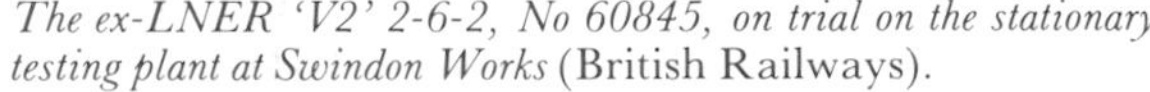

The ex-LNER 'V2' 2-6-2, No 60845, on trial on the stationary testing plant at Swindon Works (British Railways).

'desiderata' set forth by Mr Bulleid, except perhaps in view of the experience already gained with the 'Merchant Navy' Class to question the desirability of having the motion totally enclosed. When the first of the new locomotives appeared, in 1949, those who had taken a keen interest in the unorthodox steam locomotives of the past were quick to notice two feature which closely resembled points in the 'Paget' locomotive, built at Derby in 1909 to the private order of Mr Cecil W. Paget, then General Superintendent of the Midland Railway. Little had been known about this remarkable machine; but in *The Engineer* of March 26 1943 an article was published on 'Links in the history of the Locomotive' by James Clayton, who (until 1938) has been Personal Assistant of the Chief Mechanical Engineer of the Southern Railway. He had retired not long after Bulleid had succeeded R.E.L. Maunsell in that high office. In 1943 Clayton knew more than any man then alive about the 'Paget' locomotive, because from the year 1904 he had been employed privately by Paget as the design draughtsman on the project. In the article he contributed to *The Engineer* in 1943 he described the locomotive in some detail, though not to the same extent as in the sumptuously documented article that appeared in *The Railway Gazette*, also by James Clayton, in 1945.

One can be sure that Bulleid studied the 1943 article with keen interest, and that his own ideas on the boiler and cylinder design of the new locomotive were well advanced by the time the later one appeared, in November 1945. When the first of the five 'leaders' appeared in 1949 it was pointed out that elimination of the firebox legs and flat-stayed surfaces had also been done in the 'Paget'; but of course more modern constructional techniques were then available, and the boiler was welded throughout and incorporated four thermic siphons. The boiler pressure was 280 lb per square inch as on the 'Pacifics'. The accompanying diagram shows that a girder frame supported the boiler, fuel supplies and the superstructure. The bogies were each powered by a 3-cylinder engine, having cylinders 12¼ inch diameter by 15 inch stroke. The drive was on to the centre axle of each bogie, the three axles of each being coupled by chain.

There was another echo of the Paget locomotive in that the steam distribution was by a cast-iron sleeve valve, sliding inside a liner of the same material. Separate admission and exhaust ports, equally distributed around the circumference, were machined in the sleeve. The whole of the motion, including the crank axle was enclosed and continuously lubricated. In his original references to the locomotive, Bulleid stated that the cylinders would be of a new design with small clearance volume. Certainly this quantity was much reduced from that of the 'West Country', being 6 per cent as compared to 10 per cent, but it must be mentioned that on the ex-Great Western 4-cylinder 4-6-0s the clearance volume was only 5.5 per cent.

The general layout can be seen in the diagram. Access to the driving cabs was attained from the lineside by ladders at each end, and the boiler was mounted offcentre so as to provide a walkway from end to end, and to the firing platform, which was in the middle, between the firebox and the fuelbunker. The haulage capacity of the locomotive seemed a little optimistic in relation to its nominal tractive effort of only 26,300 lb, for it was stated to be capable of hauling fast passenger trains up to 480 tons over all main lines of the Southern Region, and goods and mineral trains up to 1,200 tons. The coal and water capacity were 4 tons and 4,000 gallons, considered to be sufficient for a run of 200 miles. A point that was criticised at once was the separation of the driver from the fireman. It was, of course, regular practice where small tank engines were

Southern Region: diagram of 'Leader' Class locomotive (British Railways).

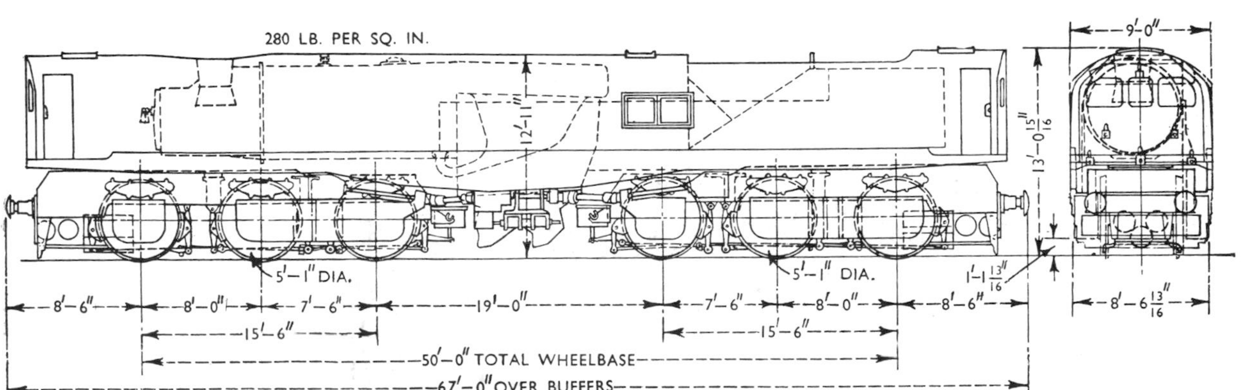

Southern Region: the only 'Leader' Class locomotive to be completed, on a test run on the Oxted line (British Railways).

incorporated in auto-train working, and the engine was propelling from the rear; but the working conditions were then very light. The practice of crew separation had been common enough in the USA on the so called 'Mother Hubbard' type on which the driver was accommodated in a cab by himself half-way along the boiler, while the fireman stoked from a platform in rear of the firebox. In this respect, and also from the temperature that reigned in the enclosed cab, the 'Leader' became unpopular from the outset.

Bulleid retired from the Southern at the end of September 1949, when the first of the 'Leaders' had been running for only about three months. He left to become 'consulting mechanical engineer' to the Irish Transport Company (CIE); but not long afterwards he was made an Honorary Member of the Railroad Division of the American Society of Mechanical Engineers. He crossed the Atlantic to give a notable address. Of the 'Leaders' he said:

'. . . The first of these new engines has run about 4,000 miles. As is to be expected, some troubles have arisen such as broken ends to the sleeve valves and spalling of the firebrick lining of the firebox, troubles which are being overcome. The engine has shown already the advantage of a double-bogie locomotive as regards freedom of running, ease in taking curves and the great value of having the total weight available for traction and braking. While in American eyes this is a small engine, its horsepower will be above 1,700 and consequently it will give at least as good results as a diesel-electric locomotive with a 2,000 hp engine. How successful we have been in the new design remains to be seen, but the new features in the engine should give us better service, help to improve the performance of the steam locomotive, and restore steam traction to favour.

'But while in this "Leader" Class of engine the development of the steam locomotive has been carried a stage further, there is still much work to be done. The use of the blast to create the draught should give way to fans, so that we can control the production of steam accurately. The exhaust steam should not be allowed to escape to the atmosphere, but the heat would be returned to the boiler. Experimental work already done encourages the thought that these two problems can be solved, and I commend them to the young engineers as worthy of investigation.

'I shall feel more than recompensed if I have shown that while the Stephenson locomotive today may in some circumstances be dead or dying, this cannot be said of steam traction itself. If new designs be developed in the light of our present greater knowledge and the servicing of the loco-

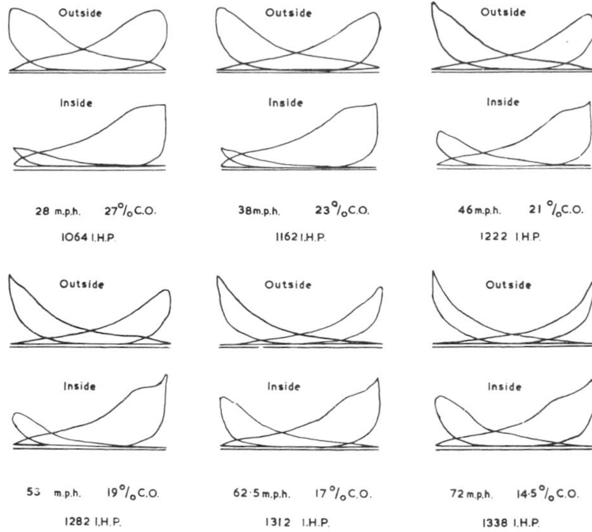

Ex-LNER 'V2' 2-6-2: examples of indicator cards—mean steam rate 18,000 lb/hr (British Railways).

motive be brought up to date—in short, if only we can demolish the conservatism which is destroying the steam locomotive rather than give up any of its customary ways—then we can look forward to the revival of steam traction.'

When he left Southern Region the first of the new engines was still having teething troubles, and without his driving force the project was doomed. The Railway Executive had nailed their colours to a very different mast, and with Bulleid gone there was nothing to deflect them; and although tests continued for another year, a failure on the road led to an instruction that all work must stop, including construction of the second and third engines, which on the former was well advanced. No official announcement was made at the time but, several months later when a question was raised in *The Railway Gazette*, the carefully worded official reply read thus:

'For various technical reasons the experiments with the prototype "Leader" Class locomotive were not as satisfactory as had been hoped, and to obviate the expense which would have been involved in continuing them for a problematical return, it has been decided not to proceed further with this novel design.'

Bulleid himself summed up this unfortunate ending to his greatest venture by saying: 'The tragedy was that it was built two years too late'; but really it was the case of the 'Pacifics' again on a much more elaborate and complicated scale. There were too many novelties packed into the one locomotive. It is true that the sleeve valve design was tried out on one of the Brighton 'Atlantic' engines, but that was only one feature. When nationalisation came a lesser man than Bulleid would probably have given up this cherished project, although five had been authorised. After all he was then 66 years of age, and the first few weeks of 1948 must have shown him that such ultra-progressive ideas in locomotive design found no sympathetic echoes within the walls of 222 Marylebone Road. But he stayed, until Ireland offered him, once again, an independent command.

After nationalisation of the railways all other work initiated by the Locomotive Testing Committee set up in January 1948 was overshadowed at first by the Locomotive Interchange Trials referred to in Chapter 13 of this book; but a review of the general practice of testing in Great Britain by D.R. Carling, Superintending Engineer of the newly opened stationary testing plant at Rugby, in a paper read before the Institution of Locomotive Engineers in September 1950, had some interesting and revealing facts to disclose about the performance of certain locomotives introduced just before nationalisation.

In Chapter 10 of this book I referred to the introduction by the LMS of the small Class 2—2-6-0, having 16 inch by 24 inch cylinders, 5 foot coupled wheels and carrying a boiler pressure of 200 lb per square inch. As originally built these engines did not steam freely, and the regrettably easy step was taken of reducing the diameter of the blast pipe orifice from $4\frac{3}{8}$ inch to $4\frac{1}{8}$ inch. This was successful so far as steaming was concerned, and in this state a series of dynamometer car test runs, using the Horwich car, were made between Crewe and Holyhead, in all cases non-stop. The distance is $105\frac{1}{2}$ miles, and the schedule time for the special

Ex-LNER 'V2' 2-6-2: examples of indicator cards—mean steam rate 23,950 lb/hr (British Railways).

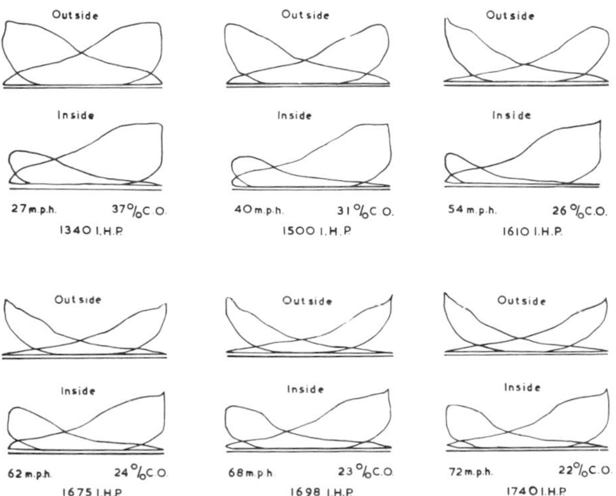

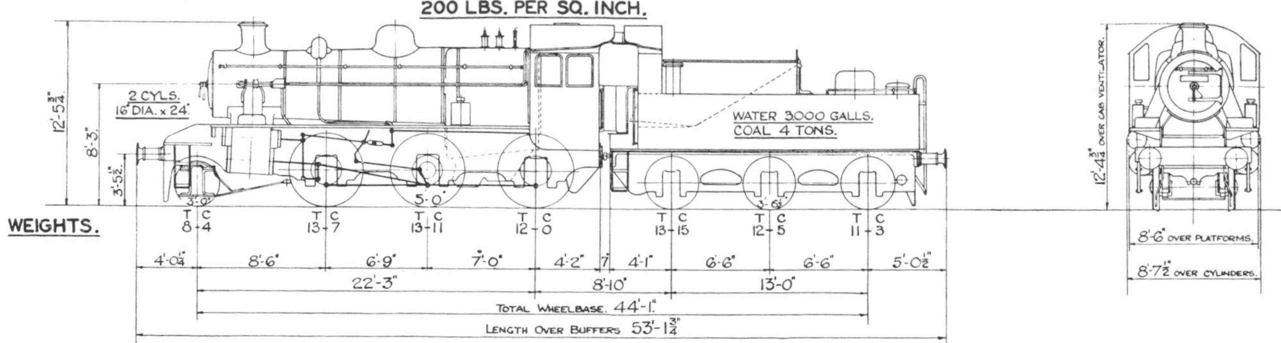

LMS: Class '2F' 2-6-0 locomotive—dimensional diagram (British Railways).

test trains was 137 minutes. This involved a not very exciting average speed of 46.2 mph over a route that is easily graded. The test load including the dynamometer car was 270 tons.

In relation to the work done it would seem that the coal consumption was heavy, amounting to 72.8 lb per square feet of grate per hour, or roughly 27 lb per train mile. Related to the work done it was a little over 4 lb per drawbar horsepower hour, at a time when locomotives in heavy express passenger work were using between 3 and 3½ lb. But the performance of the locomotive with the modified blast pipe was considered to be satisfactory, and the change was made on all engines of the class. They were intended as a general replacement for light branch line duties, and I was able to see something of their work on the heavily graded line between Penrith and Keswick, where among other steep gradients there was the 1 in 62 ascent from Threlkeld to Troutbeck, more than 4 miles at this inclination.

In 1950 the new 2-6-0 engines were being used turn and turn about with the veteran ex-LNWR 18 inch 0-6-0s of Webb's design, non-superheated, and dating back to 1880. The new engines were dimensionally more powerful, having a nominal tractive effort of 17,400 lb against 14,000. They were, of course, much more comfortable to ride. But I cannot say I was particularly impressed by their hill climbing work, in comparison with the old LNWR 0-6-0s, seeing that a span of more than 60 years separated the two designs.

My own footplate impressions were to find ample justification in the paper D.R. Carling read before the Institution of Locomotive Engineers in the autumn of that same year. British Railways had been considering the replacement of the historic 'Dean Goods' 0-6-0s of the former Great Western Railway, the origin of which extended back almost as far as the Webb 18 inch express goods engines of the LNWR to 1883, against 1880, and as originally built, with 17 inch cylinders and 140 lb per square inch boiler pressure they were not the equal of the Crewe engines. But in later years they had been thoroughly modernised, with superheaters, Belpaire fireboxes, and boilers carrying 180 lb pressure; and

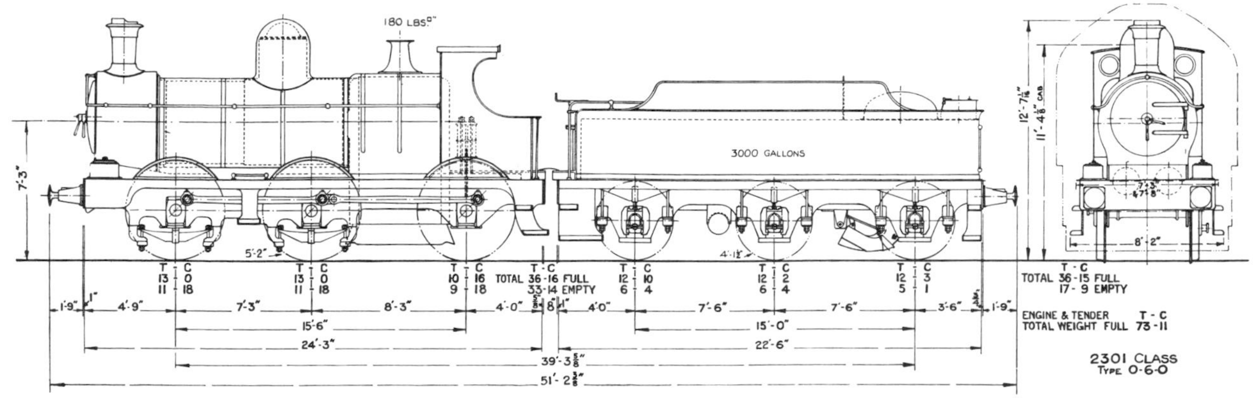

GWR: the 'Dean Goods' 2301 Class 0-6-0 dimensional diagram (British Railways).

Top *The ex-LNER 'V2', No 60845, pulling out on to the main line at Scours Lane Junction, west of Reading, on a controlled road test to Stoke Gifford, in February 1953* (M.W. Earley).

Above *The ex-LNER 'V2', No 60845, going hard in the approach to Hullavington, on a controlled road test. The load was 610 tons, the speed, 60 mph and the drawbar pull, 3¾ tons. The author was in the dynamometer car* (Kenneth H. Leech).

anything brought along to replace them would have to be very good, seeing that with a maximum axle load of 13 tons they had a very high route availability. They then carried 17½ inch diameter cylinders, and had a nominal tractive effort of 18,140 lb. Their general appearance and leading dimensions can be appreciated from the accompanying diagram (left). Moreover they had been well maintained, and were powerful and popular engines.

When one of the ex-LMS Class '2' 2-6-0 was sent to the Western Region for trial, prior to taking over some of the duties at present worked by the 'Dean Goods' it was found, to the surprise of BR Headquarters that the engine would not steam on Welsh coal and, as an expedient to enable the tests to proceed as quickly as possible, the blast pipe orifice, already reduced to $4\frac{1}{8}$ inches diameter from the original $4\frac{3}{8}$ inches, was further reduced to $3\frac{7}{8}$ inches. Even with the sharpened blast the maximum rate of steam production was appreciably less than that of the 'Dean Goods' which had a blastpipe orifice of $4\frac{1}{2}$ inches.

Careful analysis of the two designs shows that although what is termed the boiler resistance of the LMS 2-6-0 was less than that of the 'Dean Goods', the latter was able to give a greater steam output. The 'boiler resistance' of a locomotive is related to the cross-sectional area through which the exhaust gases from the firebox are drawn to the smokebox and there entrained by the blast from the exhaust nozzle of the blastpipe. The self-cleaning plates put in the latest types of locomotive to facilitate ash collection afford a small obstruction to the flow of the exhaust gases; but even taking this in account in the case of the Class '2' 2-6-0 the boiler resistance was less. And yet the engine did not steam so freely as the 'Dean Goods'. Some attention to the draughting arrangements were clearly needed. But the problem was not merely one of making a selected batch of these engines suitable for Western Region conditions and fuel, and making them at least as good as the 'Dean Goods'; the testing section at Swindon was given authority to examine the draughting because it was clear that some modification would be to the advantage of the locomotives generally, and not only for Western Region.

The examination, and comparison with WR service requirements, showed that an increase in the cylinder diameter of ½ inch was desirable. To provide the necessary steam to sustain the increased tractive effort, the draughting arrangements were modified by fitting a liner inside the chimney to reduce its diameter at the throat, but an adjustment to the position of the blastpipe enabled the original diameter of orifice, $4\frac{1}{8}$ inches to be restored. The modified design enabled both Welsh and hard coal to be used effectively. The maximum evaporation was increased by 9½ per cent for Blidworth (hard) coal and 13 per cent for Bedwas (Welsh). Those figures relate to the improvement effected with the self-cleaning plates in position, and over the former results with the reduced blast pipe orifice of $3\frac{7}{8}$ inches diameter. Strictly comparing like for like, the improvement with Blidworth, over the engine as originally delivered on the Western Region, was 23½ per cent. For Bedwas coal no comparison was possible since the engine would not steam at all with the original chimney and blast pipe cap. An engine of limited usefulness was thus transformed into a first class small power unit, which subsequently became a national standard.

The ex-LNER maximum-power mixed traffic 2-6-2 engines of Class 'V2' were generally considered to be among the most successful of all Sir Nigel Gresley's designs. As described in Chapter 1 of this book, they were introduced in 1936, and on the fast passenger schedules of the last pre-war years were often called upon to deputise for 'Pacifics'. During the war their general-utility capacity led to their being used turn and turn about with 'Pacifics' in working the extremely heavy East Coast expresses. Although suffering to some extent through reduced standards of day-to-day servicing, and some failures of the conjugated valve gear, it was only in cases of totally unsuitable fuel that there was any deficiency in the steaming. After the war, to reduce still further the attention they needed on shed, self-cleaning plates were introduced into the smoke-box, following similar measures on certain LMS locomotives; but with the 'V2' it resulted in a deterioration in steaming capacity far below the previous high standard. Various palliatives were tried, including the regrettably easy one of reducing the blast pipe orifice; none had any appreciable effect, so it was decided to send a representative engine to the Swindon stationary test plant for thorough examination. The accompanying diagram shows the smokebox arrangement of the engine, No

One of the War Department 2-8-0s, as taken into British Railways stock (British Railways).

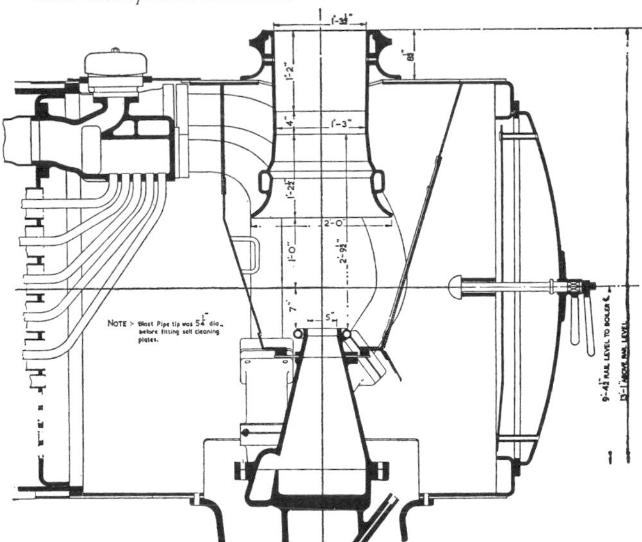

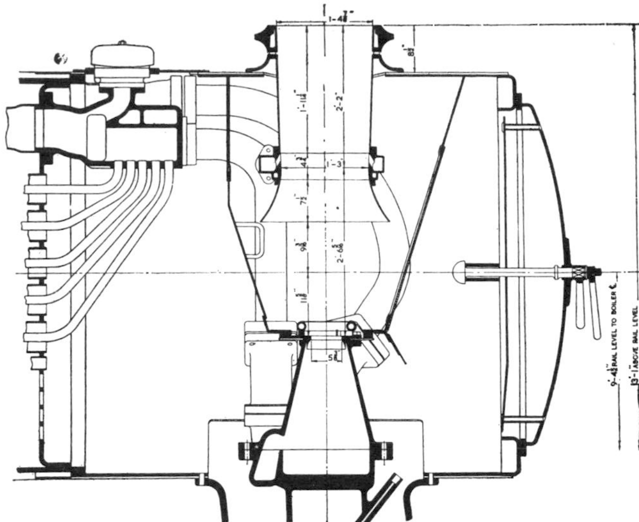

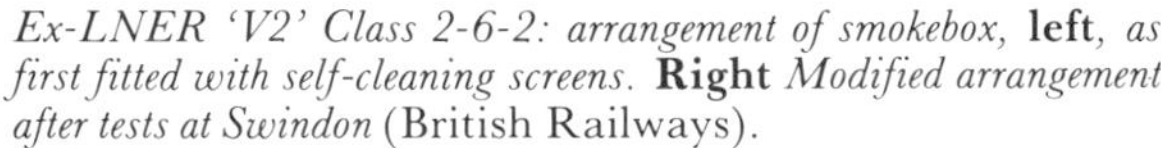

Ex-LNER 'V2' Class 2-6-2: arrangement of smokebox, **left**, *as first fitted with self-cleaning screens.* **Right** *Modified arrangement after tests at Swindon* (British Railways).

60845, as received. It was put on to the plant and the steaming was shown to be very poor, not exceeding 14,000 lb per hour, with Blidworth Grade 2B coal.

The first step was to remove the self-cleaning plates. Further tests showed a much improved evaporation, with the steam rate increased to 24,000 lb per hour; but that conditions were still unfavourable was shown by a generally discoloured exhaust at the best of times, and much black smoke at others. But the engine as received at Swindon, even after removal of the self-cleaning plates, was not restored to its original form, in the 1936 design; it retained one of the Doncaster expedients, in a reduced blast pipe orifice of 5 inches diameter, instead of 5¼ inches, and it could have been that the jet of exhaust steam was not completely filling the chimney. As originally built the 'V2' Class had no more than a very slight internal taper in the chimney, from 1 foot 3 inches at the throat to 1 foot 3½ inches at the top—an increase of only ½ inch in 1 foot 6 inches height.

Experience at Swindon in the establishment of ideal chimney and blast pipe proportions favoured an internal taper of 1 in 14, and by lowering the choke the upper divergent portion was made 2 feet 2 inches long instead of the original 1 foot 6 inches. While the original choke diameter of 1 foot 3 inches was retained, the diameter at the top of the chimney became 1 foot 4⅞ inches. The top of the blast pipe was lowered, as can be seen from a comparison with the 'as received' drawing, and its diameter increased to 5⅜ inches, that is larger than the original of 1936. The result was a complete transformation. With the self-cleaning plates in position the engine steamed freely up to a maximum of 30,000 lb per hour, with a clear exhaust, and a series of very successful tests were made on the stationary plant, and with the ex-GWR dynamometer car.

The very thorough analysis of the engine performance did not show the cylinders and valve gear up in a very favourable light, as the following comparison between indicated and drawbar horsepower reveals.

Speed (mph)	15 per cent cut-off		20 per cent cut-off		25 per cent cut-off	
	I hp	dhp	I hp	dhp	I hp	dhp
40	835	645	1,050	860	1,280	1,095
50	1,000	690	1,255	950	1,500	1,190
60	1,175	700	1,450	980	1,680	1,205
70	1,345	660	1,615	945	1,820	1,145
80	1,450	525	1,750	800	1,930	980

It will be seen that at 60 mph only between 60 and 70 per cent of the power developed in the cylinders was translated into work at the drawbar, while at 80 mph this proportion was only 35 per cent when working in 15 per cent cut-off. The irregularities in the steam distribution arising from the conjugated valve gear are vividly shown in the two sets of examples of indicator cards, at a steam rate of 18,000 lb per hour, and at 23,950 lb per hour. 'Slogger' in the pin joints of the conjugated gear results in overrunning of the piston valve of the

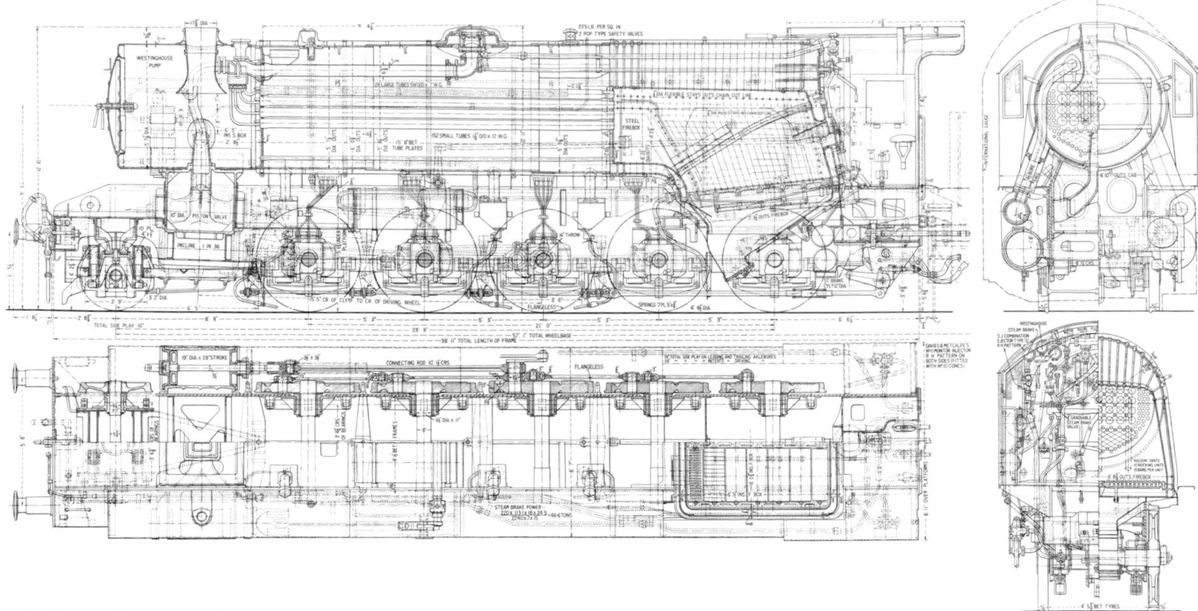

The 'Austerity' War Department 2-10-0 locomotive: general arrangement drawing (British Railways).

middle cylinder, which caused it to take an undue share of the work, and impose excessive loading on the inside connecting rod and its big-end. From an examination of the indicator cards it would seem that the valves of engine No 60845 had been set to counter, to some extent, this ill effect, though with great inequality between the power developed at the two ends of the inside cylinder.

At speeds of 60 mph and over it will nevertheless be seen how much greater an area is enclosed by the 'envelope' of the diagram taken off the inside cylinder. The extraordinary shape of the diagrams taken at 54 mph, 23,950 lb steam rate will be noted. What could be called ideal diagrams are those for the outside cylinders. Diagram shapes apart, however, the work at Swindon restored the 'V2' Class to a first rate motive power unit, with the advantage of self-cleaning plates in the smokebox.

In 1948 the nationalised British railways agreed to take over from the Ministry of Supply the 758 'Austerity' freight engines then in Great Britain, and which had been designed under the direction of R.A. Riddles during the war, when he was Deputy Director of Royal Engineer Equipment. Twenty-five of these engines were of the 2-10-0 type, the rest were 2-8-0s. Although not originally intended for service on British railways, but for war service overseas, the fact that so many of them were eventually taken into BR stock makes it necessary to make much more than a passing reference to them. The locomotive design originally selected for overseas service with the British armies was the LMS '8F' 2-8-0, adapted, and to some extent simplified for war conditions. Even so, it was something of a 'Rolls Royce' for the rough and tumble duties likely in the immediate lead up to a battle front; and by the time massive preparations for re-entry into the European continent were in full swing there was every need to economise in every feature of locomotive construction that could be simplified, and to avoid the use of specialised techniques and materials that were in short supply. Much ingenuity was shown in working out the details of design, in which Riddles had the unstinted cooperation and vast experience of the North British Locomotive Company, in producing the first engines of the new class. The broad traction requirement was for a locomotive that would haul a load of 1,000 tons at 40 mph on level track, and that should have a maximum axle load of 15½ tons, to permit its use over routes of a secondary nature.

With so many of the 2-8-0 type in post-war service on British Railways it was natural that R.A. Riddles should have wished for some positive test performance from locomotives for which he had been responsible in the war years, and arrangements were made for running trials to be carried out with both 2-8-0 and 2-10-0 units of the 'Austerity' design on the former Glasgow and South Western line between Carlisle and Hurlford (just south of Kilmarnock). The tests were carried out with the former LMS Mobile Test Plant, which enabled tests to be carried out on the road at constant speed. It was very interesting to read the comments of the testing staff included in the Bulletin issued by The Railway Executive in August 1953, particularly the criticism of the 2-8-0, because it brings into some prominence the divergence in opinion that can be formed of a locomotive type between those who test it in carefully controlled scientific conditions, and those who have to use it in ordinary day to day service, and who are 'at the receiving end', so to speak, of its general behaviour, as regards maintenance, daily attention on shed, and all other incidentals concerned with the running of steam locomotives. It was remarkable that the WD 2-8-0 emerged with a reputation diametrically opposite to that gathered by many other well known designs, in that the test results in controlled conditions could be described as 'indifferent to poor', whereas more than one British running superintendent regarded the WD Austerity 2-8-0 as the best heavy freight engine he had ever had! Relatively few of the 2-10-0s were taken into British Railways' stock after the war, but they too earned an excellent reputation.

Locomotives of both the WD Austerity types took part in the Interchange Trials of 1948. In these, as with all other locomotives involved, the method of handling was left to individual drivers, and in what could therefore be termed normal working conditions there was no trouble with steaming—rather the reverse! Reports from the routes run over included such comments as 'engine steamed freely. When working hard the firing rate had to be carefully regulated to prevent blowing off' and 'this engine was very free steaming'. The engine which was tested between Severn Tunnel Junction and Acton, and again between Bristol and Eastleigh was very run down, and was riding very roughly. It was reported that 'on the footplate considerable vertical oscillation and bumping was experienced and when steam was shut off there was a very bad fore and aft thumping movement which gradually subsided while coasting'. On the engine tested on the Eastern and LM Regions it was reported that there was lateral oscillation when running fast.

It was natural that the run-down engine tested on the Western Region routes should show a higher basic coal consumption, but in the circumstances one could not call it excessive.

1948 Interchange Trials

Coal consumption of WD Austerity locos in lb per dhp hour

Route	Engine number	2-8-0	2-10-0
WR Severn Tunnel Junction–Acton	77000	4.02	—
WR Severn Tunnel Junction–Acton	73774	—	3.59
ER Ferme Pk–New England	63169	3.56	—
ER Ferme Pk–New England	73774	—	3.09
LM Brent–Toton Yard	63169	3.55	—
LM Brent–Toton Yard	73776	—	3.65
W & SO Bristol–Eastleigh	77000	4.11	—
W & SO Bristol–Eastleigh	73774	—	3.66

Summary of freight engine performance (coal per dhp lb—all tests)

Loco	WR '2800'	ER '01'	LM '8F'	WD 2-8-0	WD 2-10-0
Coal (lb)	3.42	3.37	3.52	3.77	3.52

One of the later War Department 2-8-0s of the LMS Stanier type, which were followed by the 'Austerity' version, later in the war (courtesy of Beyer, Peacock & Co).

With his 'Austerity' engines matched against such peacetime thoroughbreds as Churchward's '2800' Class, and the Stanier '8F', Riddles could well have been satisfied with the results; but then, when two selected engines then numbered 90464 (2-8-0) and 90772 (2-10-0) were sent up to Durran Hill, Carlisle Midland shed, for full dress trials it became a very different story. There was no question of taking run-of-the-mill engines, straight out of traffic, as in 1948; both engines were given a *general* repair, and handed over for testing after being no more than run in, with 500 miles each 'on the clock'. But then what happens! Quoting from preliminary remarks in the report: 'The standard blast pipe orifice for both the WD 2-8-0 and 2-10-0 locomotives is $5\frac{1}{8}$ inches diameter. As received, the steaming of the 2-8-0 engine was poor and it was necessary to reduce the blast pipe orifice to $4\frac{7}{8}$ inches diameter before it would perform satisfactorily. Previous experience with the 2-10-0 Class also indicated that a reduction in blast pipe cap diameter was desirable, and this engine was also fitted with a $4\frac{7}{8}$ inches diameter cap. This proved very satisfactory in the initial exploratory stages of the tests and was therefore, retained for the whole series.'

Anyone who had read the report of the BR Locomotive Testing Committee on the results of the 1948 Interchange Trials, and had got no further than the introductory remarks in the Bulletin of 1953 on the testing of the 2-8-0 and 2-10-0 'Austerity' locomotives, might justifiably begin to wonder just what the Testing Committee, or that section of them who went north with the ex-LMS Mobile test Units, were really about! It seems incredible that engines newly outshopped and with an excellent reputation for free steaming should need fiddling with the blastpipe the moment they were received, before they would steam.

On reading the report, however, it becomes evident that the engines on test, both 2-8-0 and 2-10-0 were driven in the 'copybook' style with regulators full open, and the earliest points of cut-off in the cylinders that would do the work set before them. This, of course, was the very antithesis of the way the engines were handled in ordinary traffic. The tests, it is stated, set out to obtain 'data directly applicable to the immediate commercial purpose of examining train loadings and schedules to obtain reduction in fuel consumption by working the locomotives where possible nearest their point of maximum operating efficiency'. This is admirable enough in conception, and capable of translating into practice in carefully regulated express passenger train working. But the whole purpose of the WD 'Austerity' designs was to provide a simple, trouble-free locomotive suitable for the rough and tumble of ordinary freight working. One can hardly imagine a

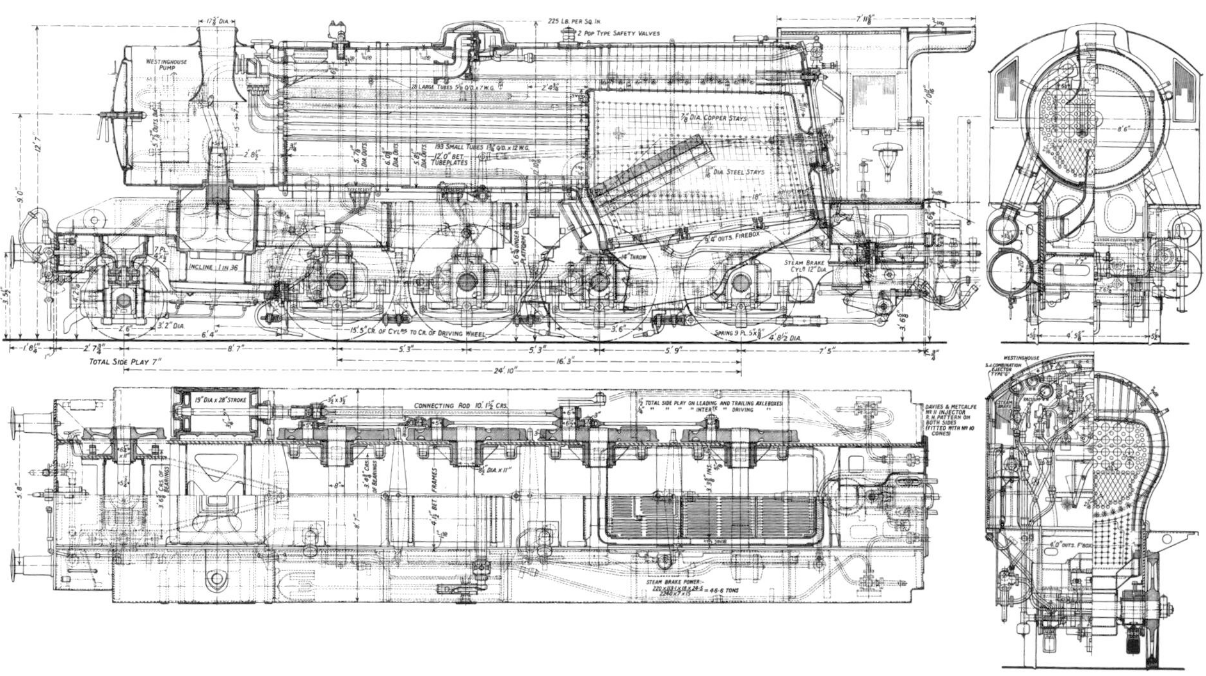

The 'Austerity' War Department 2-8-0 locomotive: general arrangement drawing (British Railways).

One of the 150 'Austerity' War Department 2-10-0s built in 1943 for war service on the continent of Europe. Gordon, *now on the Severn Valley Railway as seen here, was one of two allocated to the Longmoor Military Railway, and painted blue. After the war only 25 were taken into BR stock, but during 1945–6 the Netherlands Railways received no fewer than 103, on loan, one of which is now preserved at Utrecht* (P.J.C. Skelton).

hard-pressed yardmaster, anxious to clear his sidings of accumulating traffic, giving much consideration as to whether the train loading, or the schedules, such as they were, were ideally suited to minimum coal consumption by the locomotive!

In the tests on the WD 2-8-0 and 2-10-0, heavy loads were simulated by use of the three Mobile Test Units and the most recent of the LMS dynamometer cars. With the 2-10-0 it was shown that on level track, with a load of 1,800 tons, any desired speed up to 40 mph could be sustained while, on a rising gradient of 1 in 200, the maximum loads that could be taken at various speeds were, at 40 mph 600 tons; at 30 mph 1,000 tons; at 20 mph 1,600 tons, and at 10 mph 1,800 tons. The coal consumption was between 3 and 3.5 lb per dhp hour, whereas on level track it was a little below 3 lb per dhp hour. The 2-8-0 and the 2-10-0 had exactly the same cylinders, coupled wheels and boiler pressure, and with the same tractive effort the haulage ability on the road was naturally the same; but the 2-10-0, with the larger boiler and wide firebox, was able to sustain a higher steaming rate than the 2-8-0.

In view of the very important part the locomotives played towards the British war effort, and the skill with which such simplification and economy in construction was achieved with so little diminution in their general usefulness, the two types occupy a notable place in British locomotive history; and one is compelled to regard the performance and efficiency tests carried out in Scotland as an academic study rather than a practical exposition of the capabilities of two notable locomotive designs.

Dimensionally, both types had 19 inch by 28 inch cylinders; 10 inch diameter piston valves; coupled wheels 4 feet 8½ inches diameter, and carried a boiler pressure of 225 lb per square inch. The heating surfaces were:

	2-8-0	**2-10-0**
Heating surfaces (square feet)		
Tubes	1,512	1,759
Firebox	168	192
Superheater	310	423
Total	1,990	2,374
Grate area (square feet)	28.6	40

The maximum axle loads were 15.5 tons on the 2-8-0, and only 13.45 tons on the 2-10-0. The tractive effort was 34,215 lb on both types.

17. Scientific engine testing: the BR system

In Chapter 12 of this book, dealing roughly with a period from 1930 to 1945, the different philosophies of engine testing were discussed, showing how locomotive engineers were feeling their way towards more scientific methods, with particular regard to the practices already developed on the continent of Europe, and in the USA. In looking back upon British practice since the turn of the century it must certainly be admitted that much of it had been of a rough and ready order to obtain data for some specific object in the quickest and cheapest manner. Of the 16 main line companies in pregrouping days, only four possessed dynamometer cars; and it must be admitted that the uses to which these had been put were not very comprehensive. For example, when the London and North Western Railway carried out maximum power trials with one of the 4-cylinder 4-6-0s of the 'Claughton' Class, in 1913, although a complete record was secured of the very high power output sustained throughout the two test runs made, no record whatever was taken of the fuel consumption, an omission that leaves a serious gap in our knowledge of occasions that marked, by a considerable margin, the highest outputs of power that had been achieved by a British locomotive up to that time, and indeed until the 1920s.

In another respect, while a considerable amount of dynamometer car testing took place on the Great Western Railway in the years 1906 to 1912, Churchward himself seems to have taken little interest in the details of performance. After the tests the record charts would be laid out in the drawing office for the Chief's inspection; but apart from making a few apparently casual comments, and putting his pocket rule here and there to measure drawbar pull that would be all, and the rolls would be put away.

Much more scientific methods were being developed on the Great Western Railway in the later 1930s, and in the same era Sir Nigel Gresley and Sir William Stanier were getting together to develop more modern methods for the LNER and the LMS, which were to have been aided by the new stationary testing plant at Rugby. Construction of this latter was, however, suspended during the war years. But after nationalisation the setting up of a Locomotive Testing Committee, and the establishment of standard procedures to be used in both stationary and road testing, led to a number of very thorough tests being conducted on a variety of locomotives; what is more important from an historical point of view is that the complete results of the majority of these tests were made public in a series of bulletins. A number of these naturally concerned the new standard locomotives; but others were conducted on non-standard designs, which, by reason of the large numbers of them in traffic, or from uncertainties in their performance, made it desirable to have comprehensive records. So far as non-standard locomotives are concerned, in a few cases results were not published in bulletin form, and only a few significant details have subsequently emerged. Some well-known designs, notably the Gresley 'Pacifics' and their Eastern Region successors, were not tested at all, thus unfortunately

The Swindon stationary testing plant fully modernised. 'King' Class 4-6-0, No 6001, King Edward VII, *ran at 70 mph and developed 1,870 indicated horsepower in May 1953* (British Railways).

leaving a wide gap in the accumulated knowledge of British locomotive capacity.

As established under the general direction of the Locomotive Testing Committee of British Railways, testing work in the field was conducted in three main areas. In the Western Region the experimental section of the Locomotive Drawing Office of the former Great Western Railway had under its immediate control at Swindon the stationary testing plant, which had been thoroughly modernised in the late 1930s, and also the Churchward dynamometer car. The same testing staff operated whether in the test house or out on the road, thus making a complete degree of co-ordination a fundamental feature of all the work. It was at Swindon that the Controlled Road system of testing had been devised, and also the method of accurate measurement of coal and water consumption by what is termed the 'summation of increments' system. Both these methods were adopted by the Locomotive Testing Committee of British Railways as standard practice to be used in all locomotive testing. The 'summation of increments' was found to provide a far more accurate record that the older method of weighing the coal on and off the tender before and after a run.

Elsewhere on British Railways responsibility for testing was divided between the new stationary testing plant at Rugby, and a dynamometer car team based on London Midland Region locomotive headquarters at Derby. The new dynamometer car, No 3, built by the former LMS Railway was based there, together with the Mobile Test Units designed by Dr H.I. Andrews. The arrangement developed in supplementing tests made on the new stationary test plant at Rugby by road tests made by the Derby dynamometer car team. Advantage was taken of the facilities available in the Mobile Test Units to use them in providing all, or part of the load in road trials, and avoid the necessity of running very long trains when tests at maximum power were required. Some of the earliest road trials from Derby were carried out over a composite route southwards to Leicester, thence over the one-time Midland Counties line to Rugby, and thereafter over the former LNWR main line to Willesden; but all the later and more important trials supplementing the stationary tests at Rugby were conducted over that favourite of Midland test routes, the 'Settle & Carlisle'. A route of relatively light traffic density, the 'S & C' had the advantage of enabling test paths to be readily arranged, as well as providing severe haulage tasks in its heavy gradients.

The Interchange Trials of 1948 gave some results that were not really representative of the standard performance of some of the locomotive classes involved, particularly in the mixed traffic group. The ex-LMS 'Black Five' 4-6-0, for example, was driven in a most casual and unenterprising manner, while the ex-GWR was handicapped, on one route in particular, by the non-availability of any of the regular express drivers, and reliance having to be placed upon a 'volunteer'. At the time much was made of the disadvantage to which the engine was placed in having to use a grade B 'hard' coal, instead of the customary Welsh; but the disadvantage was actually more imaginary than real. It was all the more interesting that some of the earliest trials carried out under truly scientific conditions should have concerned the three classes of mixed traffic 4-6-0 involved in the Interchange Trials: the ex-LMS

Ready for confirmatory trials on the road—engine No 6001 with indicator shelters fitted and dynamometer car attached, outside Swindon Works (British Railways).

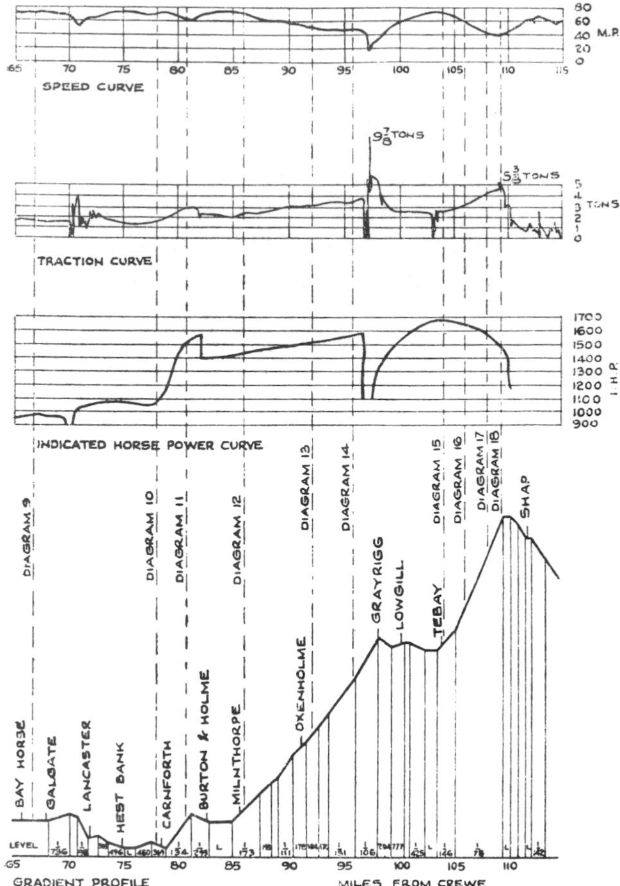

EXTRACT FROM THE DYNAMOMETER CAR RECORD ON RUN WITH NO. 1159, NOV, 4th., 1913.

LNWR: dynamometer car test run, November 1913—outstanding power output, but no coal consumption records (The Engineer).

'Black Five'; the ex-GWR 'Hall', and the ex-LNER 'B1'. The first two were tested on their own roads, while the 'B1' was tested at Rugby and on the Settle & Carlisle line. In the Interchange Trials, as previously discussed in Chapter 13, the overall results for the three classes, as summarised in coal consumption per drawbar horsepower hour had been 3.54 lb ('Black Five'); 3.94 lb ('Hall') and 3.59 lb ('B1') all engines using Blidworth coal with a calorific value of 13,940 BThU per lb.

It had been agreed with the trade unions that the maximum firing rate to be expected from a single fireman, continuously, would be 3,000 lb of coal per hour. It was generally understood that there would be times when this rate would be exceeded, briefly; but the average over an hour, or more, should not exceed the 3,000 mark. It is then very interesting to see what could be expected from each of the three classes of mixed traffic 4-6-0 in response to this rate of firing, in each case with Blidworth coal.

Performance on 3,000 lb coal per hour (Blidworth)

Engine Class	LMS 'Black Five'	GWR 'Hall'	LNER 'B1'
Water evaporated (lb per hour)	20,000	18,600	19,800
Maximum (ihp)	1,480	1,360	—
at speed (mph)	70	60	—
at cut-off (per cent)	28	18	—
Steam temperature (degrees Fahrenheit)	675	590	630
Steam per ihp hour (lb)	14.0	14.8	—
Coal per ihp hour (lb)	1.95	2.25	—
Boiler efficiency (per cent)	69	75	68
Maximum (dhp)	1,200	1,075	1,250
at speed (mph)	37	35	47
at cut-off (per cent)	39	32	35
Coal per dhp hour (lb)	2.40	2.75	2.40

The 'B1' was not indicated. From the viewpoint of complete records this was a pity, because the drawbar horsepower characteristics obtained at Rugby, and verified in trials on the Settle & Carlisle line, were very good. The Great Western engine suffers in the comparison from having no more than a moderate degree of superheat, though increased compared to earlier Swindon standards. The boiler efficiency is excellent, and in any case the basic coal consumption of 2.75 lb per dhp hour is well below the figures obtained in the 1948 Interchange Trials. With grade 1 Welsh coal the maximum drawbar horsepower was 1,270 at 37 mph 35 per cent cut-off, and the coal per dhp hour was 2.30 lb. The 'B1' in carefully controlled conditions was revealed as an efficient and effective engine, though features of its mechanical design led to rapid deterioration in service, and made it very rough and uncomfortable.

Great interest can be attached to two maximum power locomotives which were subjected to full dress trials but of which no bulletins were subse-

Right *Close-up of the attachment to the crosshead and cylinders for 'full dress' thermodynamic road testing of a 'King' Class engine* (British Railways).

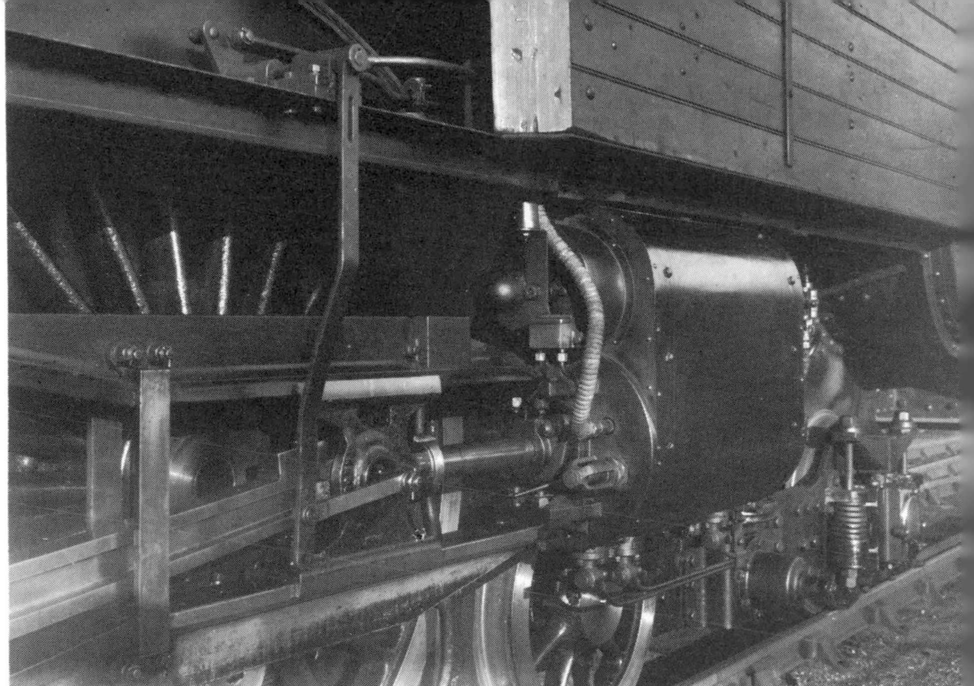

Below *The Churchward dynamometer car: close up of the instrument table, showing the fully modernised equipment for the scientific tests of the 1950s* (British Railways).

Controlled road test in 1953 with special train of 25 coaches, 795 tons, approaching Swindon at 60 mph, with engine No 6001, King Edward VII (British Railways).

quently published, namely the ex-GWR 'King' Class 4-6-0 and the Stanier 'Duchess' Class 'Pacific'. Details of the test performances of the 'King' with high degree superheat and improved draughting were given in a paper presented by S.O. Ell to the Institution of Locomotive Engineers in 1953; and some details of the 'Duchess' tests were made available to me personally at the time I was writing an engineering biography of Sir William Stanier. Further details, though not to the extent of a complete bulletin, were included in E. S. Cox's book, *The British Standard Steam Locomotives*, published in 1966. The 'King' as modified turned in a superb all-round performance. I had the privilege of seeing some of the tests in progress on the stationary plant at Swindon and also in riding in the dynamometer car during the road trials. The performance at the standard maximum firing rate was as follows:

Coal	**Blidworth**	**Markham**
Evaporation of water (lb per hour)	21,500	23,600
Maximum ihp	1,630	1,770
at speed (mph)	80	80
at cut-off (per cent)	18	20
Coal per ihp hour (lb)	1.84	1.70
Boiler efficiency (per cent)	74	71
Maximum dhp	1,210	1,340
at speed (mph)	33	35
at cut-off (per cent)	28	30
Coal per dhp hour (lb)	2.48	2.24

The 'ranks of Tuscany', as personified by E.S. Cox, did not hesitate to cheer this standard of performance, nor did he attempt to disguise his disappointment with the results obtained from the Stanier 'Duchess', which many of his contemporaries regarded as the finest of all British express passenger locomotives. His own view was that the relatively low superheat had much to do with it: '. . . the lower steam temperature being due to strangulation of the hot gases in threading their way along element fitted superheater tubes of 19 feet 3 inches in length but only $5\frac{1}{8}$ inches in diameter.' Certainly the engine tested yielded no higher indicated horsepower than 1,480, at no more than 50 mph with a maximum drawbar horsepower of 1,290 at 35 mph. In what circumstances these figures were obtained is not stated, but I can only add that in my own experience of these engines, both on and off the footplate, and that of other expert recorders, the results seem quite incomprehensibly poor and unrepresentative.

The corresponding figures of indicated horsepower at the standard maximum firing rate for a 'King' and an ex-LNER 'V2' Class 2-6-2 were 1,630 and 1,615 with Blidworth coal; but both these results were obtained at 80 mph. Why the 'Duchess'—an exceptionally free running engine—

achieved her maximum indicated horsepower at no more than 50 mph where other modern express locomotives show this quantity to have a rising characteristic, with a constant firing rate, is difficult to understand, and casts doubts, unfortunately, on the validity of the test results as a whole, on this engine at least. I have in my own records many instances of sustained outputs of 1,700 equivalent *drawbar* horsepower and more. A typical example being 67 mph 25 per cent cut-off 1,710 equivalent drawbar horsepower in an acceleration to that speed up a gradient of 1 in 335 with a gross trailing load of 510 tons. Many still more striking instances with these engines are analysed in the third volume of this work.

The results obtained with the ex-LNER 'V2', as redraughted at Swindon, have been discussed in the previous chapter. Undoubtedly the most difficult engine to test in a scientific and orderly manner was the Southern 'Merchant Navy' Class 'Pacific', which was run extensively at Rugby and in road trials on the Settle & Carlisle line. The bulletin subsequently published by British Railways was a remarkable document. It had this 'Foreword': 'This design of locomotive proved to be difficult to test owing to its inconsistent performance, especially with regard to power output. Not only was it often found impossible to obtain reasonable accuracy of repetition on different occasions but the performance would sometimes change appreciably over quite short periods of time. The changes were usually not of such magnitude as would have affected the locomotive's ability to carry out its normal duties quite effectively, but were such as to make accurate measurement exceptionally difficult, especially on the stationary test plant.

'These phenomena are of a kind known to be characteristic of this class of locomotive and are not peculiar to the one tested though their occurrence may vary from one engine to another from time to time'.

The report included the following note about the valve gear, which was described as 'a special feature of the design'.

Controlled road test: 'King' Class locomotive No 6001 at high output, continuously at 2,000 indicated horsepower (British Railways).

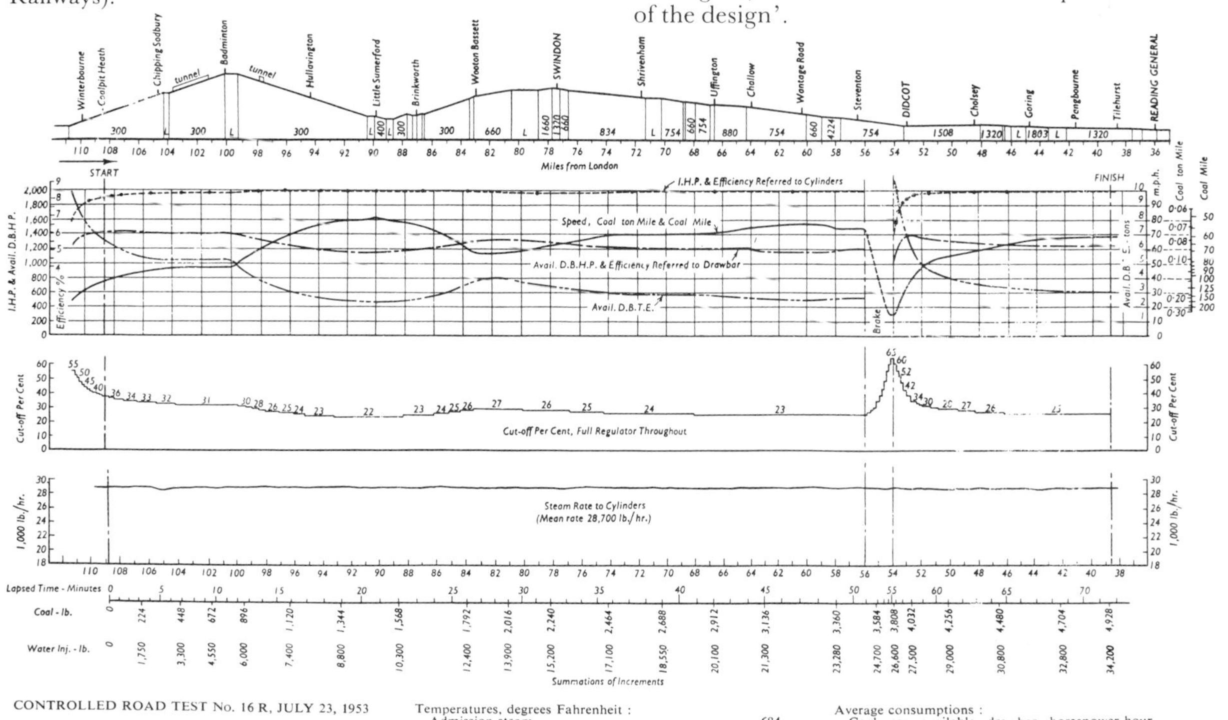

CONTROLLED ROAD TEST No. 16 R, JULY 23, 1953

Testing unit, W.R. dynamometer car ; Markham coal of 14,510 B.Th.U. per pound as fired ; live steam to injectors only ; load, 781 tons (twenty-three coaches) ; wind, average natural velocity, 7·07 m.p.h. ; average direction, 27 deg. to tail.

Mean steam and water rates, pounds per hour :

Actual feed water and cylinder steam	28,700
Equivalent f. and a. 212 deg. Fah.	39,160

Temperatures, degrees Fahrenheit :

Admission steam	684
Feed water	62

Mean coal rates :

Total rate, pounds per hour	415·0
Pounds per square foot grate per hour	121
Boiler efficiency, per cent	63

Average speed, miles per hour :

Excluding braking section	61·7
Badminton–Steventon	68·5

Average consumptions :

Coal per available drawbar horsepower hour, pounds	3·33
Coal per indicated horsepower hour, pounds	2·108
Water per available drawbar horsepower hour, pounds	23·0
Water per indicated horsepower hour, pounds	14·58

Adjustment for exhaust steam injector :
Reduce feed water consumption by 5·4 per cent.
Reduce coal consumption by 9·5 per cent.
Multiply efficiency and divide coal per ton-mile and coal per mile by 1·095.

Left *Controlled road tests with the 'Britannias': engine No 70005,* John Milton, *standing at Durran Hill yard, Carlisle, prior to leaving on a test run to Skipton, using the Horwich dynamometer car* (courtesy of A. Rimmer).

Below *The return test run, passing Badminton in heavy rain. Engine No 1009* County of Carmarthen *with a 14-coach train including the dynamometer car* (Kenneth H. Leech).

Left *A special high speed run to test the accelerated schedule for the 'Bristolian' express in April 1954. The return run, with dynamometer car, approaching West Ealing, hauled by engine No 6003,* King George IV (J.F. Russell-Smith).

Above right *Tests with the first (double-chimney) 'County' Class 4-6-0, on the stationary plant at Swindon. The draughting needed improvement* (British Railways).

'It was found that the actual cut-off bore no definite or consistent relationship to the setting of the reversing gear, not only for the locomotive as a whole but especially for the individual cylinder ends. In the shorter cut-offs particularly, there was a general tendency for the actual mean cut-off to lengthen with increasing speed but not in a smooth or regular manner. The power output in the short nominal cut-offs in the upper part of the speed range was found to be greater than that of other locomotives, size for size, and it was in some cases more than would theoretically be possible at an actual cut-off equal to the nominal cut-off, even assuming that the cylinders were completely filled up to the point of cut-off with steam at full steam chest pressure and that no early release occurred. The true cut-off must have been longer than the nominal. At times quite random changes occurred that appeared to be caused by minute changes of speed or boiler pressure. Some of these random changes were relatively small, though enough to upset the test conditions, but others were of relatively large amount. Whilst changes that occurred over a period of weeks or months might be ascribed to wear of the motion, however small, this could hardly be the case with changes from one day to the next or which occurred, sometimes more than once, in a single test period.'

Reading 'between the lines' of the official report published in the British Railways test bulletin one can sense that the engine led them a merry dance. Full dress trials, whether on the road or on a stationary plant, usually tend to give a rather more glowing picture of the capabilities of a locomotive than are realised in ordinary day to day working; but the 'Merchant Navy', like the 'Duchess' Class 4-6-2 of the LMS, for quite different reasons returned a picture that was quite the reverse. For example, on the test plant, working with a full regulator opening, the maximum drawbar horsepower was about 1,620 at 50 mph and, when working with a partly opened regulator and a nominal cut-off of 30 per cent, the maximum was no more than 1,470 at about 40 mph; yet during the 1948 Interchange Trials another engine of the class produced outputs of 1,835, 1,860, 1,920 and 1,929 equivalent drawbar horsepower on the climbs to Shap Summit, in all cases with a cut-off of 33 per cent and steam chest pressures between 180 and 225 lb per square inch. To produce the maximum of 1,620 on the test plant required a coal consumption of 4,620 lb per hour, whereas the best that could be done at the maximum standard rate of 3,000 lb per hour was only 1,100. This latter was of course an assumed continuous output, whereas the high values in the 1948 trials were no more than transitory. On the test plant the basic rate at the 3,000 lb 'single fireman' maximum, was 3 lb per dhp hour, whereas on the Euston–Carlisle test runs the rate lay between 3.41 and 3.86 lb per dhp hour.

On the test plant and on the road trials between Carlisle and Skipton the 'Merchant Navy' gave the testing staff a great deal of trouble with slipping, in some cases resulting in buckled coupling rods; and on the test plant when working at high steam there were cases of overheating. As in the 1948 Interchange Trials, however, no trouble was experienced with the totally enclosed valve gear, though leakage of oil, as always with these engines, reached the wheel treads, and caused severe slipping. In the test house the possibility that such slipping might give rise to serious damage, both to the locomotive and the plant, made it inadvisable to attempt to ascertain the maximum capacity of the boiler. It would in any case have been very far beyond the capability of a single fireman to sustain the necessary coal rate.

Although the boiler efficiency of the engine, as designed, was comparable with those of other modern locomotives some experiments were made with a special blast pipe having a single circular orifice and with a chimney of reduced diameter. What the purpose of this experiment was is a little hard to understand, because the multiple-jet type of blastpipe, derived from Bulleid's very successful modernisation of the 'Lord Nelson' Class 4-6-0, had proved very effective. In any event the experimental chimney and blast pipe, subjected to several variations during the course of the tests, proved unsatisfactory. In his comments on the Rugby tests generally, E.S. Cox refers to the 'serious inferiority of the SR 'Merchant Navy' . . .' and attributes much of it to the low cylinder efficiency, resulting from the indeterminate and random valve events; but a last thought towards the test results obtained with these engines, both at Rugby and out on the road, is to how the performance might have been influenced if they had been driven and fired by regular top link Southern Region men, as in the 1948 Interchange Trials.

In the late autumn of 1951 one of the new British standard Class '4MT' 4-6-0s was put through a series of full dress trials on the stationary plant at Swindon, followed by controlled road tests; and this locomotive, having a nominal tractive effort of 25,515 lb and a maximum axle load of 17.25 tons, put up a generally excellent performance, steaming freely up to 19,600 lb of steam per hour on both Blidworth and Bedwas coal. Details of the working are collated at the end of this chapter, in conjunction with those for the new Class '5MT' 4-6-0, and Class '7MT' 4-6-2 which were also tested in 1951–2. But, as far as the Western Region was concerned, the tests on the '4MT' highlighted the shortcomings of the indigenous Swindon 4-6-0 of similar nominal capacity, the 'Manor' Class, introduced in 1938. The basic proportions of these engines, and of the BR Standard '4MT' 4-6-0 are shown below.

Engine class	**GWR 'Manor'**	**BR Standard 4MT**
Cylinders		
Diameter (inches)	18	18
Stroke (inches)	30	28
Coupled wheel diameter (feet/inches)	5 8	5 8
Heating surfaces (square feet)		
Tubes	1,285.5	1,301
Firebox	140.0	143
Superheater	160.0	265
Total	1,585.5	1,709
Grate area (square feet)	22.1	26.7
Boiler pressure (psi)	225	225
Tractive effort (lb)	27,340	25,515
Total engine weight (tons)	68.9	67.9
Maximum axle load (tons)	17.25	17.25

A Carlisle–Skipton test special on arrival amid the snows of Blea Moor, 1,131 feet above sea level. Engine No 70005, John Milton, *taking water after an extremely strenuous ascent from Carlisle* (courtesy of W.H. King).

Right *High-power test run, Exeter to Paddington—check and reconciliation of results on the ascent to Savernake. On the graph of dhp, the dots indicate actual recordings, while continuous line represents calculated value based on steam rate* (British Railways).

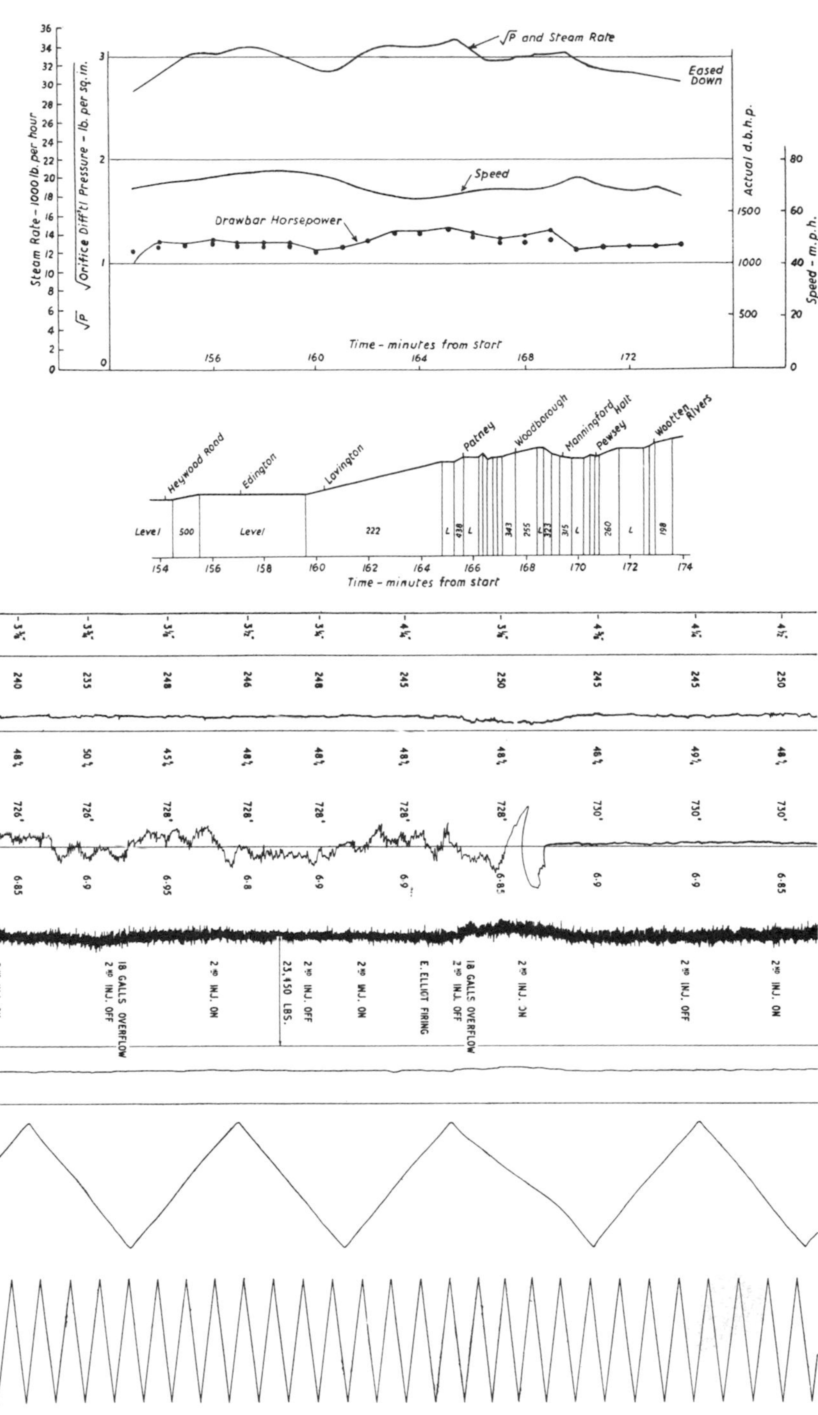

Below *Ex-LMS 4-6-2, No 46225,* Duchess of Gloucester *on a maximum power test between Settle Junction to Blea Moor. This is a portion of the dynamometer car record—continuous output of around 2,000 drawbar horsepower at 30 mph* (British Railways).

Except that the ex-Great Western Locomotive was designed to use the moderate degree of superheat traditional in Swindon products of the Churchward–Collett era one could have assumed that there would have been little in it when both engines were subjected to scientific testing. But, although most of the work on which the 'Manor' Class 4-6-0s were employed did not call for maximum power output for any appreciable time, the Running Department had generally recognised that these engines were not so free steaming as other standard Great Western designs; and the success of the new '4MT', also built at Swindon, prompted an investigation. It had rather startling results, because as designed, and running for the previous 13 years, the maximum rate of evaporation that could be sustained continuously was no more than 10,000 lb per hour, roughly half that of the 'BR4' 4-6-0. The diameter of the blastpipe orifice was $5\frac{1}{8}$ inches, but it had the jumper ring on the top which, when lifted, increased the discharge area by some 40 per cent. The blastpipe orifice was only fractionally smaller than that of the 'Hall' and 'Grange' Classes of 4-6-0, which had much larger boilers with a total heating surface of more than 2,000 square feet and grate areas of 27.07 square feet.

It was clear that the draughting arrangements had been wrongly proportioned in the first place. I must admit that in making some footplate journeys on these engines on the Cambrian line, when they were in the original condition, the steaming was very far from the solid reliability that one expected on Great Western engines. In comparing the 'Manor' with the 'BR4' 4-6-0 which had done so well a few months earlier, the blastpipe orifice (without the jumper top) was $4\frac{3}{4}$ inches diameter and the revised version for the 'Manor' was settled at $4\frac{5}{8}$ inches. An experimental chimney was made for test purposes and a new blastpipe cap fitted. The change was little short of sensational, because the maximum steam rate that could be sustained continuously was *doubled*. Details of the original and improved front end can be studied from the accompanying drawings. The changes involved nothing more than a new blastpipe cap, which could be bolted on to the existing pedestal, and a new chimney. This was of reduced diameter 1 foot 2 inches at the throat, instead of 1 foot 3 inches and 1 foot 4 inches at the top instead of 1 foot $6\frac{7}{8}$ inches. And with these relatively small, but vital changes, very cheaply made, a poor tool was changed into an extremely good one. The episode nevertheless leaves some disturbing thoughts, that a locomotive establishment with the experience and reputation of Swindon should have so neglected the principles of front-end draughting as to produce so poor a locomotive in the year 1938.

In turning to the new standard locomotives, the 'BR5' 4-6-0 mixed traffic engine was, of course, no more than a thinly disguised development of the Stanier 'Black Five' of the LMS, and it is interesting to study how men with the wealth of experience with the latter, like Riddles, Bond and Cox, sought to

Ex-GWR 'Manor' class 4-6-0, original and improved front ends (British Railways).

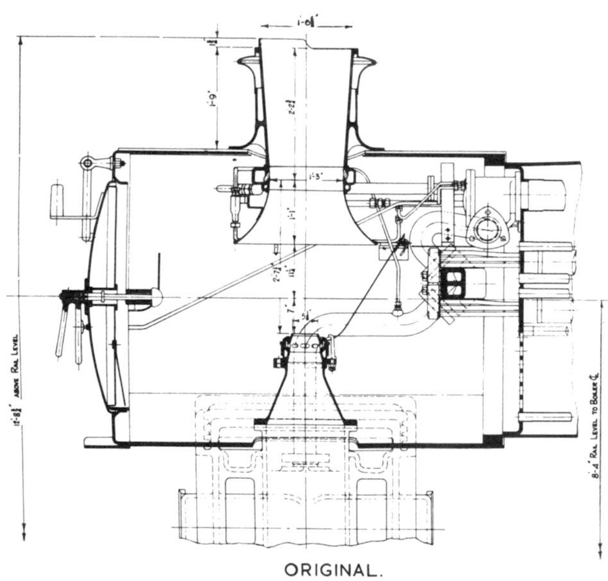

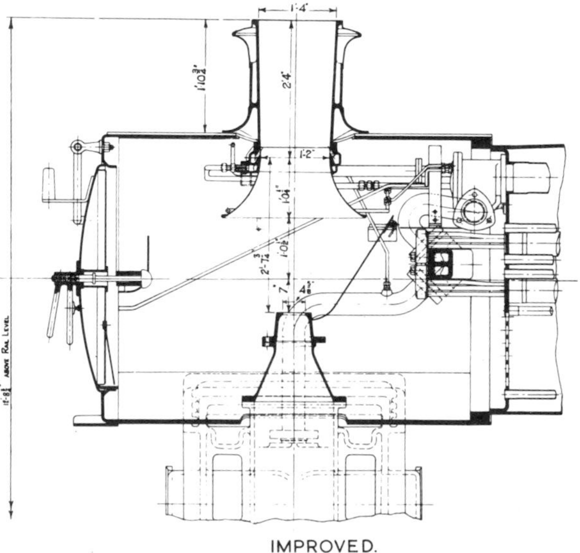

improve it, for the future. The boilers were identical, and the important dimensions that differed are set out below.

Engine class	**LMS Class '5'**	**BR '5MT'**
Cylinders		
Diameter (inches)	$18\frac{1}{2}$	19
Stroke (inches)	28	28
Coupled wheel diameter (feet/inches)	6 0	6 2
Piston valves		
Diameter (inches)	10	11
Steam lap (inches)	$1\frac{1}{2}$	$1\frac{11}{16}$
Lead (inches)	$\frac{1}{4}$	$\frac{1}{4}$
Travel in full gear (inches)	$6\frac{15}{32}$	7.73
Draughting		
Blast pipe diameter	$5\frac{1}{8}$	$5\frac{1}{8}$
Tractive effort (lb)	25,455	26,120

The introduction of larger coupled wheels and larger piston valves was no doubt intended to promote a freer running engine, bringing it virtually into the 'express passenger' category; but as originally built, to the above dimensions, it did not measure up to the high standards established by the Stanier 'Black Fives', let alone improving upon them. When firing at 3,000 lb of coal per hour (Blidworth) the maximum water evaporation reached only 18,000 lb per hour, against 20,000 by the 'Stanier', and though this was improved by use of a different type of fire-bars in the grate the steaming was still not considered satisfactory. Even with grade 1A South Kirkby coal the maximum sustained evaporation was no more than 25,000 lb of feed water per hour (26,310 lb per hour of steam to cylinders) and this needed 3,884 lb of coal per hour and the services of two firemen. At 18,000 lb per hour the engine gave an output of 1,256 indicated horsepower at 70 mph and a drawbar horsepower of 950. This was not considered good enough, and a series of experiments was initiated to improve the steaming, by the familiar process of reducing the diameter of the blastpipe orifice. Tests were made with 5 inch and $4\frac{7}{8}$ inch diameters, and the latter was subsequently adopted as standard for the '5MT' 4-6-0s. The increase in inlet steam temperature, and the resulting higher superheat, just about counter-balanced the effect of higher back pressure, and the steam consumption per indicated horsepower hour remained as previously.

The performance of the '5MT' with improved draughting as compared with the Stanier 'Black Five' can be seen from the following table, again relating to the maximum one-man firing rate of 3,000 lb per hour with Blidworth coal.

Class '5' Mixed Traffic 4-6-0s

Class	**ex-LMS '5P5F'**	**BR5**
Water evaporated (lb/hr)	20,000	19,500
Maximum ihp	1,480	1,480
at speed (mph)	70	75
at cut-off (per cent)	28	27
Steam temperature (degrees Fahrenheit)	675	643
Steam per ihp hour (lb)	14.0	14.4
Coal per ihp hour (lb)	1.95	2.00
Boiler efficiency (per cent)	69	70
Cylinder efficiency (per cent)	13.4	13.2
Maximum drawbar hp	1,200	1,180
at speed (mph)	37	37
at cut-off (per cent)	39	37
Steam per dhp hour (lb)	16.5	16.7
Coal per dhp hour (lb)	2.40	2.53

On studying the above figures the unkind thought occurs that it might have been better to have left well alone, risked the charge of pro-LMS bias, and built more 'Black Fives'!

Cox regretted that no opportunity came for testing one of the 'BR5' 4-6-0s that were fitted with the Caprotti valve gear, because he felt the results might have been quite outstanding. I must be pardoned for wondering if this would have been so. My own experiences with the 'Black Five' 4-6-0s fitted with the gear, both as a passenger and on the footplate, was that their work in hard pulling bore no comparison to that of the standard engines of the class fitted with the Walschaerts gear.

I am not likely to forget a run on the footplate of engine No 44754 with an expert Leeds crew working the Thames–Forth Express with a not immoderately heavy load of 285 tons tare, and the contrast it made to runs over the Carlisle road in the early 1930s when the unrebuilt 'Claughtons' (also Class '5') were on the job. On the long 1 in 100 ascent to Ribblehead, with full regulator and steam chest pressure between 192 and 200 lb per square inch, cut-off was finally advanced to 37 per cent and the speed came finally down to 23 mph. Yet in 1931, with an additional coach on the train (304 tons tare) one of the 'Claughtons' sustained 36 mph on the same ascent. On the faster running, and generally favourable stretch of line north of Appleby, the Caprotti engine passed Scotby, 28.1 miles from the restart, in 27¼ minutes; but another of the 'Claughtons' with a much heavier load of 352 tons tare, passed Scotby in a minute less. The respective average speeds over the 25.2 miles from Long

Marton to Scotby were 67.1 and 71.2 mph, with gross trailing loads of 300 and 375 tons respectively. There seemed nothing to account for the very poor Caprotti performance. The boiler was steaming well enough. It was just that the cylinders could not produce the power.

The 'Britannia' 4-6-2 was of course the 'flagship' of the BR standard fleet and, as mentioned earlier in this book, engine No 70005 was sent new to Rugby for testing in 1951. While performance at the one-man maximum firing rate was not noticeably better than that of other large express and mixed traffic locomotives, when fired with South Kirkby coal and steamed up to the very high water rate of 36,150 lb per hour, the coal rate, with two firemen was 5,600 lb per hour.

The accompanying diagram shows details of a remarkable performance southbound on the Settle & Carlisle line on which this high rate was sustained for more than half an hour. The approximate equivalent load was no less than 850 tons, and the cut-off, with full regulator, was never less than 40 per cent; but the basic coal rate during this mighty effort was no more than 3 lb per dhp hour. The run included some hard going at slow speed, because midway between Newbiggin and Long Marton there was a temporary speed restriction to 30 mph. The test train was slackened by brakes to observe this restriction and full steam kept on all the while. It was only when the engine slipped briefly, twice, that the constant feed from the tender was interrupted.

The numerous adjustments of cut-off, frequently by no more than 1 per cent at a time, will be noted from the diagram. When steaming with Blidworth coal the maximum feed rate that could be attained was 28,590 lb per hour, from the tender, and this needed 4,750 lb of coal per hour. At the one-man maximum coal rate of 3,000 lb per hour, the water evaporated, and the corresponding maximum

Opposite page, top to bottom

Controlled road tests with the 'BR9' 2-10-0: engine No 92178 fitted with double-chimney, Stoke Gifford to Reading, 18 coaches and the Swindon dynamometer car (Ivo Peters).

Improvements to the 'County' Class: engine No 1009, County of Carmarthen, *with an experimental, but very ugly double chimney, on a heavy load controlled road test from Reading to Stoke Gifford, passing Hullavington* (Kenneth H. Leech).

Controlled road test with No 1000, County of Middlesex, *on January 19 1954—14 coaches, 450 tons, steam rate 19,000 lb/hr, speed passing Hullavington 48 mph. The author was in the dynamometer car* (Kenneth H. Leech).

Below *'Britannia' class 4-6-2: diagram of a test at a very high steaming rate (two firemen) on the Settle and Carlisle line* (British Railways).

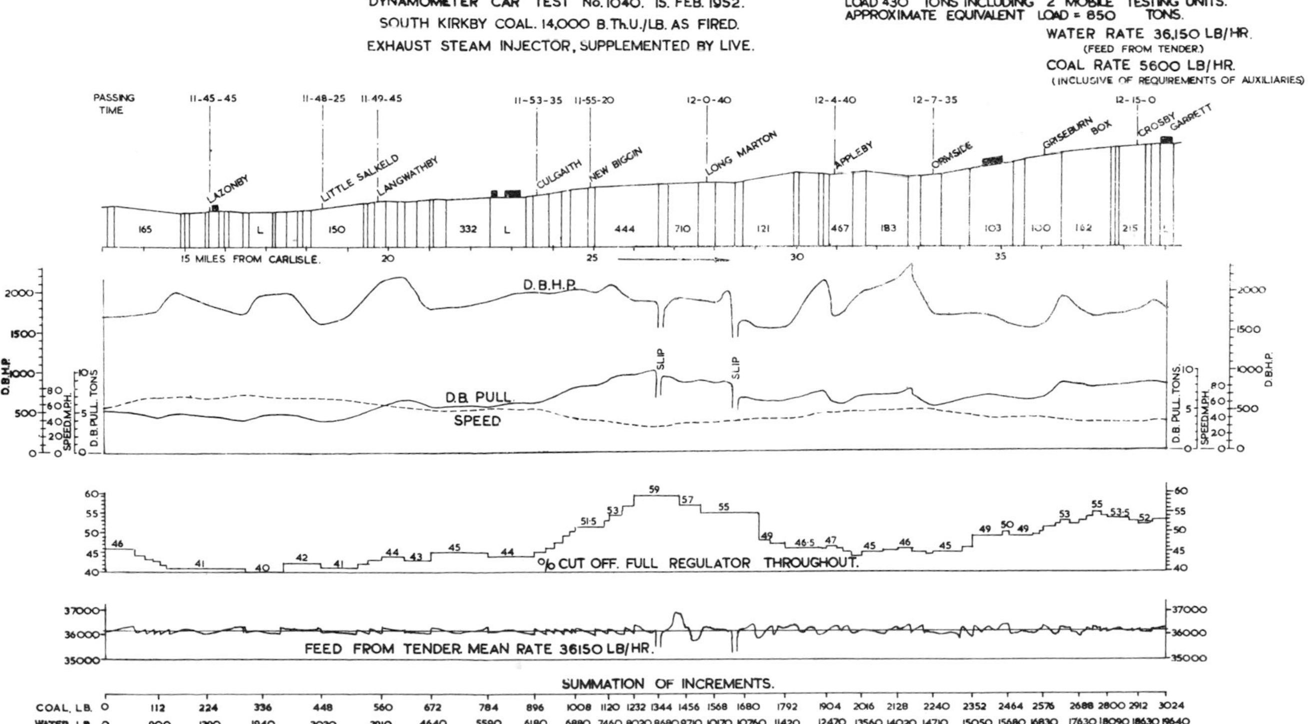

Left *Another heavy load test run with the 'BR9' 2-10-0 No 92178 getting well away on the 1 in 300 rise to Badminton, and steaming freely* (British Railways).

Left *The test run on January 19 1954 just finished, the lengthy train is coasting in to the stop at Stoke Gifford, where the train will be turned on the Filton triangle ready for the return to Reading* (Ivo Peters).

Left *One of the War Department 'Austerity' 2-8-0s, No 78621, outside Swindon Works. One of these engines was subjected to controlled road tests with the LMS No 3 dynamometer car, and Mobile test units between Carlisle and Kilmarnock. It is interesting that in this 'official' Swindon photograph of this engine the connecting rod and part of the valve gear is dismantled* (British Railways).

Right *One of the very fine War Department 'Austerity' 2-10-0s, No 73788, as first taken into 'BR' stock after the war. Engine No 90772 of this design was subjected to controlled road tests between Carlisle and Kilmarnock in 1953.*

drawbar and indicated horsepower compared with certain Regional engine classes thus, using Blidworth coal:

Engine Class	Water evaporated (lb/hour)	Maximum ihp	at mph	Maximum dhp	at mph
Britannia	19,500	1,620	65	1,240	35
LNER 'V2'	21,000	1,615	80	1,220	40
GWR 'King'	21,500	1,630	80	1,210	33

At the maximum firing rate that was expected from one man, the performance capacity of those three classes was so near as to be identical for all practical purposes, while the ex-LMS 'Duchess' and the Southern 'Merchant Navy', though producing ample steam were considerably lower, with 1,480 and 1,300 ihp respectively. Taken all round, the 'Britannia' was a successful engine, thermodynamically. It performed closely comparable work to the Gresley 3-cylinder 'V2' 2-6-2 after the deficiency in steaming on that class since the fitting of self-cleaning screens in the smokebox had been overcome by modified draughting. Power-wise the 'V2', as modernised, would certainly have been suitable for a national standard '7MT' unit; but the Gresley conjugated valve gear in any case made it unacceptable for general use on British Railways. The 'V2' could not approach the maximum evaporation rates reached by the 'Britannia', though of course these were not called for, even transitorily, in ordinary service. The tests on the later BR standard designs, the Class '8' express passenger and the '9F' 2-10-0 are discussed in a later chapter, together with those resulting from the rebuilding of the 'Merchant Navy' class with a conventional front end and Walschaerts valve gear.

British standard locomotives

Class	**4**	**5**	**7**
Type	4-6-0	4-6-0	4-6-2
At constant firing rate 3,000 lb/hour	Blidworth coal		
Water evaporated (lb per hour)	18,700	19,500	19,500
Maximum ihp	1,350	1,480	1,620
at speed (mph)	65	75	65
at cut off (per cent)	27	27	22½
Maximum dhp	1,060	1,180	1,240
at speed (mph)	35	37	35
at cut off (per cent)	39	37	35
At maximum boiler output	Blidworth coal		
Water evaporated (lb/hour)	22,490	19,500	30,000
Coal (lb/hour)	5,078	3,000	4,750
Maximum ihp	1,585	1,480	2,200
Maximum dhp	1,350	1,180	1,770

18. The last steam designs

When the construction of locomotives in the new British Railways range of so-called standard designs was well under way, there was time to consider some variations. There was a general seeking after greater thermal efficiency and more effective utilisation, and this applied particularly to the two largest designs, the mixed-traffic 'Britannia' 4-6-2 and the heavy freight 2-10-0 of Class '9F'. One senses that British Railways were slightly disenchanted over roller bearings, after their traumatic experience with the 'Britannias' in 1951. While the fitting of these bearings had been an unqualified success on the last LMS Pacifics of the 'Duchess' Class, built in Ivatt's time, and no less with a small batch of the Peppercorn 'A1' 'Pacifics' on the Eastern Region, Riddles built a batch of five 'Britannias' in 1953, with roller bearings only on the coupled axles, and followed this by a further 10 (Nos 70040–70049) with plain bearings throughout. The remarkable consensus of opinion, from running sheds and works was that roller bearings showed no advantage at all, and led to the decision to use plain bearings for the coupled wheels of the '9F' 2-10-0s.

Then there was the question of the replacement of the Class '8' 'Pacific' engine, *Princess Anne*, damaged beyond repair in the terrible double collision at Harrow in the autumn of 1952. This latter engine, No 46202, was itself a rebuild of the Stanier 'turbomotive', with conventional cylinders and Walschaerts valve gear. Until that time the design of a top-line express passenger engine in the BR range had been in abeyance. It had been considered that sufficient units of the former Regional classes existed to meet traffic requirements, in a situation where the great majority of express passenger services were still being operated at speeds considerably below the standards that had been attained by 1939. That the 'Pacific' engine, No 46202, should be replaced went without question, and Riddles seized the opportunity to make the replacement a prototype for a future Class '8' standard 4-6-2, rather than just another engine of basically LMS design. The Railway Executive agreed to this proposition and, as it was to be a replacement for an LM engine, the first moves towards the new design were taken at Derby.

By that time the British Railways' policy of breaking down regional allegiances was taking effect and the most senior influences at Derby were entirely alien. J.F. Harrison had been moved across from Doncaster to be Chief Mechanical and Electrical

Ex-LNER Class 'A3' 'Pacific' No 60055, Woolwinder, *as fitted with Kylchap exhaust system and double chimney* (British Railways).

Left-hand side view of the Crosti boiler 2-10-0, No 92024, showing no unusual appearance from this side (British Railways).

Engineer, and his chief locomotive draughtsman was C.S. Cocks from the Southern, whose ingenuity, ability and breezy good humour had been tempered in the fire of the Bulleid regime. Between them, Harrison, steeped in the Gresley tradition, and Cocks in his own style, forged the outline design of a Class '8' which was to have three cylinders 18½ inches in diameter by 24 inches stroke (à la Bulleid) 6 feet 2 inch coupled wheels, and a boiler pressure of 250 lb per square inch. The tractive effort would have been 35,380 lb—much the same as a Gresley 'A4'. Whether Harrison was thinking of the 2:1 conjugated valve gear for the middle cylinder or not was not vouchsafed on the diagram sent up from Derby to BR Headquarters in London; but the diagram did show a double chimney, and the so called 'Banjo Dome' of Gresley origin. The hand of Cocks could be discerned in the use of cylinders of no more than 24 inch stroke, while it was evidently thought that 6 feet 2 inches was large enough for the coupled wheels, seeing how freely the 'Merchant Navy' 4-6-2s could run.

One of the BR '9F' heavy freight 2-10-0s, No 92024, as fitted with the Franco-Crosti boiler. Note the special chimney just ahead of the firebox (British Railways).

As it turned out, the 6 foot 2 inch coupled wheels were about the only part of the Derby proposal that survived. While retaining three cylinders, the stroke was made 28 inches as in the 'Britannias' and the

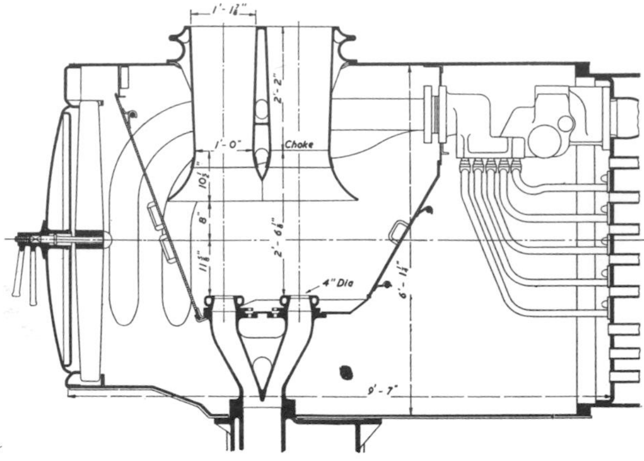

Left *BR Class '8' 4-6-2,* Duke of Gloucester—*diagram of smokebox showing draughting arrangements* (British Railways).

Below *The famous LNER 2-8-2, No 2001,* Cock o' the North, *as rebuilt, after removal of the original poppet valve gear, and fitted with standard Walschaerts motion and piston valves* (British Railways).

Right *The BR Class '8' 3-cylinder express passenger locomotive, No 71000,* Duke of Gloucester, *with Caprotti valve gear, built in 1954 at Crewe* (British Railways).

drive divided, with steam distribution by the Caprotti valve gear. E.S. Cox as Executive Officer, Design, of the Railway Executive, would obviously have liked to have avoided an inside cylinder at all. In his book on the standard locomotives, and referring to the inside big end on the Class '8' 4-6-2, he makes this rather surprising statement: 'The split brass arrangement, which assembly on to a crank axle made essential, had always been a troublesome feature throughout locomotive history, and the best way to avoid such trouble was to avoid inside big ends altogether.' When one recalls the positive swarms of inside cylinder 4-4-0s and 0-6-0s that were handling a very high proportion of the nation's traffic in the first years of this century, on many lines thrashed unmercifully too, the incidence of over-heated big ends was so small as to pass almost unnoticed. On the Great Western, Churchward's adoption of the de Glehn type of inside big end on his large 4-cylinder engines obviated any troubles in the notable development of Swindon designs, up to, and including the 'Kings'.

Although the boiler was of the 'Britannia' type, though with a larger firebox, the blastpipe was of the twin orifice type, with double chimney. The accompanying cross-sectional drawing shows the principal dimensions, and it draws attention to the remarkable contrast it made to those of the Gresley 'Pacifics' that were fitted with the Kylchap double blastpipe. By comparison the blastpipe orifices of only 4 inches diameter seem very small compared to the 5½ inches of the 'A3' Class. The chimney diameter was only 1 foot at the choke, as compared to 1 foot 3 inches and of course there were no petticoat pipes. It is not possible to judge from a single cross-sectional drawing, but in the bifurcation of the exhaust pipes, there seems to be some contraction in cross-section before it swells out again before reaching the blast cap. When the engine was on test at Swindon to produce the results discussed in the third volume of this work, S.O. Ell, who had come to be recognised as the BR expert on draughting problems, confided to me that the Class '8' had got two 'Dean Goods' blastpipes side by side. While this might have been his recommendation it was not incorporated in the actual engine, because the Dean

Goods 0-6-0 of the GWR had a 4½ inch diameter blastpipe orifice.

Use of the Caprotti valve gear was a major point in the design of the locomotive. In studying the drawings of the valve assembly, the camshaft assembly, and sectional views at the inlet and exhaust cams, one recalls the introduction, 20 years earlier, of another large British locomotive, also with 6 foot 2 inch coupled wheels, the *Cock o' the North*; that also had poppet valve gear, of the RC type. I must not at this stage anticipate the test results obtained at Swindon with the Class '8' 'Pacific' No 71000, *Duke of Gloucester*, except to say that Gresley's engine of 1934 also proved a great disappointment. Bulleid had gone to Ireland by the time No 71000 was on test at Swindon, or the results they were obtaining might have brought him vivid reminders of the adventures he had in the winter of 1934–5 when he took the *Cock o' the North* over to France for trials on the Vitry stationary testing plant, and for trials between Orleans and Tours. At this stage I will not do more than quote the basic dimensions of engine No 71000, intended to be the last word in British express passenger locomotive design and construction:

Cylinders (3)	
Diameter (inches)	18
Stroke (inches)	28
Coupled wheel diameter (feet/inches)	6 2
Heating surfaces (square feet)	
Tubes	2,264
Firebox	226
Superheater	691
Total	3,181
Grate area (square feet)	48.6
Boiler pressure (psi)	250
Adhesion weight (tons)	66
Total engine weight (tons)	101.25
Tractive effort (lb)	39,080

The engine had the massive, ponderous look of the larger British standard types. The attempts to produce a uniform design style for the entire standard range had not proved particularly successful when it came to the largest classes, such as the 'Britannias', the '9F' 2-10-0s, and now to the '8P'. When it gets to the stage of having boilers with a combined total heating surface of more than 3,000 square feet, and grate areas of more than 40 square feet, it is not easy to produce in a locomotive the canons of appearance qualifying as handsome in the traditional British style; and in trying to achieve something that was distinctive the boffins of the Railway Executive were not notably successful aesthetically.

It was on the '9F' 2-10-0s that some of the later novelties were tried out, notably the Franco-Crosti boiler. The principle of this device was that the hot gases of combustion, after passing through the flue tubes of the main boiler to the front end, were drawn backwards through the tubes of the pre-heater in which the feed water was heated before it was introduced to the main boiler. It was another way of trying to attain the economies that a hot-feed promised, and that Earle-Marsh strove after on the Brighton railway before the First World War, and which later designs of feed water heater promised, such as the ACFI. In the latter the heating cylinders were often carried on the top of the boiler but in the Franco-Crosti type, because the exhaust was at the rear end, the chimney was placed there too, with its axis horizontal, on the side of the boiler. The Italian engines so fitted, mostly of older types, had no chimneys at all in the usual place, and they always reminded me of the ghost who carried his head under his arm!

How British Railways 'fell for' this strange device I do not know, to the extent of having 10 of the '9F' 2-10-0s so fitted. But the canons of respectability had to be satisfied by the inclusion of a proper chimney, in the conventional place, if for no other purpose than fire lighting.

The accompanying diagram shows the arrangement of the boiler as fitted to the BR 2-10-0s. The enterprise seems to have originated in a holiday visit to Venice by E.S. Cox, in the course of which he visited the running sheds of the Italian State Railways on the neighbouring mainland, saw a number of 2-6-0s and 2-6-2s so equipped, and had a short footplate ride. The inventor himself, Dottore Ingeghere Piero Crosti impressed Cox with his tremendous enthusiasm, and eventually an arrangement to use the device was made, payment for which would be made according to the savings in coal consumption achieved during tests under specified conditions.

It has, however, been found in many cases that considerable economies can be made when a new device is applied to a locomotive of what may be termed 'middle-age' or one of indifferent performance; but it is another matter when the subject of the experiment is one of modern, efficient design. One thinks back to the case of one of the first applications of the Caprotti valve gear in Great Britain, on one of the original LNWR 'Claughton' Class 4-6-0s, burdened with a piston valve design of German origin that suffered from serious steam leakage as mileage mounted up, the Caprotti showed up very well; but after those piston valves had been replaced by a much simpler and far more effective design, batches of otherwise identical 'Claughtons' fitted

BR '9F' 2-10-0 locomotive—the Franco-Crosti boiler, diagram of connections (British Railways).

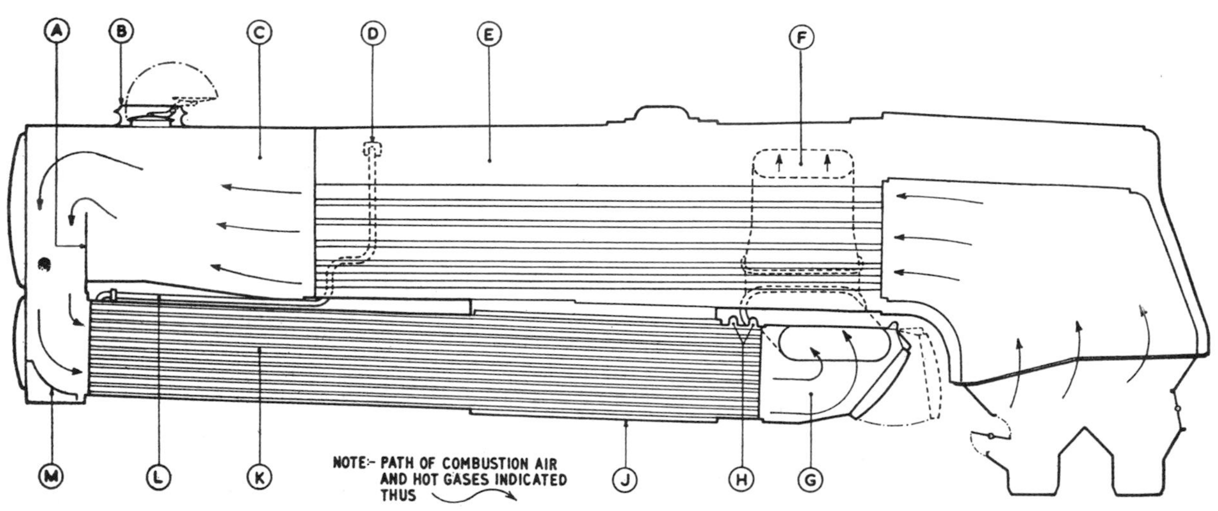

with larger boilers showed the piston valve type as more economical than the Caprotti. The '9F' 2-10-0s with the Crosti-boilers never showed economies to justify any payment to the designer.

It cannot be said that this failure was due to lack of trying, either on British Railways' part or by Crosti's firm, the Societa Anonima Locomotive a Vapore Franco. Prolonged testing was carried out at Rugby, with a 'standard' '9F' for comparison. Although it was realised that choice of the latter was unlucky for Crosti in that it happened to be one in exceptionally good condition; even so the expected economies were very far from reached. It was thought also that the choice of a sustained evaporation of 16,000 lb of water per hour as a basis of comparison, though fully representative of the requirements of heavy freight service on British Railways, did not extend the locomotive to anything near its maximum capacity. The firing rate was no more than 2,000 lb of coal per hour, whereas if the engine had been steamed up to the maximum for a single fireman, 3,000 lb per hour, an evaporation of 22,000 lb of water per hour could have been secured. An incidental question at this stage is that if an average evaporation in heavy freight service should have been no more than 16,000 lb per hour, why should it have been necessary to introduce such large freight locomotives, and eventually so many of them.

Power output apart, the Italian firm were very upset at the poor showing of their boiler, in comparison with that of a standard '9F', and apparently quite out of keeping with their experience on Italian locomotives. This was not to question the veracity of the results, nor to have anything but admiration for the diligence and care with which the tests at Rugby had been carried out. It was something that could not be understood, and they decided to ask the great French expert, André Chapelon, to examine the test results, and give his opinion. It was an extraordinary step, and his report was not forthcoming until two years later. By that time, at the end of 1957, the Modernisation Plan was under way, the end of steam prescheduled, and construction of new steam locomotives ended—except, strange to say, of the '9Fs'.

At that time, although the report was packed with the erudition that one would have expected from a man like Chapelon, it was of little more than academic interest in view of the current motive power situation on British Railways. In the meantime the 10 locomotives so equipped had become extremely unpopular with the running staffs because the exhaust fumes from that awkwardly-placed chimney not only obscured the look-out but filled the cab. The fitting of deflector plates did little

BR 2-10-0 Class '9F' with Franco-Crosti boiler under construction at Crewe Works (British Railways).

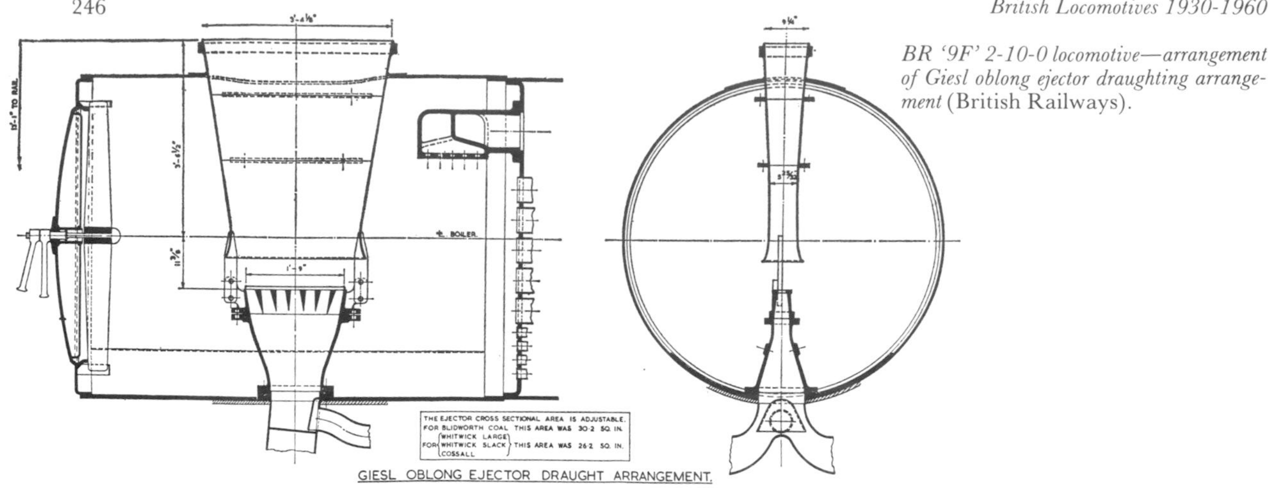

BR '9F' 2-10-0 locomotive—arrangement of Giesl oblong ejector draughting arrangement (British Railways).

to help. Eventually the pre-heating barrels were removed, and the engines converted to normal.

The engineers of the nationalised British Railways could not be accused of insularity in their attempts to improve the basic steam locomotive, and to their experimental work on the Franco-Crosti boiler, from Italy, was added the trial of the Austrian oblong ejector, invented by Dr Adolf Giesl-Gieslingen. It was yet another attempt to secure, by improved draughting, increased steaming capacity in the boiler without the attendant disadvantage of increased back pressure. From very early days when a locomotive would not steam freely, slight restrictions, often quite illicit, were inserted in the blast-pipe to sharpen up the exhaust. But in earlier chapters of this book it has been shown how more scientific methods, such as the twin-orifice blastpipe of Kylala, and the multiple-jet arrangement of Le Maitre by increasing the entraining effect of the exhaust, had achieved the desired effect without reducing the total area of the exhaust orifices. Dr Giesl, who in his earlier work on the staff of the Vienna Locomotive Works, at Florisdorf, had become particularly interested in draughting problems, conceived the idea of accelerating the flow of the exhaust gases when they emerged from the boiler tubes, so as to lessen the shock loss, when these gases met the exhaust issuing from the blast-pipe.

After much experimenting he finally arrived at a single oblong chimney that was relatively long in relation to its width, into which a row of multiple nozzles ejected the exhaust steam. The underlying aim was identical to those of Kylala, and his collaboration with Chapelon, and with Le Maitre, to produce increased draught for a given exhaust pressure, and his chimneys had been applied with great success to numerous Austrian locomotives, particularly the 4-8-0s that had the severe duty of working the international trains over the gradients of the Semmering Pass.

I had the pleasure of meeting Dr Giesl, and his family, in Vienna and on some runs on the footplate,

BR '9F' 2-10-0, No 92250, fitted with the Giesl oblong ejector and special chimney (G. Wheeler).

Above *A rebuilt 'West Country' Class 4-6-2, No 34028,* Eddystone, *when working on the Somerset and Dorset line* (Ivo Peters).

Right *A rebuilt 'Merchant Navy' Class 4-6-2, No 35028,* Clan Line, *working an inward bound Channel Islands boat express, beside Poole Harbour. A 'BR4' 2-6-0 is providing rear-end banking assistance up the 1 in 60 gradient. This 'MN' Class engine is now preserved in full working order* (Derek Cross).

Below *Southern Region: 'Battle of Britain' Class 4-6-2, No 34060,* 25 Squadron, *rebuilt with conventional Walschaerts valve gear, and 'air smoothed' casing removed* (British Railways).

sharing something of his enthusiasm and exceptionally wide knowledge of locomotive history and development. It was late in British Railways steam history, when the '9F' 2-10-0, No 92250, last of a batch built at Crewe in 1958, was fitted with the Giesl oblong ejector, and special chimney, and a very comprehensive series of tests were carried out at Rugby in 1959. As in the case of the Crosti boiler, everything possible was done to ensure a satisfactory comparison. One of the principal objects of the tests was to examine the performance of the locomotive on coal of a quality far below that of the basic Grade '2B' Blidworth, that was used as a standard of comparison on all tests of British Railways locomotives. Dr Giesl himself attended the tests, and a firing instructor from the Austrian Federal Railways, experienced in the use of low grade fuels with the Giesl ejector, was brought over to Rugby to advise. But, as with the Crosti boiler, the results were disappointing.

As it happened, however, the application to the '8F' 2-10-0 No 92250 was not the last of the Giesl ejector on British Railways. On the Southern Region, complaints were continuously being received of lineside and crop fires being caused by sparks thrown by the unmodified Bulleid 'Pacifics'. Spark arresters had been introduced but these were disliked by the running staff because they impaired the steaming qualities of the boiler. The unrebuilt 'Pacifics' of the 'West Country' and 'Battle of Britain' Classes had the multiple jet type of blastpipe but, as with other classes, the spark arrestor screens upset the balance of the draughting. But as late in British steam locomotive history as 1962, Brighton Works, where R.G. Jarvis was Chief Technical Assistant, received authority to fit one of the unrebuilt 'West Country' Class with a Giesl ejector, combined with that engineer's microspark arrestor. This, of course, meant discarding the multiple jet blastpipe, but its application to one of the 'Battle of Britain' series, No 34064, *Fighter Command*, was extremely successful, and working from Nine Elms shed the engine performed work up to the best standards of the larger 'Merchant Navy' Class. The express train schedules, particularly on the Bournemouth line, had by then been considerably tightened up, and the modified engine had no difficulty in keeping time. It was said by some critics that the steaming was too free, and that waste was occurring through excessive blowing off. This, of course, was no fault of the engine design, but rather of careless or inexperienced firing.

Through putting the modification to *Fighter Command* in immediate succession to the earlier application of the Giesl ejector, on the '9F' 2-10-0, I have stepped some seven years ahead of the very important rebuilding of the 'Merchant Navy' Class, for which work R.G. Jarvis at Brighton, was also

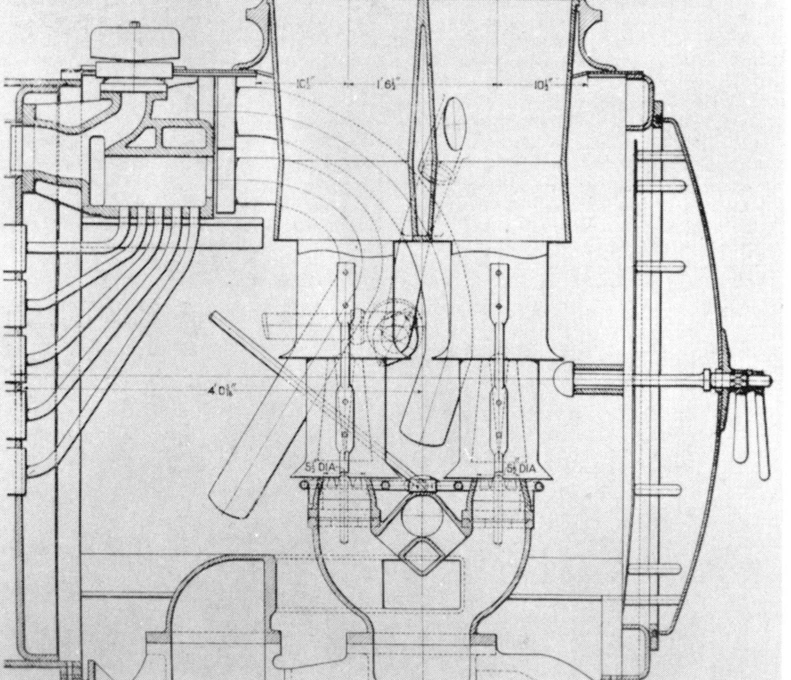

Left *The arrangement of the smokebox with the Kylchap exhaust system on 'A3' Class 4-6-2 (ex-LNER)* (British Railways).

Above right *A rebuilt 'Merchant Navy' 4-6-2, No 35026,* Lamport & Holt, *on the up 'Atlantic Coast' express, approaching Honiton tunnel.*

Right *Rebuilt 'Merchant Navy' Class 4-6-2—valve gear for outside and inside cylinders* (British Railways).

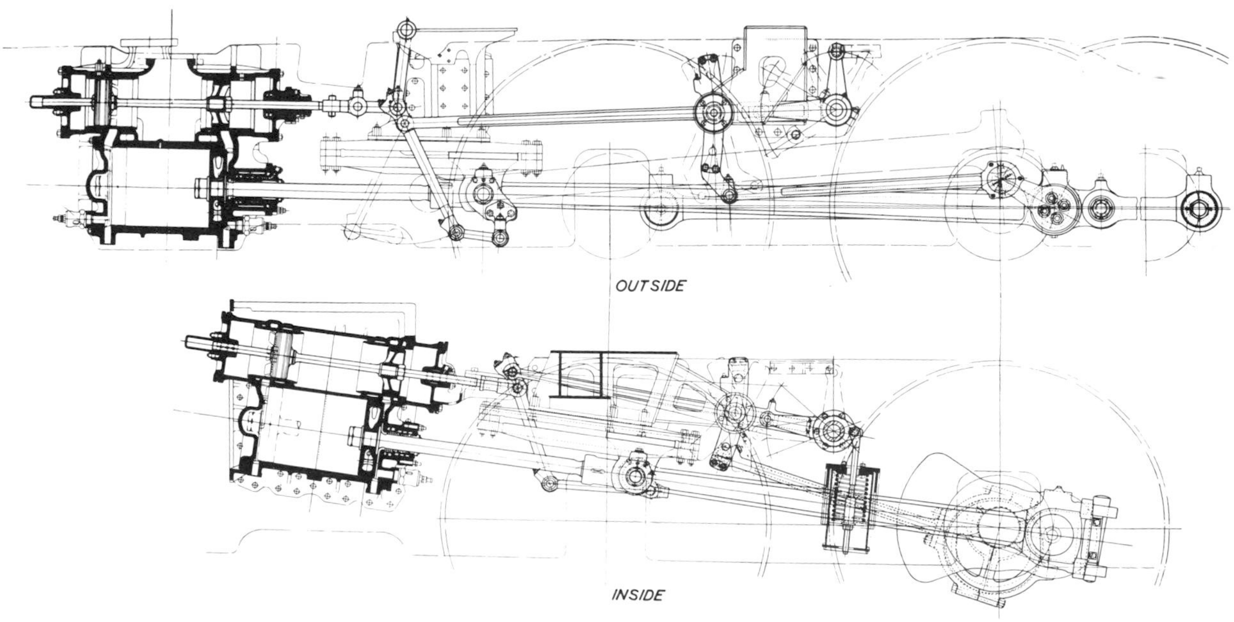
OUTSIDE
INSIDE

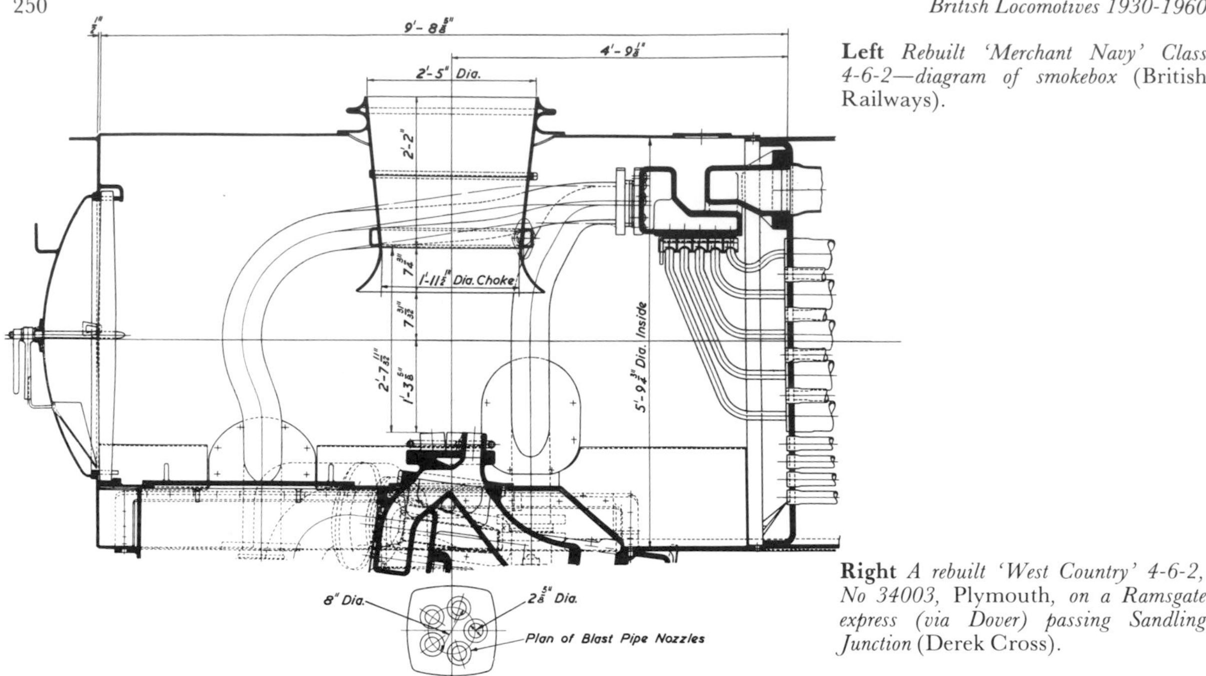

Left *Rebuilt 'Merchant Navy' Class 4-6-2—diagram of smokebox* (British Railways).

Right *A rebuilt 'West Country' 4-6-2, No 34003,* Plymouth, *on a Ramsgate express (via Dover) passing Sandling Junction* (Derek Cross).

responsible. It is no secret that the 'powers that were' at Railway Executive headquarters looked upon the Bulleid 'Pacifics' generally with the greatest disfavour. Design wise, they were the very antithesis of all the principles postulated for, and embodied in the new range of standard locomotives; and the difficulties experienced at Rugby, and when testing a 'Merchant Navy' Class out on the line, served to emphasise their general disapproval.

Yet both 'Merchant Navy' and 'West Country' Class engines had shown outstanding haulage abilities in the 1948 Interchange Trials with no mechanical troubles throughout the event; and their readiness to steam freely on inferior grades of coal should have commended them at a time when running difficulties were probably at their worst in railway history. The totally enclosed inside connecting rod and chain driven valve gear was certainly a source of trouble; but the underlying principle was so absolutely right that it is surprising with an establishment like Rugby at their disposal, that the Railway Executive did not make some attempt to eradicate the practical difficulties. After all, every internal combustion engine has its 'works' totally enclosed. There is no question of making the machinery of the family car 'get-at-able'! Bulleid, in his thinking, was many years ahead of his time with steam locomotives.

The trouble for The Railway Executive was that there were so many of the Bulleid 'Pacifics'. There was even talk of scrapping. The Modernisation Plan had not yet been launched and, had this been done, the cost of replacement would have had to be faced. Bulleid, with every justification, was very upset that he was not consulted in any way; nor was he shown the lengthy report recommending a drastic rebuilding of all the 'Merchant Navy' Class. In view of the high cost that would be involved, the proposers had to justify the steps to be taken with estimates of savings in service, and in maintenance; but when he heard through the 'grape-vine' of what was afoot Bulleid was profoundly sceptical. He wrote: 'Here a long experience in the management of the CME's department makes me extremely doubtful of all such estimates'; and in that, of course, he was no doubt thinking also of his long association with Sir Nigel Gresley on the LNER, before he went to the Southern. The report recommended that the air-smoothed casing should be removed, and that the inside valve gear and the oil bath should be replaced by three sets of Walschaerts valve gear. Also, the boiler pressure should be reduced from 280 to 250 lb per square inch. There were no changes to the basic dimensions but, because of the reduction in boiler pressure, the nominal tractive effort was reduced from 37,500 to 33,495 lb.

By the time the first of the 'Merchant Navy' Class had been rebuilt, the Railway Executive had been abolished. Riddles had resigned, and R.C. Bond was installed as Chief Mechanical Engineer of the British Railways Board. The second engine to be rebuilt, No 35020, *Bibby Line*, was put through a

series of tests by the Swindon team, under S.O. Ell, using the former Great Western dynamometer car. The engine was not put on to the stationary plant, but subjected instead to controlled road tests on the Southern main line, and then run, with the dynamometer car, on service trains between Waterloo and Exeter. The engine did not show any appreciable improvement in coal consumption over the original type, but was said to be more dependable otherwise.

With its highly distinctive air-smoothed casing removed, the rebuild was a fine-looking engine, while retaining the free steaming and free running qualities. With the experience of modern valve gears available, the rebuilt engines earned a reputation for very fast running, and more than one instance was recorded of maximum speeds of more than 100 mph.

There is an amusing story concerning the first engine to be rebuilt which illustrates Bulleid's impish sense of humour. He heard that the eccentric driving the inside valve spindle was running hot on occasions, and greatly cheered by this he proposed to write to Bond, thus: 'I understand upon good authority that you are having considerable trouble on the altered Merchant Navy with a heated inside eccentric. May I suggest you put it in an oil bath, then all will be well!' The letter was not sent.

I was privileged to ride in the dynamometer on one of the test runs made on the eastbound 'Atlantic Coast Express' from Exeter to Waterloo and noted a competent, though quite unexceptional, performance. The Southern Region traffic people set particular store upon the time keeping of their principal express passenger trains and, to lessen any chance of unpunctuality, they insisted upon reducing the passenger accommodation of the train by one coach to compensate for the addition of the dynamometer car. In contrast to the 'hit or miss' conditions that used to characterise driving methods on the original engines, the regulator and cut-off positions were quite orthodox, though I must admit not nearly so much fun!

When one looks back to the 'Merchant Navy' Class and equally to their smaller variants, it seems a great pity that the magnificent innovations of the totally enclosed valve gear and inside connecting rod was not confined at first to one or two locomotives, on which all the snags could be ironed out. With the conventional valve gear on the great majority, the original 'Merchant Navy's', with their 280 lb pressure and prolific steaming boilers, would have been a tremendous success, while the problems of the oil bath could have been studied and thrashed out on a few locomotives subjected to special scrutiny. Some of the greatest engine designs of 20th century history had been inaugurated by one or two prototypes: the Midland compounds, the large boilered GNR 'Atlantics', the Great Western 'Saints', the Gresley 'Pacifics'; whereas by the time of nationalisation Bulleid had 40 'Merchant Navy's' and 110 'West Countries' on his hands!

The rebuilding of the Bulleid 'Pacifics' was the last major project in steam locomotive design to be undertaken on British Railways, and henceforward men with a lifetime's experience in steam had to prepare, in breathless haste, for the onset of the modernisation plans, and in most cases the superseding of steam by diesel traction. The London Midland main line from Euston to Liverpool and Manchester was to be electrified, and also that of the Eastern Region, (from Liverpool Street) to Clacton. The Southern third-rail system of dc-electrification was to be extended to the main lines into Thanet, including the 'continentals' via Folkestone and Dover, and later to Bournemouth; but otherwise the entire remaining network was to be changed over to diesel traction.

The death-knell of steam, so long threatened, had at last been sounded—or so most people thought. The building programme for the year 1956 already authorised included 47 Class '5' 4-6-0s; 40 Class '4' 2-6-0s; 10 Class '2' 2-6-0s, and 25 Class '4' 2-6-4 tanks, though these orders were not actually completed until 1957. It was, however, the countinance of an extraordinary building programme for the Class '9F' 2-10-0, not completed until 1960, that seemed inexplicable in the circumstances. In the remaining years of steam it was not the new standard locomotives, but the old faithfuls that came to fairly hit the headlines.

It so happened that I was in a happy position to publicise this remarkable final burst of activity. At the end of 1958, I was honoured to receive an invitation from *The Railway Magazine* to take over the authorship of the monthly feature article 'British Locomotive Practice and Performance', which had run continuously in that journal since its inauguration by Charles Rous-Marten in September 1901. My immediate predecessor in the authorship, Cecil J. Allen, had since 1909 completed no fewer than 535 articles. At once my incoming mail was multiplied many times over. Correspondents of every age and estate began sending me details of runs they had experienced, and things they had seen. I could not use more than the merest fraction of what was sent in; but looking back at the articles I wrote in the first six years of my own authorship, it was evident that the standards of engine performance on the principal main lines had never been finer, and in many cases it surpassed anything that had gone previously.

This volume ends with the last new designs of steam locomotives in Great Britain. While the concluding and final volume will necessarily be concerned mainly with the new power—the diesels, the electrics, the HSTS and the APTs—the 'Indian Summer' of steam on the main lines, that prevailed well into the 1960s, was a phenomenon so remarkable in its technical expositions as to constitute chapters of railway history as important as any that had gone before. In the third volume of this work I hope to do final justice to it.

Left *Front view of '9F' 2-10-0, No 92024, showing the pre-heating boiler below the main boiler* (British Railways).

Right *A BR '9F' 2-10-0, No 92245, on the northbound 'Pines Express' near Midford* (Ivo Peters).

92245

Bibliography

Technical papers

Institution of Mechanical Engineers

1931 High Pressure Locomotives, H.N. Gresley

1931 Locomotive Experimental Stations, H.N. Gresley

1936 Presidential Address, Sir H.N. Gresley

1941 Presidential Address, Sir W.A. Stanier

1946 Notes on the 'Merchant Navy' Class locomotives of the Southern Railway, O.V.S. Bulleid

1947 Presidential Address, O.V.S. Bulleid

1948 Mobile Locomotive Testing plant of the LMSR, H.I. Andrews

Institution of Locomotive Engineers

1945 Modern Locomotive History (LMS), E.S. Cox

1946 Ten Years' Experience with the LMS 4-6-2 non-condensing turbine loco No 6202, R.C. Bond

1947 The Development of LNER Locomotive Design 1923-41, B. Spencer

1948 History of Southern Railway Locomotives to 1938, C.S. Cocks

1950 The late G.J. Churchward's Locomotive Development on the GWR, K.J. Cook

1953 Developments in Locomotive Testing, S.O. Ell

Journals

Engineering, The Engineer, The Locomotive, The Railway Engineer, The Railway Gazette, The Railway Magazine

Books

British Railways Standard Steam Locomotives, E.S. Cox, Ian Allan

British Steam Railway Locomotive, 1925-1965, O.S. Nock, Ian Allan, 1966

Bulleid—Last Giant of Steam, Sean Day-Lewis, George Allen & Unwin, 1964

Lifetime with Locomotives, R.C. Bond, Goose & Son, 1975

Locomotive Exchanges, Cecil J. Allen, Ian Allan, 1949

Locomotives of R.E.L. Maunsell, O.S. Nock, Edward Everard, 1954

Locomotive of Sir Nigel Gresley, O.S. Nock Railway Publishing Co Ltd, 1945

Steam Locomotive Design, Phillipson, Locomotive Publishing Co, 1936

Swindon Steam 1921-51, K.J. Cook, Ian Allan, 1974

William Stanier—An Engineering Biography, O.S. Nock, Ian Allan, 1964

Index

60030
GOLDEN FLEECE
A-4
GRANTHAM